HERB & VEGETABLE Gardening

The definitive guide to growing and harvesting herbs and vegetables

Published in 2008 by Murdoch Books Pty Limited

Murdoch Books Australia
Pier 8/9, 23 Hickson Road, Millers Point NSW 2000
Phone: +61 (0) 2 8220 2000   Fax: +61 (0) 2 8220 2558
www.murdochbooks.com.au

Murdoch Books UK Limited
Erico House, 6th Floor, 93–99 Upper Richmond Road, Putney, London SW15 2TG
Phone: +44 (0) 20 8785 5995   Fax: +44 (0) 20 8785 5985
www.murdochbooks.co.uk

Chief Executive: Juliet Rogers
Publishing Director: Kay Scarlett

Publisher: Diana Hill
Project editor: Ariana Klepac
Design layout: Jacqueline Richards, PinchMe Design
Design concept: Alex Frampton
Production: Kita George

Text: Steven Bradley, Val Bradley, Geoffrey Burnie, John Fenton-Smith, Denise Greig, Lulu Grimes,
Alison Haynes, Meredith Kirton, Dr Judyth McLeod, Roger Mann, Kim Rowney

Text and photographs originally from *Vegetable Gardening* and *Growing Herbs* © Murdoch Books Pty Limited 2004
Design copyright © Murdoch Books Pty Limited 2008

National Library of Australia Cataloguing-in-Publication Data:
Title: Herb and vegetable gardening: the definitive guide to growing and harvesting herbs and vegetables / editor,
Ariana Klepac. ISBN 9781741962284 (pbk.) Notes: Includes index. Subjects: Herb gardening. Vegetable gardening.
Other Authors/Contributors: Klepac, Ariana. Dewey Number: 635.

Readers of this book must ensure that any work or project undertaken complies with local legislative and approval
requirements relevant to their particular circumstances. Furthermore, this work is necessarily of a general nature
and cannot be a substitute for appropriate professional advice.

Colour separation by Splitting Image Colour Studio, Melbourne, Australia
Printed by 1010 Printing International Limited, China

HERB & VEGETABLE Gardening

The definitive guide to growing and harvesting herbs and vegetables

MURDOCH BOOKS

Contents

Introduction

Growing, harvesting, preparing and eating food from your own garden is all part of the same activity and a rewarding experience. It should be a grand celebration from garden to table, and the purpose of this book is to show you just how easy it is to grow your own herbs and vegetables.

All about herbs

To a botanist a herb is simply a plant that does not have a woody stem – that is, a plant that is not a tree or a shrub. Its edibility is irrelevant. However, gardeners have a different definition. To them, a herb is a plant that can be added to food or used for medicinal and household purposes, even if the plant in question is actually a shrub, such as rosemary, or even a tree, such as the bay tree.

The majority of herbs belong to three plant families: Lamiaceae/Labiatae, Apiaceae and Asteraceae, but there are ten herb families all together. The most economically important is the mint family (Lamiaceae/Labiatae), which includes herbs such as lavender, mint and rosemary.

A short history of herb cultivation

We could be forgiven for thinking that herbs are something 'new age' but, in fact, the use of herbs goes back to the very beginning of humankind, and has undergone waves of popularity and understanding throughout the ages. As hunters and gatherers, humans used and consumed wild plants, including herbs and spices. Long before recorded history, herbs were used for culinary and medicinal purposes.

With its fragrant flowers and heart-shaped leaves, sweet violet (*Viola odorata*) is an old-fashioned favourite. You can make an elegant dessert decoration with it by dipping the flowers in egg white, then dusting them with caster sugar.

Ancient times

The first documented evidence of the use of herbs in the West is in the Sumerian and Egyptian civilisations. The Sumerians under Nebuchadnezzar II of Babylon 605–562 BC, are credited with building the legendary Hanging Gardens, one of the wonders of the ancient world. Some of the plants that may have grown there include date palms, nut trees, olives, grapevines and fig trees.

The Egyptians imported herbs and spices along with the knowledge of their use from Babylon and India. Garlic, anise, caraway, saffron, coriander and thyme were used in foodstuffs, medicines, cosmetics, perfume and disinfectants, and in the process of embalming.

These traditions were picked up by the ancient Greeks. In about 500 BC, Herodotus listed about 700 herbs and their uses, many of which remain valid today. In the first century AD, Dioscorides produced a herbal guide, which is still a reference in the practice of natural medicines. Hippocrates (c. 460–c. 375 BC), a Greek physician, was perhaps the first to practise medicine as a scientific method. He often used diet and herbs as the basis of treatment.

The medical inheritance eventually passed from Greece to Rome. Physicians in Rome used herbal remedies extensively. For example, the herb mandrake (*Mandragora officinarum*) was used as an anaesthetic. Sage, fennel, betony, hyssop, borage, parsley, thyme and rosemary are just some of the herbs that were introduced into Britain by the Romans.

When the Romans landed in Britain, they found that the Druid sect had powerful priests with a deep understanding of natural remedies. The Druids collected various plants and animals, and used them to prepare concoctions for their patients. The oak tree was sacred to the Druids and the mistletoe (*Viscum album*) that grew on it played a special part in their rituals.

TOP According to Culpeper's *The Complete Herbal* (1649), both the bark and the ripe fruit of the mulberry (*Morus nigra*) are laxatives, while unripe fruit has the opposite effect.

BOTTOM In the 17th century, rue seeds, taken in wine, were used as an antidote to poison.

In Shakespeare's time, the plant we today call honeysuckle (*Lonicera periclymenum*) was known as woodbine.

Wise women and witches

Women skilled in the medicinal uses of herbs were known as wise women or midwives. They assisted women in childbirth, and tended the sick, often using prayer or charms as well as herbs. But a failure to heal could result in accusations of witchcraft.

The Dark Ages

During the Dark Ages (AD 476–c. 1000), after the invading barbarians tore down much of what the Romans had built, many of the monasteries and their gardens survived intact. The monks kept alive the Romans' knowledge of herbal remedies and treated those who lived outside the monastery walls. Some of the herbs they grew and used were poppies, burdock, marshmallow, rue, fenugreek, savory, parsley, mint, cumin, fennel and rosemary. Herbal medicines, many of which form the basis of today's liqueurs, were frequently mixed with wine to make them taste better. These herbs were often taken to combat the chronic indigestion and flatulence caused by badly prepared food.

Medieval Europe

A growing sense of peace prevailed in the Middle Ages: kitchen gardens and orchards were now planted outside the castle walls. Favourite herbs included roses, iris, lilies, columbines, lavenders, dianthus, wild thyme, avens (*Geum urbanum*), borage, parsley, orach (*Atriplex patula*), honeysuckle and fennel. The first English herbal, published in 1551 by William Turner, was a scientific study of 238 native British plants. This provided the basis of two less rigorous works, the herbals of Gerard and Culpeper, both of which are still available today.

Tudor England

In the Tudor period in England, large houses often had a 'still room'. Wines, pot pourri, medicinal salves and burning perfumes as well as culinary preparations were all made there; plants with insecticidal or disinfectant properties were particularly in demand. The still room remained a feature of large English households until Victorian times.

The age of exploration

The 17th and 18th centuries brought about much change with the discovery of the New World, when plant hunters and spice merchants crisscrossed the globe with plants, including herbs, from many continents. Seeds and recipes were brought back to Europe from America. With the help of the Native Americans (whom we can thank for the deliciously refreshing Earl Grey tea flavoured by the oil of bergamot), much was learnt about native herbs and their use.

The naturalistic movement of the 18th century, which decreed that a garden should appear part of the natural landscape, led to the decline in importance of the physic gardens as medicine and botany drifted apart. Medicinal

The flower heads of the sunflower (*Helianthus annuus*) follow the sun as it passes across the sky.

herbs retreated to the cottage garden. In rural areas, cottage owners kept gardens with many herbs and made home remedies, although this was mainly due to isolation, economic circumstances and lack of access to medicines, rather than fashion.

The modern era

By the 19th century, industrialisation had taken people away from their traditional livelihoods and sent them to work in the towns. They no longer had the room to

LANGUAGE OF HERBS A tussie mussie or nosegay is a posy of flowers and herbs that conveys some meaning or purpose. Originally it was intended to ward off disease, but its purpose evolved and eventually came to spell out a message using the language of flowers. Most often this was an expression of love, but it could also be other things, such as hate or thankfulness. For instance, lemon balm was used to convey sympathy, violets modesty, and forget-me-nots true love.

According to the language of flowers, the sweet pea (*Lathyrus odoratus*) signifies everlasting pleasure.

handy tip

Genoa or sweet basil is the perfect accompaniment to vine-ripened tomatoes. It is also a good companion plant for tomatoes in the garden.

grow herbs and so patent medicines and manufactured condiments took their place. In the early 20th century, herbs did regain importance in gardening through the work of gardeners such as Vita Sackville-West and Gertrude Jekyll, but for ornamental purposes.

Today we mostly use herbs when cooking, but don't confine your use of herbs to the kitchen. Explore their other uses as companion plants, compost accelerators, pest repellents, dyes and ingredients for home-made cosmetics, perfumes, pot pourris and household cleaners The latest trend is rediscovering herbs and their use as

a whole plant or essential oil rather than copying and isolating plant compounds. Herbs are credited with all sorts of medicinal qualities. In the past it was an essential part of a doctor's training to learn to distinguish beneficial herbs from useless and harmful ones, and these studies laid the foundations of modern botany. Some of the old prescriptions have been verified by modern science, and many modern drugs are still extracted from plants. The folklore attached to herbs is part of their charm, but don't dabble in herbal cures without seeking advice from your doctor or a reputable herbalist first.

Gardening with herbs

It is traditional to grow herbs in a garden of their own, and if you have the energy and the space, a small formal herb garden can be very decorative. But if a formal bed doesn't appeal to you, plant a potted herb garden, or use herbs as companion plants among your flowers and vegetables. Experiment with colour, foliage and form to suit the style and conditions of your garden.

OPPOSITE A formal bed in a traditional potager garden, where herbs, flowers and vegetables thrive together.

LEFT Your favourite vegetables will taste particularly flavoursome and be more nutritious when freshly picked just prior to eating or cooking.

All about vegetables

A vegetable is the edible part of a herbaceous plant and includes all parts of the plant. Fruits that are used as vegetables include tomatoes, peppers (capsicums and chillies), eggplants (aubergines), cucumbers and pumpkins. Stems or shoots include celery, asparagus and leeks. Leaf vegetables include cabbage, spinach, lettuce and chicory (endive). We eat the roots, bulbs and tubers of carrots, parsnips, beetroot, turnips, onions and potatoes. Seeds are eaten as vegetables, too, and include peas, snow peas (mangetout), sweet corn and broad beans. Flowers known as vegetables include cauliflowers, artichokes and broccoli.

A tradition of vegetable gardening

Despite frequent claims to the contrary, professions such as law and prostitution were long preceded by horticulture. And even before the horticulturists came the botanists. In early hunter-gatherer communities, human survival depended on correctly identifying edible species, and bad or inattentive botanists were inclined to be short lived, for obvious reasons. This botanical knowledge was passed on and enlarged by progressive generations, so that thousands of plants with edible roots, leaves, fruits and flowers could be identified and grown as food.

Ancient times

Prehistoric horticulture developed in the Neolithic era, which began around 12,000 years ago, arising independently in many centres of the world including Mexico, China, Egypt, Mesopotamia (within present day Iraq), in the areas now known as Turkey, Syria, Jordan and Israel, and around ancient Macedonia, Thrace and Thessaly.

Mesopotamia, 'the land between the rivers', was located between the Tigris and Euphrates Rivers. The area to the east where the two rivers nearly converge was known as Babylonia which in turn encompassed two areas, Sumer to the south, and Akkad to the

And he gave it for his opinion, 'that whoever could make two ears of corn, or two blades of grass, to grow upon a spot of ground where only one grew before, would deserve better of mankind, and do more essential service to his country, than the whole race of politicians put together'.

Jonathan Swift, *Gulliver's Travels*, 1726

north. Sumeria, which was destined to be the world's first civilisation, invented written language and was extraordinarily advanced in both the arts and sciences, including horticulture. The Sumerians' remarkable feats of engineering created sophisticated irrigation systems in order to water their dry, inland soils.

The writings of the Greeks, Romans, Hebrews and Chinese in the following historical period indicate an era when horticulture was further refined and important edible plants were introduced into cultivation including cucumbers and onions, among many others.

The surviving descriptions and frescoes of the gardens of the upper classes during this period in the Mediterranean region reveal often well designed and beautiful spaces which were retreats from the hot climate, with formal, inward-looking walled gardens which were accessed from very substantial villas. Most vegetables, though, were cultivated beyond the villa garden on farmland.

Gardening was surely one of the greatest legacies Rome left England. The English diet was notoriously limited until the Roman occupation introduced onions, garlic and leeks (and grapes for wine, of course). Rome also passed on its high level of horticultural knowledge.

After the demise of the Roman Empire, England gradually fell into disarray in the power vacuum that was left behind, with centuries of relentless struggles. During this long period of civil unrest, the monasteries became the keepers of learning, including vegetable gardening, not only in England but throughout Europe.

OPPOSITE Green oak-leaf lettuce, leeks and violas.

LEFT Ruby chard is a colourful variety of Swiss chard (silverbeet).

RISE OF THE MARKET GARDEN In the Middle Ages there was an increasing demand for more and more vegetables, as people could not produce enough food for themselves in their gardens alone. This brought about the creation of the market garden in towns and cities, where there was room enough within the town walls to build one.

The Middle Ages

The vegetable garden of a medieval monastery, known as a hortus, was well planned and functional. The plans for a Benedictine monastery at St Gall in Switzerland, drawn in c. AD 820, show a central walk bordered with nine simple raised beds on either side, each allocated a single crop such as onions or dill. Although travel was dangerous, monks did move between monasteries within their orders, and those who were assigned the role of priest-gardener ensured that new cultivars of vegetables were spread throughout Europe.

Poorer people often owned small pieces of land on which they grew vegetable crops, as well as raised animals. The Domesday Book lists large numbers of such horti and hortuli (small production gardens). Most people's diet was monotonous, mainly a mess of potage, as uninteresting gastronomically as it sounds and consisting of a thick vegetable soup based on meat broth when available, and supplemented with barley. Cabbage, leeks, broad beans and the white field pea were common ingredients.

The rich, living behind fortified castle walls, ate considerably better, with a greater variety of protein derived from seafood, mutton and beef. Simple salads were also served. But vegetables were largely neglected in favour of an array of meats. Green peas were thought acceptable but broad beans were considered the food of peasants and monks.

The Elizabethans

The Elizabethan garden of the 16th century was a remarkable place. England had both stability and prosperity under the reign of Elizabeth I. Without

Probably no section of the garden makes more demands on the soil than does the vegetable garden, with its need for constant, luxuriant growth.

the need for living under fortification, English gardens were able to expand and an appreciation of garden aesthetics and knowledge of horticulture and botany became a preoccupation of many Elizabethan gentlemen and an acceptable subject for social discourse.

European travel reinforced the fact that England had dropped well behind some other European countries in many civilised pursuits while it was occupied with its political struggles. Italy was far more sophisticated in both gastronomy and horticulture, and the newly affluent of England borrowed the Italians' ideas, as well as those of the French.

With rising prosperity came a concern for fine dining, and gentlemen of the era were likely to take a deep and well informed interest in all stages of food preparation from the raising of ingredients to their preparation.

The vegetable garden or potager of wealthier houses was laid out in a sunny position within the overview of the home, protected and discreetly screened at ground level by quickset hedges. The beds were raised, and dug through with manure to maintain fertility. Each bed was devoted to a single crop, perhaps leeks or onions, carrots, turnips, beetroot, Good King Henry (fat hen), spinach, sorrel or parsley.

Shall I not have intelligence with the earth? Am I not partly leaves and vegetable mould myself?

Henry David Thoreau, 1817–1862

Corn never occurred wild in nature. It is a crop that was synthesised in Mexico perhaps as long as 7000 years ago.

Some vegetable origins

The Americas: corn, jicama (yam bean), potato, tomato

Asia: bamboo shoots, mung beans, bok choy, daikon (white radish), garlic, lotus root, onion, radish, shallot, soy bean, spinach

Eurasia: celery, lettuce, mustard greens, turnip

Europe: asparagus, beetroot, Brussels sprouts, cabbage, carrot, chicory (endive), fennel, kale, kohlrabi, parsnip

Middle East: alfalfa (lucerne), leek

The potager was a place of pleasure, extensive, very neatly laid out, and filled with a rich array of vegetables and herbs. New crops were introduced at an astonishing rate, both from the New World and Europe. However, many of these new vegetables, such as the tomato, green bean and potato, were regarded for over a century with the deepest suspicion.

The earliest English settlements in North America were organised by Sir Walter Raleigh. The gardens of very early English settlements, such as those in Jamestown in Virginia, were modest, functional, raised, rectangular beds, filled with vegetables and herbs, placed close to the house and protected by fencing.

The New World

When Europe first encountered the Americas, there was little perception that great empires had risen and fallen for thousands of years, that extraordinary knowledge in engineering, architecture, maths and astronomy had been accumulated, or that the native peoples of the Americas had become indisputably master plant breeders.

For more than 8000 years before Columbus reached America, they had been actively engaged in cultivating and breeding plants, and collecting and testing new potential food species. By 1492, it has been estimated

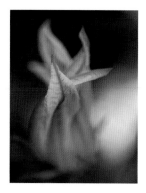

ABOVE The flower of a zucchini (courgette).

RIGHT Vegetable gardens don't always have to be green. You can either plant colourful varieties of vegetables, or interplant your greens with attractive ornamental plants, as shown here.

that the indigenous peoples had domesticated more than 300 edible species, many of which had beeen subjected to intensive selection for thousands of years to improve their taste, size, yield, appearance, and to adapt them to particular climates or soils.

The Inca civilisation which the Spanish military expedition of Pizarro and his soldiers encountered in Peru in 1532 was an empire comparable to that of Rome in size, stretching from central modern Chile in the south to southern Colombia in the north, with a population of 15 million people. It is estimated that when Pizarro encountered them, Andean Indians were growing some 3000 different cultivars of potatoes alone, and had developed the art of freeze-drying them.

According to legend, the Aztecs in present-day Mexico were told that they were to build their city in the place where they found an eagle perched on a cactus and eating a snake. They found this site in a place that was virtually uninhabitable, a snake-infested area of lakes and swamps studded with islands. However, they

DID YOU KNOW? Most vegetables are about 70 per cent water, with about 3.5 per cent protein and less than 1 per cent fat. They are good sources of minerals, especially calcium and iron, and vitamins, mainly A and C.

drained the land with canals, installed irrigation for crops, and created floating gardens – rafts anchored in the shallow areas of the lake and covered in soil on which they raised vegetables and flowers, which local people do to this day. The roots grew downwards and were fed on the nutrients in the lake water, thriving in the hottest summers. They had created hydroponics.

Although in the end the great civilisations of the Aztecs of Mexico and the Incas of South America were no match for the muskets and introduced diseases of Europe, they left an important gift to the world of more than half of our food resources, representing 10,000 years of skilled plant breeding.

The 17th and 18th centuries

As settlement progressed, American gardens of the 17th century were similar in design to those of Europe, with clipped box-hedged knot gardens and well managed orchards. The soils of Virginia were hailed as very fertile by those advocating emigration to the new colony. A number of indigenous root crops, herbs, fruit vines and salad flowers had also been incorporated into the kitchen gardens. By 1705 Robert Beverley, an early promotions expert, wrote robustly of kitchen gardens in America in his book *History and Present State of Virginia* that they 'don't thrive better or faster in the Universe than here. They have all the Culinary plants that grow in England, and in far greater perfection, than in England.' He added that a number of indigenous root crops and salad flowers had also been incorporated into the kitchen gardens.

Modern kitchen gardens

The 19th century was a period of great affluence when the British Empire was most influential. The grand houses of the era were serviced by huge walled kitchen gardens many hectares (acres) in extent, and would have included at least one hothouse where the raised temperature allowed the culture of rare plants from the colonies, and an array of hotbeds, greenhouses and cloches to protect outdoor crops from frost. Technology had entered the vegetable garden. As the century progressed, gardeners' magazines, garden knowledge and garden societies proliferated. The garden show with its giant vegetables and greatly coveted awards became the testing grounds for cultivars, theories and techniques.

Sowe Carrets in your Gardens,
and humbly praise God for them,
as for a singular and great blessing.

Richard Gardiner, *Profitable Instructions for the Manuring,*
Sowing and Planting of Kitchen Gardens, 1599

A well kept vegetable garden can be satisfying to the eye, whether you choose to plant in regimented rows or in more casual beds, as pictured here. Be sure to include paths between beds for easy access.

1

Getting started

Getting started

In order to successfully grow your own herbs and vegetables, it's important to start with the soil. If the quality of your soil isn't right for edible gardening, then all your above-ground efforts will be wasted. You can easily make amendments to the soil to achieve the right conditions or, if all else fails, plant in a raised bed.

Soil and pH

Gardening books often speak of the pH range. The pH is a measure of acidity and alkalinity, based on a scale of 1 to 14, with 1 being extremely acid and 14 being extremely alkaline.

Most soils contain some free lime, and the presence of this lime (or lack of it) will cause the soil to be either 'acid' or 'alkaline', depending on the amount present. The lime content within the soil will greatly influence the range of plants that can be grown, as well as the overall fertility of the soil, so it is important to find out the pH value before adding plants to it. Many plants will grow happily in a soil with a high lime content, but there are others that cannot tolerate it, and will die. Testing the soil will therefore save costly mistakes – both in terms of time and money.

Many herbs and vegetables do best in slightly acidic soils, so if you are serious about growing healthy crops,

Don't put all your efforts into life only above the soil. The secret to a healthy vegetable garden is healthy soil, prepared with plenty of organic material, such as compost.

step by step

TESTING SOIL PH

1 Place the soil sample in a tube (the tube should be about one-fifth full).

2 Pour in water.

3 Shake.

4 Let the sample settle. The colour change indicates whether the soil is alkaline or acidic. This test shows that the soil is alkaline.

For washing and storing the test kit, follow the manufacturer's instructions.

invest in an inexpensive pH testing kit. These can be purchased from garden centres. Gardens like regular applications of lime to maintain ideal pH levels. Lime contains an essential nutrient, calcium. This is easily lost from the soil, especially in areas of high rainfall, and will constantly need replacing. An annual application of between 50 and 100 g (1¾–3½ oz) per square metre (yard) is usually sufficient to remedy this. If you are a keen organic gardener, it is not advisable to mix lime with animal manure. This causes a release of ammonia gas and consequent loss of nitrogen. Lime is returned to the soil by adding it or wood ash to the compost heap rather than digging directly into the soil.

These days, commercially available garden lime often contains quantities of trace elements as well. The uptake of trace elements and other nutrients will only occur within certain pH ranges. Nitrogen, phosphorus, calcium and magnesium for example, need a neutral to slightly alkaline pH range for their uptake, whereas iron, manganese and boron prefer a slightly acidic soil. Nevertheless, even though pH levels may remain constant, remember that it is humus and other decaying organic matter in the soil that bacteria feed on, which in turn makes nutrients and trace elements available to the plant. Diseases indicating these nutritional shortages will soon manifest themselves if the soil is not rich in humus.

Worms and soil

Worms are natural recyclers, converting vegetative matter into nutrient-rich worm castings. Once introduced, worms will multiply rapidly and increase the aeration and nitrogen content of the soil. Compost worms will eat their way through kitchen scraps and garden waste, and produce castings that can be used on the garden. A worm farm full of compost worms is even better than a compost heap. A typical worm farm comprises three different layers: the top layer of paper scraps and organic matter, a centre layer where worms nest, and a bottom layer of castings (worm faeces). Add food scraps to the top layer and, as the worms eat them, keep adding more food. Note, however, that worms do not like banana, citrus, onion or garlic.

As chambers fill with waste, empty them into the garden or into pots. If you occasionally pour water into the farm, it will filter through the worm castings and can be collected via a tap that allows you to drain off and use the liquid waste. Use this waste diluted 1:10 with water.

Herbs and soil

Many herbs originated in Mediterranean regions where the soil is often poor and stony. These herbs – lavender, sage and rosemary, for example – prefer a spot in full sun in reasonably well drained soil. When these herbs are 'grown hard' – that is, without additional fertiliser and without lots of water – they generally have a better flavour than those grown in supposedly ideal conditions. But tropical herbs – such as lemon grass, cardamom, ginger and turmeric – need rich, fertile soil. Consult the 'Herb Directory' in the back of the book, and make sure you always check the required growing conditions before you plant.

Purpose-built herb gardens, especially those in cool regions, may have brick or stone paths and walls, which will help store and reflect the heat that most herbs enjoy. But in warm areas this is not necessary. Therefore choose the warmest, sunniest spot in your garden for herbs, and make sure that the soil there is well drained. You can

open up heavier soils by digging in plenty of compost well before planting. If the drainage is still poor because your soil is heavy clay, it's best to import some fresh soil and construct some raised beds.

BRING YOUR SOIL TO LIFE Many gardeners put all their efforts into the above-ground parts of their garden, forgetting what is going on below soil level. Half of every plant lies beneath the soil, feeding and supporting the leaf and flower growth above. To cater for your whole plant, it is important to understand soil, compost, mulching, fertilising and the organisms that make it all happen. Make sure you take the time to carry out a soil pH test so you can create the best possible growing conditions.

Starting a vegetable patch

Even the tiniest space in your garden, or a pot or container, will yield some of your favourite vegetables once you know how easy it is to grow them.

The diversity of vegetables available means that there is always a way of cultivation possible for the young, fit and healthy or the less mobile and elderly. Raised garden beds, hydroponics and no-dig gardens have revolutionised the world of gardening, and are perfectly suited for the disabled as the working area can be at any level to suit and have easy access for wheelchairs around the crops. Many groups have been established that provide horticultural therapy and these are certainly worthwhile joining. Gardening this way is also perfect for overcoming less than ideal sites which may have poor soils or climates, as weather screens, cloches and so on can be fitted.

Many vegetable crops, such as lettuce and tomatoes, will grow hydroponically; many will grow as climbers, such as beans and peas, for use as screens; other crops will even cope in a polystyrene box, like spinach Swiss chard (silverbeet).

It's also not often that one can say 'money is no object', but as almost all vegetables are available from seed, from the local supermarket or nursery, even the cost of vegetable gardening is affordable, and indeed profitable, and the net product saves you buying many of your groceries.

Easy-to-grow vegetables

Bean (green), beetroot, carrot, cucumber, garlic, lettuce, onion, pea, pepper (capsicum), radish, squash, tomato

Vegetable families

Vegetables come from a wide range of families. For example, the lily family (Liliaceae) which asparagus belongs to, the grass family (Poaceae) which gives us corn, the palm family (Araceae) where taro root and palm hearts originate, and the hibiscus family (Malvaceae) of which okra and rosella are members. Most vegetables, however, are from the following five well known families.

The daisy family (Asteraceae), apart from the wonderful array of superb flowering shrubs and annuals, also boasts globe artichoke, Jerusalem Artichoke, chicory (endive), lettuce and dandelion.

The mustard family (Brassicaceae) includes ornamentals like wallflowers and stock, as well as very important commercial crops such as canola, cauliflower, broccoli, Brussels sprouts, cabbage, radish, turnip, watercress and horseradish.

The pea family (Fabaceae) includes some beautiful flowering plants, such as wattles, cassias, brooms and sweet peas, but it is the edible beans and peas which are our staples – legumes such as lima bean, broad bean, green bean, pea, snow pea (mangetout) and soy bean.

The deadly nightshade family (Solanaceae) is unusual in that many members are highly poisonous plants, such as tobacco, deadly nightshade and Angel's trumpet. Edible fruit from eggplants (aubergines), chillies, pepper (capsicum) and tomato, as well as the favourite tuber, potato, have become important in the Western diet.

The cucurbits (Cucurbitaceae) are popular summer vegetables and include cucumber, marrow, melon, pumpkin, watermelon and zucchini (courgette) among their members.

Tomatoes are part of the deadly nightshade (Solanaceae) family.

HARVESTING ONIONS AND KALE The ornamental kale and onions (left) are ready for harvest, but the onions won't keep unless you wait for the foliage to wither. Pick leaves from the kale as needed, and let the plant continue to grow for more harvests.

salvia
Salvia spp.

sunflower
Helianthus annuus

geranium
Pelargonium spp.

amaranth
Amaranthus hypochondriacus

fig
Ficus carica

EDIBLE FLOWERS Many flowers are not only

attractive but edible, too. Roses and jasmine are made into teas. Blooms,
such as dandelion, sunflower and nasturtium, are eaten fresh in salads.
Others, like violets, lavender or rosemary, may be used in desserts or
candied as decorations.

garlic chives
Allium tuberosum

amaranth
Amaranthus hypochondriacus 'Golden Giant'

society garlic
Tulbaghia violacea

wheat
Triticum aestivum

rosemary
Rosmarinus officinalis

rose
Rosa spp.

jasmine
Jasminum spp.

lavender
Lavandula spp.

nasturtium
Tropaeolum majus

day lily
Hemerocallis lilioasphodelus

Outdoor growing tips for herbs

- Herbs grow naturally in many different soils and climates, so choose the appropriate herbs for the prevailing conditions in your area.
- Most herbs prefer full sun and free-draining soil.
- Don't pick more than one-third of a young plant or more than half of a mature specimen at the one time. The more often you pick, the bushier and healthier herbs become.
- Don't overfertilise – there will be too much soft leafy growth at the expense of essential oils.
- Snails and insects like herbs too. Be vigilant and pick off grubs by hand, and trap snails with small saucers of beer (see page 127).
- To develop full flavour, most herbs should have at least five hours of sunlight a day or 16 hours under fluorescent lights (placed 5–10 cm, or 2–4 in, above the plants).
- Many herbs grow better when planted next to other herbs, but some will struggle in the wrong combinations. For example, mint hates growing near parsley. If your herbs aren't doing well,

Herbs for all soil types

Dry soil with good drainage

Marjoram, oregano, rosemary, sage, summer savory, thyme, winter savory

Moderately moist soil

Basil, bay, bergamot, borage, burnet, chervil, chives, dill, garlic, lemon balm, lemon grass, parsley, tarragon

Wet soil

Apple mint, mint, pennyroyal, peppermint, sorrel, spearmint

Indoor growing tips for herbs

Herbs really grow best in full sun, so while temporarily growing them indoors is an option, don't expect them to last forever.

- Select a pot with plenty of drainage holes.
- Use a well drained potting mix suitable for shrubs.
- Incorporate a slow-release fertiliser at the highest recommended rate.
- Water the plant with liquid fertiliser regularly if growth is slow.
- Give the plant as much direct sunlight as possible to build in flavour.
- Choose herbs that cope with some shade, such as mint and 5-in-1 herb (*Coleus amboinicus*), also known as Spanish thyme or Indian borage.

LEFT Cress are tiny bright green sprouts with small, peppery leaves and are great in salads, sandwiches or as a garnish. Cress will germinate easily on moistened paper or cottonwool.

OPPPOSITE Get a quick start by buying seedlings of your favourite herbs in punnets, ready for planting out into the garden or in larger pots.

Comfortable conditions

Surprisingly little land is required to raise enough vegetables and herbs to keep an average family of two adults and two children luxuriously supplied with gourmet vegetables. Just 100 square metres (118 square yards) would be more than sufficient to supply abundant harvests of delicious, chemical-free food like buckets of corn on the cob rushed from the garden to the saucepan, early season asparagus, vine-ripened juicy tomatoes, intensely fragrant armfuls of herbs such as basil and mint, peas and snapping fresh beans, new-season and heirloom potatoes, and squash that has been matured under the autumn sun for thick winter soups. With intensive cultivation this area could be halved.

Don't worry if you only have a small space, as many larger vegetables can be obtained as dwarf forms which occupy less space. Clever use of vertical space and the use of large pots can also reduce the amount of land required. Replacing newly harvested crops with vegetable seedlings reduces both wastage of garden space and nutrient losses from the soil.

A well managed, organically enriched, mulched, raised garden which is continuously planted will yield far more than a larger one that is in continuous need of care. Companion planting can reduce the impact of pests and diseases without resorting to poisonous sprays, and will help to reduce crop losses. If you are using a sprinkler hose to water the garden, it is convenient to design the edible garden so that it does not extend beyond the reach of the sprinkler.

If space is very limited, imagine building one or more large, traylike, rectangular boxes with drainage provided, and filled with rich, well-composted soil. These can be rested on any surface including wooden decking, a strongly built balcony, or a brick patio, held above the surface by stacked bricks. Simply an enlarged version of a seed flat, such gardens can be enormously productive, and can be moved with the seasons to take advantage of sunlight. Drip irrigation can even further reduce the small effort in maintaining such gardens. Windowboxes and potted gardens can also be employed to produce summer herbs, tomatoes and salad greens.

Plants such as climbing peas and beans support themselves by tendrils, which are specialised organs designed to move laterally and encircle any object. Tendrils are sensitive to touch. If you stroke them lightly on the underside, they will start to turn towards that side within a couple of minutes. As a tendril brushes against any object, it turns towards it and will start to wrap itself around it.

Analysing the site

Take some time to become really familiar with a site before planning an edible garden. Good design always emerges from making the most of the opportunities a site offers and minimising its defects. Perhaps surprisingly, the quality of the soil on the site is not a major constraint as it can be considerably improved. Edible gardens may be of any shape or size, but regardless of design, they must be in a position to receive sunlight for the greater part of the day and have protection against wind. Keep clear of trees and other garden plants that will compete for water and nutrients. If topsoil is shallow or of poor quality, beds should be raised and well drained to allow root growth and prevent waterlogging after heavy rains. The following topics need to be carefully considered before you start.

Aspect

Gardens facing the east are sunniest in the morning and offer milder conditions. In the northern hemisphere, south-facing gardens receive the greatest sunlight exposure and warmth in winter while in the southern

RAISED BEDS Raised bed gardening (above) is a compromise between garden beds and containers. It can also solve the problem of localised poor soils and drainage. Beds can be constructed from railway sleepers, rocks or other strong material. Moisture levels should be monitored, as raised beds tend to dry out faster than normal ground-level beds.

hemisphere a north-facing aspect maximises growth. Most gardens offer different aspects which can be exploited by sun-loving or shade-requiring plants. The presence of walls and buildings can throw long shadows, particularly in winter. At night, sunny walls re-radiate the warmth absorbed during the daylight hours. Gardeners have long taken advantage of this effect by planting espaliered fruit trees and fruiting vines like grapes and melons against sunny walls. Rows that run east to west intercept the most light. In the northern hemisphere shorter plantings should be on the southern side, and taller plantings on the northern side. The converse holds for gardens in the southern hemisphere.

Climate

A very old adage warns novice gardeners to plant their garden to survive the extremes of the climate. But even the most experienced gardener is sometimes tempted to throw caution to the wind and plant some herbs, vegetables and fruits that will simply fail in an extreme season. This is fine, and fun, if only small gambles are taken but, generally, you will want the majority of your crops to succeed.

Some of the facts you need to know in planning are the maximum temperature extremes in the district, prevailing winds, rainfall and its distribution and historic extremes, first and last frost dates and their severity, and the length of the growing season. Soil in raised garden beds is better drained and warms more quickly in spring, so that gardens in cooler climates can be planted up to a fortnight earlier. Consider what kind of climate modifying structures might be needed on the site, like

Cool-season vegetables

Artichokes, asparagus, broad beans, broccoli, Brussels sprouts, cabbage, carrots, cauliflower, celery, chicory (endive), Chinese spinach (amaranth), kohlrabi, leek, lettuce, parsnip, pea, potato, radish, shallot, spinach, swede, Swiss chard (silverbeet), turnip, witlof (Belgian endive)

Corn likes it hot and is reasonably drought-tolerant, as it sends its roots deep into the soil, seeking moisture. Corn will be one of the last garden vegetables to wilt in the heat of the sun, but it does not fare well in heavy frost or freezes.

Warm-season vegetables

Beans (green), choko (chayote), corn, cucumber, eggplant (aubergine), fennel, lettuce, okra, pepper (capsicum), pumpkin, spinach, squash, sweet potato, tomato

Cool-season crops such as turnips will need time to mature before warm weather arrives.

Okra is a warm-season crop.

a greenhouse or polytunnel. These need to be sited in a clear sunny area that is protected from any severe winds.

Climate change is a reality for the 21st century. Current predictions by the world's most respected climate research bodies including the Intergovernmental Panel on Climate Change IPCC, the Hadley Group based in the United Kingdom, and the CSIRO in Australia have indicated an average rise in temperature of around 2°C (3.6°F) by 2030 with a rise of up to 6°C (11°F) by 2070. The Hadley Group have forecast a possible rise of 8°C (14.5°F) by 2100. These higher temperatures also predispose the world to much more extreme weather patterns, changed flows of climate which moderates ocean currents such as the Gulf Stream, and also brings for the gardener the possibility of many damaging insects previously restricted to hotter areas. Even a one degree rise can have considerable effects on climate, and historic records cannot be expected to apply as the century progresses. Planning for rather more severe conditions than those experienced in the past will allow your garden to continue to thrive.

Topography and drainage

Gardens that are located on flat, or nearly flat, land should be inspected after heavy rain so that drainage patterns in the garden can be checked. Rather than attempt the expensive business of draining areas that remain wet for some time after rain, it is better to consider these as a microenvironment to be exploited with moisture-loving plants.

Land that is too steep to be easily managed is best terraced. This will slow the flow of water off the land and allow it to percolate downwards. Steep slopes drain away rapidly and the dry soil grows many vegetables poorly. Steep slopes are also difficult to tend. The banks of terraces can either be formed into gentle slopes and grassed (a cheaper option but one which reduces the possible width of terraces), or more steeply cut and held with slightly backward-sloping retaining walls. In high rainfall areas, a drain may be used in front of a retaining wall to divert excess water.

If possible, lay a drainage system when the soil is dry, to produce easier working conditions. If working in wet

Drainage systems are often arranged with drains in a herringbone pattern of trenches. The trenches slope towards the lowest point of the garden, and the branch drains all link to a main drain.

weather, use broad wooden planks to prevent the soil becoming even more wet and sticky from being walked on. Dig the trench on a sloping site, starting from the lowest point and working upwards, so that any water is draining away from you as you work.

Drainage systems in clay soil

Heavy clay soils can hold large amounts of water, making digging and other cultivation impossible at certain times of the year. Some form of drainage system will be necessary to lower the water level, so that the upper layers of soil, at least, are drier. The siting and layering of drains in the garden is normally a fairly straightforward procedure.

INSTALLING A DRAINAGE SYSTEM

1 Using a garden line and canes, mark out the route of the drain where the drainage pipes are to be used.

2 Dig a trench about 60–75 cm (2–2½ ft) deep, and about 30 cm (1 ft) wide. Keep the topsoil and the subsoil separate.

3 Place a 5 cm (2 in) layer of gravel, ash and sand in the bottom of the trench, and lay or 'bed' the drainage pipes on top of this layer. Place the pipes so that they are touching one another end to end.

4 Refill the trench with a layer of gravel, ash or sand over the pipes to within about 25–30 cm (10–12 in) of the surface. Fill the trench with topsoil to leave a slight mound over the trench (this will settle down in four weeks). Do not press the soil into the trench, especially if it is wet. Spread any remaining soil over the site, where it will be incorporated into the topsoil over a few months. The drain should feed into a natural outlet, such as a ditch or stream.

Valued for centuries as both a useful herb and an ornamental shrub, lavender is never out of fashion.

Herb garden design

Herb gardens have special appeal, probably as a result of their long association with humankind, and certainly because of their usefulness, colour, fragrance and texture. They also evoke a sense of magic and mystery in the garden, yet team this with a practical element that only edible plants can truly provide.

Elements of design

Like any artwork, an interesting garden is made up of several design elements. Line, colour, seasonality, form, texture and grouping are all important, as are height (shorter plants in front, taller towards the back) and succession of flowering. Herbs lend themselves to fantastic garden designs.

Colour and contrast

By choosing a single colour scheme, you can create a garden that gives a sense of space, openness and brightness. Colours can also be used in combination; some colours blend together better than others. For example, a silver-foliaged plant, such as horehound, enhances red or pastel foliage or flowers. Yellow and blue is always a good combination. Orange and blue, yellow and violet, and red and green are all complementary colours and create a strong effect.

Another technique to make your garden more interesting is contrast, achieved by placing opposing elements close together to produce an intense or intriguing effect. You can contrast textures, darks, lights, colours, shapes, lines, flower form, flower height – any

Large beds of coriander, sage and thyme bookend this modern courtyard design, with four weeping birches underplanted with *Convolvulus*. The sound of water moving along the channels creates an atmosphere of peace and contemplation.

design element. For example, rounded plant forms look best next to upright ones; a plant with spiky flowers complements a plant with round flowers.

Choosing a style

Herbs are suited to all styles of garden. You can grow herbs within your existing garden, without allocating a specific area, dotted among vegetables and flowers, or in pots. Or you can use certain types of herbs as groundcovers and flowering perennials to add a decorative appeal to your garden.

A dedicated herb garden can be a feature in its own right. Although, historically, herbs lend themselves to formal layouts and cottage gardens, there is nothing to stop you using herbs in a more contemporary garden design. The criteria here are the characteristics of the site, the general surrounding landscape and the architecture of your house.

Ultimately, your choice comes down to a formal versus an informal herb garden. Formal designs have straight lines, geometric patterns, symmetry and balance. Informal designs, on the other hand, are fluid, depending on interesting plant associations for effect and allowing for a softer, freer flowing planting scheme.

You can also blend formal and informal styles, using the backdrop of rigid hedges or a strong central axis to anchor less formal plants.

Formal herb gardens

Traditional herb gardens are symmetrical and formal in design. The most common design has two intersecting paths dividing four symmetrical garden beds. These beds are not identical but appear balanced for height, foliage colour and use, with the plants often arranged in rows. Wide walkways are used to separate the beds and give the garden a sense of spaciousness. A centrepiece – such as a large urn, sundial, sculpture or birdbath – is then displayed at the junction of the paths.

Knot gardens

For a more complicated herb garden design, there are the traditional knot gardens, which were popular in 16th century England from the beginning of Henry VIII's reign. These intricate, geometric designs, contained within a square or rectangle, were usually edged with low-growing hedges of lavender or box (*Buxus*), which showed off the subtle characteristics of the herbs. No one is sure of the origins of knot gardens; classical Greek

Just part of the famous and elaborate formal gardens of 'Villandry', France, near Tours. A Spaniard, Dr Joachim Carvallo, restored the gardens in the early 20th century, basing the design on 16th century plans.

Making a simple knot garden

You can plant your own simple knot garden, to contain herbs and flowers, in any level, sunny, well drained position, preferably sited where it can be viewed from above so that you can appreciate the pattern. An area of about 12 square metres (14 square yards) is large enough for an interesting interwoven pattern.

1   Experiment first with some sketches, using different coloured pencils to represent a few different plants, such as *Teucrium*, *Santolina*, *Lavandula* and *Buxus*. Circles and squares of various sizes, overlaid on each other, will create a geometric pattern of interest.

2   Once you are happy with your design, draw the plan on graph paper so that 10 cm (4 in) represents 1 m (1 yard), and space the plants onto your design with a tube or cutting plant every 20 cm (8 in) or so.

3   Using the plan as a guide, transfer it onto the ground with sand, flour or lime dispensed from a bottle or with marking paint. A string line is the best way to create straight lines, arcs and circles (like a large compass from a set point), and a builder's square will result in accurate right angles.

4   Place your chosen plants on the markings, following the colour-coded plan you have drawn, and double-check the plants at each intersection to ensure that you have achieved the desired interwoven effect.

5   Select your specimens and plant them with extra care, as the appearance of an established hedge suffers greatly if the odd plant dies. Use water-storing crystals and slow-release fertiliser, and mulch well. Remember to check that the soil level after planting is the same as it was in the pot.

labyrinths or Celtic knots are two possibilities. However, the content of these gardens has been well documented.

Several different types of low-growing, controllable, shrubbery with contrasting foliage – such as box, cotton lavender and germander (*Teucrium*) – were used to form the outline of an elaborate pattern, which was designed to be viewed from above. The various species were then planted in such a way as to appear to cross over and under one another, like threads in a tapestry or embroidery. The spaces between the low hedges were usually left bare; occasionally, coloured gravel was used for added effect. The focus of the true knot is the interweaving pattern of the edging plants themselves.

Although some gardens contained just one square, the ideal knot garden consisted of four squares, which were each then divided into quarters. Each quarter was of a different pattern and often told a story or incorporated the owner's initials or emblem. The following combination, Jardins d'Amour or Gardens of Love, is one such design. There are box borders, in fancy shapes, accentuated by yew trees, the 'infill' planted with flowers.

- *L'Amour Tragique*, Tragic Love, with box planted as blades, swords and daggers, and red flowers representing the blood spilt.
- *L'Amour Adultère*, Adulterous Love, represented by horns and fans, with yellow flowers, the colour of betrayed love.
- *L'Amour Tendre*, Tender Love, with hearts separated by orange flames and masks.
- *L'Amour Passionné*, Passionate Love, again with hearts, but this time the hearts are shattered by passion.

By the time of Elizabeth I's reign in the latter half of the 16th century, knot gardens were the key element of English gardens. Designs by Thomas Hill, shown in *The*

A parterre garden, featuring a symmetrical grid of topiarised bay trees encircled by box hedges.

Dwarf comfrey, prostrate junipers, creeping thymes, pinks, creeping St John's wort and prostrate rosemary are all good carpeters in dry, sunny spots.

For damp conditions, try Corsican mint, pennyroyal, peppermint, ajuga and periwinkle.

Add another dimension to your herb garden by providing vertical supports for climbing herbs, such as hops, honeysuckle, climbing roses and jasmine.

Gardeners Labyrinth (1590), are based on the square, with each square often containing a circle or octagon, a pattern that is thought to represent heaven on earth and opposing life forces. The Elizabethans loved layered meanings, and enjoyed planting these knots with clusters of blossoms like a piece of tapestry.

The French equivalent to the knot garden, the parterre, was designed along similar lines, but featured scrolls and swirls rather than squares and rectangles. Both these complex designs require space and a great deal of maintenance, so be aware of this before you start creating your knot garden.

When choosing plants for a knot garden, select those that are compact, low growing and manageable. Some suggested herbs are thyme, germander, rue, hyssop, rosemary and cotton lavender. Avoid invasive herbs such as the mints. If your planting areas are wide, say, 1 m (3 ft) or more, you can edge them successfully with low hedges. Rosemary (*Rosmarinus officinalis*) is perfect for this, or the box-leafed honeysuckle (*Lonicera nitida*), cotton lavender (*Santolina chamaecyparissus*) or lavender (*Lavandula angustifolia* 'Munstead').

Herbs used for topiary

Topiary has been a popular art form in gardening since the days of ancient Greece. Topiary plants add a touch of formality and punctuation to more casual gardens, and are great architectural features in formal designs, forming living pillars, sentinels and doorstops. Bay and citrus trees were a popular feature in Renaissance and Tudor gardens, but a modern herb garden can expand on this selection by using mintbush (*Prostanthera*), coast rosemary (*Westringia*), rosemary, scented-leaf geraniums (*Pelargonium*), myrtle and lilly pillies. Spirals, mop-heads and pyramids are just a few of the shapes into which you can train your plants, and for interesting variations, why not try twisting or plaiting the trunks? For slower growing but longer lived topiary, you can use box, yew or juniper.

Informal herb gardens

These can take any form, with flowers, trees and shrubs; or you can design a theme garden. Don't limit your

Silver and grey foliage plants highlight dull corners, add light to a predominantly dark green garden bed and 'cool down' bright colours. Wormwood and artichoke, shown here, also have striking leaves.

RIGHT The grey-greens of rosemary and cotton lavender blend beautifully with the vibrant green and yellow of euphorbia.

A PHYSIC OR APOTHECARY'S GARDEN Before the days of modern medicine, the apothecary's garden once supplied the raw materials for the medicines used to heal the sick. Each herb was generally grown in its own pot or bed to make identification and harvest easier – after all, mistakes could be fatal. Before the 16th century, the apothecary was the pharmacist, and apothecaries had their own society. The most famous physic garden that is still around today is the Chelsea Physic Garden in London. It was founded in 1673 as an apothecary garden to train apprentices in identifying plants. Its location near the River Thames made the transport of patients and supplies easy, and the milder microclimate allowed many plants to survive the English winter. Over the centuries, this garden expanded, accepting offerings sent from around the world in wardian cases (portable miniature glasshouses), such as tea (Camellia sinensis) in 1848 from Robert Fortune. Today it covers 2 hectares (5 acres) and contains 300 different species, all carefully grouped according to their various uses. Grass pathways intersect the garden into square and rectangular beds, and brick and gravel paths form the main pathways. In 1983 the garden became a registered charity.

use of herbs to specific situations. You can use them to enhance most parts of any garden. Of course, some grow better as groundcovers or as edging plants; others thrive when they are intermingled with different plants in a mixed border. Most, however, are best used where their fragrance and beauty can be appreciated up close.

Paths, and accordingly the garden beds, may also be circular or free form, providing a softer effect. Use informal materials for your paths. A simple patterned brick path is attractive, or you could use a decorative pebble. Terracotta edging tiles or bricks set at an angle give a good edge to both the path and the planting area.

Herbs can work within many other garden styles. For example, tropical 'Bali' gardens and Asian styles can

Using herbs for garden 'pictures'

In the early 20th century, Vita Sackville-West (1892–1962) and Gertrude Jekyll (1842–1932) were renowned for using plants as blocks of colour, creating living pictures in the same way as an artist uses paint. Most famous of all is probably the White Garden at Sissinghurst, England, created by Vita Sackville-West in about 1946. You can create your own garden art in much the same way by using herbs.

For a white herb garden, try combining yarrow, garlic chives, chamomile, white foxgloves, sweet woodruff, white thyme, white valerian, white roses, lilies and jasmine. Or try herbs with colourful flowers in the following combinations:

- **Blue/mauve** comfrey, ajuga, borage, hyssop, lavender, rosemary, catmint, some of the salvias

- **Yellow** lady's mantle, pot marigold, curry plant, St John's wort, nasturtium, rue

- **Red/pink** pinks, bergamot, marjoram, oregano, rose, thyme, valerian, marshmallow

be achieved with underplantings of ginger, cardamom, turmeric and basil. For a modern garden, use herbs of a more sculptural habit, such as lemon grass, artichokes and the clipped shapes of box, yew and germander.

Theme herb gardens

Some gardeners prefer to select a specific theme for their herb garden and choose the herbs accordingly. Here are some ideas; however, the possibilities are limited only by your imagination.

- A kitchen garden, planted with herbs such as thyme, sage, basil, tarragon and dill
- A Shakespearean garden, planted with rosemary, heartsease, roses, woodbine and rue

The purple flowers of *Ajuga reptans* 'Catlin's Giant' and violets, punctuated by a golden-leaved box hedge.

- An apothecary's garden, including St John's wort, *Myrtus communis*, feverfew, rosemary, sage, garlic and valerian
- A colour garden, such as grey–green (planted with herbs such as horehound, lavender, wormwood and other *Artemisia* species)
- A fragrant garden, with sections for pot pourri plants, aromatherapy herbs and cosmetic plants (including mint, scented geranium, lemon balm, silver thyme and rosemary)
- A garden with different varieties of a specific herb – for example, you could combine common sage, 'Tricolor' sage, golden sage, purple sage, clary sage and pineapple sage.

Practicalities

Working on any new garden project is an exciting task, full of possibilities and promise. A herb garden is no different, and also deserves planning and thought. Once you have decided on the type of garden you want, make a rough sketch or drawing on paper. This helps you to visualise what the garden will look like and to calculate the number of plants you'll need. Next, plan your design to scale on a sheet of graph paper, with 1 cm on your paper representing 1 m (or ½ in representing 1 yard) on the ground. Clear and dig over the area and plot out your design by sprinkling flour or lime as an outline.

Some points for consideration include the following.

- **Needs** If you're a time-poor chef who still wants some fresh ingredients at hand, consider how many herbs you need. A few pots filled with your favourite herbs may be sufficient. For others, herbs dotted about an existing garden could be a practical option. A totally dedicated space, either small or large, is a delightful and useful area.
- **Time** Many people underestimate the time involved in refreshing, replanting and harvesting herbs. While many are tough, hardy perennials, they still need frequent pruning. Annuals and frost-tender herbs need replacing each season or 'bringing in' for the winter. If your garden is formal, then you'll need to regularly maintain the desired lines and shapes of your hedging.

Plants will look better if they are grouped in clumps of the same species rather than scattered through the garden bed. Edging the herb garden defines the planting area and makes the garden look as if it belongs in the landscape. If the plants are located next to a wall, a path can provide the boundary. If they are located in a lawn area, a permanent edging of brick or wood can be useful. A defined area looks more 'finished' and is easier to maintain.

Herbs with interesting leaves

- **Silver foliage** southernwood, wormwood, mugwort, pinks, curry plant, lavender, horehound, rue, sage, cotton lavender, *Thymus* 'Silver Posy' and 'Lemon Queen', *Echium*, *Euphorbia marginata*, artichoke

- **Gold foliage** golden box, golden lemon balm, ginger mint, golden sage, golden marjoram, *Thymus* 'Doone Valley'

- **Variegated leaves** *Ajuga* 'Glacier', variegated apple mint, variegated scented geraniums, *Salvia* 'Tricolor', variegated oregano

- **Purple leaves** *Ajuga* 'Purpurea', bronze fennel, Japanese perilla, purple sage, opal basil

This round, brick pond is nestled among a variety of perennials, such as salvia.

you can use any large container, but you'll have to make sure the inside is waterproofed with a sealant and drainage holes are plugged up (a cork, sealant, epoxy putty or silica gel will do the job).

Most flowering aquatic plants like the sun, with lilies, water poppies, reeds, Louisiana iris and lotus all suited to a sunny spot. If you have a shady area, you can try dwarf papyrus, arum lilies, syngonium, sedges and water lettuce. You can also use floating pond weeds, but these grow extremely quickly, so either stock fish to keep them in check, or scoop out the excess regularly to give the other plants room to grow.

Ponds take time to install but, once established, require less work than garden beds. Position is everything. Avoid placing ponds where overhanging branches will drop leaves and flowers and upset the biological balance. When selecting water plants, consider the position of your water feature. Arum lilies cope with shade, are long flowering and evergreen. Waterlilies don't like splashing water, need lots of sun and die down over winter, making them suitable for bigger ponds. Watercress prefers sun, or half sun.

Growing waterlilies

The world's most popular aquatic plant is undoubtedly the waterlily, which is a perennial aquatic herb with both traditional and modern medicinal uses, such as a poultice for bruises. Native Americans made tea from the roots of *Nymphaea odorata* to treat coughs and stop bleeding. There is a waterlily available to suit any climate, from tropical to cold zones. The miniature species *Nymphaea tetragona* (syn. *N. pygmaea*) is especially suited to pots. Very beautiful in flower, it is herbaceous, with the leaves dying back to a permanent rootstock as the weather cools. Rhizomes can be lifted during this dormancy, normally in late winter or early spring, and divided every two or three years.

You can grow waterlilies either in a large, shallow pond in the garden or in a pot on a deck or sheltered

■ **Position** Not all herbs thrive in the same growing conditions. Some like it hot, and relish basking in dry, gravelly soils. Others enjoy a cool, sheltered site and rich humus. Site your herbs accordingly, so that you work with nature, not against it. Consider the specific requirements of the herb (sun versus shade, moist versus dry soil).

■ **Use** If you grow medicinal plants, keep them separate from the kitchen herbs to avoid any unfortunate accidents.

Aquatic herb gardens

The water feature is one of summer's underrated garden essentials. The water reflects light and cools the air, and moving water creates a peaceful ambience. Many people would love to have a water feature, but the thought of pumps, huge holes, liners and the like is off-putting. Installing a pond in the garden is also fairly expensive.

The easiest and cheapest way is simply to use a large pot. Wine barrels, stone and glazed pots, and plastic terracotta look-alikes are all suitable candidates. Really,

PLANTING WATERLILIES

1 Select a waterlily root with some new shoots.

2 Insert the waterlily root into compost, and mulch with pebbles.

Waterlilies are popular and exotic herbs.

rooftop garden, as long as it is a sunny position. There are shorter-stemmed waterlilies available that are perfect for pot culture. Select a tub or decorative pot, about 20–30 cm (8–12 in) deep and at least 50 cm (20 in) wide, without a hole. Lined half barrels are ideal.

Grow waterlilies in a wire mesh basket lined with peat or coconut fibre or in a pot. Add a pinch of slow-release fertiliser to the compost and insert the waterlily root system. (Too much fertiliser will result in algal blooms in the water.) Then gently settle the basket into the water on the bottom of the pot, or to a depth of about 50 cm (20 in) if you are planting in a pond.

Then keep the water clean; some fish will keep the mosquitoes at bay. After several weeks large leaves will appear, then huge, plump flower buds. Once waterlilies start flowering they keep blooming for months, and many are perfumed.

Bog gardens

In poorly drained areas where the soil is constantly saturated, most deep-rooted shrubs and trees can't get quite enough air. Some herbaceous plants – such as

MAKING A HERB GLOBE

If space is at a premium in your garden, fill a hanging container with a range of herbs. For this project, you'll need two hanging baskets (made from heavy-gauge wire and coated in plastic), chains, a hammer, a pair of pliers, an empty plant pot, sphagnum moss, herbs, premium quality potting mix containing water crystals and slow-release fertiliser, plywood, nails and plastic-coated wire.

1 Place one basket on top of a large empty plant pot. Line the lower half with a layer of sphagnum moss and press it firmly against the wire mesh, then add some potting mix to the same level.

2 Insert the first layer of herbs by passing them roots first through the mesh, so that the roots are resting on the potting mix and the tops of the plants are hanging down the sides. Line the top half of the basket with moss and potting mix as before. Insert the next layer of herbs and top up the potting mix until it is level with the rim. Place a square of plywood over the top of the basket then carefully turn it over to form a dome. Nail the basket rim to the plywood. Leave the basket in a sheltered place and water it regularly for two to three weeks. Prepare the second basket in the same way.

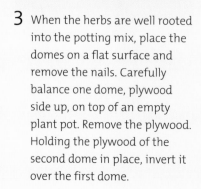

3 When the herbs are well rooted into the potting mix, place the domes on a flat surface and remove the nails. Carefully balance one dome, plywood side up, on top of an empty plant pot. Remove the plywood. Holding the plywood of the second dome in place, invert it over the first dome.

4 Slide out the plywood from the second dome and secure the two baskets together with plastic-coated wire. Attach hanging chains to the herb globe and hang it in a sunny position. Keep it well watered.

Gunnera, Alocasia, cannas, arums and Louisiana iris – will flourish here, and look great teamed with ferns, sedges and some varieties of bamboo that also thrive in these conditions.

It makes good sense to work with the conditions, so why not create a bog garden? They can look fantastic and display a wide range of flowering perennials that may be difficult to grow in hot, dry climates.

Growing herbs in containers

You can grow herbs in pots or plant several together in a large tub or a hanging basket. Group together plants that like the same conditions of sun, soil, feeding and drainage. Plant herbs that have a tendency to trail – such as oregano, thyme and prostrate rosemary – at the side of a large pot, and place upright herbs – basil, sage and sorrel – in the middle.

Add about 2 teaspoons of lime to the potting mix for a 20 cm (8 in) pot. Add more or less according to the size of the container. For herbs such as sage it may be worth incorporating some coarse sand into the mix so that the pot will drain rapidly.

Quality potting mixes contain water crystals. These act as a reservoir so that when the soil dries out, water can be absorbed from the crystals. Once you apply water the crystals are hydrated again. They continue the swelling and shrinking process, providing plants with water for up to six years. Use them at planting time.

Water the herbs well whenever they feel dry just below the surface of the soil. During windy summer heat you may need to water soft herbs such as basil, mint and parsley twice daily. However, many herbs are of Mediterranean origin and they prefer to dry out between waterings; it is easy to kill herbs like rosemary by keeping them constantly moist.

The most popular of all annual herbs is probably basil. Grow it in a rich, well drained soil and keep it watered during dry weather.

Top ten herbs

Parsley The mostly widely grown herb, growing to 45 cm (18 in) from a thick taproot. Rich in iron and vitamins A, B and C, it is great in salads, soups, stuffing and garnishes. Legend has it that you have to be wicked to be able to grow parsley successfully. Replace your parsley plants by raising fresh seed when the existing plants begin to flower.

Chives This perennial herb with fine, hollow leaves adds a delicate onion flavour to food and can be used as a companion plant for roses.

Rosemary A woody shrub that loves full sun and dry conditions. It is perfect with lamb.

Thyme A symbol of courage and vitality, this herb is used for flavouring egg and cheese dishes. It is mostly grown as an aromatic groundcover for a sunny spot.

Dill This herb is great for use in pickling, with fish and in soups. It has attractive fine foliage and needs to be forced with lots of nitrogen fertiliser.

Mint A herb that grows well in cool, moist areas, even shade, although it can become a pest if it likes the conditions too much. Mint can be used in drinks and salads and for flavouring the traditional favourite, roast lamb. (See 'Marvellous mint ' on page 78.)

Marjoram and oregano These closely related, strongly flavoured herbs are excellent for flavouring soups and pasta dishes. They make a great groundcover in a sunny spot.

Sage A close relative of ornamental salvia, with grey leaves that are useful for stuffing, as well as for flavouring soups, veal and poultry.

Basil An extremely popular cooking herb for use in soups, tomato dishes and pasta sauces, basil is a summer-growing annual and needs replanting each spring. It is also an effective companion plant for tomatoes, as it repels whitefly and other pests.

Vegetable garden design

Vegetable gardens can be delightful places and, like herb and flower gardens, they can be designed in many styles. If the vegetable patch is to be a feature of a garden, rather than just a practical production unit, many possibilities exist.

Vegetable landscaping

Even the smallest of gardens can be beautiful, eccentric, fun – and amazingly productive. Vegetables and fruits were once considered to be plants with fascinating textures, colours and interesting architectural shapes. Then for a long period they were relegated out of sight. However, in the 1980s a revolution began. Edible landscaping was pioneered, and home gardeners looked with fresh eyes at their familiar food plants. They could have a dual purpose – they could be ornamental before they were eaten.

Designing with vegetables

All sorts of unusual vegetables can be used in place of more conventional, non-edible choices in garden planting designs.

Low-growing plants for the front of a border could include a mixed planting of different-coloured lettuces and chicory (endive) – frilled and plain leaf, in greens of every shade, spotted and splashed, or brightly coloured in crimson or bronze. Edible-flowered clove pinks and violets are other possibilities.

Middle height can come from celery, chard (which comes in a rainbow of stem colours), spinach, beetroot, carrots, potatoes, curly kale, and ornamental pink-tinged or red cabbage.

Zucchini (courgettes) form a rosette of sculptural leaves and boast large golden-yellow flowers, which are also edible. Bush squash are equally handsome. Try planting them in tubs in sunny positions. Melons such as 'Sugar Bush' also do well in large containers.

OPPOSITE This potager, designed on the traditional French model, features four intersecting gravel paths. Espaliered fruit trees form a living 'fence', while the pond and statue provide a central focal point.

ACCENT VEGETABLES Edible landscaping is a style of gardening that sees beauty in the textures, shapes and colours of vegetables and incorporates them fully into the ornamental garden. The architectural qualities and beauty of plants such as artichokes, cardoons (below), corn and sunflowers are truly stunning in the flower garden. Rosette-style lettuce and chicory (endive) are particularly delightful at the front of the flower garden. Ruby chard is a dramatic introduction, together with beautiful lavender-and-white-striped or rose-coloured Italian eggplant (aubergines), tomatoes laden with glowing red fruits, golden-fruited zucchini (courgettes) and fountains of fresh celery.

Dramatic height can come from sweet corn, sunflowers, purple-flowered cardoons and artichokes, and tall, staked tomatoes. A bold planting of huge, golden-headed sunflowers and lush tall green corn all tangled with purple-flowered, purple-podded beans makes a real garden showstopper – bold and exciting, as well as edible.

Teepees

Teepees constructed of bamboo canes stuck into the ground in a circle, tied together firmly at the top, and planted with a mass of tall 'Telephone' peas, or stunning flowering beans like 'Scarlet Runner' and 'Purple King', make a spectacular feature in any garden.

Interplanting

Interplant the garden with herbs, companion plants and masses of flowers, add flowering fruit and nut trees and hedges of berries, and you have a true paradise. Whatever style chosen, separate perennial and annual crops. Perennial vegetables such as asparagus need a space devoted exclusively to their culture.

Simple vegetable gardens

Simple palette gardens consisting of a series of raised and edged rectangular beds are serviceable, easily tended, and have a simple charm when filled with vegetables and herbs. Ideally beds should be no wider than 1.2–1.5 m (4–5 ft) wide as this allows for easy

A large bean teepee can make a wonderful summer cubby house for a small child.

Interplant vegetables among other flowering plants for design and colour. Here, low-growing cabbages are planted with tall poppies.

In this attractive combination, a bed of broad bean plants is bordered with a row of low-growing, pale green oak leaf lettuces.

reach when weeding and harvesting. Old-fashioned country vegetable gardens are often set in grass, with raised rows of many vegetables and soft fruits, becoming a humming jungle of neatly tended abundance as the season progresses. The paradise vegetable garden tumbles abundance across paths, using the vertical space of walls, trellises, sheds and summerhouses to create a tapestry of rioting flowers, herbs and vegetables worthy of Eden. The formal potager garden is like a Persian carpet edged with herbs and embroidered with salad leaves and vegetables, every colour and texture chosen with care. The designs for such potagers were common in medieval and Tudor gardens, and can feature standard honeysuckles and roses, pots of topiary and a sundial to mark the alignments of axes. They have become very fashionable once more.

A potager

Luscious leafy vegetables such as cabbage, lettuce and spinach can be handsome plants, coming in a vast range of colours and textures. Blue-green, red or rich green cabbages, glossy green or reddish brown lettuces, ruby chard and purple kohlrabi are just a few that are perfect for dotting about flowers or for adding structure to formal displays. Even parsley looks great as a border.

Many herbs and vegetables have beautiful flowers in their own right. Runner beans have scarlet flowers in profusion and climbing peas have pretty white flowers that are edible. Nasturtiums have vibrant red, orange and yellow flowers, while lavender, chamomile, chives and borage will pretty up any boring vegetable patch.

Winter is the right time to be planting ornamental kale (*Brassica oleracea* Acephala Group) for a spring

Beds are raised, and rambling vines are confined to the outer fence boundaries in this well-planned, cottage-style, flower and vegetable garden. Careful consideration has been given to the colour palette, which uses a variety of pink- and white-blooming plants. Using leaves that are tinged with pink, such as ornamental cabbage, adds further beauty.

display. Its bright pink and frilly green foliage makes it an interesting potted plant but it also brightens up a vegetable garden when it is used to make decorative patterns. Grow kale in full sun, in a free-draining position, although you may need to occasionally dust with derris or diatomaceous earth to keep away the snails and cabbage moth caterpillars.

Raised beds

Using raised beds for growing vegetables, and also herbs, is an ideal way of incorporating a vegetable patch or 'edible garden' where space is limited. There are various benefits associated with growing plants in this way.

A raised bed encourages plants to root deeper into the soil, which means less watering. The plants can also be planted closer together and often in 'square' planting arrangements rather than in rows. This will aid the production of slightly smaller vegetables that are ideal for people living alone or couples. Planting at such a higher density cuts out the total amount of light that reaches the soil and thus reduces the development of weeds. This particular type of bed system will allow the growing season to be extended if necessary, as it is easy to cover part or all of the bed with either clear polythene sheeting or fleece suspended on wire hoops that are fastened to the retaining wall of the bed. The beds can be any length or height required, but the width of each bed is very important. The ideal width of each bed is about 1.5–2 m (5–7 ft), so it is possible to reach the centre of the bed from each side, rather than having to walk on the soil in the bed.

When clearing areas to make raised beds, use the removed topsoil to fill the raised beds, or mix it with new topsoil, incorporating plenty of bulky organic matter, such as compost or well-rotted manure, to encourage bacterial and worm activity. These bulky materials will also retain more moisture, reducing the need to water the plants so frequently in dry weather.

handy tip

Window gardens

Windowboxes can be filled with dwarf tomatoes and herbs, like basil, which also repel flies from windows. Trellises and the sides of garden sheds and summer houses can be covered with climbing beans and peas, annual nasturtiums in flaming reds and golds, and climbing squash.

CONSTRUCTING A RAISED BED

1 Mark out the area and
dimensions for your desired
raised bed, and remove any
surface vegetation. Level the soil
along the lines where the timber
sections are to be positioned.
Lay out the first layer of timber
to create a low wooden 'wall'
for the planting bed, and use
a builder's square to check the
right angles of the structure.
You should also use a spirit level
to check the timber sections
are level. Repeat the process,
working around the wall,
stacking timber sections to raise
the height of the wall. Drive
15 cm (6 in) nails into the corner
joints on each layer of timber
in order to keep them stable.

2 When the wall has reached
the required height, fix the
top row by driving 15 cm (6 in)
nails at an angle through the
vertical joints.

3 Dig over the soil inside the bed
area. Add some extra soil and
organic matter and mix
with the existing soil to aid
drainage and water movement.
Firm the soil well enough
to reduce uneven settling later
when the plants are in place.

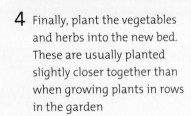

4 Finally, plant the vegetables
and herbs into the new bed.
These are usually planted
slightly closer together than
when growing plants in rows
in the garden

Growing vegetables in containers

Vegetables grow easily in containers, and many are ornamental as well as edible and can be used to lovely effect on a deck, verandah or in a courtyard. Frilly-leaved lettuces, scarlet-flowered beans, purple or borlotti beans, purple mustard and red cabbage are just a few of the beautiful vegetables which can be used with other flowers, or to lift the greens of your vegetables.

The key factor with any container is the root zone. If you nurture down at this level, plants will repay you with healthy, delicious growth. Choose a premium grade potting mix that contains fully composted organic material for water-holding ability and nutrient supply, double washed river sand for drainage and texture, slow-release fertiliser for sustained supply of nutrients, and

Chillies and other fruiting vegetables, such as cherry tomatoes, peppers (capsicum) or eggplant (aubergine), can be easily grown in containers. Rooting vegetables such as radishes, baby carrots or spring onions are great choices, too.

water crystals to stop the medium from drying out. This should be available from a garden centre or nursery.

Choosing containers

Next, ensure that the container you choose suits the crop you're trying to grow. Obviously root crops will need a deep container suitable for the length of underground tubers. Old tyres stacked on top of each other are perfect, especially for potatoes as the height can be added to, which encourages further production of tubers. Top-heavy crops such as tomatoes need weighty pots that don't blow over in the wind and can secure a stake, so large cement troughs that hold a trellis are perfect. Other climbers, like snow peas (mangetout), will trail equally as well as they climb, so large hanging baskets are a space-efficient way of growing them.

Containers don't have to be limited to the stock standard plastic pot, however. Think outside the square and imagine what's possible. Rustic-style trugs and wooden crates look great filled with leaf crops and flowering nasturtiums oozing colour. Wicker baskets (lined with perforated plastic and treated with marine-strength varnish) come in all shapes and sizes, and match cane teepees or tripods perfect for growing peas, beans, tomato and cucumbers. Even modern items such as plastic organisers and shoe pockets can have drainage

holes punctured in them to make super spots for small vegetables like lettuces and other perennial cut-and-come-agains, and they are easily transported and light which makes them ideal for mobile gardeners.

The hydroponic vegetable garden

Of course, there are also many units available for growing hydroponics, so even the indoor gardener can have pots of produce, provided an investment in the right equipment (grow lights, water recirculators and so on) is made.

Although hydroponics is thought of as a modern invention, it has been used in simple forms for many centuries. The floating gardens of the Aztecs, for instance, consisted of rafts of rushes covered with soil and planted with crops, then tethered in the shallow waters of lakes. The roots grew through the raft to obtain a continuous supply of water and nutrients.

How hydroponic gardening works

The ideal garden for most vegetable growers is a plot of rich earth in a sunny place. But for apartment dwellers who hope to raise at least some fresh vegetables, hydroponics, the art of cultivating plants without soil, can offer a solution. It is also a helpful technique in growing crops in the home greenhouse where space is limited, and for gardeners who live in arid areas where water is scarce.

In hydroponic systems, plants are supported by an inert growing medium such as scoria, perlite or pea gravel, or by an artificially created medium such as Rockwool. The open nature of these types of media allow for good aeration of the plant roots which are continuously flushed with a nutrient-rich solution. Unlike soil-grown plants, everything required for growth must be supplied by the growing system. Very precisely formulated commercial nutrient supplies are injected into the water which is pumped to the plants, and any excess is usually recycled via a reserve tank.

Because the root systems of plants grown hydroponically do not need to explore widely for

Zucchini (courgette) will grow well in a medium-sized container, showing off its striking flowers and soft, attractive leaves.

radish
Raphanus sativus

baby beans
Phaseolus vulgaris

snow peas
(mangetout)
Pisum sativum var. macrocarpon

sunflower
Helianthus annuus

cherry tomatoes
Lycopersicon esculentum

CHILDREN'S VEGETABLES
Children love to sort things and classifying the food we eat is an invaluable education. Vegetables also grow in many different ways, as vines, bushes or roots. Introducing children to home growing allows them the opportunity to pick and eat food straight from the plant, uncooked and sweet.

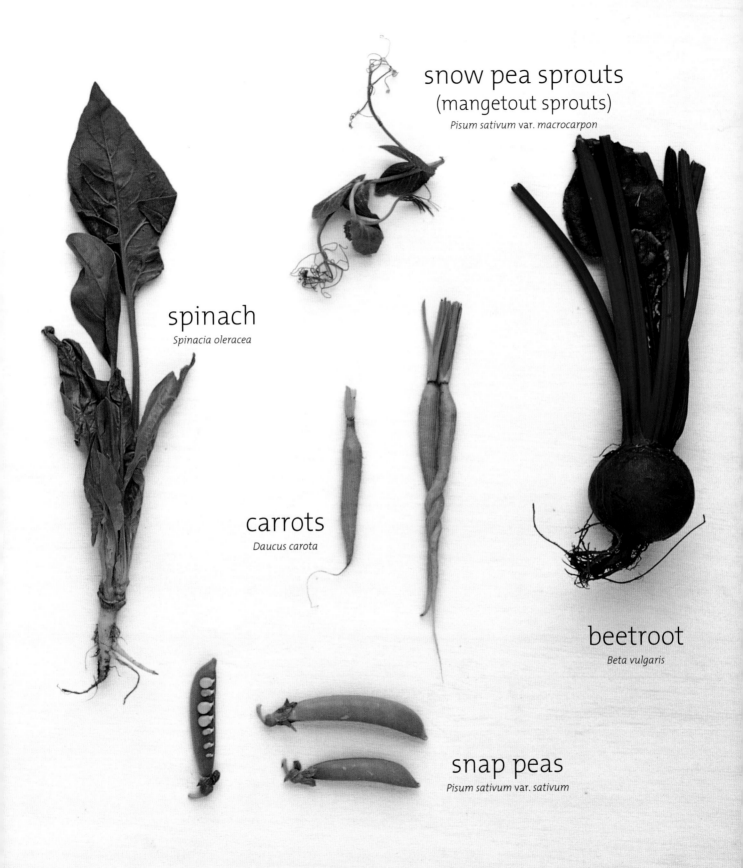

snow pea sprouts
(mangetout sprouts)
Pisum sativum var. macrocarpon

spinach
Spinacia oleracea

carrots
Daucus carota

beetroot
Beta vulgaris

snap peas
Pisum sativum var. sativum

You can use strips of pantyhose to tie tomatoes and other plants to stakes. These ties are flexible, soft and do not weather easily.

lack flavour and question their nutritional value in comparison to plants raised in rich, well-composted gardens. Due to rapid growth, plants may also lack stem strength. Salad leaf vegetables are ideal crops for raising by hydroponics. Tomatoes, cucumbers and peppers (capsicums) are also good subjects, and the vines should be supported in their growth.

A number of different commercial hydroponic systems are available for home gardeners, and these range from single pot systems to growing bags and domestic greenhouse units. These are usually powered by external pumps.

Climbing vegetables

The value of vertical gardening is often overlooked, but the space gained by going up is invaluable. Traditionally wire supports, wooden stakes, trelliswork and cane tripods carry the weight of plants such as climbing beans and peas, cucumbers and tomatoes. Even old tools, ladders and pot stands, however, can be used to add character – pretty scarlet runner beans on an arbour make a beautiful feature.

Some plants climb by themselves, given a support, such as beans and peas, due to their tendrils. Others, such as tomatoes and cucumbers, will need securing using budding tape or other flexible ties. Others happily trail on the ground, but are less likely to succumb to rot if lifted up with a support, such as zucchini (courgette).

Other edible climbers to include in your vertical garden include:

- Choko (chayote) vines on the fence, which are simple to grow.
- Sweet potatoes or yams, which can grow on 4 m (13 ft) wide trellis panels in frost-free positions.
- Malabar spinach, also known as Indian spinach (*Basella rubra*), which has green and red forms, is a vigorous climber with leaves resembling spinach perfect for tropical areas.
- Soy beans can also be grown on tripods.

nutients as do soil-raised plants, the root systems are smaller, and a higher density of planting can be made. Hydroponic plants grow rapidly as they suffer no setbacks in terms of water and nutrient supply. The inert medium in which the plants are grown ensures that there are minimal weeds and few diseases. Plants grown indoors require additional light which should be supplied by full spectrum fluorescent lights. An additional benefit is that the system can be automated, allowing the gardener to be safely away from the crops for short periods.

On the other hand, some gardeners express the opinion that hydroponically raised vegetables

Support and protection

Plants that have weak stems or a climbing habit will require some kind of support. Among these are cucumbers, tomatoes (tall varieties), peas and beans. The form of support will be determined by the plant's habit. Beans, which are vigorous growers, will need 1.8 m (6 ft) canes, tied together in a teepee shape or in a row. The canes must be anchored firmly, as the weight with the full crop is considerable. Tomatoes are best supported with a single, stout bamboo cane. Tie in the stem as it grows. Cucumbers can be trained flat to a trellis panel. With any fast-growing climbing vegetables, you will need to pinch out the growing point once enough fruiting trusses have formed, and you may have to remove some of the leaves from the sideshoots so that the fruit can ripen.

No-dig gardening

'No-dig' gardening is a specialised form of sheet composting. The technique can be used anywhere, even on the worst and most compacted soils, or directly onto lawn, to yield excellent crops. First provide an edging for the future garden. Then give the soil a good soak. As a first step, overlapping, thick layers of newspaper are laid on the ground, followed by a layer of lucerne hay, a layer of organic fertiliser, a layer of loose straw, and another thin layer of organic fertiliser. After watering well, depressions can be made in the surface and filled with compost. Well-established seedlings, large seeds, tubers and bulbs can then be immediately planted. If there is enough compost available, a layer of compost can be placed on top of the garden, rather than creating compost pockets. The contents reduce in height rapidly and will grow excellent crops.

SUPPORTING BEANS

In order to encourage green beans to grow upwards, you will need to provide some sort of support structure. Canes are ideal for this.

1 Insert the canes at least 15 cm (6 in) into the ground at appropriate planting distances, and plant the beans about 5 cm (2 in) to the side of each supporting cane.

2 The bean plant will twine itself around the cane until it reaches the top. You can then pinch out the leading shoot to prevent further growth.

SUPPORTING TOMATOES

1 To make the base, measure and cut two lengths of timber to the same width as the growing bag. Drill and screw the long and short lengths together in order to form a rectangle. Cut a section of wire mesh that will cover the top of the wooden rectangle and staple the wire mesh to the edges.

2 Turn the rectangle over and drill one 15 mm (⅝ in) hole (about 7.5 cm/3 in deep) at each corner. Place the growing bag inside the frame and insert a stout cane into each of the drilled holes.

3 Draw the two canes at each end together and tie them at the top to form an arch. Tie a cane horizontally from one cane arch to another (just above the point where the arching canes are joined.) Next, tie long strings to the horizontal cane and lower them to the growing bag.

4 Place the tomato plants into the growing bag and water them well. Tie the strings around the base of each plant, so that, as the plants grow, they can be twisted around the string and it will provide support. After three weeks of growth, the tomatoes will start to flower.

Growing bags are a great solution for balcony gardeners as they can be persuaded to fit into awkward corners and spaces.

range from long-term plants, such as apple trees with a life-span of 15–20 years, down to plants as fast growing as radishes, which grow from seed to maturity in just a number of weeks.

If you have a small patio or balcony, you could buy, or make your own, growing bag (a strong plastic bag filled with growing medium in which you simply have to cut holes). Growing bags make convenient containers for short-term plants, such as low-growing vegetables, which will usually only be in residence for a single growing season.

Although seen as short-term containers, there can be a fair amount of fertiliser residue left in the growing bags at the end of the season, especially when plants such as cucumbers, peppers (capsicums) and tomatoes have been grown in them. Therefore, they can be used twice, to grow salad crops such as lettuces and radishes without the need for any extra fertiliser.

Unfortunately, it is common to encounter problems when growing taller plants, such as eggplants (aubergines), cucumbers and peppers (capsicums), because the growing bags do not have the depth to allow for canes to be used as supports. This can be overcome by making a frame around the bag and fastening the support structure to the frame, so that the plants grow up towards the support.

Plants that are vulnerable to attacks from flying pests will benefit from being grown in a polytunnel, or covered with netting. This will also help to protect against cold. However, those plants that are insect-pollinated must have the covers removed once they flower in order to set fruit.

Making a tomato support system

In recent years, there has been a dramatic rise in growing food crops in all kinds of containers. These

Aquatic and moisture-loving vegetables

While good drainage is essential to growing most vegetables, some require quite wet soils or flourish beside or in streams, lakes and the sea.

Seaweeds

Not all seaweeds are edible, but among those eaten are species of kelp or kombu (both known as wakame when dried), papery *Porphyra* which is sold dried as nori or laver, green-leaved sea lettuce (*Ulva lactuca*), and the popular salty flavoured dulse (*Palmaria palmata*). These are used to flavour soups and stews, in salads, in stir-fry dishes and as sushi wraps. Seaweeds should only be harvested from waters known to be unpolluted.

Salicornia

Salicornia, or marsh samphire, is a succulent subshrub that colonises tidal marshes. Its bright green, thin stems led to one of its common names sea asparagus. It is used raw and crisp in salads, as a bed for fresh seafood dishes, briefly boiled and served as a vegetable with butter, or Italian-style with olive oil and a squeeze of lemon.

Sea beet

The sea beet (*Beta maritiima*) grows wild along the coasts of Europe and North Africa, as well as eastward as far as India. The coarse white flesh of this root has little to recommend it. The leaves, on the other hand, are well worth harvesting. They have a flavour comparable to their modern incarnation as chard. The leaves can be steamed and served with butter and garlic or used in any dish as a substitute for spinach.

Sea kale

Sea kale (*Crambe maritima*) grows naturally just above the tideline, and resembles a loose head of broccoli. At this stage it is bitter, but if the emerging shoots are 'blanched', by covering them from the light with pebbles or sand on the beach, or garden pots in the garden or glasshouse, for a week or more, the shoots become creamy white, tender and delicious. They are cooked and eaten like asparagus with melted butter.

Watercress

Watercress can easily be grown in well composted soil which is kept moist and located in a lightly shaded area. It is easily propagated from tip cuttings rooted in a container of water, then transplanted into the soil.

Lotus

The beautiful perennial water lotus (*Nelumbo nucifera*) has long been grown in ponds and slow-moving streams in Asia not only for its long-stemmed pink or white waterlily-like flowers sacred to Buddha, but for its edible rhizomes which are perforated in cross section, and for the nut-like seed shaken from huge pepperpot-like ripe receptacles. The sliced rhizome is cooked as a vegetable or candied.

Wild rice

Wild rice is not actually a species of rice but an annual large seeded water grass *Zizania palustris* which is native to the Great Lakes Area of North America. Wild rice can only be collected today with a licence, and gathering must be carried out using traditional techniques. Cultivated wild rice is also available.

Water chestnuts

Water chestnuts are the underwater corms of *Eleocharis dulcis*, native to Asia. They are quite easily raised in warm climates in a water container such as a wading pool with a plug, or baby bath or, for balcony gardeners, in an aquarium. They require a long growing season of 180–220 days, but the corms can be presprouted for earlier planting. Their sweet, finely textured flesh is crisp and crunchy and is sliced to add texture to Chinese dishes or eaten fresh.

LOTUS ROOT When sliced horizontally, lotus root displays a floral-like pattern of holes. This decorativeness, along with its crisp, delicately flavoured flesh, is much appreciated in Chinese and Japanese cuisine. First peel the root, then slice it before eating it raw or cooked. Add it to salads or stir-fries, or cut into chunks, or stuff. Store in water with a squeeze of lemon juice to prevent it from turning brown. The seeds are also edible, eaten out of the hand, or used in Chinese desserts and soups. The leaves are used to wrap food such as whole fish for cooking. Lotus root can be bought fresh, dried, frozen and canned.

water spinach
Ipomoea aquatica

MOISTURE-LOVING VEGETABLES

As space suitable for farming becomes more and more limited, crops that can be grown in poorly drained sites and even in the ocean will become increasingly popular and necessary. Of course, many edible plants have traditionally been grown in these environs.

wild rice
Zizania palustris

marsh samphire
Salicornia spp.

water mint
Mentha aquatica

memory plant
Bacopa monieri

taro
Alocasia macrorrhiza

dried seaweed

memory plant
Bacopa monieri

water chestnut
Eleocharis dulcis

2

Cultivating

Cultivating

Digging and cultivating techniques will help you get the most from your soil. Organic gardening practices such as crop rotation and companion planting will also benefit and increase your edible garden bounty.

Cultivating the soil

Any soil cultivation deeper than 20–25 cm (8–10 in) can be regarded as a form of deep cultivation. Deep digging is a practice that can be beneficial to heavy and compacted soils, as it can aid drainage as well as improve conditions in the root zone. The top 15 cm (6 in) of the soil is the most biologically active, containing a thriving, organically rich community of beneficial organisms such as bacteria, fungi, insects and worms. These organisms will feed on the organic matter and plant debris in the soil, breaking them down into forms which are available as food for the resident plants. Incorporating organic matter, such as garden mix or rotted manure, into this zone, or just below it, will improve natural soil fertility, as well as putting nutrients close to the roots and improving the texture of the soil. An additional benefit is that the decomposing organic matter is very good at retaining moisture close to the plants' roots. This is a factor which can be hugely advantageous during dry summer conditions. You will find that burying the manure or potting mix in the

However you choose to lay out your edible garden beds, you should make a plan – maybe numbering the beds – to show what you are planting where.

bottom of the trench during digging (providing it is not too deep) will encourage deeper-rooting plants.

The deep bed system

Organic growing systems aim to reduce the amount of soil cultivation in order to preserve natural fertility and soil structure. Materials such as manure and other organic fertilisers are crucial to organic growing practices, since they help to build and maintain a good soil structure.

When using the deep bed system, the soil structure is improved to the required depth with one cultivation, combined with the incorporation of large quantities of organic matter. From this point on, deep cultivations are kept to a bare minimum so that a natural soil structure develops and remains largely intact, and walking on the soil beds is avoided in order to prevent disturbance or compaction.

Very often the only cultivation that takes place once the bed has been established will either be digging shallow planting holes to transport seedlings of the next edible crop or digging up root vegetables when they are harvested. With further organic matter being added only as mulches and top dressings, it is quickly incorporated by the large worm population, allowing a natural soil structure to develop.

In order to achieve optimum results with a deep bed system, the soil must be loose and deeply dug, so the roots can penetrate to the required depth rather than spreading sideways.

The soil must also be enriched with plenty of organic matter such as compost or manure. To reduce pest and disease problems, crop residue should be removed and composted in a separate area before being returned to the deep bed area later.

GARDEN STRUCTURES A garden shed is very useful for storing gardening equipment and can be placed in an unproductive area of the garden. The siting of any other structures such as compost bins, garden seats, a summerhouse or a greenhouse should be considered in creating the overall design. All-weather access to the garden is essential for easy harvesting under bad weather conditions. Raised paths paved with stone or bricks, or constructed from gravel, are attractive as well as practical.

Nettles

Stinging nettles are a sign of fertile soil. For an organic liquid fertiliser, fill a bucket with water and a bunch of nettles. Allow the nettles to rot down for 2–3 weeks. Use the resulting liquid as a nutrient-rich foliar spray which is also useful against aphids, blackfly and mildew.

DEEP BED SYSTEM

1 Mark one edge of the bed with a planting line. Measure 1.2 m (4 ft) across with a planting board and set up another planting line parallel to the first. Using canes, mark a trench 60 cm (2 ft) wide; dig it out one spade deep and keep the soil to cover the last trench. Break up the exposed subsoil in the bottom of the trench with a fork, so the roots can penetrate deeply.

2 Put a 5–7.5 cm (2–3 in) layer of well-rotted manure into the bottom of the trench.

3 Leaving a cane in the corner of the first trench, measure another 60 cm (2 ft) section with the other cane, so it contains the same amount of soil. Dig the soil and transfer it to the first trench, spreading it to cover the manure.

4 Add another 5–7.5 cm (2–3 in) layer of manure to the first trench. The bulk of the manure and the loosened soil will raise the bed height. Continue to dig out soil from the second trench and cover the new layer of manure, leaving a deep bed of loose, organically enriched soil in the first trench. Scrape the soil from the bottom of the second trench. Break up the exposed soil. Repeat steps until the whole plot is cultivated. Use saved soil to cover the manure in the final trench.

DOUBLE DIGGING METHOD

1 Starting at one end of the plot, mark out an area of about 60 cm (2 ft) wide using a garden line and canes. Dig a trench of the full width, and the depth of one spade. If it is very large, the plot may be divided in two for convenience.

2 Remove the soil from this first trench and take it to the far end of the plot, laying it quite close to the area where the final trench is to be dug. When the soil is removed from the first trench, fork over the base of the trench to the full depth of the fork's tines. If required, some compost or manure may be forked into the lower layer of soil or scattered on top of it after cultivation.

3 When the base of the trench is cultivated and the compacted layer broken through, mark out the next area 60 cm (2 ft) wide with a garden line. Using a spade start to dig the soil from this second area, throwing it into the first trench, while making sure that the soil is turned over as it is moved. This process will create the second trench and the base is forked over.

4 The process is repeated until the entire plot has been dug to a depth of about 50 cm ($1^2/_3$ ft).

Double digging

With the double digging method soil is cultivated to a depth of two spade blades. This technique is most frequently used on land that is being cultivated for the first time or where a hard subsurface layer (called a pan) of soil has formed, impeding drainage and the penetration of roots.

This method of digging improves the friability of the subsoil without bringing it nearer to the surface, so the most biologically active layer of topsoil is always closest to the roots of cultivated plants. It is very important to avoid mixing the subsoil with the topsoil. If the two are mixed together, the fertility of the topsoil is diluted, rather than improving the fertility of the subsoil. Although this type of digging is hard work and can be very laborious, the benefits of double digging a plot can last up to 15 years, provided the soil is managed correctly. To double dig an area so that deeper-rooted plants such as roses, shrubs, trees or fruit bushes and trees can be grown, a number of gardeners favour adding a layer of well-rotted manure or compost into the bottom of the trench before the topsoil is reincorporated. In the edible garden, however, this organic matter may be laid over the surface of the soil after double digging as it will then be drawn into the topsoil by worms and insects. This way, the soil-borne bacteria and fungi break it down. On heavier soils a layer of ash, sand or gravel may be mixed into the bottom of the trench before the topsoil is reincorporated, to help improve the damage.

Beans prefer well drained, fertilised soil with plenty of added organic matter.

step by step

MAKING STRAW COMPOST

1 Cover the base of the area with 30 cm (12 in) of loose straw. Soak the straw with water.

2 Sprinkle a light covering of nitrogenous fertiliser over the straw to speed up decomposition.

3 Add another 30 cm (12 in) layer of loose straw to the stack, water it well and add more fertiliser.

4 As the straw decomposes, it will become covered in white mould and resembles well-rotted manure.

Organic gardening

You probably dream of a garden spilling over with fragrance and colour, brimming with luscious, juicy fruits, health-filled herbs, crisp and crunchy salad greens and perfect vegetables. This garden is alive with jewelled butterflies and pollen-heavy bees, and filled with the songs of birds.

The reality never quite matches the dream. Other creatures feast on your Garden of Eden, and nibbled leaves and fruits, webbings and pest droppings mar your visions of perfection. But the balance is easily tipped in favour of your ideal if you use simple organic techniques that will enhance the health of your garden – for example, adding slow-release organic fertilisers and soil improvers such as compost, rotted manures and seaweed supplements; reducing the potential for predators and diseases by using crop rotation and crop sanitation; and using herbs both as companion plants and in environmentally harmless, home-made sprays.

Crop rotation

Long before science and technology began taking an interest in gardening after World War II, farmers and home gardeners practised a very complex rotation of vegetable crops each season. Phases of the moon were taken into account and the whole method took on almost mystical qualities. In the garden vegetable patch it is very wise to break the crop relationship cycle. Plant a root crop such as turnip or carrots where you've just had a leaf crop such as lettuce. Plant onions prior to a crop of tomatoes, and peas and beans after cabbages and Swiss chard (silverbeet). And avoid planting anything from the same family season after season in the same bed – for example, do not plant tomatoes after potatoes, or cabbage after broccoli.

It was Charles 'Turnip' Townsend who introduced the turnip, a root crop, to England from Europe in the early 1700s and advocated its use in crop rotation. The turnip is from a different family from the potato, the most popular root vegetable, so farmers could alternate their root vegetable crops and still practise crop rotation successfully. This basic rotation of crops stops any soil-borne insects and diseases from remaining in the same garden bed year after year, and avoids the depletion of certain soil nutrients that results from planting similar vegetables in the same plot.

How crop rotation works

Different vegetable crops use nutrients in different ways, so that soil can be depleted of these nutrients despite your best preparation. The lists below will help you identify the groups to which your vegetables belong. To make crop rotation easier, keep records of what you plant and where.

CROP ROTATION This gardening technique is simple in principle: don't plant the same crop in the same bed two years running. First, this will avoid the build-up of any crop's particular pests and diseases. Second, it will help to get the best value from your compost. The need to grow vegetables quickly means they must have rich soil, and that means the edible garden will take most of your compost. But not all need their soil equally enriched. Leafy things such as lettuces and cabbages need it richest; fruit crops such as tomatoes (right), peas and peppers (capsicums) are not so greedy; root crops are less greedy still. Herbs and other permanent crops do not need to be rotated.

LEFT Perennial vegetables, such as asparagus, don't need to take part in your crop rotation plan. They can be given permanent beds in the garden.

BELOW Cabbages (top) are heavy feeders while beans and peas (bottom) are less nutrient-needy.

- Cabbage, Chinese spinach (amaranth), cauliflower, broccoli, Brussels sprouts, kohlrabi, radish, swede, turnip, mustard greens
- Tomato, pepper (capsicum), chillies, eggplant (aubergine), potato
- Pea, broad bean, dwarf bean, climbing bean
- Pumpkin, squash, melon, cucumber, zucchini (courgette), marrow
- Carrot, parsnip, celery, parsley
- Swiss chard (silverbeet), beetroot, spinach
- Lettuce, globe and Jerusalem artichoke
- Onion, garlic, shallot, leek, chive.

In the home garden crops may need to be grown in the same area more frequently than they should be, but try to rotate crops as the reduction in disease (especially soil-borne disease) is considerable. Grow your vegetables according to the appropriate season. If you try to grow them out of season the results will be very poor.

Companion planting

Grouping together plants that complement each other, thus reducing the need for chemical sprays and the overall incidence of insect and disease attack, is called

companion planting. Certain combinations of herbs and vegetables actually encourage better growth as well as repel predatory insects. Many herbs, especially those with fragrant foliage, encourage your garden to help itself by attracting beneficial insects.

Benefits of companion planting

Companion planting brings together the observations of countless generations of gardeners and farmers: plants are not the totally passive organisms that many imagine. In fact, some species are able to wage biochemical warfare on diseases and predators and can offer this protection to other nearby species. And some species produce chemicals that will stimulate the growth and productivity of another species. Putting these observations into practical terms, gardeners can place plants together so that one, or even both, partners in the planting benefit. While this seems to be a technique for small-scale gardens, it has also been used by farmers who practise intercropping and barrier

THE BLESSING OF MARIGOLDS Nematodes can be a hugely destructive pest to a variety of crops. Some species of nematode are responsible for severe crop damage, resulting in reduced growth, low yields and wilting. When infected plant roots are dug up, they appear to have tiny gall-like growths over the surface. Gardeners often mistakenly attribute these effects to drought or poor soil fertility.

However, nature has also produced a powerful nematicide, a biomolecule produced to some degree by all species of marigolds (Tagetes spp.). The substance is exuded by the roots. Marigolds can be used as barrier plantings around gardens, and the dwarf French marigold (Tagetes patula) is particularly useful for this purpose. If the brilliant golden or orange flowers upset your garden colour scheme, it is an easy matter to shear the heads off.

Here tomatoes are underplanted with French marigolds (Tagetes patula) for protection against pests such as the destructive nematode.

planting. Although companion planting has long been regarded as useful, these beneficial interactions have not been well understood until recently. If you could see all the energies weaving through your garden, and all the chemical messages moving backwards and forwards between all the plants and animals, both above and below ground, an incredibly complex and continuously changing picture would emerge.

How companion planting works

For thousands of years gardeners have known that certain plants grow well together and complement

Some effective pest-repelling herbs (from left), curry plant, southernwood and dogbane.

each other, to the extent that they appear to grow less successfully when they are growing apart. Others seem to be more successful growing on their own, and in fact, other plants seem to have difficulty growing close by them. Scientists have been able to establish that a number of plants actually produce chemicals that seep from their roots, fallen leaves or twigs and that these chemicals have an allelopathic effect on the surrounding soil. In other words, these plants use these chemicals to keep other plants from growing too close to them. This acts to reduce competition from neighbouring plants and helps to ward off pests and diseases or reduce the harm they can do to certain plants. French marigold (*Tagetes minima*), for instance, produces a root exudate that acts as a barrier to perennial weeds such as bindweed and ground elder, as well as deterring nematodes, sometimes called eelworms.

Some companion plants can be used as attractants rather than repellents. Such plants may be used as 'trap plants', to act as bait and draw a particular pest away from a valuable crop onto another plant. In effect, these trap plants will be sacrificed for the good of the main crop. Once the trap plant is completely infested with the pest, remove and destroy the plant and the pests at the same time.

However, the ideal ratio of cropping plants to companion plants is not fully documented yet. If there are too few companion plants present, only a small proportion of the crop will receive protection, but if too many have been planted, crop yield may be disappointing due to the competition between the cropping plants and their companions.

It is also worth remembering that companion planting can disrupt crop rotations, and may actually harbour some pests and diseases, enabling them to survive from one crop to the next.

Vegetable companions

These plants make good companions:

- Basil with tomatoes, asparagus, beans, grapes, apricots and fuchsias
- Beans with potatoes and sweet corn
- Chives with carrots, cucumbers and tomatoes
- Cucumbers with potatoes
- Hyssop with cabbages and grape
- Leeks with celery
- Lettuce with carrots, onions and strawberries
- French marigolds (*Tagetes* spp.) with tomatoes, roses, potatoes and beans
- Melons with sweet corn
- Mint with cabbages and other brassicas and peas
- Nasturtiums with cucumbers, zucchini (courgettes), squash and apple trees
- Onions with carrots, kohlrabi and turnip
- Peas with carrots.

Fabulous basil

Of all the olfactory confusers basil is perhaps the best. And it is impossible to have enough basil in the summer garden – as a companion plant, for the sheer sensuous delight of its fragrance, and for the kitchen. There are more than 30 different basils available. Many are decorative with ruffles, purple, red or striped foliage, and lilac or white flowers. Some have delicious scents of lemon, sweet licorice, cool sweet camphor or spice mixed with traditional sweet basil scent. Basil makes a wonderful insect-repelling centrepiece during the summer months.

Marvellous Mint

There are many species of mint, including apple mint, spearmint, eau de cologne mint (*Mentha* x *piperita* var. *citrata*), pineapple mint and pennyroyal. Mint repels most pests, especially fleas and beetles, which dislike the smell. Dried mint sachets in the wardrobe will freshen clothes and keep moths at bay. Fresh mint in the pantry will deter ants. Rub fresh mint leaves on your hands, neck and face to protect your skin from mosquitoes. Plant mints around a dog kennel or strew mint near animal cages to repel flies. Rub fresh mint around the eyes and mouths of horses or cows to discourage pesky flies.

Mint is the perfect companion plant for cabbages and tomatoes – it repels cabbage white butterfly, aphids and whiteflies.

For lovers of a fragrant garden, eau de cologne mint releases a citrus scent when you brush past it.

Spearmint.

Variegated apple mint.

Chocolate mint.

If you already have mint growing in your garden, just dig up a runner with healthy roots and replant it.

HERBS, THE GOOD COMPANIONS

The most common herb companions, together with their effects on companion crops, are listed below.

Herb	Crop	Known effect
Basil	Tomatoes	Repels winged insects
Borage	Strawberries	Improves yield and quality by improving availability of calcium and potassium; provides light shade
Chamomile	Tomatoes, roses, apples, broad beans, brassicas	Known as 'the plant doctor'; repels a number of insects
Chives (including garlic chives)	Roses, apples, carrots, tomatoes, celery, lettuce	Inhibits black spot and scab
Dill	Many	Refuge for hoverflies. Do not plant with carrots
Garlic	Roses	Broad effects
Hyssop	Brassicas	Repels cabbage white butterfly; reputed to improve grape yields. Do not plant with pumpkins or zucchini (courgettes)
Lavender	General	Repels flying insect pests; attracts bees for pollination
Marigold (*Tagetes* spp.)	Tomatoes, garlic, roses	Repels nematodes; repels whitefly
Mint	Brassicas	Repels flies and cabbage caterpillar
Nasturtium	Tomatoes, squash, radish, celery	Repels woolly aphids, whitefly and ants; trap plant for blackfly
Nettle	General	Repels blackfly
Parsley	Carrots	Deters carrot fly
Pyrethrum daisy	General	Repels a number of pests
Rosemary	Carrots	Repels carrot fly and some flying insects; appears to have general benefits; attracts bees for crop pollination
Sage	Potatoes, carrots, grapes	Repels cabbage white butterfly and a number of other harmful flying insects
Summer savory	Brassicas, beans, onions	Repels some flying insect pests; attracts bees for crop pollination

Some bad combinations to watch out for include:

- Apples with potatoes
- Beans with garlic
- Cabbages with strawberries
- Gladioli with strawberries, beans and peas
- Sunflowers with any vegetable but squash
- Wormwood with almost everything.

Herbs as companions

If you have the time to plan your garden with care, specific companion herbs can be grown in conjunction with each crop. Try some of these effective traditional planting combinations.

- Chives, nasturtiums, basil and parsley with tomatoes
- Nasturtiums with squash and radish
- Summer savory with bean and onion crops
- Horseradish and marigolds (*Tagetes* spp.) with potato crops
- Chamomile, hyssop, sage, rosemary, thyme, marigolds and savory with cabbages, kale, broccoli and Brussels sprouts
- Chives and nasturtiums with celery
- Sage, rosemary and chives with carrots.

Unsuccessful combinations with herbs

Some planting combinations are negative in effect, however, resulting in reduced growth and productivity. Herbs are not often included in these incompatible combinations, but you should avoid the following:

- Hyssop with pumpkins
- Chives with peas
- Dill with carrots
- Fennel with tomatoes.

Spatial interaction

Planting a great diversity of plants in a mosaic, rather than in blocks or solid rows of a single variety, will provide your garden with an excellent insurance policy.

The range of plants in this densely planted herb bed – lavender, mustard, cotton lavender, violas and rue – acts as a natural and attractive way to deter insects from infesting your garden.

Instead of providing insects with an endless feast with your conventional planting scheme, you will force insects to hunt for the next target crop plant. This may well be some distance away. And locating that crop may be made even more difficult by the many confusing scent signals emitted by the diverse plants in your garden. These clever tactics are easy to carry out, and remarkably effective in ensuring that you share as little as possible of your garden harvest with the insect world. The physical effects created by the way plants are arranged in the garden or in a farm crop, including the use of nurse crops, is now known as spatial interaction, and sometimes it can also offer an unexpected form of pest control. The famous traditional 'Three Sisters' garden of the Iroquois Indians, who lived in the north-eastern area of North America, combined corn, squash

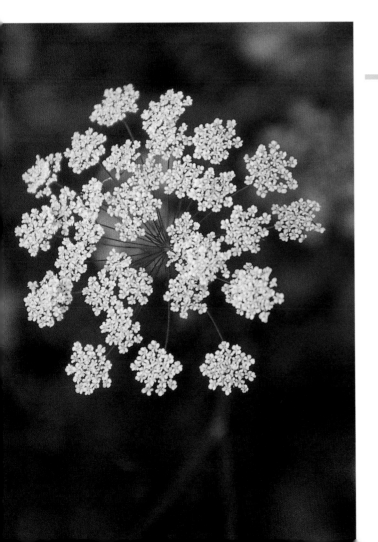

Nature in balance

Nature hates any imbalance in the environment, so destroying all insects could leave your plants vulnerable to other problems. A better way is to encourage balance.

■ Attract beneficial insects by dotting parsley, dill and Queen Anne's lace about, and by planting perfumed shrubs.

■ Birds eat lots of grubs, but will only venture into your garden if there is water to drink and some low-growing bushes for them to perch on in safety. Growing some plants that produce seed and nectar will also encourage birds to stay. And plant some herbs that attract birds – borage, dill, German chamomile, nasturtium, pineapple sage and elder.

and beans. We now know that this combination not only offers mutual protection and nitrogen benefits, but also disorients and confuses squash vine borer.

Nurse crops

The simplest beneficial effects offered by plants are purely physical, the result of something as simple as providing shelter from wind, or shading from the sun. Nurse plants in nature, for instance, may have roots that help break up and aerate heavy and compacted soils, or their canopy may offer protection to emerging plants. Farmers have traditionally used nurse crops to protect emerging plants – for instance, planting weed-suppressing annual rye grass or oats to protect and prepare the way for a perennial planting of lucerne; or interplanting raspberry plants with rows of fruit trees, so that the berries are given some protective shading.

The delicate flowers of Queen Anne's lace (*Daucus carota*) attract beneficial insects such as bees.

PEST-REPELLING HERBS

Many herbs contain phenols and other chemicals that repel pests. The most common are naphthalene (the ingredient in mothballs), pyrethrum and citronella; all three are contained in many household sprays. But other herbs deter pests. The *Artemisia* genus – which includes wormwood and southernwood – is known for its moth-, intestinal worm- and fly-repelling qualities; rue (*Ruta graveolens*) repels cats; and the *Tanacetum* genus – which includes pyrethrum, tansy and feverfew – keeps moths, flies, ants, mice, bedbugs, mosquitoes, cockroaches and mites at bay. Lavender and mint also repel flies and fleas, and look very pretty strewn throughout the house.

mint
Mentha spp.

rosemary
Rosmarinus officinalis

cotton lavender
Santolina chamaecyparissus

lavender
Lavandula spp.

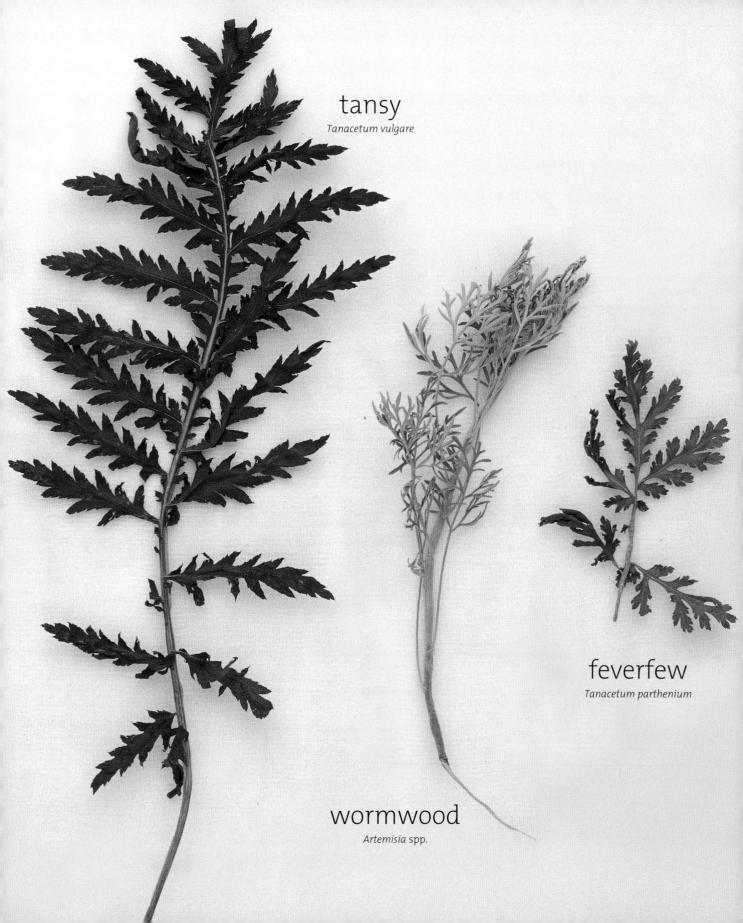

tansy
Tanacetum vulgare

feverfew
Tanacetum parthenium

wormwood
Artemisia spp.

Here small box hedges border a potager bed planted with strawberries, rosemary and varieties of lettuce.

NITROGEN FIXERS Nitrogen-fixing plants, such as peas (above) and beans, are often planted together with another crop that benefits from the improved nitrogen fertility – for example, the traditional combination of climbing beans planted with corn.

Nitrogen-fixing plants

Other useful species can offer beneficial effects to surrounding plants by improving the fertility of the soil and the health and yield of plants grown with them. Legumes such as peas, beans, lucerne and various clovers are known as nitrogen fixers – that is, they take nitrogen directly from the atmosphere and convert it into soil-enriching nitrogen compounds. This nitrogen-fixing ability is due to a bacterium called *Rhizobium* which is found growing symbiotically in the roots of legumes. In Australia, acacias, which are also legumes, are very useful pioneer species on cleared land, providing nitrogen to impoverished soils as well as shade to young plants.

Plants that retrieve nutrients

Other plant species offer benefits to surrounding plants by bringing up nutrients from deep in the ground via their exceptionally long root systems, or by actively accumulating elements useful for plants. Lucerne, also known as alfalfa (*Medicago sativa*), is an excellent example of a plant that retrieves nutrients from deep in the subsoil. It also helps break up compacted soils, while buckwheat (*Fagopyrum esculentum*), with its extensive root system, is a calcium accumulator and a useful breaker of heavy clay soils; it also attracts both hoverflies and butterflies.

Barrier crops

Many companion plants create their beneficial effects on other plants through various kinds of chemical exudates produced by the plants. These exudates can be in the form of volatile oils which form an invisible cloud of oil particles, or in the form of soluble substances released by the roots or shoots.

Soluble exudates from the leaves of some species have been found to create a 'scorched earth' effect, inhibiting the germination of their own seedlings, as well as those of other species, beneath their canopy. Species of walnuts (*Juglans* spp.) and conifers – such as some species of spruce, for instance – are well known for this activity. The black walnut (*J. nigra*) releases a chemical called juglone which suppresses the growth of many other species, as anyone who has tried to garden below the shade of this species knows. The roots also produce plant toxins.

Various species of the herbal genus *Artemisia*, some of which are known in the United States as sages, can also have this effect. Arid zone species, in particular, use this mechanism to reduce competition for scarce resources such as water and nutrients. Crop scientists are currently investigating this effect to see if it might provide a useful alternative to chemical herbicides. Recently, researchers have found that an annual rye crop, cut and left on the ground as a mulch, leaches into the soil chemicals that suppress weed germination, and provides a weed-free environment for many different transplanted commercial vegetable crops, such as broccoli and tomatoes.

The Papilionaceae family

Many genera belong to this interesting family. They are roughly divided into three groups:

1 Those with fluffy flowers, such as wattles (subfamily Mimosoideae);

2 Those with pea-shaped flowers, such as sweet peas (subfamily Faboideae); and

3 Those with orchid-like flowers, such as bauhinias (subfamily Caesalpinoideae).

Despite such showy, beautiful blooms, what makes this family so interesting is the roots. All Papilionaceae have roots with nitrogen-fixing nodules which take nitrogen from the soil and convert it into an available form for the plants to use as food.

As a result of this adaptation, many members of the Papilionaceae family are used as green manures or nutritious mulches. Lupins, peanuts, lucerne pea manure and clover all fall into this category.

The annual sweet pea (*Lathyrus odoratus*), shown here, is the most popular member of the sweet pea family, but another one to try is the perennial or everlasting pea (*L. latifolius*), a herbaceous, perennial climber with pink or purple flowers throughout summer and early autumn.

The good news for the home gardener is that these volatile oils can have a direct effect on various pests and pathogens. For instance, their smell can confuse insects so that they fail to locate their target plants. Other oils act as repellents. Most strong-smelling plants (herbs in particular) have such effects. Try placing strong-smelling herbs such as sage, rosemary, southernwood, thyme, lavender, sweet marjoram, hyssop, nasturtium, tansy (an excellent ant repellent), pennyroyal (also effective against ants) and chives throughout your garden. Plant them also as a barrier and insurance policy around your vegetable patch.

The roots of plants also exude a wide variety of active chemicals. One particularly useful example is that of the strongly scented marigold (*Tagetes* spp.). This genus exudes a chemical called thiopene from the roots which repels nematodes, microscopic worms that burrow into the conducting tissue of the roots of plants such as tomatoes, blocking the tissue and causing wilting and death. African marigold, French marigold and the weedy species *T. minuta* have all been used with considerable success to protect crops. (*Calendula*, also commonly called marigold, does not have the same effect.) You can mass plant marigold plants to clear your garden of nematodes. Chop the plants back into the soil when they are in full flower, then allow them to rot down before planting a crop.

Garlic is a crop that actively takes up substances in the soil. In California, it is grown organically in huge quantities around the town of Gilroy, not only as a very popular food flavouring exported around the world, but also as an important herbal medicine. To ensure the garlic crop is grown in nematode-free soil, a cover crop of French marigolds is used. Garlic is then planted into the nematode-free soil.

In the home garden, you can plant annual hedges of dwarf French marigold to prevent nematodes migrating into clean soil. If the prolific, brilliantly golden or orange flowers clash with your colour scheme, clip the plants back to a green hedge.

Chives and purple sage make effective barrier plants in the vegetable garden, and they will also look decorative.

Barrier crops are a very old idea, and were widely used in England from the 16th century onwards. Companion plants were used to hedge beds of vegetables and were also interplanted between rows. For example, rows of lettuce or peas were separated by rows of chives or garlic to prevent insect attack, and dwarf nasturtiums were planted between rows of broccoli. Several herbs, including sage, hyssop, thyme and rosemary, were used to suppress aphids and cabbage white butterfly, and they were traditionally planted between rows of cabbage.

Trap plants

Another category of companion plants is a group referred to as 'trap plants'. These plants will lure undesirable insects away from vulnerable species – for example, collards will protect the closely related cabbage. Other plants act as good neighbours by offering refuge to beneficial insects. Among these useful pest predators are lacewings, hoverflies, predatory mites, ladybirds, various wasp species and mantids. Around the world, researchers are currently designing planting systems that will include habitats capable of sustaining these beneficial insects, to reduce the use of insecticides.

Nasturtiums make good barrier plants as they are strongly scented. However, watch out as they can become weedy.

UNDERPLANTING TOMATOES WITH BASIL

1 Clear a space for each basil seedling.

2 Remove the seedlings from the pot. Divide them into bunches of two or three plants.

3 Plant the basil seedlings around your tomato plants and replace the mulch.

Maintenance

To cater for your whole plant it is important to understand soil, watering, compost, mulching, fertilising and the organisms that make it all happen, as well as the organisms that cause trouble. There are three main factors in improving the soil in your garden – fertilisers, compost and mulch – while watering is crucial to maintaining soil and organism health.

Watering

Watering seems to be the aspect of cultivation that causes the gardener the most problems. The best advice when it comes to watering is to use your common sense. Consider the time of year, temperature, humidity, time of day, weather, soil conditions and the stage of development of the plant.

Seeds cannot germinate without adequate moisture. Make sure you keep the seed-raising mix evenly moist, but not wet, until seedlings emerge. Once seedlings emerge, water them regularly and gently with a fine spray. You should be aware that overwatering will cause the collapse and death of seedlings. Once seedlings have

been planted out they will need regular watering until they are well established.

The age and type of plant will also affect the amount of water required. Baby seedlings with very few shallow roots will need more frequent watering than established plants that have their roots deeper into the ground. Plants with large leaves generally need more water than those with fine feathery leaves. Annual vegetables may need watering twice a week, weekly or every two or three days depending on weather and soil conditions. You should note that sandy soils dry out much more rapidly than clay soils.

It is more effective to water early in the morning or in the evening, as there will be less moisture lost through evaporation. In winter, water in the morning so that the foliage does not remain wet overnight. This also applies to plants that are prone to fungal disease; avoid overhead watering for these plants. In summer, water in the evening so the water has a chance to soak into the ground. Don't water in the middle of the day in summer or when it is very windy, as a lot of water will be lost to the atmosphere straight away.

Fertilising (left) and watering (above) are essential activities to ensure a healthy herb and vegetable garden.

Fertilising

Keep seedlings growing rapidly with fertiliser. Vegetables, in particular, must be grown quickly for maximum flavour and tenderness. There are several methods of maintaining a steady supply of nutrients. Granular fertiliser can be used prior to seed sowing by banding it along the sides of rows or by placing it in a furrow or trench well below the sowing depth. Soluble powders or liquid concentrates, which you dilute and apply in solution, can be used to boost plant growth once seedlings are growing strongly. Slow-release fertilisers can be mixed with the soil or potting mix prior to sowing or applied once seedlings have started to grow. Never apply fertiliser to dry soil as it can burn the plant roots.

While it is preferable to feed plants through their roots, some growers like to use foliar feeding (feeding plants through their leaves). When using fertiliser in solution to spray directly onto leaves, there should be plenty of moisture around the plant roots.

When growing Mediterranean-style herbs, you should generally avoid adding manure and fertiliser, but if you have an acid soil, dig in some lime prior to planting. Dig in about 100 g (3½ oz) of lime or dolomite per square metre (square yard) or a little more if the soil has a high clay content.

Composting is not the complete solution for a healthy garden. Edibles will generally require fertiliser at one time or another.

Handy feeding hints

- Always fertilise plants when the soil is moist and water thoroughly after you have completed the application.

- If in doubt about how much to use, apply fertiliser at half-strength, twice as often.

- Plants don't use much food in winter, so don't bother feeding at this time. Spring, summer and autumn feeds are generally better value.

- Nitrogen is responsible for leaf growth, but too much nitrogen can cause floppy growth and poor flowers.

- Phosphorus is vital for strong roots and stems.

- Potassium maintains the rigidity of plants and is important in promoting flowering.

Types of fertiliser

Fertilisers can be separated into 'natural' fertilisers, such as seaweed extract and animal manures, and artificial combinations or chemical fertilisers. Organic fertilisers can encourage soil organisms and lead to better structured soils. Chemical fertilisers can be fast acting and balanced, and many are designed to cater for the specific needs of certain plants. Fertilisers are classified according to their component ratio of nitrogen, potassium and phosphorus (known as the NPK ratio). These are particularly important elements, as they are needed for basic plant growth and function and are used in relatively large quantities. The 'big three' are all highly soluble, so if you apply excess fertiliser it washes straight into waterways and eventually causes algal growth. It is particularly important to remember this when you are feeding your lawn.

Mineral fertilisers

Even though you feed your soil with good quality compost, it may still lack mineral nutrients if the original soil is poor. A soil test will show major deficiencies, which then can be remedied by the use of rock dusts and other adjuncts.

Calcium is best supplied by dolomite derived from dolomitic limestone and this form also supplies magnesium to the soil. Ground limestone can be used as an alternative. Phosphate is usually supplied by the dust of natural rock phosphate. Potassium can be added to the compost heap in the form of wood ashes. Sulphur comes in the powdered form 'flowers of sulphur', which is mined from volcanic deposits.

Many soils, particularly in old geological areas, lack one or more trace elements. Rock dusts of the individual trace element can be added but dispersal is difficult. Thankfully, liquid seaweed fertilisers are an excellent means of supplying them, together with seaweed meal. But such additions should never take the place of regular doses of compost.

Liquid fertilisers

Liquid fertilisers give a rapid growth boost to plants that have been stressed or are under insect attack. Perhaps the finest organic liquid fertiliser is seaweed fertiliser which is readily available commercially. Some products incorporate fermented fish and other seafood wastes and, though the smell is memorable for the first hour or two, many of these are quite excellent, stimulating not only plant growth but also desirable microbial activity. Plants suffering from black spot and other fungal diseases respond rapidly with a clean flush of new growth after a spray of these substances, diluted as recommended.

It is quite simple to brew your own seaweed fertiliser. If you live nearby, take a visit to the beach, and gather a sack of seaweed that has been washed up onto the tideline. Tie the sack tightly, immerse it in a large container of water, and leave it for approximately 7–14 days. It will make an invaluable, although strong smelling, liquid garden feed.

A similar process can be used with a bag of manure. The resultant 'manure soup', needless to say, also can have a somewhat evil odour initially. But it's an absolute treat for organically grown produce.

Blood and bone.

Chicken manure.

Slow release fertiliser.

The magic of compost

Nature constantly makes compost – that almost magical, soil-like material which results from the decomposition of organic material and forms the basis of the healthy organic garden.

However, the natural composting process is fairly slow. Relying on the backyard 'rubbish heap' is rarely satisfactory. It can take 12 months or more to complete the recycling process and produce usable compost – and most of us want results a little quicker than that.

There are a variety of ways to produce good compost, but all techniques fall into one of two baskets depending on whether they rely on bacteria that are aerobic (oxygen users) or anaerobic (non-oxygen users) to break down the raw materials.

Aerobic composting is very efficient. It generates sweet, nutty-smelling compost rapidly, and with none of the feared evil smells that accompany some backyard disasters. The compost can reach temperatures of 70°C (138°F), hot enough to sterilise weed seeds and kill many disease organisms.

One of the most valuable things you can do to assist the health of your edibles, is to start a compost heap.

step by step

BASE DRESSING

Base dressings of fertiliser are applied to the soil before plants or seeds occupy the site. This helps to maximise nutrients in the soil.

1 First sprinkle a measure of the appropriate fertiliser onto prepared soil in the area you intend to plant or sow.

2 Incorporate fertiliser into the top few centimetres (inches) of soil using a garden or wooden rake.

TOP DRESSING

Most vegetables grow relatively quickly and will almost certainly need an extra feed during the growing season. A top dressing of fertiliser applied around the plants will help to increase both bulk and yield.

1 First, carefully sprinkle the fertiliser onto the soil around the plants. Make sure the fertiliser does not land on the foliage as it will burn it.

2 Use a hoe or tined cultivator to incorporate the fertiliser into the soil. Do not cultivate too deeply or some plant roots may be damaged.

Anaerobic composting is much slower and takes place at cooler temperatures. This method is prone to undesirable odours, and depends on very ancient and less efficient species of bacteria.

What goes in the compost heap?

Some people say that anything that has lived before can be put into a compost heap, and it is a good general guideline.

So what exactly can go in the compost heap? For a start, if you eat plenty of fresh fruit and vegetables in your diet, every night will produce a bowl full of vegetable and fruit peelings. Other kitchen waste – like crushed eggshells, tea leaves and coffee grounds – is also ideal.

Time spent working in the garden will yield picked weeds, soft and hardwood prunings, as well as the remains from harvested vegetable crops. Mowing the lawn will also contribute a pile of fresh, moist grass that is high in nitrogen. In autumn, add piles of leaves high in carbon from deciduous trees.

Clockwise from top left, mushroom compost, prunings, liquid fertiliser, kitchen scraps.

MAKING BLACKJACK

Blackjack is an excellent, nutritious plant 'pick-me-up', which is very useful during flowering or fruiting periods. Although it is not sweet-smelling, your plants will be very grateful for the application.

1 To create blackjack, you will first need a quantity of animal manure that has been well rotted down.

2 Add some soot (which provides nitrogen) and wood ash (good for potassium) to the manure. Put the mixture into a plastic-net bag.

3 Seal the bag carefully and suspend it in a barrel of rainwater. Leave it in position for several weeks.

4 Once the solution is ready, decant it as required into a watering can, diluting it to the colour of weak tea, and apply it to your plants.

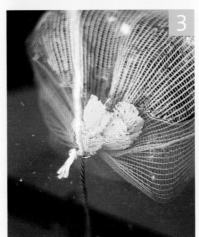

Worm farms

Worm farming can be an excellent way of dealing with modest amounts of household scraps, and producing quantities of an excellent natural fertiliser. Commercial worm farms are available and it's quite a simple matter of following the instructions in order to assemble them. But a worm farm can be made from a simple bin or box, vented with air holes around the side and about 5 cm (2 in) below the rim. You should also make a row of drainage holes. Keep in mind that the worms are active only between the temperature range of 12–25°C (50–77°F). Make sure the bin is moved into a warm area and insulated throughout winter in colder regions, and placed out of the sun and in a cool area during hot summers.

Only species of worm adapted to living in decomposing organic matter are suited to worm farming, such as *Lumbricus rubellus* and the red wiggler worm or Brandling worm *Eisenia foetida*. These are available at some garden centres and can also be mail-ordered.

When you start composting it is inevitable that you will become expert at scavenging. Garden materials bagged and waiting to be sent by neighbours to waste disposal sites will develop a magnetic attraction. Before long even the shyest gardeners will find themselves knocking on doors to ask for those unwanted bagfuls.

A day fossicking beside the seaside can provide seaweed, torn off by wave action and stranded along the tideline (see page 90 for more details).

Waste paper and cardboard can also be composted, but sheets should be individually crumpled up before use so that they increase the aeration of the heap. Colour printed material was once considered undesirable in the compost heap as it might contain toxins, but modern processes have reduced that likelihood. However, you

LEFT Aerobic composting is much faster in warm weather. The time taken in hot, humid summer areas may be as short as 14–20 days, and in somewhat cooler areas around 2 months.

OPPOSITE If space permits, particularly in cool areas, it works well to have three compost bins adjacent to each other for maximum efficiency. The first two bins alternate to hold the compost heap when it is inverted. The third bin is used to build a new heap.

must avoid including in your heap any materials that may have been sprayed with chemicals.

Sawdust and wood shavings are still relatively easy to acquire. Timber mills have found that these are a saleable commodity, so that free clean sawdust is often difficult to acquire. But large bales of dried sawdust are still quite cheap and make an excellent addition to the compost heap.

Spoiled hay and straw are often available at a reduced price after a period of rain. These are bales that have become wet and already started to break down naturally, so that they are no longer of any value to farmers as animal feed. Spoiled alfalfa (or lucerne) hay is particularly valuable for the home gardener since it is high in nitrogen and other minerals.

Mushroom growers often advertise spent mushroom compost but some care should be exercised in choosing your supplier. Mushrooms are often grown with surprisingly high levels of insecticidal chemicals, the compost is often almost exhausted of nutrients, having grown successive flushes of mushrooms, and the pH of spent mushroom compost can be stongly alkaline, making it unsuitable for acid-loving plants. If you choose to use mushroom compost, it is a good idea to recompost it and leave the pile for a few months before using it on your edible plants.

NO GO! There are exceptions to what materials can be composted – at least in backyard compost heaps which do not always reach high enough temperatures to break down all manner of organic refuse. Fish and chicken bones, meat scraps, cheese and other protein-containing material will almost inevitably attract unwanted attention from hungry animals (including rats) and should be excluded from the pile. And never place severely infected prunings or plants in the compost heap. The infective organisms need to be burned to prevent the spread of the disease.

Animal manure

One of the most vital ingredients, animal manure is a must for making good compost. There was a time when, even in large cities, extraordinary amounts of unwanted manure were yours for the asking, as long as you were willing to gather it and take it away yourself. Now that so many gardeners are learning the benefits of compost for their garden, there is increased competition for such raw materials. Obliging stables, dairies, poultry farms and other once easily accessible sources now often have an agreement to supply professional compost companies. But keep an eye out for farms on the outskirts of cities and large towns which still advertise sacks of horse, sheep and cattle manures at their gates. Just a couple of sackfuls can go a long way towards building excellent compost. Pigeon fanciers and poultry farmers may also be willing to allow you access to droppings, to take away for your garden.

ZOO POO Not so long back, many zoos around the world were having trouble disposing of the vast amounts of manure accumulated on a daily basis. Now many enterprising major zoos are recycling their animal wastes through composting destined to supply public gardens. But they also sell bagged, mixed manures of the most exotic kinds, from elephant and zebra droppings to those of peacocks, marketed under labels such as 'Zoo Poo' – and it is brilliant for the compost heap.

A mixture of manures works best. Poultry manures are particularly high in nitrogen and will allow the compost heap to reach high temperatures. Horse and cow manures are a more even mixture of nitrogen and carbon, and while of good quality will not create such high temperatures.

Keeping the compost moist

Well made compost heaps are moist and hold water like a squeezed sponge. If the pile has been made off the ground, any excess water which would displace air from the pile cannot accumulate. If your compost heap gets excessively wet, it will not heat. As a result, it will become anaerobic, start to smell unpleasant and both you and your heap will end up rather unpopular with your neighbours.

Speeding up the process

The greater the surface area of material exposed to the activities of composting micro-organisms, the more rapidly will they be able to convert a compost heap to usable compost.

A shredder can be invaluable to help reduce woody materials to chips, which have an infinitely greater surface area than the original stems and branches. Alternatively, chop larger pieces of prunings and clippings with a spade.

And get the hammer out to break up the tough stems of corn stalks and cobs, broccoli and Brussels sprouts stems, and other tough vegetable remains. Eggshells can be crushed in your hands before adding to the compost container in your kitchen.

Maintaining the right temperature

Compost heaps are often hidden in dank corners, commonly behind shrubberies and in the dripline of branches. It's far better to place them in a warm, wind protected, but not overly hot situation, which would dry the heap unnecessarily.

And size does matter if a compost heap is to heat effectively. Little compost heaps never reach the desired temperature, so save up materials to make a larger heap. Ideally the heap should be at least 1 m (3⅓ ft) wide, long and high.

Larger heaps are even better. To prevent a particularly big heap falling over as it decomposes, and to make it less vulnerable to family pets and small children, you can enclose the pile within a compost bin.

Building a compost heap

A good compost heap is like a well laid fire in a fireplace, allowing oxygen to be drawn up and vented though the heap.

The easiest way to achieve this is to build the compost pile on top of an open 'mattress' of thick, branched sticks. Larger tree and woody shrub prunings are ideal for this purpose. Alternatively, you can use a section of heavy gauge wire lattice balanced over bricks placed at each corner.

To provide venting inside the heap, stick four or more stakes, depending on the intended size of the heap, vertically into the pile after the first layers have been established. Continue to build the pile around the stakes, and when it is complete, wriggle the stakes loose and carefully pull them out. This creates 'chimneys' through the pile which will draw air upwards. Material like freshly mown grass, which is moist and tends to compact in the pile, should be mixed with drier materials like sawdust or straw.

Some gardeners dismantle the heap when it begins to cool down, and invert the pile by forking the outside to the inside and vice versa. This fluffs up the pile and makes air readily available. Material turned into the centre is also exposed to the warmer, moister heart of the pile where the greatest microbial activity is taking place. The pile will heat up for a second time. But if such physical work is difficult for you, the pile can be left as is, although complete composting will happen more slowly.

Commercial compost bins

Commercial bins are popular with some organic gardeners. They don't take up much space and they effectively exclude animals – both household pets and vermin. Resembling garbage bins, they do provide some insulation and allow microbes to remain active longer in the season. And they can look very neat and tidy, if that is a priority for you.

The plastic compost bin here blends into a cottage-style garden, flanked by the blooms of pink society garlic (*Tulbaghia violacea*) to soften its appearance.

LEGUMES
Legumes are the edible seeds and pods of plants such as beans and peas.

borlotti bean
Phaseolus vulgaris

shelling pea
Pisum sativum
'Earlicrop Massey'

bush bean
Phaseolus vulgaris
'Blue Lake'

broad bean seeds
Vicia faba 'Aquadulce'

snow pea (mangetout)
Pisum sativum var. macrocarpon

bean seeds
Phaseolus vulgaris 'Redland Pioneer'

pea seeds
Pisum sativum 'Greenfeast'

left to right:
dwarf snow pea seeds, snake bean seeds, broad bean seeds

butter bean
Phaseolus lunatus

lima bean seeds
Phaseolus limensis

beanettes

sugar snap peas
Pisum sativum var. sativum

red kidney bean seeds
Phaseolus vulgaris

bean seeds
Phaseolus vulgaris 'Scarlet Runner'

MAKING LEAFMOULD

1 Rake up fallen leaves into heaps. The best time to do this is just after it has rained, when the leaves are moist; but they can also be collected dry, and wet later. Remove any foreign material, such as plastic wrappers, from the heaps. Collect the leaves and place them in plastic bags or black bags. The latter are better as they block out most of the light and encourage fungal activity.

2 To every 30 cm (1 ft) layer of leaves add a small amount of organic fertiliser, such as dried, pelleted chicken manure or a measure of organic nitrogenous fertiliser, such as sulphate of ammonia (which contains 16–21 per cent nitrogen).

3 When the bag is almost full, place it in the position where it is to eventually be left while its contents decompose, and water it thoroughly so that the contents are soaking wet.

4 Over a period of about two years, the pile of leaves will decompose and settle in the bag. These leaves will be pressed tightly together, with some remaining almost whole and others disintegrating completely. When the leaves are ready for use, the bag can be split open and the leaves used as an effective mulch or soil conditioner.

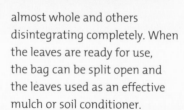

Compost tumblers

Compost tumbling systems are usually fairly low volume but will still handle all the household scraps generated by a small family. Under ideal conditions they will convert organic material to compost in as short a period of time as three weeks – approximately the time of a well constructed aerobic compost heap.

The bin is rotated on a daily basis, remixing the contents and maintaining high microbial activity. Pack the bin loosely to ensure that adequate turning of the contents will take place. A mixture of about half dry and half green material is needed. You can store material for future batches in bags until required – or set up a two-bin system.

Constructing a compost bin

There are a number of methods for 'binning' compost, but in many ways, simple wire netting compost bins are ideal. They are very easy to make and to dismantle, allow excellent access for air, and are not themselves composted. What's more they are cheap to build and the materials can be readily recycled for other purposes. Tall, vertical, metal star posts or wooden posts are embedded into the soil to make the corners. Wire netting is used to form the sides, and wire ties can be used for the construction.

Compost boxes can also be made by constructing the sides with open fence palings, but in time these will rot.

Some gardeners construct the walls of the heap with bales of straw arranged with small gaps between. Less air is accessible but the walls themselves contribute to the compost and are easily dismantled when composting is completed. The partly composted hay bale walls can become the foundation of the next compost heap. In cool climate areas, hay bale walls have the added advantage of helping to insulate the pile from heat loss.

You should never construct a compost bin around a tree. The bark will compost, allowing in unwanted disease organisms.

The far end of the heap is ready to use, and the autumn leaves, still fresh, will be composted by spring.

When is the compost ready?

You know the composting process is completed when the pile has completely cooled and the content has the appearance and texture of rich brown, crumbly earth. It is not unusual to find the remains of a few tough, fibrous ingredients like corn cobs. If you want, you can sift the compost by tossing it in forkfuls through a panel of wire netting. Then just add any uncomposted remains to a new pile.

Protect the top of the finished pile of compost with a plastic sheet or tarpaulin. Otherwise, if the pile is left exposed to the rain, the nutrients will be leached out.

Leafmould

Leafmould is one of the most valued sources of organic matter that a gardener can use. It makes an excellent soil conditioner, but also has low levels of nutrients (0.4 per cent nitrogen, 0.2 per cent phosphate and 0.3 per cent potassium), and is usually slightly acidic.

Leafmould is a material that would slowly form naturally beneath trees in a woodland setting over many years. Making your own is quite a long-term project, as the leaves take time (up to two years) in order to decay into a dark, coarse and crumbly compost-like material.

Trench composting

Trench composting can be an ideal answer for those who have larger gardens and for the more patient among us who are willing to wait for results.

This method of composting is an anaerobic technique, so keep in mind that the compost materials will not reach the temperatures needed to kill weed seed and pathogens. Dig a trench about 20 cm (8 in) deep.

GREEN MANURES *Green manure crops are planted to improve the quality of the soil – and enhance plant growth. They are usually nitrogen-fixing plants, often with strong, deep rooting systems that help to break up compacted soil and draw nutrients up to the soil surface where they are available to future plantings. Good choices for green manure crops are dense plants that will also out-compete weeds.*

Fill the trench with vegetable wastes from the kitchen and garden, before covering with a layer of soil. In a few months, the materials will be fully incorporated.

As this is a cool process, earthworms will actively contribute to turning the organic matter through the soil. You could add commercially obtained earthworms to the trench, but populations of native worms will be attracted to the organic waste and multiply rapidly of their own accord.

Mulch – and more mulch

It is impossible to overestimate the value of mulches in the garden. Mulches can be divided into organic mulches such as leaf litter, hay, straw, composted sawdust and wood chips, and inorganic mulches such as rocks and river pebbles.

Both kinds of mulches are invaluable in conserving soil moisture so that plants are less prone to water

GREEN MANURE CROPS

Type	Length of growing period	Soil	When to plant	Benefit
Alfalfa (lucerne)	Perennial	Neutral to alkaline, well drained	Spring to midsummer	Nitrogen-fixing, exceptionally deep-rooted
Buckwheat	Annual (2–4 months)	Good on poor soils	Spring to midsummer	Improves soil structure and attracts pollinating bees
Crimson clover	2–5 months; will overwinter	Sandy loam preferred	Spring to late summer	Nitrogen-fixing, attracts pollinating bees
Lupin (*Lupinus angustifolia*)	3–5 months	Acid, sandy to sandy loam	Spring to midsummer	Nitrogen-fixing
Phacelia tanecetifolia	2–4 months; can ovewrinter	Wide tolerance	Spring to summer	Attracts beneficial insects, soil structure improved
Rye	Overwinter	Wide tolerance	Early to late autumn	Fibrous root system improves soil structure
White radish (daikon)	3–5 months	Tolerant	Spring	Flowers attract beneficial insects. Huge roots break up soil for water penetration

TRENCH COMPOSTING

1 In the late summer or early autumn, mark out the area which is to be dug over in a series of trenches and mark the lines of the parallel trenches.

2 Dig out a single trench about 30 cm (1 ft) deep, and move the soil from the trench to the end of the plot, which will be the very last section to be trenched.

3 As they become available, gradually fill the trench with plant debris, vegetable scraps and kitchen waste.

4 Dig out a second trench in a similar way to the first one. Cover each additional layer of material in the first trench with the soil which has just been dug from the second parallel trench. After the first trench is full and the second trench has been dug, start filling the second trench by creating a third trench. Each completed trench will gradually settle over a month or two as the plant material decomposes. Woody material such as prunings will decay quicker if they are shredded before being buried, and a small nitrogenous fertiliser may also need to be incorporated to speed up the whole process.

down quickly and so need to be replaced every few months. Never use peat moss as a mulch as it repels water once it is dry; rather, blend it into the soil and use it as a soil conditioner.

Inorganic mulches – such as black plastic, weed control mats, scoria and decorative gravels and pebbles – are not really 'garden friendly'. They add nothing to the soil structure and, once these mulches are in place, soil additives are difficult to incorporate. They tend to raise the soil temperature and some can even stop your soil from breathing, which can lead to serious problems.

Depending on the time of year at which you mulch your garden, you can influence soil temperatures. For example, if you mulch at the end of autumn, you will keep the soil warmer for longer, while mulching in early spring will keep the soil cooler and prevent heat being trapped in summer.

stress, and thus do not suffer reduced productivity and susceptibility to pest and disease attack.

Mulches also minimise erosion, help maintain an even soil temperature, and reduce soil splash on plants, which can spread soil-borne diseases.

Organic mulches have some additional benefits. As they break down they provide organic matter to the soil, protect and improve soil structure, encourage beneficial micro-organism activity, and are also invaluable in suppressing weeds.

Types of mulch

Mulches are available in many forms, both organic and inorganic. Organic mulches include leaf mulch, pine bark, red gum chips, alfalfa (lucerne), straw, newspaper, compost, rice husks and sugar cane. An effective mulch should not be dislodged by wind and rain and should have a loose enough structure to allow water to soak through easily.

Some mulches – for example, alfalfa (lucerne), compost and sugar cane – have a high nitrogen content. These mulches improve the soil fertility, but they rot

You should always wet the soil down well before applying mulch, and also wet the mulch down when the job is completed. Dry mulches can be water repellent.

Pennyroyal and other low-growing plants, such as *Ajuga*, can be used effectively as a living mulch in your garden beds.

Applying mulch

You should apply organic mulches at least 10 cm (4 in) thick. To assist in excluding light from the soil surface and aid with weed suppression, lay down overlapping layers of newspapers before applying the mulch.

Mulches should not be laid until the soil has warmed up after the winter months. And be careful not to place mulch too close to the trunks of shrubs and trees – it can cause collar rot.

Fruit trees benefit greatly from a mulch of nitrogen-rich alfalfa (lucerne) hay, which can be weighted down with stones. Make sure you rake up any fallen fruit and leaves at the beginning of winter and compost them. If you leave them as a mulch they will act as a reservoir of disease for the following season.

Sawdust and wood chips are commonly used as mulch. However, when either raw sawdust or wood chips begin to break down, the soil bacteria responsible for this process require nitrogen. They will rob the soil, and plants that have been mulched with raw sawdust or wood chips will exhibit yellowing due to this temporary withdrawal of nitrogen.

Once the process has been completed, the nitrogen is made available to the soil. You can either add a sprinkling of blood and bone to provide the required nitrogen, or partially compost the sawdust or chips in a pile for a month before use. Sprinkle the pile well with liquid seaweed fertiliser to boost the partial composting process. Sawdust and wood chips often contain levels of tannins high enough to inhibit plant growth and these are also partially leached during composting.

While mulch is invaluable, it is better not to simply throw masses of garden refuse on the soil. Compost it first. Piles of rubbish will often decompose anaerobically into a slimy mess that will encourage disease. Of all mulches, none is better than compost (which can be applied when quite roughly textured) and alfalfa (lucerne) hay.

Living mulch

Many low-growing plants make ideal living mulches. Groundcovers such as *Ajuga* planted into mulched soil are excellent for excluding weeds in ornamental gardens. Blue-flowered periwinkle is ideal for dry shade areas and is easily controlled at a suitable height with a string trimmer used twice a year. Other 'cover crops' such as any of the prostrate-growing plants are effective in reducing weeds.

Actually, weeds may not always be a nuisance but in fact can be helpful. A carpet of weeds can be a protective blanket, another 'living mulch' of sorts.

Mulching not only keeps the soil healthy, but also makes less work for the gardener by reducing weed infestation.

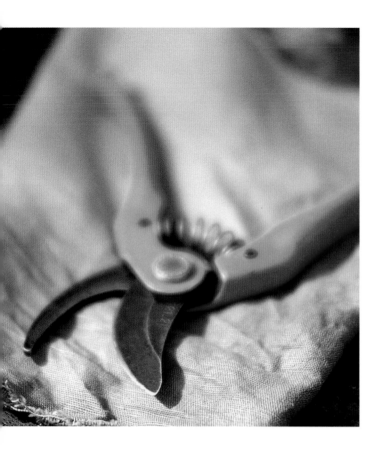

Pests and diseases

Organic growers long suspected that the more healthy a plant is, the more resistant it would be to pest and disease attack. Recent research backs this up. Insect pests are attracted to the weakest, most stressed plants in a crop, apparently detecting them by subtle differences. Improving soil structure and fertility with organic matter makes for healthier soil and this in turn makes for strong, healthy crops – and minimal crop damage.

Organic gardening techniques also produce plants that grow steadily rather than rapidly, as they do with chemical fertilisers. The plants do not become soft and sappy and prone to attack.

Compost and mulches retain soil moisture so that plants are not water-stressed on hot days. It is also important to water in response to the needs of the plant. Plants that are regularly wilted and stressed, as well as ones that are overwatered, are much more susceptible to attack by insects.

A plant in the wrong position is also liable to be attacked. We all succumb to the temptation to buy and plant things which are marginal for our climate, do poorly in our type of soil, or need conditions we cannot offer, like wind protection or an open sunny site. But plants that survive these impulsive gardener moments remain marginal in the garden and will always be more vulnerable to pests and diseases.

And it pays to plant crops at the optimal time. Plants may well survive being planted too early or too late, but they will never thrive as they should.

You can also choose cultivars that have been selected for resistance. Many strains of vegetables are able to resist attack to some degree. If you garden in an area regularly affected by a particular pest or disease, some research and careful selection will reward you with stronger, less susceptible plants. Neighbourhood plant nurseries can be invaluable sources of good advice.

The virtues of weeds

Many gardeners make their lives a misery worrying about weeds in their garden beds. They see them as the gardener's curse, and throw their hands up in despair. Or they may decide that the occasion calls for a military-style attack.

Organic gardeners tend to be a bit more relaxed about 'invasion' by 'unwanted' plants. They know that weeds are essential to the health of the soil. Bare earth is easily eroded by wind, compacted by heavy rain or foot traffic. It is more easily leached of soluble nutrients and can also lose important gases.

If an area is to remain bare for a while, allowing it to become covered in weeds may not be the neatest solution, but it is sound ecologically. The weeds can be slashed just before they begin to flower and left on top of the soil as a green mulch, or dug through to add valuable organic matter.

ABOVE LEFT Make sure that you keep your gardening tools and implements scrupulously clean, to avoid the spread of disease.

OPPOSITE BOTTOM There are numerous types of caterpillar pests that can completely defoliate whole vegetable plants.

THE FARMER'S FOOTPRINTS There is an old saying that goes: 'The finest fertiliser is the farmer's footprints'. In other words, the farmer who regularly walks their land, observing carefully and monitoring their crops, is the most important factor in producing a good crop. Therefore, be vigilant, and constantly walk around your garden and check to see that your plants are healthy and hearty.

Good garden housekeeping

Many diseases and plant pests can be eliminated from the garden simply by good housekeeping practices.

All garden wastes, including spent crops, should be composted. If material is infected, it should be placed into the centre of the compost heap where the high temperatures reached will kill all spores. Infected woody prunings, however, are unlikely to break down fully in the compost and should be disposed of.

Viral diseases are passed on mainly by sap-sucking insects. As soon as a virus-infected plant is detected, it should be removed and added to an activated compost heap. Or better yet, dispose of diseased plant material.

Seasonal tasks

Dealing with garden problems as they arise will ensure that you have fewer pests and diseases to be dealt with as the seasons progress.

Autumn is an especially valuable time for the gardener. A thorough clean-up at the end of summer or early in autumn can do much to prevent pests and diseases in the next growing season. Digging the garden over at this stage not only aerates the soil but can expose overwintering larvae of various pests.

After pruning deciduous trees, check for the presence of borer and destroy any you find by poking a wire into any holes. Use a wire brush to remove any loose bark which often shelters overwintering pests. Make sure that no vegetables are left on the ground. Any mummified vegetables should be disposed of.

Biologically friendly pest control

If excessive pest damage does occur in your garden, usually the result of unusual seasonal conditions, there are many additional measures that you can adopt, none of them dangerous to the environment or your family. The more we have come to know of the life cycles and behaviour of insect and animal pests, the more we have been able to develop environmentally friendly ways of minimising the damage they can cause.

Barriers and traps

Among the most useful advances in recent times has been the development of finely woven, transparent cloths to protect vegetables and fruit trees. These are woven to allow water and maximum light and air through while excluding insect pests. Floating row covers are ideal for the vegetable garden.

Other relatively newly developed barriers are sticky, non-drying glues that trap insects migrating up the stem or trunk. The glue is placed on a paper collar around the base of the plant. A simple non-sticky collar can be made from a cardboard cup with the base cut out. Placed around the base of a seedling, this is sufficient to protect it from cutworm damage.

In some areas, carrot fly is a real problem. But the female fly hovers low over the crop in order to detect the odour of carrots. Erecting a simple, temporary barrier fence of hessian around the row will force the female fly to hover too high to detect the scent.

 TRAP PLANTS Some plants are very attractive to pests – perhaps because of their colour, smell or taste – so that they preferentially attract them, thereby protecting other plants. Bright yellow nasturtiums, for instance, attract aphids away from cabbages. Zinnias have long been used as trap plants to lure Japanese beetle. Dill (above) is traditionally used to lure green tomato caterpillar. In themselves, trap plants are not sufficient protection for your garden – but they do contribute towards maintaining healthy crops.

Yellow objects attract many flying insects, and sticky yellow paper ('fly paper') makes an effective trap. These traps can be bought from most garden centres.

Insect-repelling 'teas'

'Teas' can be made with plant material known to be insect repellent. The leaves are chopped roughly and covered with water in an enamel saucepan. They are simmered for 15 minutes, then strained and the resulting tea cooled for use as a spray. Eucalyptus, wormwood, southernwood, black sage (*Salvia mellifera*)

and *Equisetum* are all used in this way. Quassia tea is prepared from wood chips of the species *Picrasma quassioides*. The tea is made with 100 g (3½ oz) of chips very gently simmered with 3.5 L (3½ qt) water for two hours. After straining and cooling, the tea is diluted 1 in 5 with water for spraying against pests. It has the advantage of being non-toxic to bees and ladybirds.

Warning! Take care that no-one is tempted to drink these teas, and that they are kept well labelled.

To spray or not to spray?

If you are planning to have an organic garden with the minimum of problems, never spray with chemical sprays. They will upset the ecological balance in your garden and you will end up with a cascade of further problems. Beneficial predators will also be wiped out so that pests previously under control may take over.

Instead, you can try one of the organically acceptable sprays. These include garlic spray, wormwood spray, pepper spray, pyrethrum spray, and the fungicides lime sulphur and Bordeaux mixture. The latter contains copper and hydrated lime and is used on potato blight and other fungal problems. Bordeaux spray should be restricted in use as it builds up levels of copper in the soil. And lime sulphur should only be applied when a plant is dormant.

Pyrethrum is derived from the white flower heads of an African daisy species and is useful against aphids including greenfly and whitefly. But note that pyrethrum can also kill useful insects.

Another useful item in the organic gardener's arsenal is insecticidal soap derived from plant fatty acids and used against red spider mite, greenfly, whitefly, blackfly and soft scale. More delicately textured plants can be susceptible to damage from insecticidal soap.

Another spray, derived from rapeseed oil, is used against whitefly, blackfly, greenfly, red spider mite and scale. Soapy water spray made from soft soap (not detergent) is useful against aphids

CONTROLLING PESTS

Pest	Description	Controls
Aphids	Small sap-sucking insects about 1–2 mm (1/32–1/16 in) long; may be green, black, yellow, pink or grey. May appear in small numbers but rapidly increase to form large colonies. They cause curling and distortion of leaves. New shoots can be thickly coated with aphids.	Encourage natural predators like ladybirds, praying mantises or lacewings. Remove with a strong jet of water from hose, or squash with fingers. Use an insecticidal soap or spray containing pyrethrum, imidacloprid or rotenone (Derris dust). These will kill the pests on contact.
Cabbage white butterfly	The cabbage white butterfly is frequently seen in gardens. It has creamy white wings with a black spot on the wing tips. Its wingspan is 4–5 cm (1½–2 in). The caterpillars are green with a pale yellow marking down the side. The caterpillars chew the leaves, especially of cabbages and other brassicas. The caterpillars are often well camouflaged. Look for tell-tale droppings.	Keep gardens as weed-free as possible, as many weeds will act as host plants for the pest. Pick individual caterpillars off plants by hand and destroy. You can also spray with the bio-insecticide *Bacillus thuringiensis* (BT). This is not a knock-down spray but the caterpillars will stop feeding almost at once. Carbaryl in the form of a dust or spray is an effective method of killing all types of caterpillars
Cutworms and armyworms	The larvae of nocturnal moths, which are about 2.5 cm (1 in) long. The moths are greyish brown with dark and light markings. The caterpillars are smooth-bodied, 3–4 cm (1¼–1½ in) long and may be olive green to brown or black. The worms chew the stem at the soil surface.	Try to catch the caterpillars at night. Protect seedlings with barriers around them (small milk cartons or plastic drinking cups with bottoms cut out) and pushed into ground over plant. Or spray or dust plants with Carbaryl late in the afternoon before the caterpillars come out to feed at night.
Root knot nematodes (eelworms)	These pests are root feeders. Feeding nematodes inject saliva into plant roots, causing the development of abnormal cells. The lumps, or galls, should not be confused with the nodules of legumes such as peas or beans. Plants become stunted and wilt even when there is ample water in the soil. The nematodes are tiny, thin transparent creatures that are not visible to the naked eye.	Rotate vegetable crops and do not repeatedly plant susceptible varieties in the same area. Onions, cauliflowers, cabbages and sweet corn are tolerant of root knot nematodes. If there is no alternative food source, nematodes will feed on marigold roots (*Tagetes* spp.), which exude a substance that is toxic to them. For chemical solutions, you could apply fenamiphos granules to the soil.

Pest	Description	Controls
Snails	Snails chew holes in leaves and may also completely destroy seedlings. They also move up plant stems to feed on foliage. Wherever they move, they leave behind them a silvery, slimy trail of mucus. The soft body of the snail is enclosed by a broad, spiral shell, inside which they are able to seal themselves through very long periods of dry weather. Snails feed mostly at night when conditions are moist. They are most active when there are heavy dews or showery weather. Snails can live for several years.	Go into the garden at night with a torch to look for snails, particularly after a shower of rain. Squash them or drop them into a bucket of heavily salted water. A short piece of terracotta pipe with a little canned pet food inside will attract snails, which can be cleaned out with a stick. Bury a jar or margarine tub in the soil and pour in ½ cup of beer. Check the jar daily for snails and top up the beer. You can also use snail pellets containing metadehyde or methiocarb sparingly around plants. Make sure that the pellets are not accessible to children or pets by placing them inside a length of plastic pipe no more than 5 cm (2 in) in diameter.
White curl grubs	These are the larvae of the scarab or cockchafer beetle. They are whitish grey grubs with an orange-brown head and three pairs of jointed legs. They grow to about 2.5 cm (1 in) long, and are usually seen in a curled or semicircular position. They chew the roots of plants.	Dig over the soil and pick out the grubs. Where the grubs are found in potted plants, remove all the potting mix and replant in a clean pot with fresh potting mix. Chemical controls for this pest for the home garden are hard to find.
Whiteflies	Whitefly nymphs sap suck, causing leaves to become mottled and slightly papery. They suck sap from plant leaves, secreting honeydew on which sooty mould feeds. The tiny, white flying insects have a wingspan of about 4 mm ($\frac{1}{8}$ in). When disturbed, they rise in a cloud from the plant. They can cause problems in greenhouses. Tomatoes and beans are frequently attacked.	Parasitic wasps are available that prey on whiteflies but these are better for controlled environments like greenhouses. Use yellow sticky traps. Or spray affected plants with cyfluthrin or dimethoate to control whitefly infestations.

CONTROLLING DISEASES

Disease	Description	Control
Anthracnose (*Colletotrichum* spp. and related genera)	This fungus manifests itself as dark patches or spots on both foliage and fruit. Often the spots will enlarge until they run together, forming black patches. On some plants, as the spots enlarge, the centre becomes dry and papery, eventually falling out. Ripening avocados first show small brown spots that rapidly enlarge and blacken, becoming slightly sunken. Beans may show dark spots or patches on the leaves, stems and pods until leaf veins turn black.	Prune off any dead leaves that may harbour fungal spores. Rake up and destroy any fallen leaves or fruit that may be carrying spores. Water plants with a soaker hose or by drip irrigation. Sprays of copper oxychloride or mancozeb can be effective. Spray approximately once a month or more often during wet weather.
Grey mould (*Botrytis cinerea*)	The symptoms of this fungal disease vary to an extent depending on the host plant, but grey mould is generally characterised by grey, furry growth. Grey mould affects a wide range of vegetables. This fungus can survive on both living and dead plant material.	Rake up dead leaves from the ground beneath plants. Affected leaves should be cut off and destroyed. Allow good spacing between plants to ensure good air circulation. Don't water from overhead or late in the day as the increased humidity will remain around the plants overnight, maintaining conditions favourable for the spread and growth of this fungal disease.
Leaf spot (*Septoria* spp., *Mycosphaerella* spp. and *Cercospora* spp.)	Fungal leaf spots on plants have many and varied forms. The spots are brown to black in colour, but several types then produce a secondary ring or halo around the original spot. Sometimes these haloes are pale yellow but they may also be black, brown or grey. In severe cases the spots coalesce so that large areas of the leaf are affected. On some plants the dead tissue at the centre of the spot falls out, making holes in the leaf. These diseases do well in warm and cool humid conditions.	Prune off and destroy any affected leaves. Avoid overhead watering or watering late in the day. Thin out the foliage of dense plants to allow better air circulation and allow adequate spacing between plants. Where vegetable crops have been affected, practise crop rotation. If a chemical control program is selected, thorough spraying with mancozeb or copper oxychloride should prevent this fungal disease from spreading through your edible plants.

Disease	Description	Control
Mosaic virus (many strains)	The symptoms of viral diseases are variable and may manifest themselves as yellow streaks, rings, wavy lines or sometimes a mottling of pale and dark green. Some of the discoloured leaf areas turn brown or black as they age. The leaves of cucurbits (such as pumpkin, cucumber and zucchini/courgettes) show some mottling. Viral diseases are spread through the plant sap. Aphids provide a means of transmission for many viruses as they move from plant to plant, but infected sap can also be transmitted via your hands, secateurs or any garden cutting tool. Many weeds act as hosts.	You should remove or isolate any infected plants. Wash your hands and disinfect any garden tools that have been in contact with diseased plants. Keep the garden free of weeds. For chemical controls, since aphids are the main means of infection, the best treatment is to spray to control aphids with pyrethrum, imidacloprid or dimethoate. However, when aphids are the means of transmission they have normally infected a plant by the time they are noticed.
Powdery mildew (*Oidium* spp., *Sphaerotheca* spp. and related genera)	This is a fungus. Grey-white powdery spots appear on leaves. If humidity is high, these spread until large patches or whole leaves are covered. Young leaves can become curled and misshapen, sometimes folding in on themselves. Buds, stems and fruit may also be affected, becoming covered in a powdery coating. It occurs in high humidity. Strains may attack cucurbits (cucumber, zucchini/courgette, pumpkin and marrow).	Where possible, plant varieties that are resistant. Plant breeders continue to work to develop resistant strains of plants. There are cucurbits with good resistance. Wettable sulphur provides good control of powdery mildew but it cannot be used in temperatures over 24°C (77°F) or it will burn the plants. Choose cool weather if using this method of control. There are some sprays containing triforine that are registered for the control of this fungal problem.
Rust (*Puccinia* spp., *Uromyces* spp. and related genera)	Rust is a fungal disease and is generally first noticed when pale, often yellow, spots appear on the upper surface of a leaf. On the underside of the leaf there will be a reddish brown, powdery pustule. This reddish brown powder is made up of the fungal spores that will be rapidly spread by the wind. Leaves on some plants eventually wither and may die.	Plant resistant varieties where possible. Remove and destroy infected leaves or whole plants as soon as the problem is noticed. Avoid overhead watering and improve air circulation around plants. For chemical solutions, spray affected plants with mancozeb or copper oxychloride, following the manufacturer's directions on the product labels.

3

Propagating

Propagating

There is nothing more satisfying than planting a tiny seed, caring for it and watching it gradually grow into a herb or vegetable that you will eventually be able to harvest and eat or use. There are several other ways of creating new plants, including taking cuttings, layering and dividing.

Growing from seed

We are still dependent on seed crops for survival – all agricultural production starts with seeds, and vegetable, grain and cereal crops are grown from seed. On another, more personal level, raising plants from seed is a thrill for the home gardener. All gardeners find it very satisfying to see something as small as a pinhead emerge into a lovely flowering plant or something good to eat. Nothing beats the taste of fresh produce from the garden or the delight of seeing a floral display you've grown from seed.

So many herbs are easy to propagate from seeds or cuttings. But if saving seed, you should weigh up the advantages – low cost, access to interesting new genetic material, and variation and variety – against the possible loss of particular characteristics (such as flower colour) that may change in the second generation, particularly in the case of annuals and biennials.

Pumpkin seed can be sown all year round in hot climates and throughout spring in warm zones but, in cold regions, plant pumpkin seed only in early summer.

About seeds

A seed is a miniaturised plant, packed and stored within a protective coat, waiting for the perfect conditions that will give it its start in life. Some plants will easily self-seed, while others may need to be collected, treated, sown and transplanted.

All seeds have an optimum temperature range at which they germinate best. This range is between 15°C (59°F) and 25°C (77°F), so spring and early autumn are generally the most appropriate times to sow seeds.

Certain seeds need to be stimulated out of dormancy before they will germinate successfully. Some cold climate herbs need an artificial cool time (called stratification) for germination to occur in milder climates. This is an adaptation to prevent seeds from germinating until the last of the cold weather is over, so that late frosts or snow don't harm the young seedlings. Other seeds respond to heat and smoke or drought. Hard seed coats can prevent plants from germinating by keeping out air and water, two vital ingredients in the process, and the seeds will therefore need to be chipped or rubbed with abrasive paper (a process called scarification) before sowing.

Pricking out, or removing seedlings from trays, can be done after the first set of true leaves appears (these develop after the baby pair of leaves, or cotyledons) and before the third set has arrived, to minimise root damage. The more leaves a seedling grows, the more roots it develops; therefore, it's possible that transplanting might disturb these roots.

You should always harden plants off before planting them out. A spell in an open, shaded position toughens them up and is particularly important if you have covered your seedling tray with glass to retain warmth and moisture. Try to gradually acclimatise the seedlings to cooler growing conditions, and watch that your seedlings don't dry out or get eaten by pests at this stage of their growth.

ABOVE One way of separating herb seeds enclosed in fleshy fruit from the pulp is to place the fruit in a colander and push the pulp through the holes with your fingers. Hosing helps.

MASHING SEEDS Herb seeds that are enclosed in fleshy fruits or berries, such as elder (right), will need more vigorous treatment. First you need to mash the fruit. With your hand inside a large jar, mash the berries with your fingers. Add some water to the jar, replace the lid, and give the jar a good shake. The pulp should float to the top, leaving behind the seeds, which can then be dried and stored in paper bags. Alternatively, small amounts of fruit can be macerated in a blender. Some seeds will settle at the bottom of the blender and can be gathered.

SOWING LARGE SEEDS IN THE GARDEN

1 Rake a fine tilth in the soil in a garden bed.

2 Level the bed with a straight piece of timber.

3 Use the edge of the timber to create seed drills.

4 Plant the seeds in the drill. The distance between the seeds will vary according to what you are planting.

5 Backfill and water the seeds gently. Keep the soil moist until seedlings appear.

Advantages of using seed

Growing plants from seed is economical. If you are starting a new garden or have large areas to plant, growing from seed will save you money. Plant a few seeds at a time over a period of several weeks to ensure a long cropping period. This makes more sense than having 10 lettuces or 10 cauliflowers ready for harvest at the same time, which is what will happen if you plant established seedlings.

Growing plants from seed is also often the only way that you can obtain a range of unusual plants for the garden. Seed companies produce a very large range of seeds for plants that are not available as seedlings or ready-grown plants. The seeds often include unusual colour ranges or unusual forms of familiar plants.

When to sow seed

It is important to check seed packets for the correct sowing times. Most seeds are dependent on temperature and/or day length for their germination and development. For a better chance of success follow the directions on the packet. Bear in mind that there can be some climatic variations from year to year which have a bearing on soil temperature and sowing times, as well as regional differences. If you live in a cool climate, mark on your calendar the date of the last expected spring frost. Then, working backwards, calculate when you need to sow seed. Check the Herb Directory and Vegetable Directory at the back of this book for details about when to sow specific crops.

handy tip

The top of the refrigerator is just the right temperature to give bottom heat for trays of germinating seedlings.

Seed-raising mixes

For seed raising in trays or pots you can make your own mix or purchase a ready-made commercial seed-raising mix. These mixes are ideal for germinating seed and raising seedlings of vegetables, but are not generally suitable for long-term growth.

The simplest seed-raising mix is made up of two parts coarse washed river sand or propagating sand with one part peat moss or coconut fibre peat. You will find these items at nurseries and garden centres. Beach sand is unsuitable for use in seed-raising mixes, as is builder's sand, which sets like concrete if wet and dried again. Coconut or coir fibre peat is often sold as cocopeat. Well aged, crumbly garden compost can be used as a substitute for the peat.

To grow some of the more unusual types of eggplant (aubergine), you'll need to start plants from seed.

ABOVE Growing plants from seed is interesting and straightforward. Begin by sowing easy-to-handle seeds that are known for their reliable germination. Vegetables that are easy to handle include beans, peppers (capsicum), cucumber, melons, peas, pumpkin, sweet corn, tomatoes and zucchini (courgette). Good herbs are basil, chives, dill, mint, sage and thyme.

RIGHT Sow broad bean seeds directly into the bed where they will grow to maturity.

Vermiculite is also used in seed-raising mixes as it is able to absorb large quantities of water and can hold nutrients in reserve for developing seedlings. Perlite is another good addition. It is extremely light but can hold 3–4 times its own weight of water. It has no nutrients but aids in the aeration of mixes. Both perlite and vermiculite are used in seed-raising mixes at the ratio of 1 part added to 2 parts of sand.

Garden soil, however good it is in the garden, is generally unsuitable for seed raising. Both drainage and aeration can be poor, leading to very low seed germination rates. Seed-raising media must always drain well and be well aerated. Even the best soil tends to compact to a certain degree when placed in containers. It is also impossible to guarantee that garden soil does not contain pathogens. Soil should only be used if it is pasteurised, which means that it has been kept at a temperature of 60°C (120°F) for 30 minutes to kill off any pathogens. Soil can be baked in the oven or in a microwave, but you should note that this is a messy business and the soil will still be unsuitable for using on its own for seed raising.

Depth and spacing

Seed packets give useful details of suitable planting depth and spacing for that particular plant. The rule of thumb is that seeds are planted at a depth of roughly twice the diameter of the seed. Fine seed is generally planted no more than 5 mm (¼ in) deep with a very light covering of soil or potting mix. Large seeds are planted deeper, according to their size. However, if you plant seeds too deeply they won't germinate and may rot in the soil. Some seeds need light to germinate and should therefore not be covered at all. Good soil preparation prior to sowing is vitally important. If the soil is heavy and the drainage poor many seeds will fail to germinate.

SEEDS AND SEED PODS

The seeds and seed casings from many herbs make wonderful spices. Some are richly textured, some sweet, others fragrant, and of course, all have the added benefit of being longer lasting than fresh and dried foliage herbs. Incorporate seeds and seed pods into dressings and pickles, curry pastes and stews, or even add them to pot pourris. Alternatively, combine a pod with one other ingredient: add a vanilla pod to a jar of sugar, which will then become infused with the vanilla flavour.

1 Star anise.   2 Cardamom pods and seeds.   3 Juniper berries.   4 Brown mustard seeds (top) and yellow mustard seeds.   5 White sesame seeds and black sesame seeds.   6 Blue poppy seeds and white poppy seeds.   7 White peppercorns (top), pink peppercorns and green peppercorns.

1 Nutmeg.   **2** Allspice.   **3** Cubeb pepper.   **4** Pomegranate seeds.
5 Vanilla pod.   **6** Aniseed.   **7** Celery seeds.   **8** Dill seeds.
9 Caraway seeds.   **10** Fennel seeds.   **11** Cumin seeds.
12 Barberry seeds 'Zareshk'.   **13** Coriander seeds.
14 Fenugreek seeds.   **15** Nigella seeds.

1

2   3   4

5

6

7

8

9

10

11

12   13   14   15

step by step

SOWING FINE SEEDS OUTDOORS

1 Create a fine tilth in the soil in a garden bed. Draw a drill in the soil.

2 Encrust a piece of sticky tape with fine seeds. Simply lay the tape in the drill.

3 Backfill lightly.

4 Water in the newly planted seeds.

Seeds in containers

In the past, seed boxes were always made of timber. Timber boxes are easy to build. They should be 8–10 cm (3¼–4 in) deep with a width and length that make them convenient for you to lift and move around. The timber pieces that form the base of the box should be spaced slightly apart to allow for drainage.

Plastic trays such as those that are used at nurseries to hold seedling punnets are ideal if you can get hold of some of them. You should line the base of the trays with a single sheet of newspaper to prevent the seed-raising mix from falling through the holes.

Cell trays that hold individual seedlings can be purchased or recycled. These make transplanting very easy and are most suitable when you want to raise only a few plants at one time. You can also sow individual seeds in egg cartons – these can easily be pulled apart so that you can plant the seedlings without disturbing their roots. The cardboard carton will break down in the soil.

Peat pots in which seeds can be sown are available commercially. Once the seedlings are large enough, plant them – still in the peat pot – straight into the garden.

Clean, used margarine or butter tubs are useful containers for seed sowing. Make sure that the tub will drain well by perforating the base with a skewer in several places.

Seed-raising kits are also available, which provide you with everything you need to get started. These are available at garden centres.

Sowing herb seeds in pots

Many herbs grow well from seed, and packets of herb seeds are readily available from garden centres and even most supermarkets. When you buy packets of seed, you should read the information on the packet to ensure that you are planting in the right season, and that the aspect and climate are appropriate. Most seeds germinate best in a warm place that is out of direct sun. Once

handy tip

Recycled seed trays

Egg cartons are ideal seed propagation trays. The whole cup can be planted in the garden at the appropriate time. Just cut out the bottom.

the seedlings appear, gradually move the tray to a sunnier position and into more normal conditions.

You will need to buy some seed-raising mix and good quality potting mix. You can start seeds in any clean, flat container with adequate drainage. Plastic trays are ideal and are easy to wash clean. If you are reusing old containers, scrub them clean with a brush and a little detergent before potting to remove any disease pathogens.

The seedlings may need daily watering until they are firmly established, then less frequent watering according to the weather conditions, exposure and plant type. They should be established – that is, obviously strong and growing – after about 7–10 days. You can then begin to fertilise them with soluble plant foods, especially seaweed-based ones, a sprinkling of blood and bone, or pelleted poultry manure.

ABOVE LEFT There are both annual and perennial varieties of chamomile (*Anthemis nobilis* and *Chamaemelum nobile*) that can be grown from seed sown in spring. They need full sun and do not like a lot of fertiliser.

LEFT Sow fresh seeds of the chestnut (*Castanea sativa*), as dried ones may not germinate. Although the chestnut has medicinal uses, always discard the fruit casing as it is poisonous.

Sowing herb seed step by step

1   Use a seed-raising mix to fill clean punnets or seed trays. You can purchase this from a garden centre but it's easy to make your own. Use 2 parts of coarse washed sand to 1 part of peat moss or a substitute such as coconut fibre peat (cocopeat).

2   Bring the mix to within 2.5 cm (1 in) of the top of the tray and firm it down.

3   Gently sprinkle a few seeds over the surface and lightly press them into the mix so that the seeds come into good contact with it.

4   Finally, add a light sprinkling of mix on top of the seeds.

5   Carefully water the container with a fine spray, or soak the bottom of the container in a dish filled with water so that moisture will be drawn up into the mix. When the soil is completely moist, lift the container out of the dish and leave it to drain.

6   Keep the soil damp, but not wet, until seedlings emerge. This could occur within a week for fast-germinating seeds, but may take up to six weeks for parsley.

7   Once the seedlings have developed a few leaves and a root system, and are big enough to handle, transplant them into a pot or garden bed. It is best to do this in the cool of the day. Again, use a good quality potting mix if you are planting your herbs in pots, or into a garden bed that has been dug over with some organic matter added. Make a hole with your finger, just big enough to accommodate the seedling. Gently lower it into the hole and press the soil mixture around the roots.

8   Gently water the seedlings in; this will also settle the soil around the roots.

9   Place your potted herbs in a sheltered bright spot, away from direct sunlight, until they are well established.

Good herbs for containers

The following is a selection of popular herbs that are suitable for growing in pots.

Anise

Sow seeds of anise (*Pimpinella anisum*) in spring in a well drained mix with lime added. Anise needs full sun and regular water but should be allowed to dry out between waterings. Harvest it in autumn: hang the stems to dry, remove the dried seeds and store it in an airtight container.

Basil

Sow the flavoursome herb basil (*Ocimum basilicum*) in spring but not too early as this herb prefers warmth. Space the plants about 20–25 cm (8–10 in) apart in full sun, and water and fertilise them regularly. Don't allow basil to flower too early or it will stop growing. Remember to pinch out the growing tips often for bushier basil plants.

Bay

Bay (*Laurus nobilis*) trees planted in the open ground will grow into very large trees. However, you can grow a bay plant in a container, and it will last there for many years.

ABOVE The leaves of coriander are widely used in Thai and Asian cooking. The seeds are common in many spice mixes.

OPPOSITE Onion chives belong to the same family as onion, garlic, leek and shallot.

Bay strikes readily from cuttings in late summer and autumn. A fairly slow-growing tree, it can be trimmed to a formal shape or left to develop its own neat style. It is quite tolerant of neglect and does not mind if a few annuals or herbs are tucked into its pot to grow alongside. Plant bay in full sun, in a well drained mix, but give it plenty of water in warm weather. Pick the leaves as you need them.

If your bay plant is attacked by scale insects, spray it with white oil, but not on a very hot day.

Caraway

Sow caraway (*Carum carvi*) in spring and again in autumn in warm areas. Provide full sun and wind protection, as these plants are tall. Space them 15–20 cm (6–8 in) apart. Water regularly but don't keep the soil wet. When the seeds are ripe, cut off the seed heads and dry them thoroughly before storing.

Chamomile

Sow chamomile (*Anthemis nobilis*) seeds 15 cm (6 in) apart in spring, and provide full sun, regular water and good drainage. Pick the flower heads on a warm, dry day and spread them to dry.

BUGS AND SNAILS Watch out for bugs and snails. These pests can be quite a problem with seedlings, particularly in wet weather. You can protect new shoots with snail pellets, but if you're concerned for children or pets, hide the pellets in a piece of open pipe or inside an old terracotta pot. Snails love these places. Chewing caterpillars can also be a pest. Search for them, by torchlight if necessary, and destroy them. If you cannot find the pests, dust the plants with Derris dust on several consecutive nights. One good solution for snails and slugs is a beer bait. In order to make one, simply place some beer in a bottle and half-submerge it in the soil so that the snails and slugs can get inside, but can't escape. Or use a shallow dish full of beer.

Lemon grass is an untidy grower but you can keep it presentable by trimming the foliage back in spring.

Chervil

You can sow chervil (*Anthriscus cerefolium*) seeds in spring, and again in autumn in warm districts, about 10 cm (4 in) apart. Chervil will enjoy a semi-shaded position, but is frost tender. It needs plenty of summer water. Pick the leaves as needed, or clip before flowering and hang them to dry.

Chives

Chives (*Allium schoenprasum*) can be propagated from spring-sown seeds but it is easiest to divide old clumps in late winter when the plants are still fairly dormant. Space them 2.5–5 cm (1–2 in) apart to allow for increase. Full sun, regular watering and fertiliser will ensure a regular supply for months. Chives are rarely attacked by insects, although aphids can be a problem.

Coriander

Sow coriander (*Coriandrum sativum*) seeds about 25–30 cm (10–12 in) apart in spring, and again in autumn in warm areas. Coriander requires full sun, wind protection and regular water to maintain growth. It may need staking. You can pick the leaves often, but be careful not to denude the plant. Collect the seeds when they are dry and ripe.

Dill

Sow dill (*Anethum graveolens*) seeds in spring 20–25 cm (8–10 in) apart. Dill seeds need full sun and wind protection, and may also need staking or support. Add lime to the potting mix. Allow the mix to dry out between waterings. Pick leaves as you need them but let the seed heads ripen before drying and storing them.

Lavender

Lavender (*Lavandula* spp.) must have full sun, good drainage and lime added to the mix. Grow it from tip cuttings taken from late spring to autumn. Lavender plants can grow quite large so you will need to repot them as they outgrow the smaller pots. Allow them to dry out between waterings and give little or no fertiliser. Pick the blooms or cut back after flowering.

Lemon grass

You can start new lemon grass (*Cymbopogon citratus*) plants easily in late winter or spring by cutting a few fleshy stalks from a clump below soil level. Make sure each piece has a root attached to it. It is sometimes easier to remove the plant from its pot and divide it, and then replant the separated pieces. You can also strike a piece bought from a fruiterer. Look for a piece that is fresh, with a good fleshy base. Insert it straight into moist potting mix, then keep the pot in a warm, shady place. Roots will form within 2–3 weeks.

Mint

Mint (*Mentha* spp.) will grow from any piece of root planted in semi-shade with moist soil. In fact, it can become quite invasive. (See 'Marvellous mint' on page 78.) Keep it well watered throughout the growing season, then cut it back hard in winter. Caterpillars like the leaves, and rust can be a problem. If rust occurs, remove the affected leaves or, if the rust is too advanced, pull the plant out.

Oregano

A perennial herb, oregano (*Origanum vulgare*) needs full sun and lime added to the potting mix. Grow it from seeds sown in spring or from cuttings taken in late spring or summer. The plants need regular cutting back; they become woody after 3–4 years, and are best started again. Allow the mix to dry out between waterings, and give the plants little or no fertiliser.

Parsley

Sow parsley (*Petroselinum* spp.) seeds in spring and again in autumn in warm areas. The seed can be slow to germinate and must be kept damp at all times, though flat-leaf parsley germinates much faster and may take only a few days. Although parsley is a biennial, it is best treated as an annual and replanted each year. It prefers sun, but will tolerate half a day's shade.

ABOVE Rocket, or arugula, has been a favourite salad herb in Italy since ancient Roman times.

BELOW Italian lavender (*Lavandula stoechas*) is a good companion plant to *Erigeron* and *Ajuga*, as all three of these decorative plants flower simultaneously.

Rocket

Rocket, or arugula (*Eruca vesicaria* subsp. *sativa*) resents heat, so sow seeds in spring or early autumn. It likes some shade, regular water and fertiliser. Rocket plants can grow quite tall as they go to seed and will need some protection from wind. Keep the pot near the kitchen door and pick the leaves as you need them.

Rosemary

Best grown from cuttings taken from late spring to autumn, rosemary (*Rosmarinum officinalis*) needs perfect drainage and full sun. Add lime to the mix, and allow it to dry out between waterings; don't overwater in winter. Cut sprigs for fragrance or for cooking, and cut the bushes back after flowering in spring to maintain compact growth. Rosemary plants can become large, and will need potting on to larger containers as they grow.

LEFT Traditionally, rosemary was thought to bring one good fortune and fertility.

BELOW *Thymus* 'Mount Tomah' is a creeping thyme with dark green foliage, which turns golden in winter.

HERBAL MEAT TENDERISER *The Elizabethans used to wrap tough meat in sorrel leaves. This served both to tenderise the meat as well as imbuing it with a piquant flavour.*

Purple sage (*Salvia officinalis* 'Purpurascens') has attractive foliage and pale mauve flowers.

Sage

Sage (*Salvia officinalis*) must have full sun and free-draining potting mix; it will not tolerate wet 'feet'. Grow from seed in spring and from cuttings taken in late spring or autumn. Add lime to the mix. Water regularly until the plants are established, but then only water if the soil is very dry. Pick the leaves as required or pick sprigs of young leaves before flowering and dry them in a dark airy place.

Sorrel

Sow sorrel (*Rumex acetosa*) seeds in spring or divide roots of existing clumps in autumn or late winter. This herb prefers full sun but will tolerate half sun. It needs regular water in hot weather and occasional fertiliser. As flower stalks appear in summer, remove them at the base or the plant will stop growing. Snails and caterpillars can be pests.

Thyme

You can grow thyme (*Thymus* spp.) from its very small seeds in spring, from cuttings taken in late spring or autumn, or from root divisions. It needs full sun, perfect drainage and lime added to the mix. Water regularly to establish the plant, but when it is growing well, water only occasionally and don't add any fertiliser.

Watercress

Grow watercress (*Nasturtium officinale*) from seed or root division in flowing water or in a container half-filled with potting mix, in sun or half sun. As seedlings grow, gradually increase the water in the container. At least once a week, change the water completely. Keep harvesting the stems to maintain growth.

Sowing seed outdoors (in containers)

Most seeds should be sown in a seed tray or in punnets initially, then pricked out and planted into larger containers as the seedlings develop.

When sowing fine seeds add fine dry sand to make spreading the seeds easier. Just tamp these seeds down slightly after sowing, rather than covering them over. Add sand to hairy seeds to stop them sticking.

Cold frames

In colder climates, cold frames are ideal for raising seeds. A cold frame is a raised enclosure, framed in brick or timber, with a glass or plastic cover. The frames are built higher at the back so the cover slopes, allowing rain to run off. If the frame is being used for seed raising, fill it with seed-raising mix. There will be less temperature fluctuation and fewer problems with the growing medium drying out.

You could also use a seed bed, which is essentially the same. A seed bed is a raised bed, probably no more than 1 m (3⅓ ft) square, enclosed by brick or timber. A removable cover of 30 per cent shadecloth or flyscreen wire will provide light shading for seedlings and reduce the impact of heavy rain. The cover can either be attached to a metal or wooden frame with legs or it can be supported on bricks.

Slightly larger seeds can be sown straight from the packet or container. Draw a line (called a drill) in the soil with a pencil or stick, sow the seed, then backfill slightly. After the first set of true leaves appears (which appear after the baby pair of leaves, or cotyledons), and before the third set has arrived, you can remove the seedlings from the trays (or 'prick out' as its known) in order to prevent as much root damage as possible. The more leaves a seedling has, the more roots it has developed below the surface; if you transplant too late, you might disturb these roots.

You should always harden your seedlings off before planting them out into the garden. You can simply place them in open, shaded position for a time. This is particularly important if you have covered your seedling tray with glass to retain warmth and moisture. Gradually acclimatise the seedlings to cooler growing conditions.

Sowing seed indoors

If you sow seed indoors, it allows you to start the new season earlier than if you have to wait for the weather to plant outdoors. You will also be able to control your environment, so seeds will germinate more strongly.

Vegetable seeds need quite a warm place to germinate (between 24 and 32°C (75 and 90°F), so try and find a suitable spot indoors. On top of the fridge or above a water heater are both good positions. At some garden centres, horticultural heating mats are available. Be sure to place these mats on a heatproof surface.

Once the seeds have germinated, keep them by a sunny window, or under special fluorescent plant lights. The seedlings will require between 10 and 16 hours of light a day.

As mentioned above, if the seedlings start to become crowded, transfer them to their own containers.

About two weeks before you plan to transplant the seedlings outdoors, start to reduce watering and fertilising. A week before you move the plants outside, take the seedling containers outdoors and put them in a position protected from full sun or wind. Just leave them outdoors for an hour to start with, then bring them indoors again. Over the following week, gradually leave them out for longer and longer. At the end of the week they should be ready for transplanting outdoors.

Sowing seeds outdoors (direct method)

You can plant large easy-to-handle seeds directly into the garden at the appropriate spacings where they are to grow without any need for you to transplant them.

Propagating your own plants from seed, in a greenhouse or cold frame, will give you immense satisfaction.

SOWING SEED OUTDOORS (BROADCAST)

Broadcast sowing is a useful technique for salad vegetables such as radishes and spring onions, and green manure crops such as comfrey or mustard.

1 Rake the soil to form a seed bed with a fine tilth. Remove any large stones and break down large clods of earth. This will leave the soil with a fine layer on the top surface.

2 Pour a few of the seeds from the packet into the palm of your hand.

3 Sow the seeds by scattering them evenly over the soil surface. Sow from a height of about 30 cm (1 ft) above soil level.

4 Lightly rake over the seed bed in at least two different directions to incorporate the seeds into the soil and to avoid gathering them into clusters. Label the seed bed.

SOWING SEED OUTDOORS (DRILL)

Drill sowing is a good technique for growing most vegetables, allowing you to see immediately when seeds have germinated and to remove week seedlings from between the drills easily.

1 Rake the soil to form a seed bed with a fine tilth; break up large clods of earth and remove any large stones. Mark out the rows with a garden line (keeping it taut).

2 Using a draw hoe or cane, make a groove in the soil to form the seed drill.

3 Sow the seeds thinly into the drill by hand, aiming for a set distance between the seeds. Never sow them directly from the packet.

4 Using a rake, draw the soil back into the drill, covering the seeds. Gently pat and firm the soil over the seeds using the back of the rake.

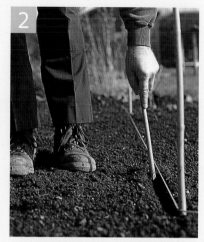

GERMINATION TIME In the right conditions many plants will germinate in as little as 5–10 days. Beans and peas are among this group. Other plants are quite slow, taking 3–4 weeks.

For the maximum number of seeds to germinate successfully, the environment must be right. The soil making up the seed bed must be moist and firm, with a fine, crumbly texture without being too light and fluffy. It should not contain too many stones, as this will make it difficult to draw out a seed drill row to place the seeds into. The smaller the seeds to be sown, the finer the tilth of the seed bed should be.

If you are planting seeds directly into the garden, make a furrow about 15 cm (6 in) deep, sprinkle a little fertiliser into the base of the furrow and then refill it with soil almost to the original level of the ground. You can then sow your seed and firm down the soil surface. This is the method most often used by vegetable growers, as vegetables must be grown rapidly in order to ensure the very best quality produce.

Different seeds for different climates

There can be a big difference in performance of plants grown from seed, depending on the source of the particular seed. Some plants may grow well in a range of different climates, but this is not always the case.

Seeds that are sourced from plants originating in milder regions with light, free-draining soil may not perform well in areas that have heavy frosts or in areas with heavy clay soils, whereas seeds sourced from warm, low altitudes may not thrive in colder, high-altitude regions. Seed companies aim to supply seed that

Eggplant (aubergine) seeds will require warm soil conditions in which to germinate successfully.

performs well in a range of climates, and they choose strains of seed with proven superior qualities.

Cool climate plants

Seeds of some plants are very sensitive to high temperatures and won't germinate if the weather conditions are too warm. Lettuce, peas and spinach are in this group.

Some cool climate plants will grow quite well in warm climates but will never flower, often because the lack of chilling prevents the development of flower buds. In nature, chilling stimulates growth and flowering in many species of plants. Seeds that mature in autumn sit in the ground (or in their containers), are dampened by rain, then chilled by frost or snow in winter, and finally burst into life in spring. Some seeds will not germinate unless they have had a sufficient period of chilling followed by a period of rising soil temperature and increasing day length.

Warm climate plants

Plants that will not germinate in low temperatures include beans, eggplant (aubergine) and tomato. Grow warm climate plants in cool climates with the protection

witlof (belgian endive)
Cichorium intybus

fiddlehead fern
Dicksonia antarctica

bamboo shoot
Phyllostachys **spp.**

SHOOTS AND SPROUTS
We all enjoy young, fresh produce and juicy shoots and sprouts are the best of all. Sprouts come from all sorts of plants, including broccoli, onion, alfalfa, beans, peas and wheat. These are literally just germinated from their seed. Shoots refer to the tender new growth on more mature plants, such as the underground spears of the bamboo plant or asparagus, which sends up new spears from a perennial plant each spring.

lemon grass
Cymbopogon citratus

snow pea sprouts
(mangetout sprouts)
Pisum sativum var. *macrocarpon*

spring onions
Allium fistulosum

asparagus
Asparagus officinalis

mung beans
Vigna radiata

celery
Apium graveolens

broccoli sprouts
Brassica oleracea Botrytis Group

garlic chives
Allium tuberosum

alfalfa
Medicago sativa

Raising seedlings in containers in a protected environment will mean they are more sturdy when you come to transplant them into the open garden.

of a glasshouse, at least through the vulnerable stages of germination and establishment. Soil temperature is important for many summer flowering and cropping plants. Seeds of these plants will simply not germinate if the soil is too cool. Cold soil can result in the failure of many summer annuals and vegetables if you sow seed too early in spring.

Seed viability

Seeds vary greatly, too, in their viability or ability to grow. Some have a very short period of viability while others may maintain their ability to grow over many years. Seeds from commercial growers have a use-by date on the packet which indicates how long the unopened packet should last in good condition and still give good germination rates. Fresh seed usually gives the best results, and after opening a packet it is advisable to use the remaining seed within six months.

Seeds must be stored in a cool, dry place, even in the refrigerator. Enclose packets of seed in sealable plastic bags before storing them in the fridge. You can also store seed in the freezer for long periods. Commercially packaged seed is contained and sealed in airtight foil envelopes to ensure that the seed remains dry and clean.

High temperatures and damp conditions are the worst enemies of stored seed. In damp conditions seeds absorb moisture, providing ideal conditions for fungal organisms to take hold. If conditions are too wet the seeds may absorb enough moisture to swell and start to germinate; they will then rot, and the whole batch of seed will be lost.

Seed companies grow their own seed or contract special growers to produce their seeds to ensure that the packeted seed is of the highest quality. Their seeds are tested regularly for purity and germination rates.

Pricking out seedlings

Container-grown seedlings must be thinned out to wider spacings once they are growing strongly. This process, which is known as pricking out, allows for optimum development of the seedling. If the seedlings are very crowded, prick them out as soon as you think they are large enough to handle. At this stage they will probably be about 1.5–2 cm (⅝–¾ in) high and have their first true leaves (that is, the leaves that emerge above the seed leaves). Plant them out in another container to grow on until they are ready for their intended growing positions. Seeds that have been planted at adequate spacings, usually large seeds, can be left to grow on where they are until they are 8–10 cm (3¼–4 in) high. At that stage they will be ready to be planted out in their permanent positions either in the ground or in containers.

When pricking out and replanting tiny seedlings, work out of the sun and out of the wind. Spread out a sheet of plastic or newspaper so that you have somewhere to place the small bundles of seedlings once they have been removed from the seed pots or trays.

Fill a seed tray or pot with a suitable potting mix and, using a pencil or stick, make holes in the mix ready to

THINNINGS *The thinnings of many vegetables are delicious in salads, or lightly wilted. Try chicory (endive), turnips, radish, Swiss chard (silverbeet) and beetroot.*

Germination tips

Problems with growing media, soil or mix

May be too wet Heavy, poorly drained soil or mix holds too much water, causing seeds to rot. You should use good quality seed-raising mix or open up heavy soils by adding organic matter. Water only often enough to keep the seed moist but not wet.

May be too dry Seeds cannot germinate without moisture. Once seeds swell and start to germinate they will die if they dry out. You should check moisture levels regularly. Cover sown seed with shadecloth, glass or even paper to conserve moisture.

Soil-borne fungal disease Sow seed only in fresh seed-raising mix in clean containers or in the garden in well-prepared, well-drained soil. Don't sow seed in areas where disease has been present. You should practise crop rotation to avoid continuing problems. Avoid overwatering and don't sow seed in poorly drained sites.

Growing medium too loose or too compacted
If you haven't firmed down the mix after seed sowing there will be too much air around the seed – this lack of contact with the mix means seed will dry out. If the mix is too compacted drainage will be poor and seeds will be deprived of oxygen.

Planting depth A good general rule of thumb for seed sowing is to plant at a depth of twice the diameter of the seed. Very fine seed should just be pressed into the surface of the mix. If you sow seed too deeply it may not have enough food reserves to provide the energy needed in order to reach the surface. Shallow-sown seed is more likely to rot if given constant watering. By the same token, if the sowing depth is too shallow, the seed is then at risk of drying out, unless you are vigilant about watering. The lower soil temperature at a greater depth may also affect seed germination.

Other problems

Pests Animal pests, such as cats and dogs, often dig up freshly tilled soil. It is therefore strongly recommended that you cover your seed beds with wire netting to prevent this kind of damage. You can also place strong smelling mothballs or other animal repellents around the bed to further discourage pets. Contrary to popular belief, the plastic bottle of water method does not work.

Snails and slugs can totally demolish young seedlings that are emerging from the soil. You can use physical barriers such as sharp shell grit scattered around the sown area, or you could sprinkle commercial snail baits on the seed bed. It is vital to ensure that neither children nor dogs are able to reach the baits.

Fertiliser Fresh fertiliser in the soil can burn seeds and emerging roots. To avoid this problem, apply fertiliser in bands on either side of the planting row. You also have the choice of waiting until the seedlings have emerged

and are growing strongly before you apply any fertiliser. Do not allow the fertiliser to touch the leaves or stems of the seedlings, as it could scorch them.

Alternatively, you can place the fertiliser in a furrow well below the seed-sowing area. Make the furrow about 8–10 cm (3¼–4 in) deep, place the fertiliser along the trench, then backfill with soil. Firm the soil down with your hands and sow the seed.

Seed viability problems The seeds of many plants lose their viability quite quickly once you have opened the sealed packet. Lettuce and parsnip are two plants that rapidly lose their freshness and ability to germinate. Generally, once you have opened the foil packet of seeds it is a good idea to try to use the seed within six months. Store the seeds in a cool dry area to prolong the period of viability – both heat and moisture will cause rapid deterioration of seed.

Heirloom crops

One of the rewards of growing your own organic crops is being able to indulge in the incredible richness and diversity of our inheritance of traditional and heirloom vegetables and fruit. The beauty and flavour of heirloom produce is almost beyond dreams. For tomatoes, imagine translucent apricot-striped green 'Zebra'; huge clusters of tiny 'Red Currant' glowing like jewels; big pink 'Brandywine', an Amish heirloom considered to have the finest and most intense flavour in the world; emerald green 'Evergreen' with strong, fresh, sweet flavour for salads and the equally delicious 'Aunt Ruby's German Green'; huge pleated fruits the size of plates like rich crimson 'Zapotec Ribbed' and 'Ruffled Yellow'; tiger gold and red striped 'Tigerella'; mahogany red richest-flavoured 'Black from Tula'; and delicious black varieties like 'Black Russian' and 'Black Krim'.

There are hundreds of heirloom tomato cultivars being rescued from extinction around the planet, along with thousands of ancient and heirloom forms of every other vegetable, grain, herb and fruit.

Carrots need a deep, stone-free soil if they are not to grow forked and misshapen. However, if you have unsuitable soil, you can get round this problem by growing the round or stump-rooted varieties.

receive the plants. Make the holes 3–6 cm (1¼–2½ in) apart. The wider spacing will be needed for plants with large leaves such as lettuce or cabbage. Use a flat blade or a stick to separate and lift out a bunch of seedlings from their original container. Place them on the sheet of paper or plastic that you have previously spread out in readiness and gently separate them. Hold the seedling firmly but gently and lower its roots into the hole, then backfill the hole by pushing the potting mix around the roots with a stick or with your fingers.

Gently water the plants with a fine spray and set the container in a sheltered spot. The container should receive some sun but preferably only early morning sun until the seedlings have recovered from their move.

Once the plants have recovered from transplanting shock, gradually expose them to more sunlight and give them some liquid fertiliser at half strength. When the plants are growing strongly and have reached a height of 8–10 cm (3½–4 in) they are ready to be planted out into their permanent positions.

Watering and fertilising seedlings

Watering at this stage is very important, and you should check the soil around plants by scratching away the

TRANSPLANTING YOUNG PLANTS

Once plants raised in a seed bed become sufficiently large you will need to transplant them to allow them space to carry on growing.

1 Lift the seedlings carefully, holding the leaves rather then the stem, which will bruise easily.

2 Make a hole in the new position and insert the plant, firming down the soil around it. Water plant in well.

surface to feel or see whether it is moist. As you want to encourage your plants to put down deep roots it is better to thoroughly soak the area every few days rather than sprinkle it daily. Of course, the frequency of watering will depend on the season and the weather, as well as the conditions of your local climate.

After a few days, when the seedlings have recovered from the move, you should give them a dose of half strength liquid plant food. It is also important to keep the area free of weeds so that the young plants are not competing for water or nutrients.

Transplanting seedlings

When transplanting the seedlings into the ground or into their permanent containers, you should make sure that everything is ready before removing them from their trays or pots. Have the garden soil well prepared, marking out planting holes with a narrow-bladed trowel or your fingers.

Lift the seedlings with a trowel or flat blade, disturbing the roots as little as possible and leaving soil attached to the roots. Lower the plant into the hole and firm the soil around the roots, leaving a small depression around the plant to ensure that water is directed to the root zone. Give the plant a thorough watering. If you have some old compost or manure you can sprinkle this around the plants as a mulch to help conserve moisture – just make sure that you leave a little space around the plant stem. It may also be a good idea for you to sprinkle some snail bait around the newly planted seedlings, especially if the weather is damp or dewy.

Planting patterns

Interplanting means to plant more than one type of plant in the same place, in among each other. Ideally, mix early and late-maturing types, such as carrots with cucumber.

Succession planting means planting a second crop after you've harvested a first, in the same position, so you get two crops from the same space in just one season.

Successive sowing means you plant the same vegetable, successively, at several locations, at 10–14 day intervals for a continuous harvest.

Propagating Vegetables

TRANSPLANTING VEGETABLES		
Transplanting	Row width	Plant spacing
Cauliflower	45 cm (1½ ft)	60 cm (2 ft)
Celery	45 cm (1½ ft)	45 cm (1½ ft)
Garlic	20 cm (8 in)	20 cm (8 in)
Onion sets	20 cm (8 in)	15 cm (6 in)
Potatoes	50 cm (1⅔ ft)	30 cm (1 ft)

RAISING VEGETABLES FROM SEED		
Seed sowing	Row width	Plant spacing
Beetroot	30 cm (1 ft)	10 cm (4 in)
Broad bean	30 cm (1 ft)	23 cm (9 in)
Broccoli	40 seeds per tray sown indoors	
Brussels sprouts	40 seeds per tray sown indoors	
Cabbage (summer/autumn)	45 cm (1½ ft)	30 cm (1 ft)
Cabbage (winter)	45 cm (1½ ft)	45 cm (1½ ft)
Carrot	15 cm (6 in)	10 cm (4 in)
Cauliflower (summer)	40 seeds per tray sown indoors	
Cauliflower (winter)	30 cm (1 ft)	15 cm (6 in)
Cauliflower (spring)	30 cm (1 ft)	15 cm (6 in)

Seed sowing	Row width	Plant spacing
Celeriac	40 seeds per tray sown indoors	
Celery	40 seeds per tray sown indoors	
Cucumber (ridge)	1 seed per 7.5 cm (3 in) pot sown indoors	
Eggplant (aubergine)	1 seed per 7.5 cm (3 in) pot sown indoors	
French bean	30 cm (1 ft)	7.5 cm (3 in)
Kale	60 cm (2 ft)	45 cm (1½ ft)
Kidney bean	30 cm (1 ft)	15 cm (6 in)
Kohlrabi	30 cm (1 ft)	15 cm (6 in)
Leek	10 cm (4 in)	2.5 cm (1 in)
Lettuce	30 cm (1 ft)	30 cm (1 ft)
Marrow	1 seed per 7.5 cm (3 in) pot sown indoors	
Onion salad	10 cm (4 in)	5 cm (2 in)
Onion seed	30 cm (1 ft)	10 cm (4 in)
Parsnip	30 cm (1 ft)	15 cm (6 in)
Peas	13 cm (5 in)	13 cm (5 in)
Pepper (capsicum)	1 seed per 7.5 cm (3 in) pot sown indoors	
Radish	15 cm (6 in)	2.5 cm (1 in)
Swede	38 cm (1¼ ft)	23 cm (9 in)
Sweet corn	1 seed per 7.5 cm (3 in) pot sown indoors	
Tomato	1 seed per 7.5 cm (3 in) pot sown indoors	
Turnip	30 cm (1 ft)	15 cm (6 in)

In hot weather do your transplanting in the evening as this allows plants some time to recuperate. Plants may well wilt the following day when the full heat of the sun is upon them, but if the soil is moist they should recover once the sun moves off them. If it is extremely hot you could consider providing plants with some form of shading through the middle of the day.

Seed saving

Various techniques are used for seed collection – depending on the growing and seeding habits of the individual plant.

Plants in the Apiaceae family (previously known as Umbelliferae) including celery, carrots, celeriac and parsnips form lacy heads of tiny flowers followed by progressively ripening seed. To prevent much of the seed spilling on the ground, pick the entire head once the most mature seeds are fully sized and brown, place in a paper bag, tie with string and suspend upside down in a well ventilated area out of the direct sun. The seeds will all fall into the bag.

For stronger crops, let your very best plants go to seed each year, and use those seeds for the next planting season.

Clean the seeds, looking for any insects, place in an airtight container, label (including a date), and store in a dry, cool place. Apiaceae seed is generally viable for only one year, so plant a crop every year. Seed of the onion family Alliaceae is treated in the same way.

Pepper (capsicum) and chilli pepper seed can be removed from the fully ripened fruit and dried for storage (gloves are recommended for the process, as the chilli oils are hot).

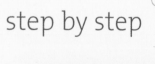
step by step

SAVING TOMATO SEED

1 Remove the sac of jelly which contains germination inhibitors. Squeeze the seed from ripe fruits into a non-metal container.

2 Add an equal amount of water and allow it to ferment for 3–4 days, then pour through a sieve, and dry the seed on a plastic or china plate. Store the seed in an airtight labelled container. Tomato seed will last for three or more years if properly stored.

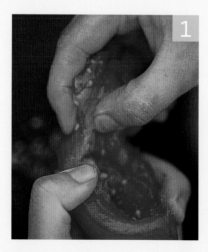

Peas and beans are left growing in the field until the pods are dry. Pull the bushes from the ground at the end of the season and thresh on a sheet to release the seed.

Brassicas, too, should be left in the garden. They will explode their seed as soon as fully dried so be sure to enclose heads in large paper bags to capture as many seeds as possible.

Cross-pollination of vegetables

It is important to prevent cross-pollination between closely related cultivars. Fortunately, three of the most collected groups, tomatoes, peas and beans, are normally self-pollinating and their seed can safely be saved. Other groups including cultivars of squash, brassicas like cabbage, broccoli, Brussels sprouts, chillies and peppers (capsicums), beetroot, corn and eggplant (aubergine) are likely to cross between cultivars.

There are various ways to prevent this happening. The easiest is to allow only one cultivar of each type to reach flowering in any season. Plants can be isolated by net cages, or newly opened flowers can be hand fertilised and prevented from cross-fertilisation by covering them with white paper bags or net.

In long season areas, it is often possible to plant two cultivars several weeks apart so that their flowering periods do not coincide. This technique is often used by gardeners for corn. However, in corn-growing districts, wind-blown pollen is carried far and wide and only hand pollination of newly emerged cornsilks protected beneath paper bags or paper cones will ensure that seed is not accidentally contaminated.

Planting edible tubers

Tubers can either be swollen roots or swollen stems for storage. The humble potato is the most commonly grown tuberous plant in the world, and the most consumed vegetable in the Western world. Tubers themselves are a starch-based storage system for the plant to adapt to extremes of climate such as cold and drought and help the plant vegetatively propagate itself. They should be grown quickly to produce sweet-tasting crops and need large amounts or potassium and phosphorus in the fertiliser used to help promote root development.

Hand-pollinate sweet corn by carefully taking pollen from the tassels and sprinkling it on the silks.

Edible tubers

Beetroot	Kohlrabi
Burdock	Parsnip
Carrot	Peanut
Cassava	Potato
Celeriac	Radish
Dandelion	Rutabaga
Galangal	Salisify
Ginger	Scorzonera
Ginseng	Swede
Hamburg parsley	Sweet potatoes
Horseradish	Taro
Jerusalem artichoke	Turnip
Jicama (yam bean)	Yam

Like other vegetables, root crops need a full sun position. The soil needs to be well worked over prior to sowing seed and most crops enjoy liberal quantities of organic matter dug through. Even small clods of earth can misshape crops such as carrots, radishes, swedes and turnips, so make sure a fine tilth is created before sowing seeds in shallow drills. Potatoes and Jerusalem artichokes are less fussy with soil, and any well drained area will suffice.

Tuberous vegetables have long been of use as food, especially as winter vegetables, as they keep so well once dug and in cold areas form the basis of many staple dishes. Despite their popularity as winter fodder, there are root vegetables for all seasons. From spring to autumn beetroot, carrots, potatoes, sweet potatoes, Jerusalem artichokes, kohlrabi, radish and parsnip make great eating, and as the season progresses, swedes and turnips come to the fore. Don't overlook the more unusual root crops either. Salsify, scorzonera, horseradish and dandelions make pleasant accompaniments and yams, cassava, taro root and jicama (yam beans) are exotic root crops worth sourcing in hot or tropical climates.

Potatoes

Potatoes are the most widely eaten vegetables in the Western world. Potatoes are tubers, a root modified as a starch storage vessel. They can be propagated from the 'eyes' of seed potatoes, normally purchased in your local nursery as certified disease-free. For a similar flavour, try Jerusalem artichokes.

Beetroot is an edible root vegetable that grows well in cooler climates and tolerates frost.

PLANTING SEED POTATOES

1 Keep some seed potatoes until they sprout. This is called 'chitting' potato tubers and will give your plants a head start.

2 Using a spade or hoe, double dig a trench. Create a wide, flat-bottomed or V-shaped 15 cm (6 in) trench with a trowel.

3 Cut the seed potatoes into pieces so that each piece contains an eye.

4 Plant the pieces of seed potato in the trench. Backfill the trench with soil and water in thoroughly.

Water chestnuts (*Eleocharis dulcis*).

Alliums are all extremely adaptable to climate and soil types, providing the correct variety for the time and place is chosen. They also make an excellent winter crop and many varieties store well. To grow alliums, prepare the bed well, removing clods and scattering a preplanting fertiliser high in potassium. The soil pH needs to be around neutral, so liming may be necessary for acid soils. Sow the seed in drills very lightly on the surface onto dark, damp soil and after two weeks young seedlings will have emerged. Thin seedlings out as they develop so that each plant has about 10 cm (4 in) to grow into. Leeks are ready to harvest from about three months, while onions take up to eight to fully mature. Don't be tempted to hill plants or mound earth around them, as bulbs like to sit on the surface.

Corms are similar to bulbs but do not have the fleshy scale leaves; instead, they are a swollen stem. Water chestnuts are a type of corm, and not related to the

Although readily available in shops, home-grown spuds can be harvested early, to eat as 'chats', which are sweet baby potatoes. Other interesting potatoes include Desiree, which has pink skin; Purple Congo which has purple or bluish skin; and sweet potatoes.

Planting edible bulbs

Bulbs are swollen underground stems and each leaf is a fleshy scale, folded one on top of another and encasing a flower. These are full of plant foods such as starch, protein and sugar, which not only provide nutrients for new plants, but also in the case of the *Allium* genus, make a delicious ingredient in cooking.

Historically, records show that onions have been eaten for thousands of years, with references to them in the Bible and an inscription on the Great Pyramid. Their volatile acids give them their strong flavour and antiseptic qualities.

ONIONS Onions need the richest soil of all root crops, so give the bed a dressing of manure before planting. Sow seeds in spring, thinly along the rows, and mulch well. Onions are shallow-rooted and are easily damaged when you are weeding.

Edible bulbs

Chives, garlic, leeks, onions,
ramp (Canadian wild onion), shallots,
spring onions, water chestnuts (corms)

Garlic oil, bulbs, fresh garlic with stems, and peeled cloves.

chestnut family at all. The dark brown 'nut' grows at the base of a water plant with reed-like leaves and has sweet white flesh which can be eaten raw or cooked once the skin is peeled. They grow best in warm to hot areas in a container or pond that stays moist.

The Liliaceae family

The members of the *Allium* genus – onions, spring onions, leeks, shallots, garlic and chives, among others – belong to the lily or Liliaceae family. Some of the most stunning ornamental plants are to be found in this family, such as hyacinths, tulips and lilies. Like their family members, many edible plants in the Allium genus sport exquisite, showy flowerheads.

Garlic

The sulphur content of garlic acts as a strong disinfectant. In the Middle Ages it was hung outside the door to stop the plague and the juice has been used to heal gunshot wounds. Garlic is also said to prevent leaf curl in peaches and ward off black spot on roses. The longer garlic is cooked, the milder the flavour. Reduce

Earthing up

Other vegetables are covered with earth, but it's the stems and leaves that are eaten, not the roots. With asparagus, celery and witlof (Belgian endive), you can really surpass shop-bought specimens if you take a little time with the growing process. The taste of these vegetables can be improved enormously by a technique called 'earthing up' – mound the soil around the plants as the shoots emerge and the stalks will become elongated, white and tender. Asparagus, however, won't be ready for full harvesting for five years.

'garlic breath' by eating parsley, basil, mint or thyme, or use the Chinese method and chew cardamom pods.

Layering

Some plants, such as mint, send out runners that develop small plants. About six weeks after the runners have taken root, carefully cut them from the parent plant and repot them. You can encourage this by securing runners to the soil with a U-shaped piece of wire.

1 Select a suitable shoot to be layered. At a point at least 30 cm (1 ft) back from the tip of the shoot, use a knife to make an angled cut (about 20 degrees) on the underside of the shoot. The cut should penetrate about one-third of the way through the shoot.
2 Dig a shallow hole and position the injured section of the shoot in the bottom of the hole.
3 Peg this shoot firmly into place with a wired hoop.
4 Replace the soil in the hole around the shoot and firm the area well.
5 Once the shoot has formed roots, use secateurs to sever the new plant from the parent. Leave the

ABOVE It's a good idea to secure the layered shoot with a U-shaped wire hoop like this one.

RIGHT Propagate perennial sweet violets by dividing old clumps in late winter, keeping the crown of the plant clear of the soil. Plant them 15–20 cm (6–8 in) apart in sun or shade. Violets flower in late spring and summer. They need ample summer moisture and a sprinkle of blood and bone for best results.

plant in the same position for another growing season before transplanting it to a new site.

Division

Divide clumps of perennials herbs – such as chives, valerian and sweet violets – in late autumn or late winter before they start to make fresh growth.

1 Lift the plant and shake off the excess soil.
2 Gently spread the roots apart and break or cut the clump to separate the young, healthy plants from any dead old wood.
3 Cut off any torn or damaged roots cleanly with secateurs or a sharp knife.
4 Pot each new plant with its own root system in a clean pot.
5 Water it in well and place it in a shady spot for a few days to recover.

Some plants with a fibrous root system, such as thyme and oregano, need not be lifted. Choose a new

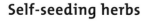

Self-seeding herbs

If you want to encourage a relaxed, cottage feeling in your garden, try to encourage herbs to self-seed. This may mean putting up with some messy plants as you wait for the seed heads to form fully. It also means weeding and disturbing the soil as little as possible, as tiny plants are hard to see and can easily be damaged. Try to keep the garden moist, and wait until spring before mulching so that young seedlings are large enough to be noticed and left undisturbed.

This self-seeding process can often produce chance associations that are far more effective than anything you could design. And often these plants are the ones that remain in old gardens. Johnny-jump-up, or heartsease (*Viola tricolor*), is a self-seeding viola that will keep popping up in unexpected spots.

shoot of young growth with roots already attached and use a sharp knife to cut it from the base of the plant.

Cuttings

A cutting is a small piece of stem taken from a healthy plant that grows roots when it is inserted into a suitable cutting medium. Taking cuttings is an easy and cheap method of propagation and provides you with a plant that is exactly like its parent. It is the best propagation method for woody-stemmed herbs, such as lavender and rosemary. To strike a herb from cuttings, take the cuttings from a strong healthy plant early in the morning. The cuttings should be 5–10 cm (2–4 in) long. If you can't plant them straight away, wrap them in damp newspaper and store them in a cool place.

Cuttings in water

Some herbs will send out roots if their stalks are placed in water. Make sure that the leaves do not touch the water. You can make a support by stretching some plastic wrap over a jar and poking cuttings through it into the water. Water roots are more delicate than ordinary roots, so take care when transplanting.

Root cuttings

Propagating from root cuttings is simple. It is the standard method of propagating a few plant species, mainly herbaceous perennials and alpines.

The great advantage of propagating from root cuttings is that you can produce a large number of new plants without disfiguring the plant itself. The roots of suitable plants contain dormant buds that have the capacity to produce new shoots and stems.

The best time to take root cuttings is in late winter and early spring when the plant is dormant. There are two ways of taking root cuttings:

- From plants with thick fleshy roots, such as the horse chestnut (*Aesculus hippocastanum*) and *Echinops*, that are inserted vertically into the mix
- From plants with thin wiry roots, such as sea holly (*Eryngium maritimum*) and dame's violet or eveweed (*Hesperis matronalis*), that are laid horizontally on top of the propagation mix.

1 Carefully dig around the roots of the plant with a garden fork until they are exposed.

2 Using a pair of secateurs, cut through some of the strongest and healthiest roots, and remove them.

3 Carefully wash the roots and remove as much soil as possible. This makes it easier to see where to cut.

4 With a sharp knife, cut the roots into 5 cm (2 in) long sections. Make the cut on an angle at the bottom end and at right angles at the top: this will make it easier to put the cuttings into the propagation mix the right way up.

5 If the cuttings are thick and fleshy, gently push them into a pot of propagation mix so that the top of each cutting is level with the surface of the mix. If the cuttings are thin, lay them over the surface of the mix.

6 Cover the cuttings with a layer of grit. This will allow air to reach the top of the cuttings without letting them dry out.

Striking herb cuttings

1 Prepare a small pot with a mix of two-thirds coarse sand and one-third peat moss, and remove the lower leaves from each cutting. If you wish, dip the base of each cutting in hormone rooting powder or liquid.

2 Make a hole in the mix with your finger or a pencil, insert each cutting to about one-third of its length and firm the mix around it. Set the cuttings about 2.5–3 cm (1 in) apart.

3 Water well, and then cover the pot with a plastic bag to create a mini-greenhouse effect. Don't place the pot in direct sun.

4 Keep the mix damp but not wet. Once roots have formed, plant the herbs out.

Leaf cuttings

You can propagate new plants from the fleshy leaves of some herbs, including violets. Although you can take leaf cuttings at any time of the year, spring and summer are the best times.

1 Remove a mature leaf and its stalk, known as the petiole, from the plant.

2 Cut straight across the stalk and dip the end in rooting hormone.

3 Insert the stalk in some cutting propagation mix and firm the mix well around it. Several leaves can go into the one pot but make sure they don't touch each other.

4 Cover the pot with a plastic bag and place it in a well lit spot away from direct sunlight.

5 Be sure to keep the propagation mix moist. New leaves will grow from the stalk, feeding off the original leaf until they develop roots.

6 Once roots have developed, pot them up and place them on a sunny windowsill. Soon you will have flowering plants.

These stems of black willow (*Salix nigra*), a traditional medicinal herb, have produced roots after a few weeks in water.

step by step

STRIKING LEAF CUTTINGS

1 Insert each stalk, or petiole, in the cutting propagation mix and firm the compost around it.

2 Water the cuttings in well.

Horn of plenty mushroom.

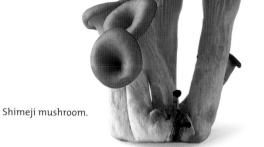
Shimeji mushroom.

Mushrooms

Mushrooms can be grown and harvested from kits all year round. Many types of mushrooms are highly poisonous, so only experts should forage in the wild. A much safer bet is to plant your own. Fungal spore can be purchased for a whole range of mushroom varieties, with more of the exotic Asian types, such as shiitake and oyster, coming onto the market daily. All they need is a cool, dark place, such as a garden shed or cellar, in which to grow.

Culivated mushrooms

Cultivated mushrooms are available in varying stages of development. The smallest, button mushrooms, have a mild flavour and keep their pale colour when cooked. Use raw in salads or cook in white sauces. Closed-cup mushrooms are good for slicing and adding to stir-fries. The larger open-cup mushrooms are more flavoursome and are ideal for adding to stews and casseroles. Flat (open or field) mushrooms have a good earthy flavour and a meaty texture. Chestnut (crimini) and portobello mushrooms are relatives of the button mushroom. They have a creamy brown cap, buff-coloured stalks and a more pronounced flavour than button mushrooms.

handy tip

Cultivated mushrooms don't need to be washed before use – simply wipe over them with a paper towel or damp cloth to remove the soil and grit.

Wild mushrooms

There are many unusual forms of wild mushroom available. Cep (porcini) mushrooms, with a brown cap and thick white stem, are rich, sweet and nutty in flavour and are sold fresh and dried. Enoki mushrooms grow and are bought in clumps. They have tiny cream caps on slender stalks and a delicate flavour. Shiitake mushrooms have dark brown caps and are sold fresh or dried. Oyster mushrooms are large flat mushrooms. Shimeji mushrooms are a type of small oyster mushroom with long stalks.

MIXED MUSHROOM STIR-FRY ➤ Trim and clean 500 g (1 lb 2 oz) mixed mushrooms, slicing any larger ones. Melt 25 g (1 oz) butter in a frying pan and add 1 tablespoon olive oil. Add 1 finely chopped chilli, 1 finely chopped shallot and 1 garlic clove and fry briefly. Add the mushrooms and toss over high heat until cooked through and beginning to brown (if you are using shimeji or enoki mushrooms, put them in at the end). Add 1 tablespoon chopped coriander, 1 tablespoon soy sauce, season well and drizzle with sesame oil. Serve tossed through noodles or pasta or on bruschetta. ➤ Makes enough for 12 bruschetta or 4 appetiser noodle or pasta serves.

MUSHROOM KIT

1 To make the mushroom kit you'll need peat, lime, mushroom spore and a suitable container, such as an old wooden box, lined with plastic. Moisten the peat with a little water until it feels damp all over and releases some water when you squeeze it.

2 Thoroughly blend the peat and lime together.

3 Spread the peat and lime to a depth of about 15 cm (6 in) over the mushroom spore.

4 The completed mushroom kit is now ready to be stored in a cool, dark place.

5 The fruiting bodies, or actual mushrooms, appear about 4 weeks later.

4

Extend
the season

Extend the season

Keen gardeners like to squeeze a little bit more time from the growing season. With protective structures like greenhouses and cold frames you can get a head start in spring, and stretch the season end in autumn.

Protecting your crops

With the help of a wide variety of quite simple protective structures, other than in areas with the very coldest of winters, it is possible to achieve a flow of fresh herbs and vegetables into the kitchen for most of the year. These range from modest devices like cold frames and cloches, to larger structures such as polytunnels and greenhouses.

Rather than harvesting a matured vegetable crop in late autumn, many vegetables can be left in the soil during the winter months if they are provided with the protection of cloches and portable frames. These crops can be supplemented with vegetables such as kale and winter cabbage, which are exceptionally cold-hardy and grow outdoors without the benefit of frost protection, together with various crops from warmed greenhouses.

Protective structures such as greenhouses, conservatories, cold frames and cloches are truly multifunctional. Seedlings of spring crops can be raised well in advance of open sown seedlings, extending the

Tomatoes are a favourite greenhouse crop and there are specific varieties available that are suited to greenhouse growing.

growing season by a month or more. Vegetables and herbs requiring a warm growing season or long summer growing period can be matured satisfactorily, and winter crops of edibles raised.

Greenhouses

Greenhouses can be either freestanding, or a lean-to construction built against a sunny brick wall to take advantage of the solar heat absorbed by the bricks during the day and re-radiated at night. Re-radiation from brick walls can raise nearby temperatures by 5°C (9°C) at night. Choose a position that is open to the sun all year when siting a greenhouse.

Greenhouse design

Home greenhouses can often be quite small, around 1.8 x 2.4 m (6 x 8 ft), but as they are multipurpose you are unlikely to regret not building one at least double this size. The frame is built either with rot-resistant timber like cedar, or with galvanised steel or aluminium. Glass is still the preferred glazing although polycarbonate is also used. The latter transmits lower light levels but has useful insulating properties. Unless greenhouses are well ventilated, the internal temperatures can rise too high and cause damage or death of plants. Ventilation is essential not only to lower heat but also to moderate high humidity which encourages fungal infections. Ventilation can be achieved via louvres, or temperature-regulated, automated roof vents may be installed. The floor should be easy to clean to prevent build-up of fungi and algae.

Greenhouses can be quite elaborately designed. Waist-high benching makes work more easy. Benching may be made of treated wood with slatted tops. Steel benches are virtually indestructible. Wooden pallets raised on bricks can be a useful temporary solution but may need replacing.

A greenhouse is the hallmark of the serious gardener. Greenhouses may be simple structures, or have sophisticated heating and ventilation apparatus. They allow you to have a supply of fresh and juicy edible crops year-round.

A MAGIC ENVIRONMENT *While smaller structures have the advantage of mobility and low cost, and are most commonly used to protect in-ground crops, greenhouses and polytunnels (right) allow the gardener to share the protective environment with their plants in cold weather. There is the smell of humus and the green fragrance of young plants mingling with that of potted flowering plants. It is the perfect retreat from the cold of a winter world.*

Greenhouse irrigation equipment

Gently hosing plants is a pleasant chore, but other methods of delivery can be more reliable. Drip irrigation is particularly useful for larger pots and growing bags. Capillary matting is ideal for delivering water to punnets of seedlings and smaller pots on benches. Misting units on timers can also be attached along benches. Plants will require less water in winter than summer, and a simple sensor which monitors soil moisture can be used to activate watering according to the needs of the plants.

Greenhouse insulation and heating

In cold areas, additional insulation during winter months is advisable. Cheap, temporary solutions in use at the moment are polystyrene blocks or sheets used to line the lower walls, and sheets of clear polycarbonate or bubble plastic used to insulate the inside of the roof. In addition, lengths of fleece can be draped over any plants at risk during a cold snap. Even a small heater can allow many quite exotic plants to be grown, and reduces the possibility of cold damage or death of plants.

Summer heat can be regulated with a cover of shadecloth, in combination with good ventilation. Shade cloth comes in a variety of densities from 10 to 90 per cent. Many gardeners still use the older but effective method of painting the glass roof with shading paint in summer. In some areas, low light intensities or short day lengths in the middle of winter can make supplementary lighting necessary to maintain healthy growth and to germinate seedlings. Full spectrum fluorescent lamps are ideal to supplement existing daylight. They should be arranged well above the level of foliage.

A heated bench is a small luxury well worth building or buying. It consists of a strongly built, usually galvanised tray on a bench, containing soil-warming cables buried in approximately 15 cm (6 in) of sand or fine quartz gravel. The bottom heat provided by a heated bench speeds up both the germination of seed and the rate at which cuttings form roots. Some seeds, such as those of peppers (capsicums), are difficult to germinate without considerable warmth and benefit from bottom heating. Heat mats are also available to place under pots.

Polytunnels

Polytunnels are cheaper to construct than greenhouses, consisting of a covering of heavy grade, ultraviolet-

structures like greenhouses, their fittings should be easily moved. With this in mind, they can be equipped and modified for seasonal changes in much the same manner as greenhouses. Some growers treat full-sized polytunnels as the equivalent of a giant tunnel cloche. The soil under cover is dug, enriched with organic matter, and crops planted in rows. Every few years the polytunnel can be dismantled and moved to another site to prevent the build-up of soil-borne diseases.

Growing plants in greenhouses and polytunnels

The moisture and warmth in polytunnels and greenhouses encourage the growth not only of plants, but also of pests and diseases. For this reason care should be taken not to introduce infested plants into these structures. If plants are being introduced from elsewhere, check them carefully. A good precaution is to isolate new introductions for a fortnight to ensure no infections develop before placing them in the greenhouse. Regular inspections for potential pests and diseases are advisable. Sticky insect trapping strips can be suspended to provide a sample of any flying pests such as whitefly. Biological control agents are particularly effective in the closed system of a greenhouse or polytunnel.

Try to keep the greenhouse or polytunnel very clean and weed-free, and wash down all surfaces with hot soapy water at least four times a year. Make sure there is nowhere for snails and slugs to hide by day. They can devastate the plants at night.

Summer heat often encourages spider mites. Water well under the leaves of affected crops with a foliar spray such as seaweed solution, Drenching both sides of the leaves, in the cooler hours, is also helpful.

Regular watering in greenhouses and polytunnels readily leaches nutrients from pots, and higher temperatures rapidly reduce organic matter levels. Applications of foliar sprays such as commercial seaweed solution will help to maintain good nutrition. If crops are grown in beds, strict attention needs to be paid to crop rotation to prevent the build-up of pests and diseases in the soil.

resistant, plastic film stretched over a frame of galvanised iron or steel hoops. The skin is anchored around the outside by embedding it in a trench and backfilling with soil. Doors are provided at both ends for ventilation as polytunnels maintain higher humidity than glasshouses. It is for this reason that wider, shorter polytunnel structures are preferred for home use. According to the quality used and the conditions, the skin should be replaced about every 3–7 years. Reinforced PVC covers are also available.

To improve accessibility in the polytunnel, straight-sided rather than curved polytunnels are preferred by some gardeners, although they are more expensive. As polytunnels are more temporary in nature than larger

RIGHT If you live in a cold climate, you can lift mint and chives (pictured here) in autumn, then pot them and place them in a heated greenhouse.

OPPOSITE In cold climates, conservatory extensions of the kitchen, or the sunny side of the house, provide a place to enjoy warmth and light, as well as fresh, juicy vegetables, such as peppers (capsicums), even in the coldest months.

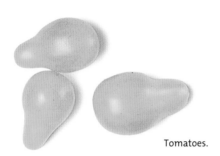

Tomatoes.

Crops for greenhouses and polytunnels

Many crops that fail or are unreliable under conditions where the summer is too short or cool, can be successfully grown under greenhouse or polytunnel conditions. Tomatoes are a prized greenhouse crop, along with peppers (capsicums) and eggplants (aubergines), salad vegetables like lettuce and chicory (endive), cucumbers, Asian greens, basil, coriander, mint and chives.

Lettuce.

Vegetable gardens for dry areas

Gardeners in hot, dry climates have an abundance of sunshine although arid inland areas do have cool to cold nights. The greatest limiting factor for successfully raising vegetables is lack of water, and a three-pronged approach to drought-wise or xeriphytic gardening will ensure success for your edible crops.

Choosing vegetables

First, the right choice of vegetables is important. Becoming known as 'xeric vegetables', these are cultivars which are promoted as drought tolerant or drought resistant. Water delivery systems which minimise water usage or, alternatively, watering regimes that encourage deep rooting into moister soil layers, form the second approach to consider, and increasing the water holding capacity of the soil provides the third.

Species that originate from areas with hot dry summers such as the Mediterranean Basin, the Middle

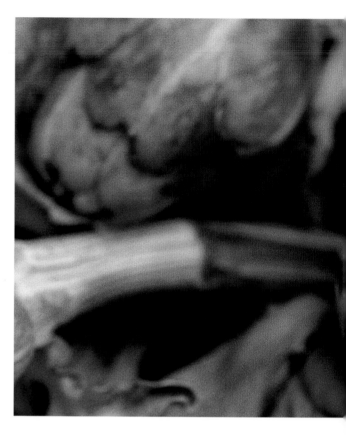

East and Mexico are likely to thrive in any part of the world with a comparable climate. They include vegetables such as artichokes, cardoons, many Mexican beans, peppers (capsicums), chillies, eggplants (aubergines), tomatoes and corn.

Drought tolerant cultivars

Search among old cultivars recommended by experienced farmers and gardeners in your district to find reliable performers. Joining organisations preserving and exchanging heirloom seeds is very worthwhile as it will

Mulches are critical to success in dry climates. They can greatly reduce moisture loss from the soil.

Artichokes are considered the vegetable of the gods, especially beloved by the ancient Greek god, Zeus.

preferable. Recyled grey water can be critically useful in extreme drought, along with the collection of all rainwater via guttering and downpipes to holding tanks.

Drought-prone soils usually lack organic matter, which acts in the soil like a sponge to hold moisture. Soil that is well enriched with compost will greatly reduce the water needs of the garden. If pumice stone is available, it makes an excellent natural addition to the soil as it is able to absorb any extra water and release it back to plants as the soil dries.

Mulches reduce the loss of moisture from the soil and suppress weeds which steal water from crops. At the same time, they reduce daytime soil temperatures and hold in warmth absorbed from the sun, releasing it in the cool to cold night hours. Plants grow better when the root systems are exposed to less extreme daily fluctuations. Organic mulches such as hay or compost are ideal for garden beds. Keep mulches away from tree trunks to prevent collar rot and insect damage under the bark.

Disturb the soil as little as possible. Cultivation increases the rate of loss of moisture. Wind can also be a major factor in drying garden soil, and well placed windbreaks can counteract much of this problem.

give access to cultivars that have been reselected by many generations of farmers and gardeners to meet the most extreme demands of a particular climate. Often doing no more than changing over to these cultivars known to perform well in drought will ensure success.

Growing tips

In arid areas or during prolonged droughts, encourage plants to explore deeply into the soil to reach cooler, moister soil levels. This can be done by reducing the intervals between watering once plants are well established, but watering deeply. Plants that are watered lightly and frequently have their root mass near the surface. This is the ideal for perennial vegetable crops. Annual vegetable crops rarely penetrate deeply into the soil, and drip irrigation is

Zucchini (courgette) flowers.

Drought-tolerant vegetables

▪ Artichoke	▪ Cardoon
▪ Chillies	▪ Corn
▪ Eggplant (aubergine)	▪ Peppers (capsicums)
▪ Tomato	▪ Zucchini (courgette)

COLD FRAMES *Many modern cold frames are made from polycarbonate materials, which are much more durable than glass. These materials make the frames less of a safety hazard for children, as there is far less chance of them being injured than if glass was used and accidentally broken.*

made frames are quite often sturdier and offer better insulation. They are easily constructed from recycled materials. A finish with white paint ensures that the maximum light is reflected onto seedlings. Movable wooden frames can also be placed onto garden beds to protect crops.

While frames are most commonly used for seed and cutting propagation, larger ones can be used as they were in the past to raise melons in areas where they would not mature fruit in the open, and to produce extra early and late season salad greens and herbs. Frames should be located where there is good light in both spring and winter. When supplied with bottom heat, cold frames are known as hot frames.

Constructing your own cold frame

Seeds and cuttings can be started into growth 3–4 weeks earlier than if they were growing outside in the open. The frame will also keep the air humid around the tops of cuttings and prevent them from drying out. Some gardeners prefer to construct their own cold frame, either from timber with a soil base or a brick-built frame with a concrete base and wooden lid with glass panels. These structures are excellent for protecting plants, but they are usually fixtures, and unless the frame is correctly sited, they can have limitations, such as lack of light at certain times of the year.

An alternative is to get a self-assembly 'kit frame', available from many DIY centres. Most are made with materials which have good insulation properties while still allowing good light transmission, and are quite light and easy to move about the garden, giving the gardener greater flexibility.

Cold frames

Cold frames have long been popular with gardeners. They can be easily made in a range of sizes, and are a cheap alternative to large structures like greenhouses. Traditionally, they consist of a low, rectangular, bottomless structure with wood or brick sides, and topped with one or more wood-framed windows which are usually hinged so that they can be easily propped open in balmy weather. Lightweight, rigid plastic sheets are sometimes used now in place of glass windows. Timber-constructed cold frames can be placed on a brick or pebble base to ensure they do not rot. Lightweight commercial versions are available but home-

CONSTRUCTING A COLD FRAME FROM A KIT

1 Remove the contents from the package and check that all the items listed on the assembly instructions sheet are present.

2 Using the corner clips provided, fit the grooved aluminium edges to the two lid sections (with the hinged bars at one end of each panel). Following the assembly instructions, fit the grooved aluminium edges to the top and bottom of each of the base panels (with the hinge bar on the top of the rear panel).

3 Using screws, fasten the corner brackets onto the side base panels. Make sure that they are fixed firmly into position before sliding the front and rear base panels into the corner brackets and fastening them into position using screws. Attach the lid to the frame's base by sliding the two hinge grooves together on the frame's rear panel. Repeat with the second section of the lid so that the frame is complete.

4 Fasten a spacing bar on to the lid of the frame (this is to allow the frame to be ventilated in gradual stages). Place the frame in its allotted position and add plants which need protection or shelter.

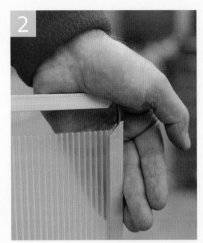

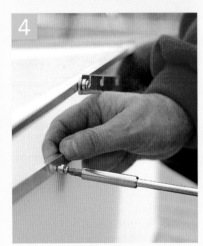

purple kale
Brassica oleracea

radicchio
Cichorium intybus

chives
Allium schoenoprasum

CUT AND COME AGAIN
VEGETABLES
The 'cut and come again' method of growing vegetables will provide a continuous supply of certain perennial leafy greens. As the plants grow, harvest just the outside leaves of the plants, or cut off the tops of the leaves with scissors, leaving the rest of the plant to continue on growing in the ground, to be harvested again later.

swiss chard
(silverbeet)
Beta vulgaris var. *cicla*

white frilled kale
Brassica oleracea

chervil
Anthriscus cerefolium

mizuna
Brassica juncea

water spinach
Ipomoea aquatica

rocket (arugula)
Eruca vesicaria subsp. *sativa*

red chard
Beta vulgaris var. *cicla*

white chard
Beta vulgaris var. *cicla*

baby rocket (arugula)
Eruca vesicaria
subsp. *sativa*

yellow chard
Beta vulgaris var. *cicla*

purple mustard
Chorispora tenella

garlic chives
Allium tuberosum

chicory flower
Cichorium intybus

flat-leaf parsley
Petroselinum crispum var. *neapolitanum*

curly endive (frisée)
Cichorium endivia

chicory 'pane de sucre'
Cichorium endivia

MAKE YOUR OWN CLOCHE

1 Place the prepared wire mesh sections over the plants to be protected, with the plants occupying the central position within the cloche. Position the sections together with their ends touching, adding as many sections as required to cover the row of plants.

2 Take a sheet of clear plastic, unfold it and draw it out over the wire mesh carefully, so that it does not tear. Allow at least 60 cm (2 ft) of surplus plastic at each end of the cloche.

3 At the sides of the cloche, lay down a section of 25 x 45 mm (1 x 2 in) wooden batten drilled with holes at 30 cm (1 ft) intervals. Position these at the edges of the plastic. Anchor the plastic along one side of the cloche by pushing 15 cm (6 in) nails or plastic pins through the holes and plastic into the soil below.

4 Stretch the plastic taut on the remaining side of the cloche and pin it down with battens, before cutting off any excess plastic. Gather up the surplus at the ends of the cloche. Bury it in the soil or peg it down with pins and battens using the same method as on the sides.

Cloches

Cloches are small, mobile greenhouses and they are only limited in form by ingenuity. Some are designed to cover single plants while others may enclose an entire row. Bell cloches, used popularly in Victorian times, were originally made of glass and shaped like large bottomless bottles.

Cloches are now quite often made of heavy clear plastic but can still be purchased in glass. A low-cost version is made from recycled plastic drink containers by cutting off the bases. The bottle's screw top is removed to allow heat to escape.

Tunnel cloches are popular, usually now made of corrugated clear plastic strengthened by supporting hoops, and wide enough to cover a row of herbs or vegetables or a garden bed. In general, traditional glass cloches offer better cold protection and allow better access to light, but plastic forms are cheaper and lighter.

Growing plants in a cloche

Cloches can be easily constructed on any sheltered area of the vegetable garden and are ideal for giving plants an early start in the spring. They can often promote growth up to three weeks ahead of unprotected plants. This type of temporary shelter can be important for protecting early herbs and vegetables from late spring frosts.

Some gardeners are put off using a cloche as they can look quite forbidding and difficult to use. However, if the cloche is well constructed and positioned, it should be quite easy to maintain your plants within it. When you need to tend your plants, simply lift up the plastic covering and remove the wire mesh.

As a precaution on sites that are particularly windy, it is best to position the cloche tunnel so that one end faces squarely into the prevailing wind. This will present a much smaller surface area to the wind than if the cloche is positioned side-on, making it less vulnerable. It is also much easier to reinforce the smaller ends of the tunnel than the sides.

In Victorian times, perfectly miniaturized greenhouses were devised and can still be purchased. Modern cloches are more simple A-frame structures or tunnels made from plastic.

Row or crop covers

Row covers or crop covers are the simplest of all forms of frost protection. They consist of lightweight fabrics that can be laid over the top of crops to provide protection against frost. They have the advantage of being easily applied and as easily removed in response to changing weather conditions, and can serve a secondary purpose in protecting crops from insect attack. Row covers can consist of long life, fine mesh plastic which will also exclude larger insect pests, or very fine gauge mist netting which will exclude small insect pests. Both allow good air flow. Fleece covers are also available and are the best option for frost protection. On the other hand, they are more opaque, cause excessive humidity and need to be replaced quite frequently. Row covers can be pegged down, or the edges weighted down with bricks or wooden boards. Row covers should be removed as soon as all danger of frost has passed unless being used as an insect barrier.

Vegetables for tropical areas

Gardening at lower altitudes in the tropics is both a blessing and a curse. High humidity and summer temperatures combine with torrential seasonal rain. In the wet season, growth rates can be astonishing but so too is the growth of weeds and pests. Other problems can include damage to soil structure, erosion of garden beds, severe storm damage, leaching of nutrients from the soil, and rapid decomposition of soil organic matter. In many tropical areas there is also a marked dry season. The illusion of gardening in paradise is short lived for many gardeners.

A major problem for vegetable growers in the tropics lies in plant selection. Few of the vegetables originating from outside the tropics will thrive. But the tropical pantry is so rich in exciting flavours, with a tropical vegetable equivalent for all those used in milder regions, that the key is to grow only tropical species, or cultivars proven to succeed under tropical conditions. Many tropical food species have been selected over thousands of years and excellent cultivars exist.

Leafy vegetables substitutes

A variety of leafy vegetables is available to replace cabbages, spinach and iceberg lettuce. Suitable substitutes include Malabar spinach (*Basella alba* and *B. rubra*), collards and Ethiopian kale, tampala spinach (*Amaranthus giganteus*), bush okra or jute mallow (*Corchorus olitorius*) and katuk (*Sauropus androgynous*), a staple vegetable in Borneo, where it is grown as an edible hedge and the leaves, tips and flowers used cooked or raw. Katuk tastes of green peas and is now being commercially grown in Hawaii, while Borneo is exporting it to Japan as 'tropical asparagus'. It has an astonishing growth rate, tolerates full sun to shade conditions, and seems to be virtually disease- and pest-free. Warrigal greens or New Zealand spinach (*Tetragonia tetragonioides*) is an excellent hot climate spinach substitute which will continue to thrive in the dry season.

Some cultivars of true lettuce succeed well in the tropics. Almost all are open-hearted in form and include 'Anuenue' (from Hawaii) and 'Mairoba' from Brazil. 'Montello' is an excellent hearting lettuce cultivar which has done well in many tropical areas including southern Florida and the Caribbean. Brazilian spinach (*Alternanthera sissoo*) is often preferred in Brazil to lettuce and is eaten in similar ways.

Other vegetables

Most modern tomatoes are exceedingly difficult to grow in the tropics, but the 'wild tomato', a large vining type producing sweet, cherry-sized fruit in great abundance, never fails and is remarkably pest and disease resistant. The currant tomato, a closely related species, is also highly productive.

Onions are more difficult to raise in the tropics as their growth pattern is day-length dependent. Short-day cultivars will form bulbs but long-day cultivars will only form small bulbs. In some tropical areas, gardeners raise onions as sets (baby onions), replanting them at the beginning of the rainy season to complete their growth.

Biennial vegetables, which normally complete their lifecycle over two growing seasons, often fail to develop or set seed in the tropics. Some tropical carrot cultivars have been identified which complete their seed to seed cycle in one season. Jicama (yam bean), cassava (*Manihot esculenta*), taro (*Alocasia macrorrhiza*), yam (*Dioscorea* spp.) and sweet potatoes (*Ipomoea batatas*) are admirable substitutes for the cooler climate potato. Tropical sweet corn cultivars are also readily available.

Taro shoots.

RIGHT Taro plant and tubers.

ABOVE Cassava (*Manihot esculenta*) is a tropical vegetable and an admirable substitute for the cooler climate potato.

Growing tips for the tropics

Mounded beds are necessary for good drainage during the wet season, but tend to be flattened by heavy rain. Beds edged to a height of around 25 cm (10 in) will hold soil in place. Tropical soils easily become leached of vital nutrients and are structureless after pounding rains. The regular addition of organic matter is essential to growing vegetables in the tropics, replacing both lost nutrients and humus in the soil. Inorganic fertilisers will do nothing to save the soil's structure, or its moisture and nutrient retentive properties. Mulches are also vital. Not only do they reduce soil temperatures and retain moisture in the dry season, but they reduce the impact of heavy rains on soil. Partially composted chopped palm and banana leaves are useful for this purpose. Weeds are also suppressed by the use of mulches, a necessity as they can overwhelm a crop in a short period of time and incur much hard labour.

5

Harvesting and storing

Harvesting and storing

After spending so much time and trouble tending your herbs and vegetables in the garden, you should take the same care in harvesting, and possibly preserving your crops. No matter what herbs and vegetables you grow, it's likely there is a successful method of preserving and storing.

Harvesting and preserving herbs

The range of uses for herbs is extraordinary. It seems such a waste not to harvest and use them all year round, especially when an enormous amount of plant material can be preserved, allowing it to retain much of its fresh glowing colour, form and fragrance.

The traditional method of harvesting and storing herbs is to air dry them, but more recently, freezing has become popular as a means of storing herbs for use over longer periods when they are out of season. This method is particularly suitable for tender herbs, such as basil and parsley. You can also use a desiccant such as sugar or salt to preserve herbs.

Although the leaves of herbs are typically collected, you can use other parts of the plant too – flowers, stems, roots and seeds. For instance, use herb flowers for both

The flower heads of *Allium* can be left to dry naturally. The stems emit a slight garlicky smell when they are cut, but immersing them in water dispels the odour.

flavour and decoration – add fresh nasturtium flowers to salads, or freeze borage flowers in ice cubes and add them to summer drinks. You can also harvest root herbs, such as horseradish, in winter when the plants are dormant, and the seeds of herbs such as angelica, dill and fennel. And for fragrance, lavender (spring) and yarrow (spring and summer) will continue to fill the room with their perfumes in dry form. Silvery foliage is also often aromatic.

When harvesting herbs, cut them with sharp tools: anything that crushes or bruises the stem will make the herbs bleed sap, which will result in loss of flavour and possibly in a mouldy stem. Only cut the freshest, leafiest, upper stems of the plant. Harvest them in the morning on a dry day, when the herbs are full of moisture but the dew has evaporated.

Do not harvest leaves or stems that are brown, wilted, damaged or showing signs of pests and diseases. Store the dry herbs in dark glass jars with screw-top lids.

handy tip

Most culinary herbs can be stored in the fridge. Just place them in plastic bags or lidded containers, and wash them before using. Basil turns black quickly, however. Try storing it as a bouquet in a glass of water or wrapping it in damp paper towels.

Air drying herbs

As soon as a flower or leaf is detached from the plant, changes begin to take place within the cells because the supply of moisture has been cut off.

The quicker a piece of plant material can be dried, the quicker this process is frozen, trapping the oils within the cells. If the material is dried too quickly, the moisture evaporates too quickly, taking the oils with it. If the material is dried too slowly, the oils are destroyed by decomposition.

The most obvious method of preserving herbs is air drying. Just hang bundles of herbs to air in a dry, dark, well ventilated place. If it is damp or humid, the material will rot, especially where the stems or flowers are touching – for example, at the tying point of a hanging bunch.

Or you can choose other methods that utilise modern technology. Dry herbs in a slow conventional oven, or even in a microwave oven. Wrap the chopped herbs loosely in paper towel and cook them for a minute at a time on High. Always have a cup of water in the microwave, as herbs do not contain much moisture and the oven could be damaged.

Leaves

Harvest leafy herbs when the concentration of aromatic oils reaches its highest point, in midsummer just before flowering. After flowering starts, the chemical balance

Harvest nasturtiums for your next salad. The leaves have a peppery flavour and the edible flowers add a decorative touch.

An old clothes horse makes a suitable drying rack for the flowers and foliage of herbs and other plants.

within the plant changes and the oils in the leaves are not as potent. They should be mature but not beginning to show signs of ageing. This timing will give you the best flavour or fragrance from plants such as bergamot (*Monarda didyma*), rosemary (*Rosmarinus officinalis*) and sage (*Salvia officinalis*).

With most plants, it is easier to cut whole stems because you can handle them without damaging the individual leaves. Remove all the lower leaves and wipe away any moisture on the stems with some paper towel. Bundle them together in bunches of 5–10 stems,

depending on their thickness, and secure them with an elastic band (if you tie them with string, the stems may fall through the loop as they dry and shrink). Hang the bunches upside down in a dark, well ventilated place at a temperature of about 20°C (68°F) until they are dry.

The drying time will vary from days to weeks, depending on the thickness of the stems. Crumble herb leaves that are intended for cooking between your finger and thumb, then store them in a dark and airtight, labelled glass jar. For pot pourri the leaves can be kept whole.

HARVESTING AND DRYING ROSEMARY

1 Cut the herbs.

2 Make up small bunches of clean, dry stems, varying the number according to their thickness. For instance, bundle rosemary up to 10 stalks at a time, and for bay leaves, dry separate bunches.

3 Hang the bunches of herbs upside down in a dry, dark, well ventilated place. The temperature should be between 21° and 32°C (70 and 90°F) for around 5–14 days until they are dry and crisp. When totally dry, remove the leaves from the stems by rubbing them through your hands. Place them in dark, airtight glass jars. Label the jars with the name of the herb and the date of harvest, so that they can be used in order of freshness.

Flowers

Again, be sure to only harvest flowers when they are at their peak. Pick flowers in the middle of a dry day just before their prime. Do not collect them when the air is damp or if they are still covered in morning dew, because they will become mouldy and discoloured instead of drying properly. To avoid damaging the petals, remove

When drying the flowers of herbs, make sure that you select blooms when they are at their peak.

Herb vinegars

Freshly picked herbs make a wonderful addition to a good white wine vinegar or cider vinegar. Use herb vinegars infused with herbs such as basil, chives, dill, fennel, mint and tarragon to add flavour to salad dressings, marinades and sauces.

1   Pick the herbs, wash them and pat them dry.

2   Loosely fill a clean jar with them, pour on enough vinegar to fill the jar, then replace the cap.

3   Store in a warm place for about three weeks or until the vinegar is full of flavour. If you desire a stronger flavour, just strain the vinegar and add some fresh herbs.

4   When the vinegar is ready, strain it and pour it into some clean, attractive bottles.

5   Finally, label each bottle.

the whole flower with some of the stalk, then check each flower carefully and discard any damaged ones. Place the flowers in an open container, as they may sweat and rot in a closed container.

You can dry large flowers by hanging them in bunches in the same way as for leaves, in a dark, well ventilated area. However, don't be tempted to interfere with the flowers until they have completely dried out, otherwise they will simply droop and disintegrate. It works well to lay small flowers such as borage (*Borago officinalis*) and violets (*Viola* spp.) on sheets of muslin stretched over a wooden frame or metal cooling rack. If you dry the flowers correctly, they should retain

almost all their colour. Once dry, the petals or whole flowers should be ready to use. If you're storing flowers for future use, some herb flowers, such as lavender (*Lavandula* spp.) and chamomile (*Chamaemelum nobile*), can be stored intact; others, however, such as marigold (*Calendula officinalis*) should be stored with their petals removed.

For best results, cut and dry flowers while they are in peak condition. For instance, lavender (*Lavandula angustifolia*, featured in the step by step sequence on page 184) is ready to be cut when the flowers are half to three-quarters open. They will continue to open while they are drying.

HARVESTING AND FREEZING HERBS

Chop up leaves and freeze them with water in ice cube moulds, or bundle them into plastic bags and place them directly in the freezer. Suitable herbs are parsley, chives, basil and borage.

1 Collect young tender shoots and keep them out of direct sunlight so they stay cool and fresh.

2 Wash the herbs thoroughly in cold water before cutting them into small sections using a sharp knife or secateurs. Place the chopped herb into the compartments of an ice cube tray and fill each with water. Place the trays in the freezer.

Seeds

Harvest seeds such as juniper berries, vanilla pods, dill seeds, nutmeg and cloves when they are fully ripe, with no visible sign of green. Collect them on a warm, dry day by shaking the seed head into a paper bag, or by cutting whole seed heads and laying them on paper in a seed tray. Put them in a dark, warm, well ventilated location and allow them to dry. Not all seeds turn brown or black when they are dry, so test them for firmness rather than rely on colour. Store the dried seeds in packets or envelopes in a dark airtight jar.

Roots

Harvest the roots and rhizomes of plants such as angelica (*Angelica archangelica*),

handy tip

Once herbs have been frozen, decant them into plastic bags and keep them in the freezer, then reuse the ice cube trays.

Sunflower seeds.

Ginger.

ginger (*Zingiber officinale*), violet (*Viola odorata*) and valerian (*Valeriana officinalis*) in autumn, when the foliage is dying down and the concentration of oils is at its strongest.

1 Remove the required amount and replant the rest of the plant so that it will survive until the next season.

2 Wash the soil from the roots, handling them very carefully to avoid damaging or bruising them.

3 Lay the roots on baking trays and dry them in an oven at about 50°C (120°F), turning them regularly until they break easily.

4 Cool and store them in an airtight glass or metal container.

Using desiccants

Desiccants draw the moisture out of herbs while supporting them, and can result in a replica that is close in colour, size and texture to the original. A safe drying agent such as sugar or salt can be applied to accelerate the process.

First, ensure that all the material is in perfect condition. Next pick the desired plants in the afternoon when they are completely dry. Place a layer of salt on the bottom of an airtight container and gradually pile the salt around the plant material, using a fine brush to make sure that every part of the flower or leaf is fully immersed. Once the plant material is completely covered, replace the lid and seal it with tape. Test the

step by step

WIRING FLOWER STEMS

1 Wire the flower heads upright before drying so they won't become brittle. All you need is some fine wire and your chosen blooms.

2 Using a piece of fine wire about 50 cm (20 in) long, push one end through the centre of the stem just under the flower.

3 Twist the ends of wire around the stem. For thicker stems, use thicker wire. If wiring for a bouquet or a vase, use green budding tape to disguise the wire.

HARVESTING AND DRYING LAVENDER

1 On a warm, sunny day, when the whole plant is dry, cut the stems with sharp secateurs to avoid bruising the stem or flower stalk. Working on a clean flat surface, sort through the flower stalks, stripping off the leaves and discarding any bruised or broken stems.

2 Grade and sort the stems for size and length, gathering 15–20 stems together at a time. Tie them firmly with an elastic band. Do not use string – as the stems dry and shrink, they will slip through the loop.

3 Hang your bunches from nails or hooks in a dry, dark place with good ventilation. Leave them for 2–4 weeks, depending on the plant and the dryness of the atmosphere. When the stems are completely dry, sort through the bunches again and remove any withered flowers and stems before bunching the lavender into bouquets of about 80–100 stems.

flowers or leaves every couple of days, as they can become too dry and thus very brittle.

Using glycerin

Another way of drying herbs and flowers is to preserve them with glycerin, but make sure you only use this method for decorative purposes. This process depends on replacing the water in the plant with glycerin, which keeps the plant in a stable condition over a long period.

Make up a solution of 60 per cent glycerin and 40 per cent hot water and stir the mixture thoroughly. Cut stems at a sharp angle, and hammer the ends of any woody stems to crush them flat. Place the cut stems in a vase containing about 10 cm (4 in) of the hot solution so that the stems are firmly supported by the sides of the container. Place the vase in a cool, dark place for a minimum of six days so that absorption can fully take effect. At the stage when little beads start to form on the upper part of the plant material, it has absorbed all the glycerin it needs. Remove it from the vase immediately and wash it thoroughly.

The leaves of deciduous and evergreen plants and trees can be preserved in glycerin. This method is particularly good for branches or twigs of beech, eucalyptus, bells of Ireland, ivy, mahonia, choisya, fatsia, pittosporum, aspidistra and holly.

Harvesting and storing vegetables

A bountiful harvest is the reward you reap for all your hard work. You can either feast on the freshly

handy tip

Note that immature plant material cannot be preserved with glycerin, so spring leaves are not suitable for this kind of treatment.

harvested vegetables or freeze, dry, bottle or preserve them for later use, until your cupboards are bursting.

Naturally, you harvest each vegetable just when it is at its peak of maturity and flavour. Often this only lasts for quite a short period, and you may well have made successive small plantings so you have a series of harvests. This is a sensible practice, but with vegetables that freeze well, such as peas, beans, cauliflower or Brussels sprouts, you may prefer to make one big planting, gather your harvest in all at once, and freeze what you don't need for the kitchen immediately.

It is important that only the best of the crop are selected for storage, although produce with some marking or slight damage can still be used immediately. Any parts of the plant that are brown, wilted (when they are not supposed to be), damaged or showing any signs of pest and disease damage should not be stored, as these problems may be transferred to the healthy plants in the store.

The harvesting and storage of vegetables will depend on a number of factors, particularly the climate and the type of vegetable. In cooler climates, where crops mature fairly slowly, it is possible to leave them growing and harvest them only when required, especially as many are not eaten until they reach maturity. Others, such as the salad types of vegetable that are harvested while semi-mature, are cut while they are still quite young.

The biggest problem, especially with leafy vegetables or those that are harvested when quite young, is one of short-term storage; that is keeping the soft, edible tissue fresh and palatable until it is eaten.

Some vegetables, such as beans, cabbage, chillies, garlic, marrows, onions, peas and tomatoes, will keep quite well if they are stored in a dry condition and allowed to dry slowly in a cool, dry, frost-free place, but others will need to be kept in airtight containers.

Storing root vegetables

Many root vegetables are stored in boxes over winter to protect them from frost and, for convenience, these

How you choose to harvest and store your vegetables will make a difference to their quality and flavour.

HARVESTING LEAFY VEGETABLES

1 Start in the morning while the weather is still cool and, with a sharp knife, cut through the stem just above ground level and trim off any damaged or dirty leaves.

2 Wash the vegetables in cold water, and leave them to soak in the water for 30 minutes after they have been harvested. This will lower their temperature dramatically and prolong their keeping qualities.

3 Remove from the water, and allow to drain.

4 Store the vegetables in clear, open plastic bags and leave them in a cool, damp place, until required.

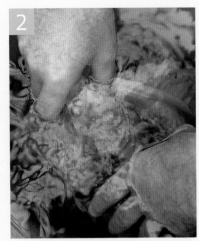

DRYING BEANS

1 Start by carefully removing the bean pods from the plant, using both your hands.

2 Place the bean pods in a tray or in a container of your choice. Leave them to dry in a cool, dry room. When the pods split, remove the seeds for storage. Discard the pods.

DRYING VEGETABLES OUTDOORS *Vegetables can be dried outdoors in warm, dry, windy weather conditions for a period of 24–36 hours. Some vegetables suitable for drying include beans, beetroot, carrots, chillies, corn, mushrooms, okra, onions, peas, peppers (capsicums) and pumpkin.*

boxes are usually placed in sheds or cellars. It is often easier to go and collect vegetables stored in this way than to go outdoors in winter weather to collect 'field-stored' vegetables stored in a clamp (see pages 190-91).

Boxes or barrels of slightly moist sand are used to keep produce fresh and to extend its storage life. Ideally, these containers should be kept in a frost-free place in order to protect their contents as much as possible. Vegetables stored in this way must be handled carefully to reduce the risk of bruising and any soil must be cleaned off the produce before it's stored. Soil left on the roots may contain fungal or bacterial spores, which can attack the produce and cause it to rot while it is in storage. Never store any vegetables that

STORING ROOT VEGETABLES IN SAND

1 Harvest the vegetables that are to be stored. Handling them carefully, brush off any lose soil. For vegetables such as beetroot, carrots, parsnips and turnips, trim off leaves and stalks and remove any long, thin roots. Discard all vegetables that show any signs of rot or damage. Wash the vegetables to remove any remaining soil and leave them until the water has drained away, but the surface of the vegetable is still moist.

2 Place a sturdy container, such as a barrel or box, in a frost-free site, where the temperature is just above freezing. Cover the bottom of the container with a 10 cm (4 in) layer of damp sand. Remove any stones or gravel to avoid them damaging the vegetables.

3 Place a layer of vegetables on the sand, with the root tips facing the corner of the container. Cover with a layer of sand, and another layer of vegetables. Make sure the vegetables are not touching one another, as this will help prevent the spread of fungal or bacterial rots. Place the largest vegetables at the bottom and the smallest at the top (the smallest ones are prone to drying out and should be used first). Repeat this

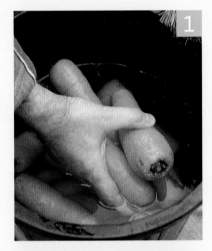

process until the container is filled to within 15 cm (6 in) of the upper rim. Place at least 5 cm (2 in) of sand between each layer of vegetables and the sides of the container.

4 Cover the topmost layer of vegetables with a 15 cm (6 in) layer of damp sand. Gently pack the sand down to remove as much air as possible and lightly water it to form a surface crust or 'seal' to reduce moisture loss. Check frequently to see if it is drying out. If it becomes too dry, gently moisten it with a fine spray from a watering can.

STORING VEGETABLES IN A CLAMP

1   Clear and level the area of ground where the vegetables are to be stored (it is important to select a site with a free-draining soil).

2   Spread out a layer of dry, loose straw to cover the area to a depth of approximately 20 cm (8 in).

3   Build up a mound of vegetables on the straw to form a cone shape to the required height (carrots should not be stacked more than 75 cm/2½ ft high). Once the mound of vegetables has reached the required height, cover the whole mound with a 15 cm (6 in) layer of dry straw.

4   Cover the mound with a layer of soil about 10 cm (4 in) deep. The soil is provided by digging a trench around the base of the clamp for drainage, and throwing the resulting soil up over the straw-covered mound.

5   Finally, firm the soil over the mound by patting it down with the back of a spade. This helps keep the straw dry and reduces the chances of rain washing the soil down from the top of the mound. Leave a small area of straw exposed at the top of the clamp, as this will keep the vegetables cooler.

are showing signs of rotting or severe damage. These 'suspect' vegetables will be a source of primary infection, causing rotting among the healthy plants, and should be discarded straight away. Use any lightly damaged vegetables as they will also rot quickly.

Vegetable storage clamp

The traditional method for storing root vegetables in cold areas is in a clamp or 'pie'. This is a low mound of vegetables, laid on a bed of loose straw for insulation, and encased in a layer of soil or sand to hold the straw in place and provide extra protection. In the olden days of large families, the root crops were often left in the ground and stored in this way.

These clamps can be made either outside on a well drained site or under cover in a shed or outhouse. Although the storage conditions are very similar to those in the ground, a clamp is often more convenient. It is easier to remove vegetables from the storage clamp in severe cold weather when the ground is frozen than it is to dig them out of the soil in the vegetable plot.

Unfortunately, the amount of waste from rodents and rotting can be high. For extra protection, a clamp may be formed against a wall or hedge, and if long-term vegetable storage is your objective, choose a north-facing site (south-facing in the southern hemisphere) if possible, as this will receive much less sunlight in the winter months.

Root vegetables that can be stored using this method include potatoes, parsnips, carrots, Swede and beetroot.

Parsnips.

 BEETROOT This colourful root vegetable, once highly valued by the ancient Greeks and Romans, is considered a caretaker of the immune system. Both the leaves and root are edible and packed with goodness. Beetroots should be harvested when they are about 2.5 cm (1 in) in diameter. When removing the tops from the root, leave about 2.5 cm (1 in) of stem attached to the root to prevent 'bleeding'.

galangal
Alpinia galanga

mini
round
carrot
Daucus carota

white radish (daikon)
Raphanus sativus var. longipinnatus

radish
Raphanus sativus

beetroot
Beta vulgaris

parsnip
Pastinaca sativa

red onion
Allium cepa Cepa Group

purple
carrot
Daucus carota

nicola
potato
Solanum tuberosum

kohlrabi
Brassica oleracea Gongylodes Group

garlic
Allium sativum

sweet
potato
Ipomoea batatas

shallot
Allium cepa

kipfler potato
Solanum tuberosum

spring onion
Allium fistulosum

baby
garlic
Allium sativum

swede
Brassica napus Napobrassica Group

yam
Dioscorea spp.

TUBERS, ROOTS
AND BULBS
The underground part of a plant is easily overlooked, but can often be the most important component. In the world of vegetables, roots really come into their own, whether they are potato tubers, onion bulbs, or roots such as carrots.

beetroot
Beta vulgaris 'Chioggia'

beetroot
Beta vulgaris

golden beetroot
Beta vulgaris

STORING VEGETABLES

Vegetable	Storage method
Artichoke, globe	Harvested buds will keep in a cool place for several weeks or in the refrigerator for no more than two weeks. Keep them dry in an airtight crisper or plastic bag.
Asparagus	Fresh asparagus will keep in the refrigerator for 7–10 days after being harvested. Break off the rough ends and stand upright in 3 cm (1¼ in) water.
Bean, broad	Freshly harvested pods will keep in the refrigerator for up to two weeks. Shelled beans can be dried, or preserved by bottling.
Bean, green, dwarf	Do not wash the vegetable after harvest. Freshly picked beans will keep in the refrigerator for up to a week or they can be successfully bottled or pickled when mature.
Beetroot	Swollen roots of the beetroot will keep for up to three weeks in the refrigerator and the leaves for up to a week if stored in an airtight plastic bag. Roots can be pickled or bottled.
Broccoli	Heads will keep in the refrigerator for up to a week, after which broccoli gradually turns yellow and becomes tasteless.
Brussels sprouts	Early winter sprouts left on the stem and hung in a cool dry place will keep for up to a month. Singly harvested, they will keep for 7–10 days in the refrigerator. In both cases, first remove all the loose and discoloured leaves from the plant and only wash the vegetables just before you are ready to use them.
Cabbage	Cabbage will keep for several weeks in the crisper compartment of the refrigerator. Pickled as sauerkraut, cabbage makes a delicious preserve.
Carrot	Like potatoes, carrots can be stored in the ground in cool-winter areas. Leave the leafy tops attached. Once cropped, the top can be removed and the carrots stored in containers packed with dry sand. Carrots will keep in the refrigerator for four weeks if stored in plastic bags.
Cauliflower	Heads will keep up to a week in the refrigerator.

Vegetable	Storage method
Celery	Celery stalks will keep crisp for up to 10 days in the refrigerator. Leaves can be dried and chopped and used as a dried herb for flavouring purposes. Seeds are also dried and used in soups and pickles.
Chicory (endive)	Will keep for up to two weeks in the crisper compartment of the refrigerator, the inner leaves being best for salads.
Chillies	Keep in a cool, dark place for up to a week or in a sealed container in the refrigerator for three weeks. Chillies are also excellent when dried.
Chinese broccoli (gai larn)	Keeps in crisper compartment of the refrigerator for up to a week.
Chinese cabbage (wong bok)	Keeps fresh in the refrigerator for several weeks, and keeps for months in cool, dry places such as a cellar. When ready to use, discard outer discoloured and battered leaves to reveal firm, central head. Never store Chinese cabbage in plastic bags.
Chinese spinach (amaranth)	Leaves go limp soon after harvesting. Young shoot thinnings are best eaten straight away and are good in salads. Older leaves can be stored in refrigerator crisper but will not keep for more than a few days. Steam or cook in the same way that you would cook other leafy vegetables.
Choko (chayote)	Freshly picked choko will keep in the vegetable crisper of refrigerator for 1–2 weeks.
Cucumber	Will keep in refrigerator for 7–10 days but at very cold temperatures the flesh will turn soft and translucent, rendering the cucumber inedible. It is ideal for pickling, especially if fruit is picked when young, at the 'gherkin' stage and 5–7 cm (2–2¾ in) in length.
Eggplant (aubergine)	Recently cropped fruit will keep for 7–10 days in a cool spot. It is ideal for pickling.
Fennel	Fennel leaves do not keep for more than a couple of days in the refrigerator. The bulb will last for about five days.
Garlic	Leaves are left attached to the bulb then left to dry in clumps in full sun for a few days. On no account let bulbs get wet. Move inside if rain threatens. Hang in an open mesh bag in a dry, airy position.

Vegetable	Storage method
Ginger	Mature ginger rhizomes store well in a cool, dry place. If stored in the natural state for too long, however, the flesh will become dry and the flavour turns towards bitterness, so try to use ginger when it is still young and fresh. Dried ginger can be ground into powder.
Jerusalem artichoke	As with other root crops, the simplest method of storing is to leave the tuber in the ground, digging up only when necessary and thus having a ready supply out of season. Harvested vegetables will keep for a month in dark, cool places away from intense cold. Pack into boxes and surround tubers with peat moss.
Kohlrabi	Bulbs can be stored in the refrigerator for 7–10 days.
Leek	Will keep 7–10 days in the refrigerator.
Lettuce	Will keep 7–10 days in the crisper section of the refrigerator.
Marrow	Handle carefully and do not wash or brush skin of the fruit before usage to prevent skin damage. Marrow will keep for up to a week in the refrigerator.
Mushroom	Mushrooms can be stored in the refrigerator (not in plastic bags or they will sweat) for around 5–7 days. They can also be dried or pickled and stored in bottles.
Okra	You can successfully store okra in the refrigerator for up to three days. Pods may be used fresh or dried.
Onion	Store bulbs in a cool, dry place in an open-weave mesh basket to allow free air circulation around them. Do not store close to other vegetables.
Parsnip	Parsnips can be kept in the ground 2–3 months after reaching maturity in cool to cold climates, but see that beds are kept reasonably dry during this storage period. Low temperatures convert starches to sugars, giving a sweet root. Freshly cropped vegetables will keep in refrigerator 2–3 weeks, slightly less in cool dry cupboards where they tend to lose their firmness.

Vegetable	Storage method
Pea	Pods keep for a short time in the refrigerator. The seeds will lose a great deal of their sugar content within a few days, converting it to starch.
Pepper (capsicum)	Peppers will keep for up to a week in the refrigerator. They can also be grilled or baked and, with the skins and seeds removed, preserved in spicy vinegars. Hot peppers can be dried successfully.
Potato	Keep crop in a cool, dark, airy place and exclude sunlight to prevent skin becoming tinged with green. Young or 'new' potatoes will not store for long periods.
Pumpkin	Handle carefully and do not wash or brush skin of fruit before storing. It will keep for several months in a cool, airy place or in boxes. Check occasionally for rotting or damage to skin and flesh by vermin.
Radish	Radish will keep for a week to 10 days in the crisper section of the refrigerator.
Shallot	Bulbs will keep in a cold, dry place for several months or the flesh may be chopped and frozen.
Snow pea (mangetout)	Pods keep for a short time in the refrigerator
Spinach	Spinach leaves keep in the refrigerator for up to a week but are better eaten immediately.
Squash	Handle carefully and do not wash or brush skin of fruit before usage to prevent skin damage. They will keep for up to a week in the refrigerator.
Sugar snap pea	Pods keep for a short time in the refrigerator. The seeds will lose a great deal of their sugar content within a few days, converting it to starch.
Swede	Swedes have a long storage time and can be kept in or out of the refrigerator.
Sweet corn	Sweet corn means there is plenty of sugar in the vegetable when it is harvested. The sugar soon turns to starch and the vegetable loses a great deal of its flavour, so freshly picked corn should be eaten as soon as possible. Storing in the refrigerator for a couple of days will slow down the sugar loss. Alternatively, kernels can be stripped from the cob and then snap frozen..

Vegetable	Storage method
Sweet potato	Very easy vegetable to store, but do not wash before putting away. Will keep for at least four months in this condition. Do not store in refrigerated conditions below 10°C (50°F).
Swiss chard (silverbeet)	Swiss chard (silverbeet) will keep for up to two weeks in the crisper drawer of the refrigerator, but it is best eaten when freshly picked before the leaves become limp. You can start picking some of the older, outer leaves first, and leave the younger ones in the middle to keep growing and just harvest them when you need them.
Tomato	Tomatoes will keep between 2–4 weeks in the refrigerator although they tend to lose their flavour over long periods. They can be pulped then bottled or processed into soups and sauces and frozen. Tomatoes are best left at room temperature. One easy method is to wrap individual tomatoes in newspaper and then layer them in boxes.
Turnip	Turnips do not store as long as swedes but, like that other vegetable, can be kept in or out of the refrigerator. You can store them, with the tops on, for 4–5 months.
Water chestnut	Examine the vegetable for rotten spots and remove damaged corms. The unpeeled crop will keep in bags in the refrigerator for up to two weeks. If peeled in advance of use, store in cold water in the refrigerator to prevent browning, again for up to two weeks, but water must be changed daily. Chestnuts can be dried and ground to a flour. Commercial crops are cooked and preserved by canning – flavour and texture being lost in the process.
White radish (daikon)	If the root has developed a hollowness inside, it will not store long, but generally will keep in the refrigerator at very low temperatures for several weeks. White radishes can be eaten raw, cooked, dried, pickled, fermented or preserved in brine.
Witlof (Belgian endive)	Witlof does not store well and becomes limp soon after exposure to light. It may be kept in the refrigerator for a few days but a greening of the leaves from exposure to light indicates a developing bitter taste.
Zucchini (courgette)	Handle carefully and do not wash or brush the skin of fruit before usage. They will keep for up to a week in the refrigerator.

FREEZING VEGETABLES

Vegetable	Freezing method
Artichoke, globe	Remove outer leaves. Wash, trim stalks and remove 'chokes' and blanch them, a few at a time, for seven minutes. Cool in iced water for seven minutes, drain. Pack in freezer bags, remove air from bags, seal and label. Freeze for up to six months.
Asparagus	Wash and remove woody portions and scales of spears, cut into 15 cm (6 in) lengths and blanch in boiling water for three minutes. Cool in iced water for three minutes, drain. Place on a tray in a single layer and freeze for 30 minutes. Pack into suitable containers, seal and label. Freeze for up to six months.
Bean, broad	Shell beans and after washing blanch in boiling water for 1½ minutes. Cool in iced water for 1–2 minutes. Place on a tray in a single layer and freeze for 30 minutes. Pack into freezer bags, remove air, seal and label. Freeze for up to six months.
Bean, French climbing, dwarf	Remove any strings and top and tail. Blanch for two minutes and cool in iced water for two minutes. Drain, spread on tray in a single layer and freeze for 30 minutes. Pack into freezer bags, remove air from bags, seal and label. Freeze for up to six months.
Beetroot	Only freeze young tender beetroots, those that are not more than 5–7.5 cm (2–3 in) across. Cook until tender and slice, chop or leave whole. Cool and transfer to plastic containers, cover with lids and label. Freeze for up to six months.
Broccoli	Choose tender young heads with no flowers and tender stalks. Wash well and divide into sprigs. Blanch for three minutes in boiling water. Cool in iced water for three minutes. Drain and spread on a tray in a single layer. Cover with plastic wrap to stop the strong smell of broccoli penetrating the freezer, and freeze for 30 minutes. Pack in freezer bags, remove air from bags, seal and label. Freeze for up to six months.
Brussels sprouts	Remove outer leaves and cut a cross at the stem end of each sprout. Wash thoroughly and then blanch for three minutes. Cool in iced water for three minutes, drain and spread on tray in a single layer. Cover with plastic wrap to prevent strong odour of sprouts penetrating the freezer. Freeze for 30 minutes, remove from tray and pack into plastic bags. Remove air from bags, label and seal. Freeze for up to six months.

Vegetable	Freezing method
Cabbage	Remove outer leaves and wash the remainder. Cut into thin wedges or shred. Blanch for 1½ minutes if shredded, or two minutes if cut into wedges. Chill in iced water for 1–2 minutes. Drain and pack in freezer bags, label and seal. Freeze for up to six months.
Carrot	Wash and scrub carrots and cut large carrots into pieces. Blanch for three minutes in boiling water. Chill in iced water for three minutes, drain well. Spread on a tray in a single layer and freeze for 30 minutes. Pack in freezer bags, remove air from bags, label and seal. Freeze for up to six months.
Cauliflower	Divide into florets and wash. Blanch for three minutes in boiling water. Chill in iced water for three minutes. Drain and place on a tray in a single layer. Cover with plastic wrap to prevent odour of cauliflower penetrating the freezer. Freeze for 30 minutes. Transfer to freezer bags, remove air from bags, label and freeze. Freeze for up to six months.
Celery	Use young tender stalks. Remove any string and wash and cut into 2.5 cm (1 in) pieces. Blanch for two minutes in boiling water. Chill in iced water for two minutes. Drain and place on a tray in a single layer. Freeze for 30 minutes. Pack freezer bags, remove air, label and seal. Freeze for up to six months.
Chicory (endive)	Do not freeze.
Chillies	Remove seeds, wash, dry and spread on a tray in a single layer. Freeze 30 minutes, pack in freezer bags, remove air, seal and label. Freeze for up to six months.
Chinese broccoli (gai larn)	Remove any coarse leaves and thick stems. Wash and blanch in boiling water for two minutes. Chill in iced water for two minutes. Drain and spread on a tray in a single layer; freeze for 30 minutes. Pack in freezer bags, remove air, seal and label. Freeze for up to six months.
Chinese cabbage (wong bok)	Only freeze crisp and young cabbage. Wash and shred finely. Blanch for 1½ minutes. Chill in iced water for 1–2 minutes. Drain, and place in freezer bags, label and seal. Freeze for up to six months.
Chinese spinach (amaranth)	Wash and trim leaves off stalks. Blanch for one minute. Chill in iced water for one minute. Drain, pack in freezer bags and remove air from bags; seal and label. Freeze for up to six months.

Vegetable	Freezing method
Choko (chayote)	Cook sliced chokos until tender in boiling water. Drain well, then mash and cool. Pack into plastic containers with well fitting lids, leaving space at the top. Freeze. Alternatively, roast the whole choko, with seeds removed, in a moderate oven until just tender. Cool, pack in containers, leaving room at the top, seal and label. Freeze for up to six months.
Cucumber	Peel and chop in food processor. Pack into plastic containers with well fitting lids, label and freeze. Freeze for up to three months.
Eggplant (aubergine)	Cut into slices, sprinkle with salt and allow to stand for 20 minutes. Drain off excess liquid and fry eggplant gently in butter or margarine until just tender. Cool, then pack in plastic containers, seal and label. Will freeze for up to three months.
Fennel	Use fresh young stalks. Wash thoroughly. Blanch for three minutes. Chill in iced water for three minutes. Drain, pack in freezer bags and remove air. Will freeze for up to six months.
Garlic	Place cloves, separated from bulbs, in freezer bags. Remove any excess air from bag, seal and label. Freeze for up to three months.
Ginger	Separate ginger into convenient-sized knobs. Place in freezer bags. Remove excess air from bags, seal and label. Freeze for up to six months.
Jerusalem artichoke	Peel and slice. Place in cold water with the juice of ½ lemon to prevent discolouration. Blanch for two minutes in boiling water. Cool in iced water for two minutes. Drain and spread on a tray in a single layer. Freeze for 30 minutes. Pack into freezer bags, remove air, seal and label. Freeze for up to six months.
Kohlrabi	Wash well, peel and cut into pieces. Blanch for three minutes. Chill in iced water for three minutes. Drain and spread on a tray in a single layer. Freeze for 30 minutes. Pack in freezer bags, remove air, seal and label. Freeze for up to six months.
Leek	Remove tough outer leaves, wash remainder. Cut away green part of stem, slice white flesh, or cut in half lengthways. Blanch two minutes (slices), or three minutes (halves); chill in iced water 2–3 minutes. Freeze on trays in a single layer for 30 minutes. Remove, pack in freezer bags, expel air, seal and label. Freeze for up to six months.

Vegetable	Freezing method
Lettuce	Do not freeze.
Marrow	Peel, cut into pieces and cook in boiling water until just cooked. Cool and place in freezer bags, remove air from bags, seal and label. Alternatively, bake in oven until almost cooked. Cool, package in freezer bags, seal and label. Freeze for up to three months.
Mushroom	Cultivated mushrooms need no preparation. Pack clean mushrooms in freezer bags. Remove air from bags, seal and label. Freeze for up to six months.
Okra	Wash well and trim off stems. Blanch in boiling water for 3–4 minutes. Cool in iced water for 3–4 minutes, drain and pack in freezer bags. Remove air from bags, seal and label. Freeze for up to six months.
Onion	Peel, chop or cut into rings. Wrap in layers of plastic wrap, place in a plastic container. Label and freeze for up to three months. Alternatively, package small onions in their skins in freezer bags. Remove air from bags, label and seal. Freeze for up to three months.
Parsnip	Peel and dice. Blanch for two minutes, chill in iced water for two minutes, then spread on a tray and freeze for 30 minutes. Pack into freezer bags, remove air, label and seal. Freeze for up to six months.
Pea	Shell, wash and blanch for one minute. Chill in iced water for one minute, drain, spread on a tray. Freeze for 30 minutes. Pack into freezer bags, remove air, seal and label. Freeze for up to six months.
Pepper (capsicum)	Wash, remove seeds and cut into slices or leave whole. Place on a tray in a single layer. Freeze for 30 minutes. Pack in freezer bags, remove air, label and seal. Freeze for up to six months.
Potato	There are a number of ways of freezing potatoes: **1** Scrub new potatoes. Cook in boiling water until almost cooked. Drain, cool, pack in freezer bags. Seal, label and freeze for up to six months. **2** Prepare chips and deep fry for about four minutes until cooked, but not brown. Drain and cool on paper towels. Place on a tray in a single layer and freeze for 30 minutes. Pack in freezer bags, remove air, label and seal. Freeze for up to three months. **3** Potatoes may also be mashed or prepared as Duchesse Potatoes and then frozen for up to three months.

Vegetable	Freezing method
Pumpkin	Peel and cook in boiling salted water until tender. Mash, cool, then pack into plastic containers, leaving space at the top. Freeze for up to three months. Alternatively, peel and cut into pieces. Bake until almost cooked. Pack into freezer bags when cool, remove the air, seal and label. Will freeze for up to three months.
Radish	Do not freeze.
Shallot	Separate cloves from bulb. Place in freezer bags, remove excess air. Freeze for up to three months.
Snow pea (mangetout)	Use tender pods. Wash and top and tail. Blanch for 30 seconds. Chill in iced water for 30 seconds. Drain, pack in freezer bags, remove air, seal and label. Freeze for up to six months.
Spinach	Wash well and trim leaves off stalks, blanch in small quantities in boiling water for one minute. Chill in iced water for one minute, drain, then pack in plastic bags or containers; label and seal. Will freeze for up to six months.
Squash	Peel and cook in boiling salted water until tender. Mash, cool and pack into freezer containers, leaving room at the top for expansion. Seal and label. Freeze for up to three months.
Sugar snap pea	Remove pods, wash and blanch for one minute. Chill, drain and spread on a tray. Freeze for 30 minutes, then pack in plastic bags, remove air from bags, seal and label. Will freeze for up to six months.
Swede	Only use tender, young swedes. Cut to required size and blanch for three minutes. Chill in iced water for three minutes. Drain, place pieces on a tray in a single layer and freeze for 30 minutes. Pack in freezer bags, remove air, seal and label. Freeze for up to six months.
Sweet corn	Remove leaves and threads and cut off top of cob. Wash, blanch a few cobs at a time for 5–7 minutes, depending upon size. Chill in iced water for 5–7 minutes, drain, then wrap each cob in plastic wrap. Pack wrapped cobs in freezer bags, remove air from bags, label and seal. Freeze for up to six months.
Sweet potato	After scrubbing and peeling, bake or roast until just tender. Drain on absorbent paper and cool. Pack into plastic bag or container. If using plastic bags ensure that air is removed before sealing. Label and date. Will freeze for up to three months.

Vegetable	Freezing method
Swiss chard (silverbeet)	Wash the leaves well and trim leaves from stalks. Blanch in small quantities of boiling water for one minute. Chill in iced water one minute, drain, then pack in freezer bags or containers. Remove air from plastic bags, label and date bags or containers and freeze. Will freeze for up to six months.
Tomato	There are various ways of freezing tomatoes. **1** Wash, remove stems, cut into halves or quarters or leave whole. Dry and pack into freezer bags. Remove air, label and seal. Freeze for up to 6 months. **2** Dip into boiling water for one minute, remove and peel. Place whole tomatoes on a tray and freeze for 30 minutes. Place in plastic bags, remove air, seal and label. Freeze for up to six months. **3** Simmer chopped tomatoes in a pan for five minutes or until soft. Push through a sieve or food mill to remove skins and seeds. Cool, then pack in plastic containers, leaving space at the top of container. Freeze up to six months.
Turnip	Peel and trim young, tender turnips. Cut to required size and blanch for three minutes, chill in iced water for three minutes. Drain, place pieces on a tray in a single layer and freeze for 30 minutes. Pack into plastic bags, remove air, seal and label. Freeze for up to six months.
Water chestnut	Bring chestnuts to the boil. Drain and peel off shells. Freeze for up to six months.
White radish (daikon)	Do not freeze.
Witlof (Belgian endive)	Wash well. Blanch for three minutes. Drain, place on a tray in a single layer and freeze for 30 minutes. Pack in freezer bags or plastic containers, remove air, seal and label. Freeze for 2–3 months.
Zucchini (courgette)	Slice into 2.5 cm (1 in) slices without peeling, then sauté gently in a little melted butter until barely tender. Cool, then pack into plastic containers, leaving space at the top of the container. Freeze for up to three months.

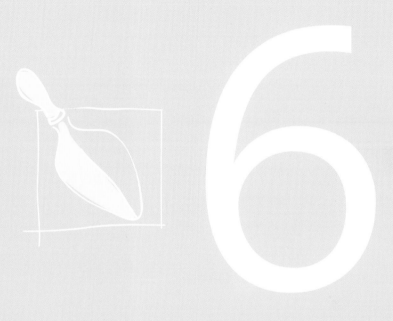

6

Using
herbs

Using herbs

Herbs have been used in cooking for thousands of years, by virtually every cuisine in the world. However, there's no need to confine your use of herbs to the kitchen. Consider their many other values – as natural dyes, remedies and medicines, air fresheners and deodorisers. You can also use them to make cosmetics, perfumes, pest repellents and even cleaning products.

Medicinal herbs

For as long as humanity has suffered pain, discomfort and diseases, cures have been sought from the world of plants. There are no records of our earliest experiments with plants, but since herbs have great power to harm as well as heal, the journey to knowledge must have been incredibly risky.

The ancient world

Our earliest records of herbal medicine go back to the ancient worlds of Mesopotamia and Egypt. The Sumerian civilisation in Mesopotamia was extraordinarily advanced in science, mathematics and the arts. The Sumerians were also remarkable agricultural engineers

Echinacea thrives in full sun and a regularly watered soil. The medicinal plant species are all perennial, and quite beautiful in the garden with their very large daisy flowers of lilac, pink or white. The plants can be raised from seed.

and constructed what must have been inspiring and very productive stepped pyramid or ziggurat gardens (the Hanging Gardens of Babylon, one of the wonders of the ancient world, were in this style). They also constructed vast public parks filled with exotic trees and shrubs brought back by travellers to distant lands. The oldest herbal we have, dating back to 2500 BC, came from Sumer. It includes plants such as bay, caraway, thyme, mandrake, saffron, sesame, poppy and coriander.

Assyria also amassed a remarkable knowledge of medicinal herbs. Tablets that originally came from the library of Ashurbanipal, King of Assyria (668–626 BC), describe more than 250 medicinal plants and 180 mineral-based cures.

The Egyptians too were advanced in their knowledge of agriculture, irrigation and the construction of villa-style gardens for the rich, with water features, grape-shaded walks, and trees such as palms and figs. Included in these gardens were aromatic-leaved herbs and fragrant-flowered plants, their scent trapped by tall protective walls. Egypt also imported from Babylon many dried medicinal herbs, as well as spices and fragrant oils, and specialists called rhizomatists or root gatherers collected herbal plants from the wild. As in Sumer, science and mathematics in Egypt were very advanced. The earliest recorded Egyptian physician of genius was Imhotep, who served the Pharaoh Zoser around 2600 BC. He was also a powerful astrologer and magician, and with time he became more god than man as he entered into the mythology of Egypt. A thousand years later the first surviving Egyptian herbal, the *Papyrus Ebers*, was written.

Greek medicine

The Greek civilisation was built on the foundations of Mesopotamia and Egypt, and it gave rise to several great healers and schools of medicine. Asclepius, probably born in Epidaurus about 1250 BC, was famed in his day

The wild poppy (*Papaver rhoeas*) is probably better known to us today as the Flanders poppy, an emblem of those who died in World War I. One of the flower's modern medicinal uses is as a treatment for coughs and insomnia.

However, Theophrastus of Eresus, who was born on the beautiful Greek island of Lesbos in 372 BC, left us two outstanding herbals, *Historia Plantarum* and *De Causis Plantarum*, describing 500 plants. He was a pupil of Aristotle (from whom he inherited his famous garden), and incorporated Aristotle's writings on botany into the herbals.

The most celebrated medical school of its age was the Alexandrian School. Founded in 331 BC in the Egyptian city of Alexandria, the school was famed far beyond the region and attracted leading scholars and physicians. They brought with them healing traditions from many

for what seemed like miraculous cures; after his death, legend enveloped his memory. He was said to have been slain by Zeus, the ruler of the heavens, for daring to rival the god in healing. Asclepius's mythological daughter was Hygieia, the goddess of health.

However, perhaps the greatest of all Greek physicians was Hippocrates, often referred to as the 'Father of Medicine', and remembered now for the Hippocratic oath, which has long defined the ethical behaviour of doctors.

Hippocrates was born in 460 BC, and practised for much of his life on the Greek island of Kos, near Rhodes. His surgery was situated beneath a spreading plane tree in the town square. There were notable physicians before him, but Hippocrates clearly delineated the change to a scientific approach to medicine. He was a man of good sense, and much that he espoused in his approach to healing would be endorsed by modern holistic medical practitioners. He developed a systematic approach to diagnosis, working in a rational, orderly manner, and restoring health not only through the use of herbs but also through changes in a patient's environment, diet and lifestyle. Sadly, he did not leave us a herbal.

The fig tree (*Ficus carica*) grows wild throughout the Mediterranean. The milky juice from the leaves will remove warts, and a syrup made from the fruit is a mild laxative.

sources, which were integrated within the Alexandrian School, in turn initiating new lines of research.

In the first century AD, Dioscorides, a Greek physician with the Imperial Roman Army, wrote the most influential of the herbals, *De Materia Medica*. This vast work of scholarship attempted to place in one book all the knowledge accumulated by the Alexandrian School, the teachings of Hippocrates, and Dioscorides's own observations and discoveries as a doctor working in Spain, France, Germany and the Middle East. He described with precision some 600 medicinal plants. This monumental work remained the standard for the medical profession for the next 1500 years. In the same period the Roman writer Pliny produced the less scientific but charming 37-volume *Historia Naturalis*, seven volumes of which were devoted to herbal plants.

Physic gardens

The Roman conquest and occupation of much of Europe lasted for 400 years. The Romans were sophisticated in the use of culinary as well as medicinal herbs, and their armies carried with them many herbs for their own use. During the Roman occupation of England, approximately 200 herbs were introduced, many of them naturalising in their new land. Christianity arrived

VALERIAN *Valerian (Valeriana officinalis) is an attractive perennial plant with coarse, green fern-like leaves forming rosettes, from which tall stems of large, lacy white heads of tiny flowers emerge. The dried roots were used to make a sedative in World War I to treat shell-shock victims. It is now used as a mild remedy for insomnia, and to relieve stress headaches. However, prolonged continuous use is not advised by some authorities. Both dogs and cats find the odd smell of the root irresistible; it is reputed to be the magical attractant carried by the Pied Piper of Hamelin, the character in the poem.*

officially in England in the sixth century AD, and Roman herbs became the foundation of the physic gardens created by the great monasteries and nunneries for supplying medicinal plants to the infirmary.

We can visualise these physic gardens from the plans produced in AD 820 for a great monastery of the period, St Gall in Switzerland. They were intended not only for the reconstruction of the monastery but also to act as an idealised template for the design of Benedictine monasteries throughout the Carolingian Empire.

The design incorporated consideration of all the bodily and spiritual needs of the monks according to the strict Rule of St Benedict. The plans included a physician's house opening out onto a garden of herbs, and the herbarius, consisting of geometrically arrayed, raised rectangular beds, each devoted to a single herb such as fennel, pennyroyal, rue, sage and cumin, or to Gallica roses and Madonna lilies (both of which were used to decorate the chapels on feast days). The physic garden was surrounded by borders of rosemary, savory, mint, costmary, lovage, *Iris germanica* and other herbs. Other common plants in such medieval monastic gardens included gilvers (flowers which we now call

Arthritis herb

Arthritis herb (*Hydrocotlye asiatica* syn. *Centella asiatica*) is a creeping herb with scallop-edged, fan-like leaves, widespread from India to Hawaii. It appears to occur in several strains with differing herbal activity. One strain, known as gotu kola or Indian ginseng or pohe kula, is considered to have properties similar to those of true ginseng, and it has been included in the daily diet (two leaves in a salad or similar) in many Asian countries as well as Hawaii for centuries. It is believed to retard ageing, relieve depression and improve energy levels and memory. The strain found in the wild in Australia has developed a reputation for assisting in increasing mobility and decreasing the pain of arthritis, and has become known as arthritis herb.

The apothecary's rose (*Rosa gallica* var. *officinalis*), grown as a medicinal plant in medieval times, was listed in John Gerard's *Herball* (1597). It is possibly the red rose that was used as the emblem of the House of Lancaster.

carnations and clove pinks), peonies, columbines and bugloss (*Anchusa officinalis*).

When the Roman Empire crumbled, research in medicine in Europe all but ceased for 600 years. Monasteries and nunneries became the keepers of the flame, protecting the herbal, medical and horticultural knowledge of the past, maintaining libraries and archives and, with the help of skilled calligraphers, copying and distributing treatises between monasteries. They also became the hospitals of their day, treating not only the inmates but also the people of nearby towns, passing pilgrims and travellers.

Medieval England

One of the earliest lists of herbs grown in medieval England was provided in the *Glastonbury Herbal*, written in Anglo-Saxon in the 10th century. It listed both useful

The garden in a Norman castle often included a flowery mead, which was a highly contrived grass meadow richly spangled in spring with a mixture of gentle wildflowers and exotic plants from Europe and the Middle East.

native plants and introduced species, and showed evidence of sophisticated horticultural techniques. The *Leechdom*, also written in the 10th century, is a wonderful compilation of medical, herbal and veterinary knowledge. A third important herbal emerged from the Welsh Physicians of Myddffai, a great Welsh school of medicine which rivalled the finest medical schools of medieval Europe.

The Norman invasion of England in the 11th century saw the art of gardening raised to a new elegance. The massive, highly defended castles were virtually fortified

ECHINACEA *Echinacea (above) was highly valued as a medicinal herb by Native Americans and by early settlers in America, who used it for healing weeping wounds, boils and abscesses, and to treat snakebite. There are nine species of echinacea, of which three are used medicinally (*Echinacea angustifolia, *E. purpurea* and *E. pallida*). Today it has a well researched and confirmed reputation for enhancing immune function, and is used as a preventative for influenza and colds. Echinacea is also considered to be useful in the treatment of upper respiratory tract infections. It is not recommended for those who have diabetes mellitis or diseases of the immune system, such as AIDS and MS.*

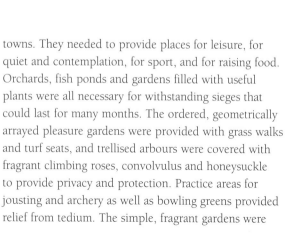

towns. They needed to provide places for leisure, for quiet and contemplation, for sport, and for raising food. Orchards, fish ponds and gardens filled with useful plants were all necessary for withstanding sieges that could last for many months. The ordered, geometrically arrayed pleasure gardens were provided with grass walks and turf seats, and trellised arbours were covered with fragrant climbing roses, convolvulus and honeysuckle to provide privacy and protection. Practice areas for jousting and archery as well as bowling greens provided relief from tedium. The simple, fragrant gardens were

Lenten rose (*Helleborus orientalis*). A tincture of the root is used in homeopathy.

Common sage

Sage (*Salvia officinalis*) is well known as a culinary herb, especially in combination with poultry and pork. Salvia's name comes from the Latin word *salvere*, meaning 'good health'. An old English proverb asked, 'Why should a man die whilst sage grows in his garden?'.

Recent research has confirmed many of the traditional medicinal uses of sage. Sage has antioxidant properties; its reputation for prolonging one's life span and improving memory is probably related to this. In the 17th century, the Chinese, who believed firmly in the anti-ageing properties of sage tea, traded with the Dutch as many as seven shiploads of their own *Camellia sinensis* tea leaves for one shipload of European dried sage. The plant also contains natural oestrogen and has been used as a tea to treat symptoms of menopause. Sage is both antibacterial and antifungal in activity, vindicating its traditional use in the treatment of sore gums, and as an effective gargle for sore throats. Sage has also been used as a tonic for the liver and nerves.

filled with herbs and flowers to be used by the lady of the house in producing medicines, toiletries and fragrances in her still room.

English herbals

Greek texts were used virtually unamended and unchallenged for many centuries in England. William Turner's *New Herball*, published in 1551, was the first scientific study to break new ground in England, and it included descriptions of 238 British plants. Two famous herbals, books that were individual and independent in both their ideas and opinions, were to follow.

John Gerard was a physician, and the superintendent of the gardens of Lord Burghley, Secretary of State to Elizabeth I, and an apothecary to James I. His delightful *Herball* was first published in 1597. He based his book on the research of the Flemish physician Dodoens, to which he added his own original voice and scientific discipline. His trials and experiences with the American plants that were now beginning to flood in from the American colonies are part of the *Herball*'s fascination. His own large garden was also filled with a major collection of European plants, and his fresh, intimate observations remain as valid today as they were in the 16th century.

FOXGLOVE Foxglove (Digitalis purpurea) is known by many delightful folk names, including fairy thimble, in its native lands of western and central Europe. However, some of the plant's names, such as dead men's bells and witch's gloves, hint at its dark side. The leaves are highly poisonous, containing a variety of glycosides, and have been used to strengthen the heart muscle in the treatment of heart disease. The plant is the source of important modern heart-regulating drugs, which are only issued under medical supervision. In the past it was used in the treatment of dropsy, and in cases of pneumonia.

Nicholas Culpeper was a physician whose herbal was published in 1653. He was a man of decided opinions and of a less scientific bent than Gerard. His herbal included astrology, and subscribed to the old doctrine of signatures in which herbal plants supposedly resembled the disease or part of the body they were intended to cure. The book is a curious mixture, at odds with a time that was so forward looking.

The first herbal written in America appeared in 1569, written by Spanish physician Nicholas Monardes, whose name is honoured by the delightfully aromatic herbal genus *Monarda* (bergamot).

Arab physicians

During the long centuries when science was stifled in Europe, the enquiring spirit of Greece passed to the Arab world. All the major treatises of Greek medicine, including the herbals, were translated by c. 900 and had been distributed to the famed libraries of Baghdad, Damascus and Cairo. It was a time of Muslim expansion and conquest across North Africa and as far as Spain. The Arab world drew on the accumulated knowledge of both Europe and the Orient, combining this with its own very advanced medical and herbal knowledge. Among its most brilliant practitioners were Abulcasis, in Spain, whose reputation drew the sick from all over

Europe; the great clinician Rhazes, who was a royal physician in Baghdad; and Avicenna, who wrote the *Canon Medicinae*, which brought together the integrated medical and herbal knowledge of the whole Arab world.

The green tradition

There is a hidden tradition of herbal medicine that too rarely receives mention. Women figure little in the early story of medicinal herbs, yet for the poor they were often the only skilled help available. Herbal knowledge was handed down by verbal tradition or in family recipe books. Women skilled in the healing arts were known as wise women, cunning women or midwives.

Like male physicians for thousands of years before them, these often skilled herbalists frequently included

the use of prayer, charms and incantations to assist their medicine. However, they walked a fine line. If their skills failed, village gratitude for help through childbirth and illnesses could quickly turn to accusations of satanic involvement as fear fed on ignorance.

Charges of witchcraft in England and America reached their height in the 17th century, particularly in Essex around the town of Colchester, where the self-appointed Witchfinder General operated his reign of terror; and at Salem in Massachusetts, where an outbreak of ergot in cereal crops was almost certainly the initial cause. Ergotised grain, caused by infection with the fungus *Claviceps* spp., is well known to cause violent and intense hallucinations as well as the sensation of burning in the extremities. The condition was often called St Anthony's fire in Europe. Such an outbreak, in a population of staunchly evangelical puritans (mainly settlers from 17th century witch-fearing Essex), was an inflammable and fatal mixture.

The word 'witch' is derived from the Old English *wicca*, which means wise. Most modern Wiccans

WHITE YARROW   Yarrow (Achillea millefolium) is native to southern Europe but is also widely naturalised in Australia, New Zealand and North America. It has been used in herbal medicine to improve blood circulation, and as a tea to relieve stomach cramps and treat menstrual problems. One of its earliest recorded uses was to staunch the flow of blood from wounds, especially those caused by metal swords and knives. It was last used in an official military capacity for this purpose in the American Civil War. The pulped leaves have been used for their astringent properties – applied as a poultice to sores, ulcers, piles and acne. (Yarrow should not be used by pregnant women.)

Yarrow makes dense rosettes of fine, feathery, strongly scented foliage, eventually making a neat mat in full to half sun. It bears dense, flat inflorescences of pretty pink, lilac or white flowers. Yarrow is propagated by seed and by division.

see themselves as seekers of wisdom, attuned to and protective of the natural world, and preservers of ancient knowledge and herbal traditions. Far from being devil worshippers, the Wiccan religion's creed is 'Harm no one', and their worship is of the harmonising male and female power of the cosmos, a belief that echoes the universal yin and yang forces that form the basis of Chinese medicine.

Chinese herbal medicine

The medical knowledge of the Ming dynasty, a period corresponding to the 17th century in Europe, has been estimated to have been 1000 years ahead of that of Europe. But by the turn of the 20th century, the West had made giant strides while China had languished under the Manchu reign. Fortunately, the great herbal and medical traditions of China have survived, and now flourish around the world.

China and Europe approached healing with somewhat different philosophies. Chinese medicine was based on the principles of holism and harmony. The legendary Emperor Shen Nong, who lived approximately 5500 years ago, is credited with testing many species of plants for their curative properties, developing a pharmacopoeia, and founding organised medicine. Shen Nong also derived the idea of two opposing and equal principles in nature. Life was seen to be in eternal flux, constantly renewing the delicate balance between these opposing forces.

The great sage Confucius (551–479 BC) created a doctrine of universal order and a complementary code of social ethics. He, too, taught that the two opposing forces of the cosmos, yin and yang, must be balanced to maintain harmony at all levels. A contemporary, Lao Zi, the founder of Taoism, created a philosophy of universal law and order, a world in which harmony is forever being created by the delicate rebalancing of yin and yang forces. He advocated taking the path of least resistance, allowing this rebalancing to occur without our intervention.

It was against this background that Chinese medicine developed. The body was seen as a part of a greater whole, and health was seen as the result of harmony both within and without. The quick fixes sought by patients of Western medicine were never the true aim of Chinese

Marshmallow

Marshmallow (*Althaea officinalis*) belongs to the same genus as hollyhock, and it closely resembles a small-flowered perennial hollyhock. The original marshmallow, which was eaten as a sweet, was made from the dried and powdered root of this plant. It contains a mucilage that acts as an excellent thickening agent. This species was introduced early into the American, Australian and New Zealand colonies. Marshmallow tea was used to soothe sore throats, as well as to relieve coughs and diarrhoea. A poultice made from the dried powdered roots was used to soothe inflamed skin, and a decoction of both the leaves and the roots was often included in lotions as a time-honoured remedy for sunburn as well as for chapped hands. The flowers of the true hollyhock (*A. rosea*) were similarly used for their soothing properties, and a poultice of the boiled leaves of the related Australian native hollyhock (*Lavatera plebia*) was traditionally used as a bush medicine to draw boils and soothe irritated skin.

medicine. Disharmony at deeper levels was considered to constantly re-express itself in one medical problem after another unless a state of balance was reached. Chinese medicine involved the careful holistic evaluation of a patient, and changes in diet, attitude and lifestyle were prescribed together with herbal mixtures.

The great herbal tradition of China remains of the highest value. The Chinese were using narcotic anaesthetics over 700 years ago, ephedra (source of ephedrine) for asthmatics 1800 years ago, iodine for the treatment of enlarged thyroids a millennium ago, and fermentations containing antibiotic substances have long been in use to combat infections. As the quintessential 700 or so herbs employed by Chinese herbalists are tested by Western science, the efficacy and uses of many have already been fully validated.

BELOW The apothecary's rose (*Rosa gallica* var. *officinalis* 'Versicolor') is an old herbal rose.

ELDERBERRY This herb (above) dates back to ancient Greek times, and is shrouded in mystery and folklore. It is said that Christ's cross was made of elderwood, and that elder would only grow where blood had been spilt. In fact, elderberry (Sambucus spp.) grows happily in any temperate climate in sun or shade, and once established, will cope with frosts.

There are a few different species of elderberry, but if you intend to make elderberry wine, sorbet or jelly, make sure that you plant the edible S. nigra *(pictured above) rather than the other species, which are poisonous.*

The bark of *Acacia decurrens* is collected from a tree that is at least seven years old. It must then be matured for another year before it can be used for medicinal purposes.

The New World

In 1747 a small group belonging to a religious sect called The Society of Believers In Christ's Second Coming left Manchester in England for the New World of America, where they dreamed of creating 'heaven on earth'. They were led by a woman of indomitable spirit, called Ann Lee. The group became known as the Shakers, their name deriving from their trance-like possession during prayer sessions.

In time the Shakers were to found many communities, spreading from Maine to Florida. The Shaker villages became models of self-sufficiency. The communities were committed to providing a simple, virtuous, rewarding and creative life. Even the simplest items were made with an eye to improvement of design, ease of use and harmony of form.

The involvement of the Shakers with the herb industry of North America began modestly, as part of their need to provide the best possible care for their communities. The Shakers were deeply interested in the herbal knowledge of the First Nation (the Native Americans, as they are now known) and gathered many herbs from the wild, growing them in their herb gardens. From the beginning, the Shakers took meticulous care in identifying plants, collecting the correct, medicinally active part of the plant, and harvesting plants at the peak of medicinal activity or culinary flavour. At their largest,

plantings of herbs in Shaker settlements occupied some 68 hectares (150 acres).

Shaker herb gardens were managed organically. The medical profession welcomed the high quality of their herbs, and the catalogues they issued were amazing in their day. The Canterbury Village catalogue listed over 200 different herbs, and its botanic garden was said to have the largest collection of medicinal plants in New England. In 1831 the New Lebanon Shakers were exporting top quality dried herbs around the world and offering 137 different herbs. The Shakers were the first professional herbalists of America, and thanks to them interest in herbs in the United States never abated.

Early Australian settlers

Life was daunting for the early pioneers of Australia; they were thrown almost entirely on their own resources. Free settlers arrived equipped with the seeds and precious potted roots of many valuable medicinal, fragrant and useful herbs. Chinese immigrants following the huge Australian gold strikes of the 19th century brought with them their own armoury of herbal medicine; it is sometimes forgotten that a strong tradition of Chinese medicine has existed in Australia for almost as long as European settlement.

There's a belief that early settlers lived in an encapsulated European world. It is true that many pined for a lost homeland, but early paintings of colonial gardens depicted the inclusion of many native flowers. Desperation or a thirst for knowledge drove some to seek information from the original owners of the land, the Aboriginals.

Dysentery was a major killer in the colonies, but a decoction made from the bark of the green wattle (*Acacia decurrens*) was found to be so effective that it was exported and even included in the *British Pharmacopoeia*. Aboriginal herbal medicines employed in the colony included the hardened gum that oozes from wounds in various species of eucalyptus. Known as kino, the substance was a very effective treatment for diarrhoea, and became a successful export in the 19th century. Aboriginal herbal knowledge was extensive, based on

tens of thousands of years of experimentation, and the Australian bush proved to be a fully stocked medicine chest for virtually every ill.

Modern herbalism

Interest in modern medical herbalism has been remarkable in the last 20 years. Extensive and exciting research is being carried out on the medicinal herbs of South America, Mexico, North America, Africa and Australia. In response to strong consumer demand, many reputable companies now supply high quality, standardised herbal products to cope with everyday ills.

The term 'aromatherapy' was coined in 1928 by the French chemist Dr René-Maurice Gattefossé, who studied and documented the use of essential oils in maintaining good health. Aromatherapy has ancient roots, and today it is a rapidly growing field of herbal treatment and research, uniting the knowledge of the herbalists with that of the essential oil practitioners. Increasingly it also involves the 'hard sciences', providing evidence of the healing activity of the plants and aromatherapy treatments. The medical profession in France has incorporated essential oil therapy into medical practice and a Chair of Phytotherapy (literally, 'plant therapy') has been established at the University of Paris Nord, where postgraduate studies are undertaken in this field. A major revival is now apparent in the great traditions of herbal medicine.

FEVERFEW *Feverfew (left) is one of the prettiest and easiest herbs to grow, with dark green, deeply cut foliage and masses of small, golden-eyed, sparkling white daisy flowers. Feverfew (*Tanacetum parthenium *syn.* Chrysanthemum parthenium*) has been used for many centuries to treat severe headaches and migraines. This has been verified by a number of clinical trials, and several valuable medicinal compounds have been isolated from the plant. Many migraine sufferers have reported good results after including a raw leaf in a daily sandwich. The leaves are quite bitter. The success of the herb in the treatment of headaches is attributed in part to the ability of feverfew to relax smooth muscle spasms.*

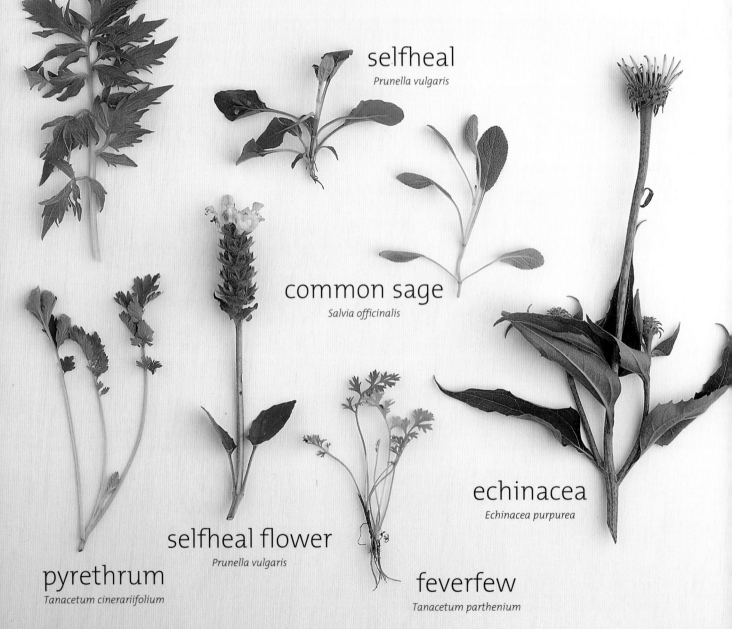

MEDICINAL HERBS

Herbs have been used for thousands of years to treat a wide range of illnesses – from menopause and menstrual problems (evening primrose and lady's mantle) to fevers (feverfew and yarrow), and from mood swings and mental disorders (St John's wort and valerian) to injuries (arnica and comfrey).

valerian
Valeriana officinalis

selfheal
Prunella vulgaris

common sage
Salvia officinalis

echinacea
Echinacea purpurea

selfheal flower
Prunella vulgaris

pyrethrum
Tanacetum cinerariifolium

feverfew
Tanacetum parthenium

marshmallow
Althaea officinalis

christmas rose
Helleborus argutifolius

wormwood
Artemisia absinthium

foxglove
Digitalis purpurea

white yarrow
Achillea millefolium

arthritis herb
Hydrocotlye asiatica syn. Centella asiatica

Cosmetic herbs

The use of herbs in essential oils, perfumes and cosmetics dates back to ancient civilisations. There are many simple herbal preparations that you can use to tone, clean, moisturise or simply refresh your skin. Hair rinses and bath preparations, too, can be quickly made from your garden herbs.

Cosmetics through the ages

Herbs have been used in perfumes and cosmetics for thousands of years. The ancient Egyptians held their preparations in high regard and were entombed with them so they could continue to adorn themselves in the afterlife. They treated wrinkles with a mixture of frankincense, wax, moruga oil, cyperus grass and fermented plant juice, and chewed herbs for bad breath. A cure for baldness required placing chopped lettuce

on the bald patch, while grey hair was treated with an ointment – juniper berries and two other plants were kneaded into a paste with oil, then heated before being applied to the hair.

The Greeks used fragrant oils to ward off illness, sprinkled furnishings with scented waters and placed garlands of flowers around the necks of their guests. The Greek philosopher and scientist Theophrastus (c. 370–c. 287 BC) wrote an early study of perfumes, *Concerning Odours*, in which he described how a poultice on the leg could sweeten the breath – the essences permeated the skin and then entered the circulatory system.

The Romans adapted many of the Greek uses of perfumes. Both the Greeks and Romans used the powdered root of sweet flag (*Acorus calamus*) as talcum powder, and it was widely used in Elizabethan times.

OPPOSITE In the 16th century, an Italian perfume – called 'Frangipani' after its Italian creator, the Marquis Frangipani – was used to scent gloves. When the frangipani flower was discovered in the Caribbean, its perfume was considered reminiscent of the scented gloves, so the flower was called frangipani. However, the genus name, *Plumeria*, commemorates Charles Plumier, a 17th century French botanist. *Plumeria rubra* is pictured here.

Roses, hyacinth, myrtle and jonquil were popular in seventh century Eastern civilisations; the wealthy surrounded themselves with plants that were either aromatic or produced strongly fragrant flowers. Musk was the most popular fragrance, and when building their places of worship, followers of Mohammed mixed it with mortar for a lasting fragrance. Since the days of the Prophet, Muslims have used miswak, a natural brush and toothpaste from *Salvadora persica*, a tree that is native to southern Egypt and the Sudan.

GRASSE The first perfume laboratory in Grasse, France, was set up by the Italian Catherine de' Medici in the 16th century. She had come to France to marry Henry II. As there was also an established tanning industry in Grasse at the time, the two industries joined forces to produce perfumed gloves, which aristocrats held to their noses to screen out the often overwhelmingly unpleasant smells of urban living. In the 18th century the leather industry declined, and the craftsmen turned their attention to manufacturing perfume.

In medieval Europe, herbs were commonly used for cosmetics, perfumes and washing. Chamomile was used in water for handwashing; lavender was used in personal baths and scent; and nutmeg was set in silver and used as scented jewellery. Rosemary leaves were boiled in white wine and used as a face wash, while thyme was used as an astringent.

Perfumes came into general use around the time of the reign of Elizabeth I of England, when exotic new fragrances were brought back from the New World by Spanish and English explorers.

Scented flowers and aromatic gardening fell into decline during the 18th century when landscape gardening, with its emphasis on dramatic vistas rather than floral displays, became popular. The Victorians

The musk rose (*Rosa moschata*) inspired many of the great English poets, such as Keats and Shakespeare.

The dried flowers of *Lavandula angustifolia*.

remedied this to some extent with their love of flower beds, although they tended to concentrate on colour rather than fragrance.

By the turn of the 20th century, however, the aromatic garden had become popular again and in more recent times there has been a revival of interest in both aromatherapy – the use of aromatic plant extracts and essential oils for healing and cosmetic purposes – and also gardening.

Commercially, the interest in aromatic plants has never been more intense. Today perfume is a huge industry. The town of Grasse in southern France is one of the largest centres in the world for the production and development of fragrances, and it heavily invests in plant-breeding programs designed to produce varieties with greater concentrations of sought-after oils.

Home enfleurage

To produce small quantities of your own essential oil, follow these steps.

1 Gather the fresh flowers of the plant you wish to use, remove the stalks and place the flowers in a glass jar half-filled with good quality grapeseed or jojoba oil.

2 After 24 hours, remove the flowers, squeeze them (allowing the liquid to run back into the jar) and then discard the flowers.

3 Add some fresh flowers to the jar.

4 Repeat this process until the oil is saturated with perfume.

5 Finally, add an equal quantity of pure (ethyl) alcohol, tightly screw a lid onto the jar and shake daily for two weeks.

6 Pour the fragrant alcohol off the oil and use it as required.

Hyacinths, with their stunning fragrance are commonly used in perfumes.

I know a bank whereon the wild thyme blows,
Where oxlips and the nodding violet grows
Quite over-canopied with luscious woodbine,
With sweet musk-roses, and with eglantine

A Midsummer Night's Dream, William Shakespeare

Essential oils

Essential oils are the concentrated natural chemicals within the plant that contain fragrance. Although they are often used simply as perfume as well as in the manufacture of cosmetics, some also have therapeutic value. When applied by massage or in baths, the oils penetrate the skin and quickly enter the bloodstream and lymphatic system. Inhaling the aroma is also believed to affect your emotions and mood.

Types of oils

Essential oils may be held within various parts of the plant, including the flower, leaf, bark, roots and rind. In flowers, the oil is stored in cells on both surfaces of the petals, although the concentration is usually greater on the upper surface. In leaves, the oil is stored in one of three ways:

- deep within the leaf or in capsules that require some pressure to release the oil
- in cells on or near the surface, to be released when the temperature rises
- in glandular hairs on the underside of the leaf.

Obtaining essential oils

Removing essential oils from the plant without losing the fragrance is at the heart of perfume production. Commercially, this may be done by several methods, including extraction, distillation and expression. If you wish to make your own essential oils, you can use a simple home enfleurage process.

Lavender, mint, rosemary and marigold are relaxing, while sage and lovage (shown here) are said to stimulate.

Buying and storing oils

If you buy essential oils rather than make your own, always read the label beforehand to check where the company sources its ingredients and whether it runs checks for purity. If the oil is labelled as 'aromatherapy oil', it has probably been mixed with a carrier oil such as grapeseed oil. Although this is necessary if you wish to apply the oil to the skin through massage, for example, you should remember that it reduces the life of the oil from years to months.

All essential oils oxidise over time, so look for oils sold in dark-tinted glass bottles and avoid any that have been on display in a hot window, since heat and sunlight accelerate the deterioration process. Keep the bottles firmly sealed, and store them in the fridge.

When blending your own oils, it's a good idea to use a glass eye dropper to measure the quantities, and always shake the bottle well before use. Remember to label the bottle, too, and add the date of purchase.

Using essential oils

You can use essential oils in many ways around your home. Depending on which fragrance you select, the effect can be stimulating or relaxing.

Massage

Essential oils are highly concentrated and when used on the skin should be diluted in a carrier oil, such as grapeseed or jojoba. Olive oil aids itchy skin but its smell will overwhelm that of the essential oil. For use on the body, for every 50 ml (2 fl oz) of carrier oil, add 20 drops of essential oil; 10 drops for use on the face; and 5–10 drops for use on children.

Vaporisation

Ceramic burners usually consist of a shallow saucer over a night-light candle. The heat from the candle causes drops of oil (either used alone or in a small quantity of water) to evaporate and scent the air. Or you can place a few drops of oil in a dish of water on a radiator or a sunny windowsill. Try some of these.

- Eucalyptus for its refreshing scent
- Basil for concentration
- Rose for improving your mood
- Lavender for relaxation
- Peppermint for staying alert.

Warning

Do not apply undiluted essential oils to the skin. If you have sensitive skin, use a small amount of oil to check for a reaction. Never massage areas of the body that have broken skin, rashes, swollen joints or varicose veins. Anyone with a heart condition should avoid massage. Pregnant women and people with high blood pressure or epilepsy should consult a qualified aromatherapist before using essential oils.

handy tip

Each essential oil has its own property and can be matched to a purpose. Try clary sage and basil for tiredness; peppermint and ginger for nausea and digestive problems; and sweet marjoram and rose for insomnia.

Perfume

In order to preserve the scent of essential oils as perfume, you need to mix them with alcohol in a ratio of about 1:5. A simpler method is to add a few drops to a tissue tucked discreetly into your clothing – it will last for several hours. You can also create a unique fragrance by mixing oils together. Try the recipe for eau de cologne, below.

Chamomile flowers and rosemary and sage leaves are useful in hair rinses. Perfumes are also well known for their use of herbs. In Victorian times vanilla pods were rubbed all over the body, and from the 19th century lavender fields in Provence have been harvested for this industry. Rose, boronia and jasmine oils are three other well known plant extracts in the perfume industry.

EAU DE COLOGNE ➤ Combine 150 ml (5 fl oz) vodka, 60 drops orange essential oil, 30 drops bergamot essential oil, 30 drops lemon essential oil, 6 drops neroli essential oil, 6 drops rosemary essential oil in a bottle and leave for a week. Shake daily. Add 50 ml (2 fl oz) distilled or boiled water, shake and set aside for 4–6 weeks. Strain through a filter and funnel into a second sterilised bottle.

According to Dioscorides, the Greeks and Romans used the rhizomes of *Iris germanica* in perfumery.

lavender

Lavandula spp.

marigold petals

Tagetes spp.

borage

Borago officinalis

elder flower

Sambucus nigra

aloe vera

Aloe vera syn. *A. barbadensis*

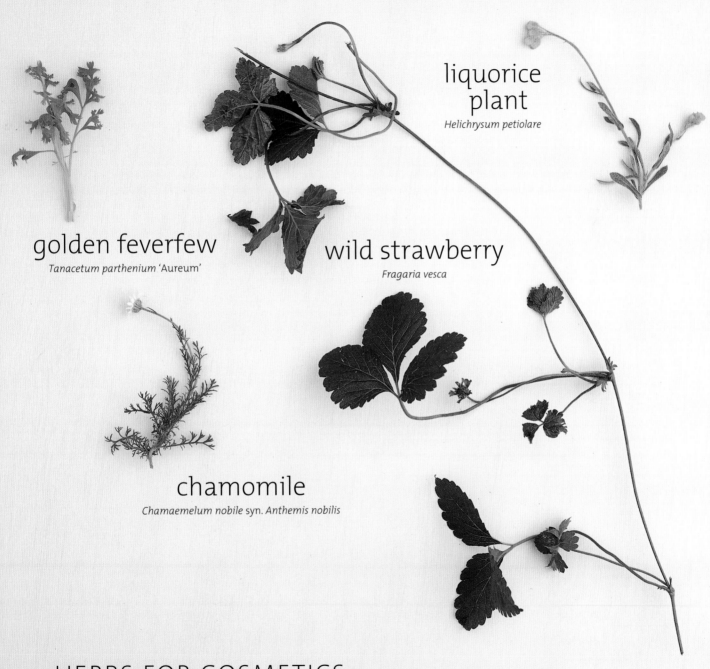

liquorice
plant
Helichrysum petiolare

golden feverfew
Tanacetum parthenium 'Aureum'

wild strawberry
Fragaria vesca

chamomile
Chamaemelum nobile syn. *Anthemis nobilis*

HERBS FOR COSMETICS
Herbs can be used to beautify our bodies. Some, such as aloe and wild strawberry fruit, are known for softening and whitening the skin. Others, such as borage, are key ingredients in facials, while fennel seed, feverfew leaves and calendula flowers make natural face cleansers.

Cosmetic recipes

Ready-made toiletries and cosmetics are welcome conveniences of 21st century life, but home-made ones are luxurious and making them can also be fun. If you are sensitive to the ingredients used in commercial preparations, making your own helps you to avoid any known irritants and allergens.

The earliest cosmetics were made at home and housekeeping manuals traditionally included recipes for head to toe care. Some of them contain ingredients we'd have difficulty finding today, but many, including those given, use simple ingredients that are still appealing.

Bath oil

Legend has it that Cleopatra enjoyed bathing in asses' milk. This would be rather difficult to arrange today, and possibly distasteful as well. A simple bathing indulgence, more attuned to our modern senses and circumstances, involves adding drops of essential oil to a hot bath.

After a busy or stressful day, add 5–10 drops of your favourite essential oil to a filled bath, then lie back and relax. Make sure the water is not too hot or the fragrance will be quickly lost.

CHILDREN'S BUBBLE BATH ➤ Place 4 tablespoons flower petals or heads (e.g. rose or lavender) in a bowl, cover them with 300 ml (10½ fl oz) boiling water and leave for approximately 15 minutes. Strain the flower water into a second bowl. Add 300 ml (10½ fl oz) bottle of baby shampoo and 12 drops essential oil (e.g. lavender). Pour the mixture into plastic bottles. Shake each bottle for several minutes. Make sure that you store any extra bottles that are not in use in a cool, dark place. Children can help make this as long as a supervising adult deals with the boiling water.

Bath bags

An aromatic herbal bath can be both pleasurable and therapeutic, especially after a busy day in the garden. Gather a square of muslin into a little bag shape, fill it with flower petals, tie the bag and hang it under the running water as you fill the bath. For example, try a mix of oatmeal and petals of rose, lavender and chamomile. The oatmeal is a gentle cleansing agent. Or experiment with fresh herbs. You can either mix them together or use each one individually.

CHAMOMILE FACE MASK ➤ A very simple face mask can be made from chamomile flowers, honey and bran. It softens the skin and leaves it feeling beautifully smooth and refreshed. Make an infusion, using 1 tablespoon dried chamomile flowers or 3 tablespoons fresh ones and 1 cup boiling water. Allow the infusion to stand for about half an hour and then strain. Warm 1 teaspoon honey in a pan and mix it with ⅓ cup of the chamomile water and 2 tablespoons bran. Spread it on your face, leave it for about 10 minutes and then wash it off.

FENNEL FACE CLEANSER ➤ This fresh mixture made from fennel seed, buttermilk and honey is a lovely way to cleanse your face naturally. Crush or roughly chop 1 tablespoon fennel seed and then pour 1 cup boiling water over it. Let it stand for about half an hour before straining it into a small bowl. Add 2 tablespoons buttermilk and 1 teaspoon honey to the fennel seed water and mix it all together. Pour the mixture into a completely clean container and refrigerate it until it is cool. Store it in the fridge and use it as needed.

FEVERFEW MOISTURISER ➤ This complexion milk acts as a moisturiser and will help to discourage blackheads and fade skin blemishes. Place ½ cup fresh feverfew leaves and 1 cup milk in a saucepan. Simmer for about 20 minutes and leave it to stand. Strain the liquid into a clean container and refrigerate. Apply it to the skin with cotton balls and let it dry. Rinse off with lukewarm water.

SCENTED CREAM ➤ Add 8 drops essential oil (e.g. lavenderor chamomile) to 50 ml (2 fl oz) unscented base cream (available from chemists). Stir well. Once open, this cream must be kept refrigerated as it does not contain any preservative.

RIGHT Lime (*Tilia* spp.) flowers.

OPPOSITE The flower heads of lavender.

AROMATHERAPY OILS IN THE BATH Essential oils and aromatherapy oils are sold in an extremely concentrated form. They are ideal bath mates when added drop by drop to running water. But their soothing qualities can turn toxic if too much is used. Never use more than 10 drops of oil in a bath.

ROSE WATER AND GLYCERINE HAND LOTION ➤ Add 150 ml (5 fl oz) rose water and 1 drop pink or yellow food colouring to 100 ml (3½ fl oz) glycerine little by little. Mix together with a hand whisk.

TANSY-LEAF SKIN FRESHENER ➤ This easy-to-make skin freshener has a strong tansy fragrance. Place 1 cup fresh tansy leaves, 1 cup water and 1 cup milk in a small saucepan and bring to the boil. Simmer for 15 minutes, then leave the mixture to cool. Strain the liquid from the saucepan into a clean container and then refrigerate it. Splash it onto your skin straight from the fridge.

Paw paw.

PAW PAW MASK FOR OILY SKIN ➤ Using a wooden spoon, rub the flesh of half a ripe paw paw (papaya) through a sieve, then add 1 tablespoon fuller's earth and 1 tablespoon natural yoghurt. Mix thoroughly, before adding 1 tablespoon orange blossom water. To use the mask, smooth it over your face and leave it for 15 minutes until it is almost dry. Break the mask up by rubbing your hands all over your face, then rinse with warm water. Finish off with a cold splash.

When used in a herbal bath, fennel (*Foeniculum vulgare*) has a stimulating effect on the skin and body.

Some home-made cosmetics (left to right): feverfew cleanser, rosemary hair rinse and some chamomile leaves.

HAIR RINSE ➤ There are a number of herbs you can use to make fragrant hair rinses. Shampoo your hair first. Chamomile rinses brighten fair hair, rosemary rinses help control greasy hair and also add shine to any hair, and sage rinses darken grey hair. Always use an old towel to dry your hair after using a herb rinse – sage, in particular, will stain the towel. Place 5 cups water and chamomile flowers, fresh rosemary tips or sage leaves in a saucepan and bring the mixture to the boil. Simmer it for 15 minutes and let it cool. The sage rinse should stand for several hours. Strain and bottle it, ready for use.

handy tip

Sterilising glass jars

To sterilise a glass jar, place it in a saucepan with enough water to cover. Bring it to the boil, then boil for five minutes. Use tongs to remove the jar. Dry it in a warm oven.

Scented herbs

Scents are extraordinarily evocative and can bring to mind memories of childhood, places or people long gone. Their power should never be underestimated. The one element that all fragrant plants require is shelter – the more sheltered the position, the stronger the scent will be.

How plants use scent

Everything in nature evolves for a reason and the fragrance in plants is no exception. Scent performs two main functions: it attracts pollinating insects and protects the plant from pests. But why do some plants have a strong fragrance while others have none at all? And why are there so many different fragrances? You can discover the answers to these questions by looking at the life cycle of the plants themselves and also the environment they inhabit – for example, bees are attracted to the colour blue, so some plants that grow in areas colonised by bees produce blue flowers and therefore have no need of scent.

Protection

Plants can use the essential oils in their leaves and stems to deter attack by pests and browsing animals. For example, ants appear to intensely dislike the scent of mint (*Mentha*) and will avoid it at all costs. Try deterring ants by growing mint near the entrances to your home.

Many highly aromatic plants, such as herbs, originate in hot, arid areas. In these conditions they protect themselves from drying out by releasing oils that remain in a vapour around the surface of the leaf. The effect is then further enhanced if the leaf is covered with hairs that can trap the vapour.

Pollination

All plants rely on pollination to ensure the continuation of the species, and the majority rely on insects. This allows cross-pollination between individual plants so that genetic material is constantly mixed and the plants that result are strong and healthy.

Scent is an important way of attracting insects. The more sheltered the location, the more the plant relies on

ABOVE Butterflies are especially attracted to shrubs with a sweet scent such as lavender (*Lavandula*), lilac (*Syringa*) and butterfly bush (*Buddleia*), and to herbaceous perennials such as pinks (*Dianthus* spp.). Here, a monarch butterfly (*Danaus plexippus*) is pollinating a butterfly bush flower.

OPPOSITE Lemon savory (*Satureja biflora*) is a lemon-scented groundcover that flowers in spring and summer.

Spearmint (*Mentha spicata*).

Leaf perfumes

The perfume of leaves is subtle compared to that of flowers. However, while a flower's perfume reduces when dried, leaf fragrance is persistent and can increase as the water evaporates, concentrating the essential oils. Some of the same oils are found in both leaves and flowers, so some leaf fragrances conform to flower scent groupings. Apple mint (*Mentha suaveolens*) smells of apples and falls into the fruit-scented group, as does clary sage (*Salvia sclarea*), a hardy biennial with leaves that smell of fresh grapefruit when bruised.

Following are the main types of leaf perfume:

- **Turpentine group** These plants have a resinous aroma – for example, that of rosemary.

- **Camphor and eucalyptus group** Plants in this group – such as sage (*Salvia officinalis*), chamomile and thyme – have a medicinal scent which clears the nasal passages.

- **Mint group** A tangy, fresh scent such as that found in mint.

- **Sulphur group** A heavy, cloying smell, as in onions and garlic.

fragrance to attract insects, since they are less likely to be conveyed on the wind. The most fragrant plants are those that grow in shaded places or flower during the night. Most night-flowering blooms open for a single night and die after fertilisation. The lower temperatures and higher humidity levels of evening and night-time trigger the release of a flower's fragrance. The heaviest fragrance occurs in white flowers and those with thick, waxy and velvety petals: thinner petals cannot retain essential oils, so the fragrance is quickly lost. The more pigment or chlorophyll present in the petal, the less oil is produced, so those flowers with little or no colour contain the most oil.

Insects and birds are involved in the pollination process, and each is attracted by a different means. The competition to attract them is fierce and some plants have developed very specific relationships with their pollinating agent. A mutual dependence can evolve so that the life cycles of both the insect or bird and plant are closely connected.

- Bees are primarily attracted by certain colours, particularly blue, and by markings that direct the insect to the centre of the flower. Blue flowers often have very little scent because the colour is sufficient to attract bees.

- Flies are attracted by disgusting smells with no appeal to other insects. Some malodorous herbs that attract flies are stinking Benjamin (*Trillium erectum*), lords-and-ladies (*Arum maculatum*) and bugbane (*Cimicifuga*).

- Many birds appear to be blue/green colour-blind; the flower colours that attract them are crimson and gold. Fragrance has no part to play.

- The few flowers that rely on beetles to pollinate them usually emit a fruity scent, such as lemon balm (*Melissa officinalis*).

OPPOSITE Potted kumquats, underplanted with lobelia, punctuate alternating clumps of lavender and violas along this pathway.

Making the most of fragrance

With some careful planning, you can enjoy scented herbs both day and night in key areas of your garden. Here are some ideas.

Paths

Whether they lead to utility areas, such as the compost bin or the garden shed, or are designed to meander through different areas of planting so you can enjoy your garden to the full, paths are an essential part of the garden. Even the dullest looking path can be enlivened with careful planting. Use an edging of fragrant, low-growing plants that can be clipped back if they start to encroach too much on the path itself. Some aromatic herbs suitable for spilling out onto paths are thyme (*Thymus*), chamomile (*Chamaemelum*), lavender, marjoram (*Origanum majorana*) and lemon balm. These herbs release fragrance when they are bruised.

Bergamot

Native to North America, bergamot (*Monarda* spp.) replaced Indian tea in many American households following the Boston Tea Party of 1773. The common name, bergamot, comes from an Italian word because the crushed leaf resembles the small bitter Italian orange that is used in aromatherapy, perfumes and cosmetics. Native Americans used bergamot for colds.

Outdoor entertaining area

If you regularly cook outdoors on a barbecue, plant a range of fragrant and delicious herbs nearby. In the heat of the day these herbs will smell wonderful as they release their essential oils into the air, and they will

In China, waterlilies are traditionally grown in large glazed pots, raised on plinths in the middle of a courtyard, allowing them to be admired without any distractions.

Special features

If you have a special feature or focal point in your garden, such as a statue or water feature, you could experiment with planting fragrant plants in order to build up the intensity of the aroma or fragrance as you approach the feature. Try not to overdo it, though: an overpowering fragrance can make it unpleasant to linger in one spot; the idea is to enhance, not compromise, your garden feature.

Choose plants whose fragrance you most enjoy, but ensure that they are suitable for the situation. For instance, try some strikingly beautiful waterlilies (*Nymphaea* spp.) – see page 44 for more information – or the pretty cinnamon-scented sweet flag (*Acorus calamus*) around a water feature.

A fragrant lawn

Low-growing, matting plants such as thyme release their fragrance when crushed underfoot, and provide an unusual cover for many situations. Here are some ideas.

- A path of pennyroyal
- Carpeting patches of thyme between stepping stones
- Corsican mint as a groundcover in a fernery
- A herbal carpet in an area too small for a lawnmower
- A spectacular carpet of thyme on a sunny bank (there are many types to choose from: creeping thyme comes in pink-, crimson- and white-flowered varieties, and there are also golden, orange-peel scented and variegated leaf types)
- A fragrant chamomile footrest beneath the garden seat.

Choose herbs that grow from stolons or runners so that they can cover any bare patch that may develop. The mint family will grow in areas with poor drainage or dappled shade, otherwise most herbs like good drainage and plenty of sun.

always be ready for you to use. If you plant a herb like mint, which repels ants, then you'll have a dual-purpose herb garden.

Typical summer herbs are dill, basil, mint, oregano and parsley; spring herbs are chives, sorrel and chervil; and typical winter herbs are sage, rosemary and thyme.

Scent at night

Some plants are scented only in the evening so that they can attract night-flying insects, such as moths. For instance, evening primrose (*Oenothera*), mignonette (*Reseda*) and sweet rocket (*Hesperis*) all smell delightful in the evening. Plant them near open windows and doors, or near an outdoor sitting area.

The carpeting thymes were favourites of Edna Walling, the Australian garden designer. *Thymus carnosus* has tiny aromatic leaves. It is slow growing and very compact, with pure white flowers in summer. 'Pink Chintz' was another of Walling's favourites. *Thymus × citriodorus* 'Silver Queen' has silver-white foliage and 'Aureus' has tiny golden yellow leaves. All carpeting thymes are deliciously fragrant when they are crushed.

Consider growing a lawn of thyme – imagine stretching out on a herb lawn, with the crushed leaves releasing their subtle perfume as you relax. Or try one of these:

- *Chamaemelum nobile*
- *Mentha requienii*
- *Chamaemelum nobile* 'Treneague'
- *Thymus praecox*
- *Mentha arvensis*
- *Thymus pseudolanuginosus*
- *Mentha pulegium*
- *Vinca minor*.

Success with a herb lawn

1 To prepare a herb lawn, first remove all weeds from the site, then use a product containing glyphosate to poison any that have bulbs so they won't reappear.

2 Plant your herb lawn in a well drained soil that is rich in humus, or dig in plenty of compost or manure.

3 Rake the soil to a level finish and plant herbs 20 cm (8 in) apart.

4 Water well and refrain from walking on the lawn for about one month or until the plants are established.

5 Weed regularly and plant any bare patches with rooted pieces from well grown plants.

PLANTING A HERB CARPET

1 Position your chosen herbs until you are happy with the result, then dig a hole for each herb and plant it. Backfill with soil.

2 Finish with pebble mulch and water in.

3 Granite sets provide an attractive foil for the carpeting herbs.

Fragrant hedges

A garden hedge is more than just a boundary to a property, keeping out unwanted animals and people, and providing privacy. A hedge can also be used as the 'skeleton' of your landscape, helping to create garden rooms for you to decorate, conceal utility areas and unsightly views, and act as a windbreak.

Whether you are planting a low hedge for edging a path or a tall one to act as a privacy screen and property boundary, you can add another dimension to your living fence by choosing fragrant plants. Lavender, for instance, has a bushy habit that makes it ideal for growing as a fragrant hedge in an informal garden. However, it doesn't respond well to excessive pruning, making it unsuitable for a formal hedge. Some alternatives to lavender are rosemary, cotton lavender and salvia, which also make good low, informal hedges.

If you are growing a hedge for its aromatic leaves, you can prune it regularly to maintain the shape without affecting the production of fragrance. If you have selected a particular hedging plant because of its flowers, however, the timing is critical: the buds and flowers should not be removed before their best display.

Pruning hedges

Hedges require regular trimming to keep them looking good. Start trimming from the bottom so that the clippings fall clear. A hedge should be wider at the base than at the top. This allows vital light to reach all parts. Hedge trimmers and shears give more control, especially if you want a particular shape. Don't use a mechanical

This low-growing hedge surrounding a small lawn combines rosemary and cotton lavender.

How to plant a hedge

1 For a really straight hedge, mark out the run with a string line. Dig a trench at least 60 cm (2 ft) wide and 45 cm (18 in) deep.

2 Incorporate lots of well rotted manure or compost. Fill in the trench. This will create a small mound.

3 Using a measuring stick, space out all the plants. Dig a hole for each plant, add some slow-release fertiliser and water crystals, and plant, ensuring that the soil is not built up around the trunks.

4 Tip prune all new shoots to encourage branching. Do this for the first few seasons so that you develop a well branched hedge that is thick to the base.

5 Trim the hedge to shape. Secateurs allow precise cutting and are suitable for pruning all informal hedges. They are ideal for the initial shaping of young plants. For larger plants in an informal hedge, use shears: they produce the best shape and leave the foliage unmarked. They can also be used on formal hedges for a perfect, but time-consuming cut, or you can use electric hedge trimmers in slow, even cuts.

pruner on large-leafed plants as it damages the leaves
If your hedge has grown out of control, check that your
particular type of shrub will reshoot after pruning. Start
by cutting the top of the hedge first, then one side. Wait
until that side has greened up before you prune the
other side.

Remember to regularly feed your hedge and mulch it
to keep it looking good for years to come.

handy tip

*To get the best effect from a fragrant hedge,
grow it in a formal design, keeping it quite
closely clipped to the desired height and outline.
Trim the plants at least once a year, or more
often for the more vigorous herb varieties.*

Lavender hedges were once used as clotheslines: laundered items
were placed on the bushes to dry, and in the process they became
impregnated with lavender oil.

 *FRAGRANT ROOTS Several herbs have fragrant
roots, although the scent is not detectable unless
you dig up the plant. Avens (Geum urbanum) is a
herbaceous perennial with short, thick rhizomatous
roots that smell of cloves when they are dried.
Chocolate root (Geum rivale) is moisture loving
and has thick, rhizomatous roots that smell of
chocolate. Sweet flag (Acorus calamus) roots
produce a camphor-like smell and was once used as
a strewing herb for floors.*

scented-leaf
geranium
Pelargonium 'Graveolens'

heliotrope
Heliotropium arborescens

curry plant
Helichrysum angustifolium
syn. *H. italicum*

rosemary
Rosmarinus officinalis

white heliotrope
Heliotropium arborescens 'White Lady'

pink
creeping thyme
Thymus serpyllum 'Pink Chintz'

pink thyme
Thymus x citriodorus

french
lavender
Lavandula dentata

floral and herb pot pourri

citrus-scented pot pourri

lavender and herb pot pourri

POT POURRI
You can make wonderful pot pourris from herbs, usually combined with rose petals or geranium leaves. With so many herbs to choose from, you can customise a pot pourri for any part of your home. For example, you could have a warm mixture in the hallway or a sweeter bedroom bouquet. Herbs such as lavender, violet, rosemary, basil, mint, sage, thyme, cinnamon, clove, juniper and star anise are all favourites.

LEFT AND BELOW Experiment with different materials. If you don't like sweet fragrances, a citrus pot pourri may appeal to you.

Pot pourri recipes

Here are some recipes to get you started. Once you've mastered the basic principles of making pot pourri, you can try out different combinations, depending on what you grow in your own garden.

Dry pot pourri

Use dried flowers, leaves, berries, spices, peel or bark to make dry pot pourri mixtures. You'll need a fixative to preserve the blend. Fixatives are available as powders and are often perfumed, which you should take into account when choosing your ingredients. The most common fixative is orris root, which has a violet scent. Use it in a ratio of about 1 tablespoon of orris root to every 1 cup of plant material. Essential oils are ideal for refreshing pot pourri but add only a few drops at a time or the fragrance will be overpowering. You can purchase fixatives and essential oils from health food shops, some Asian supermarkets and some craft shops.

HERB AND LAVENDER POT POURRI ➤ Mix 1 cup lavender flowers (*Lavandula angustifolia*), ½ cup dried spearmint (*Mentha spicata*), ½ cup dried marjoram (*Origanum majorana*), ½ cup dried oregano flowers (*Origanum vulgare*), 2 tablespoons powdered orris root and 2 teaspoons lavender essential oil together, then place the mixture in a plastic bag for 2 weeks to mature. Shake regularly. Transfer to an ornamental bowl.

FLORAL AND HERB POT POURRI ➤ Place ½ cup rose petals, ¼ cup violets, ½ cup marigold flowers, ½ cup lavender, ¼ cup cornflowers and ¼ cup sweet mixed herbs in a bowl and gently mix them together with a wooden spoon, being careful not to break the flower petals. Place 1 tablespoon orris root powder and 2 teaspoons cinnamon powder in another bowl and, using an eyedropper, add 5 drops rose oil, 3 drops lavender oil and 2 drops lemon oil. Mix everything together thoroughly. Add the orris root and cinnamon mixture to the dried materials and stir with a wooden spoon. Place in a brown paper bag, fold over the top and fasten with a clothes peg. Store in a cool, dark place for 2–4 weeks, shaking the bag gently every few days to blend the ingredients. It should then be ready for use.

LEMON-SCENTED POT POURRI ➤ Mix 4 cups lemon verbena leaves, 1 cup lemon-scented geranium leaves, ½ cup basil and ½ cup lemon thyme together. Mix ½ cup dried lemon peel (freshly ground) and ½ cup dried orange peel (freshly ground) with ½ cup caraway seeds. Tear 1 cup oakmoss into small pieces, place in a bowl and add 2 drops lemon verbena oil and 2 drops bergamot oil. Rub the oil through the oakmoss, then mix thoroughly with the leaves, peel and seeds. Place in an airtight container for about a month, stirring occasionally. It will then be ready for use.

Herbs for household use

For thousands of years, herbs have been used in households as fabric dyes, insect repellents and air fresheners, even furniture polishes and general cleaners. Try out some of these safe, non-toxic recipes using herbs from your own garden.

Fabric dyes

Before synthetic dyes were developed in the 19th century, dyes were made from plants, animals, insects and minerals. For instance, red fabrics from Tutankhamen's tomb that have been chemically analysed show the presence of alizarin, a pigment extracted from madder (*Rubia tinctorum*). The plants were dug up, and the roots were washed and dried before being ground into a powder. By the 19th century the most widely available fabrics were dyed with madder, known as 'turkey red'. Madder was used until the late 19th century when synthetic dyes were developed.

By the fourth century AD, other plant dyes – such as woad (*Isatis tinctoria*), weld and indigo – were in use. Purple dye was once extracted from a Mediterranean mollusc called a purple fish (*Murex*), found near Tyre in Phoenicia in the Mediterranean. This dye was so expensive only royalty could afford it, hence the association of purple robes with kings and queens.

Until the Middle Ages, woad was used in Europe to dye fabric blue. The leaves were dried and ground, then mixed with water to make a paste. By the 1630s, woad

*SAFFRON The Romans prized saffron highly and used it in cooking, dyeing and in oils. Saffron is the dried stigma of the autumn crocus (*Crocus sativus*), which flowers only in hot, dry weather. It is expensive, as more than 70,000 blooms are needed to produce just 500 g (1 lb 2oz) of saffron. The Romans liked to show off their wealth by strewing saffron on the floors of their villas.*

was replaced by indigo; the leaves were fermented and the sediment purified. The material remaining was made into chunks or 'cakes'. Indigo was a popular dye because it was colour fast to both washing and light, and being a substantive dye, it did not need
a mordant in order to fix the colour. The manufacture of indigo lasted until the early 1900s: in 1905 the scientist who developed aspirin, Adolf von Baeyer, won the Nobel Prize for developing a process which produced indigo synthetically.

If you want to experiment with dyes using herbs from your own garden, try some of these ideas.

- Pink: strawberries, raspberries, cherries
- Green: spinach leaves, grass
- Red: dandelion root, beets, rose hips, red onion skins, madder

handy tip

Boil 8 cloves in 2 cups of water for a few minutes to rid the kitchen of an offensive cooking smell.

- Blue/purple: red cabbage, elderberries, blueberries, cherry roots
- Yellow: onion skins, marigold blossoms, celery leaves
- Brown: sumac leaves, walnut hulls, tea, juniper berries, coffee grinds.

Air fresheners

These days flowers and aromatic herbs are popular in pot pourris and linen sachets, but they were once used as 'strewing' herbs. The Koran mentions that the floor of the Garden of Paradise is covered with wheaten flour mixed with musk and saffron. In medieval Europe, the packed earth floors and small windows of the times meant that buildings and churches smelled musty, so fragrant seasonal flowers, herbs and sweet-smelling grasses and rushes were strewn on the pews and floors. Herbs were particularly useful for strewing as they released their fragrance when someone walked on them, crushing the leaves. Thyme repelled unpleasant odours, and wormwood deterred fleas. So important was this aspect of domestic life that royal households had an official 'Strewer of Herbs'.

The scented rush (*Acorus calamus*) had many uses in addition to strewing: it also yielded a volatile oil from the leaves, and the root could be used to flavour beer and wine, or could be dried and powdered for use as talcum powder.

Other plants were used only for their repellent qualities. Dried tansy flowers were sprinkled on pantry shelves in order to deter flies. Green rushes strewn on the floors could attract fleas and other insects, therefore it was customary to burn repellents such as fleabane to avoid infestation.

Pomanders were another popular device for warding off disease, and Elizabethan pomanders consisted of an apple, orange or lemon stuck with cloves and then dried, or a container with a sponge soaked in scented vinegar. Later, silver pomanders were fashioned, based on the orange, with filigree segments hinged at the base and held by a clasp at the top, each of which could hold a separate perfume.

LEFT The autumn crocus (*Crocus sativus*). Each flower has three, distinctive red stigmas.

RIGHT A pomander could also be used to disguise unpleasant smells, from overpowering body odours to streets with open sewage drains.

Scented sachets

Fragrant sachets in drawers and wardrobes not only make your clothes smell fresh, but they also help deter moths and silverfish. Here are some suggestions that are quick and easy to make.

- To add a fresh smell to your wardrobe or chest of drawers, take a couple of teaspoons of pot pourri or dried lavender, place in a piece of lightweight fabric, such as muslin or cheesecloth, and tie with a ribbon.
- Or fill light sachets with mixtures of ground cloves, nutmeg, mace, caraway seeds, cinnamon (30 g or 1 oz each) and orris root powder (90 g or 3¼ oz).

POMANDER ➤ Wash and dry a firm-skinned orange and stud it evenly all over with fresh cloves. Place 1 teaspoon orris root powder and 1 teaspoon ground cinnamon in a brown paper bag with the orange, and shake the bag to coat the orange. Store the bag in a dark place for a month, then remove the orange and brush it free of powder. Tie a ribbon around the orange and finish with a loop at the top.

DYEING HERBS

Using natural plant dyes is an art. The delight of harvesting berries and leaves, and mashing, chopping and boiling like an alchemist can only be understood once you've experienced it, and the satisfaction of watching these concoctions turn fabric into colour swatches is well worth the time.

elderberry
Sambucus nigra

sorrel
Rumex scutatus

juniper berries
Juniperus spp.

comfrey
Symphytum officinale

chamomile

Chamaemelum nobile syn. *Anthemis nobilis*

st john's wort

Hypericum spp.

dianella

Dianella spp.

onion skins

Allium cepa

marigold flowers

Tagetes spp.

LAVENDER BAG ➤ The essential oil of lavender kills germs and provides fragrance. Put lavender sachets or bags in a drawer to prevent the contents from becoming musty. This lavender bag will retain its scent longer if you keep the stalks on. Cut lavender in full bloom and spread the stems out to dry on newspaper, either in the sun or in another warm place. Cut fabric, such as muslin or fine cotton, to the size and shape required for a bag. When the lavender is dry, insert a bunch into the bag so that the stems stick out of the opening. Close the opening with hand stitching or a length of ribbon. Trim stalks to a length of 4 cm (1$^1\!/_2$ in).

MOTH SACHET ➤ A sachet filled with this mixture will repel moths for up to a year. Make several and tuck them among your woollen clothes and stored blankets. Crumble 1 cup rosemary, 1 cup tansy, 1 cup thyme, 1 cup mint and 1 cup southernwood together and mix with $^1\!/_2$ cup cloves (freshly ground) and $^1\!/_2$ cup dried lemon peel (freshly ground). Spoon the mixture into sachets and tie with a ribbon.

ABOVE Herbal moth deterrents include sachets of cedar chips, dried rosemary or southernwood (*Artemisia abrotanum*), pictured here. Place these fragrant herbs among your clothes. If these cause irritation you may need to store vulnerable clothing in sealed plastic bags.

BELOW Rose-scented geranium leaves add a sweet perfume to a pot pourri mixture.

Pyrethrum

Many modern insecticides are now synthesised
forms of pyrethrum. To make your own
spray, follow these steps. Use the mixture as
needed as a contact spray for aphids and other
sapsuckers. Other foul-tasting concoctions can
be made from chilli, garlic, wormwood and
quassia chips.

1   Finely chop the flowers and leaves of the
    pyrethrum daisy.

2   Immerse them in water overnight.

3   Strain the water through a muslin cloth
    and store it in a container. Spray it on
    plants as required.

HERB PILLOW ➤ Some herbs are thought to
promote peaceful sleep and sweet dreams, and
so a pillow filled with sleep-inducing herbs can
be a practical addition to your bedroom. Place
the mixture in a muslin sachet and tuck it into
the pillowcase with your usual pillow. Mix 1 cup
dried rosemary, 1 cup dried lavender, 1 cup dried
lemon verbena, 1 cup dried lemon thyme and
3 cups dried scented geranium leaves together in
a large bowl. If you like, add a preservative such
as orris root and a drop or two of essential oil.

Herbal insecticides

Many herbs have properties that make them
useful for repelling pests. The naturally occurring
insecticide pyrethrum is made from the dried
flower heads of *Chrysanthemum cinerarifolium*
and *C. coccineum*. Other plants with pungent oils
that can deter pests are garlic, lavender and rue.
The spicy heat of the chilli pepper can be used
effectively to deter animal and insect pests.

CHILLI AND SOAP SPRAY

1   Gather the ingredients
    and materials you'll need:
    chillies, soap, grater, sharp
    knife and chopping board.
    You'll also need a spray
    bottle and some water.

2   Grate some soap (or use
    pure soap flakes instead).
    Add soap flakes to a spray
    bottle that is nearly full
    of water.

3   Chop about 8 chillies. Add
    the chillies to the bottle
    and screw the lid back
    on. Shake the contents
    vigorously and spray your
    home-made insecticide
    onto any plant.

Warning: It's important to
wash your hands thoroughly
after handling chillies.

RUE A sturdy evergreen herb with blue metallic, feathery leaves, rue (Ruta graveolens) is useful as a disinfectant and as an insecticide. In medieval Europe, rue was used in the sickroom to drive away disease-carrying insects. Plant it by doors and windows to repel mosquitoes, flies and other insects, and rub it over pets to help reduce fleas.

handy tip

Chilli tea

For a spicy insecticide or as a deterrent to rabbits and other animals, use a food blender to purée 20 or so chillies to form a paste. Mix the paste with water, then leave it to stand so the pulp can settle. Use the strained 'tea' as a spray on a still day so that it won't blow into your eyes.

step by step

CHIVE TEA

Make your own chive 'tea' for treating mildew on plants.

1 Harvest a generous amount of chives from your vegetable garden, or buy some. Roughly chop the chives.

2 Add the chives to a watering can. Cover with boiling water and steep for at least 1 hour before using.

To remove the smell of onions from your hands, rub them well with celery or parsley.

ALL-PURPOSE INSECTICIDE ➤ You can make an all-purpose insecticide for spraying any plants plagued by caterpillars, aphids or flea beetles. Combine equal quantities of mint, chopped onion, garlic and lavender tops and stems in enough water to cover. Leave the mixture for 24 hours, then strain it.

GARLIC SPRAY ➤ Use this garlic spray for aphids, mites and small caterpillars. Garlic also provides some fungicide protection. Soak 12–15 chopped garlic bulbs in 2 tablespoons mineral oil for 24 hours. Dissolve 7 g (¼ oz) soap in 600 ml (21 fl oz) water and slowly add it to the garlic mixture. Strain the mixture through fine gauze, before storing it in a china or glass container. Dilute it before using – 1 part soap and garlic mixture to 50 parts water.

Diluted tea tree oil keeps the toilet brush and bowl germ-free.

Cleaning preparations

Essential oils are used in cleaning preparations for both their fragrance and their disinfecting qualities.

BASIC HOUSEHOLD SOAP CLEANER ➤ Grate 100 g (3½ oz) pure soap into a large saucepan and cover with 2 L (3½ pints) of cold water. Bring to the boil, add 1 cup washing soda crystals and stir until dissolved. Stir in 3 teaspoons eucalyptus oil or tea tree oil, 1 cup white vinegar and a few drops lemon or lavender essential oil for fragrance. Pour into a bucket, add 9 L (16 pints) hot water then stir in 10 L (18 pints) cold water. When cool, transfer to smaller containers and label.

Use this versatile cleaner in the following ways.
Laundry detergent ➤ Suitable for machine washing or hand washing, for front loaders and top loaders. Use about 2 cups per load.
Prewash ➤ Soak heavily soiled items in a solution before washing.
Washing up liquid ➤ Make up a solution of 1 teaspoon to 5 L (9 pints) of water.
Dishwasher detergent ➤ Use 1 cup per load. (Note: It doesn't remove tea and coffee stains.)
Carpet or upholstery stain-removing foam ➤ Add 1 cup of hot water. When cool, beat to a light foam and spoon over the stain. Leave it for 10 minutes then wipe with a sponge dipped in white vinegar.

ALL-PURPOSE SPRAY CLEANER ➤ This cleaner is suitable for the kitchen and bathroom. In a bucket, mix 2 tablespoons cloudy ammonia, ½ cup white vinegar, 2 tablespoons baking soda, 2 drops lavender or lemon oil and 2 tablespoons basic household soap cleaner into 4 L (7 pints) hot water. Cool, then fill spray bottles.

7

Eat the garden

Eat the garden

The fruits of your labour finally make it to the dinner table. Your herbs are fragrant and your vegetables fresh and juicy, with all the advantages of flavour and nutrition that home growing provides. You will definitely feel it was well worth the effort.

Cooking with herbs

Culinary herbs are so versatile that you can use the leaves, flowers, seeds and stems of this group of plants in a bewildering array of dishes from all over the world. Particular herbs suit different styles of cooking and every cuisine has its favourites.

Most herbs are best when fresh. Buy them cut or grow them in pots on the windowsill or in the garden. If fresh herbs are unavailable, use dried, but these are often more concentrated in flavour (unless, of course, they are stale) and you only need to use half or less of the quantity specified for fresh herbs. In some cuisines, dried herbs are preferred – for example, the Greeks prefer dried oregano (rigani).

Obviously you can use herbs at any time, but the type of recipe they suit often depends on the time of year. Typical summer herbs are basil, dill, mint, oregano and parsley; spring herbs are chives, sorrel and chervil; sage, rosemary and thyme often suit winter dishes.

Boil artichokes with the juice of 1 lemon for 40 minutes. Serve with a vinaigrette of lemon juice, olive oil, finely chopped onion and finely chopped parsley.

The leaves, seeds and roots of coriander all have distinct culinary uses, and are often found in Asian dishes.

Scented-leaf geranium.

Storing culinary herbs

- Herbs sold in plastic boxes or cellophane bags keep well in them.
- Put loose herbs in plastic bags and store them in the vegetable crisper of the fridge. Herbs with more robust leaves will keep longer than those with more fragile ones.
- Big bunches of mint, parsley and coriander will keep in a jug of water for a few days. Remember to change the water daily.
- You can preserve fresh herbs by setting sprigs into ice cubes.

Cooking tips for herbs

When you crush, chop or heat the leaves of a herb, an oil is released, and it is this oil that imparts flavour.

- Chop herbs with scissors, a flat knife or a mezzaluna. Chop large bunches of more robust herbs like parsley in the food processor.
- Fine herbs, such as tarragon and chives, can be left in large pieces, shredded or snipped.
- Coarse herbs such as rosemary and parsley benefit from fine chopping.
- Flavour vinaigrette or mayonnaise by finely chopping or pounding the herbs in a mortar and pestle, then add the rest of the ingredients.
- Herbs such as basil, coriander and sage discolour if they are chopped too early before use.
- Whole leaves of mint or basil can be steeped in water to make 'tea'. Crush them gently in your hand first to release the aromatic oils.

Agar-agar

Agar-agar (pictured above) is a flavourless vegetarian gelling agent made from seaweed. It is used to set ice cream, Asian desserts and jellies. Foods set with agar-agar will remain set at room temperature, which is a useful attribute in hot weather, unlike those containing gelatine. Desserts that have a high acidic content, such as lemon jelly, may need more agar-agar before they will set. Agar-agar flakes, strands, powder or blocks are sold in health food and Asian shops.

Angelica

The angelica variety of most interest to cooks is *Angelica archangelica*, an aromatic herb that resembles a tall parsley plant. It is native to the northern hemisphere and grows well in Scotland, Germany, Scandinavia and Russia, but can be cultivated in warmer climes. In medieval times, it was thought to be an antidote to poison. According to one legend, the Archangel Raphael was supposed to have revealed in a dream that angelica was a cure for the plague.

Today, angelica is regarded more for its culinary qualities: the fresh stems and leaves are used as a flavouring for pastries, confectionery and liqueurs; oil from the seeds and roots is used in the preparation of liqueurs; and the leaves are used fresh in salads. Angelica's most popular use is in cake decoration, where its green stalks are blanched, peeled and boiled, then candied in sugar to produce a vivid green colour.

Annatto

Annatto is a bright orange food colouring, which is extracted from the dark red, triangular seeds of a small tree (*Bixa orellana*), native to South America. Although the seed is edible, it has little flavour and its culinary value lies more in its colouring properties. Also known as achuete and anchiote, annatto is used as a colouring agent in Filipino, South American, Southeast Asian and Caribbean cooking. Usually the seeds are fried in oil or lard and then discarded, and the remaining yellow fat is used to fry vegetables or meat to give them a golden yellow colour.

When ground into a powder or paste, annatto is used to colour butter, margarine and smoked fish. Washed-rind cheeses, such as Livarot, are sometimes dipped in annatto colouring to deepen the colour of their rind, while the colouring of some cheeses, such as Red Leicester, is also enhanced with annatto.

Cupcakes decorated with strips of candied angelica.

Arrowroot

A starch powder obtained from the root of a tropical plant (*Maranta arundinacea*), arrowroot is used as a thickening agent. It is tasteless and the fine powder becomes clear when cooked, making it useful for thickening clear sauces. Arrowroot must be slaked (mixed with a small amount of water to form a smooth paste) before it is mixed with a hot liquid for use in sauces, puddings or pie fillings. Heat the sauce only until thick and remove it immediately, as overcooking will cause it to thin again.

Bay leaf

The glossy green leaves of an evergreen tree (*Laurus nobilis*), bay leaves are used to add a strong, slightly peppery flavour to many dishes. The bay leaf was probably introduced into Europe by the Romans, who held the bay tree in high esteem: they used it to make laurel wreaths to crown their poets as well as their athletic and military victors. The berries of the bay tree and the leaves of other laurels (such as the bay rum tree) are poisonous.

The flavour of bay leaves goes well with fish, lamb, marinades, pork, potato, soup and tomato.

handy tip

Making a bouquet garni

Wrap the green part of a leek around a bay leaf, a sprig of thyme, a sprig of parsley and celery leaves. Tie the bundle with string, leaving it long at one end for easy removal. Vary the herbs to suit the dish.

Bay leaves can be used fresh or dried, and are usually removed before the dish is served. Add one or two to the pot to enhance stews or stuffings, add to a bouquet garni, insert a leaf under chicken skin, use to flavour rice, or add to the milk infusions used in baked custards or béchamel sauce.

Fresh bay leaves have a stronger flavour than dried. Wash fresh leaves well and store them in the fridge for up to three days. Dried bay leaves will keep in an airtight container for up to six months.

Bouquet garni

Used for flavouring sauces, stews, soups or stocks, a bouquet garni is a bundle of herbs tied together with string. It should be removed at the end of cooking so, to make this easier, tie the end of the string to the handle of the saucepan. If you are using dried herbs or peppercorns, first wrap them in muslin and tie off with some string.

Chrysanthemum greens

The young leaves are used in salads and stir-fries and the edible flowers are used in Chinese cooking. Chrysanthemum greens are also known as chop suey greens and garland chrysanthemum.

Edible flowers

The use of edible flowers in cooking is a tradition that dates back several centuries in Europe. Flowers can be added to food merely as decoration, or to give it texture, flavour and colour. Always confirm the identity of the flower and check it is edible before use. Take care that any flower used as food – wild or cultivated – has not been sprayed with poisonous chemicals.

Some flowers used in cooking are roses, violets, marjoram, lavender, mint, oregano, fennel, marigold and nasturtium. Add marigold and nasturtium to salads, but toss them in after you have added the vinegar dressing or they will turn brown.

Jamaica flower or rosella

Not to be confused with the ornamental hibiscus plant that grows in tropical areas worldwide, Jamaica flower (*Hibiscus sabdariffa*) is a tropical and subtropical plant grown for its enlarged, fleshy, deep red sepals. The sepals are edible, slightly tart in flavour and may be bought fresh, dried or frozen. When dried, they may be infused in teas; used fresh, they may be cooked into jams or a sauce similar to cranberry sauce. In the West Indies, the flower is used to make wine. It also adds colour and flavour when mixed with rum and spices to make drinks. In Mexico, the Jamaica flower is used to make a drink by infusing the flower in boiling water, then adding sugar.

Lavender

Apart from being universally recognised as an ornamental shrub, with its silver foliage and unmistakable perfume, lavender can also be used to great effect in the kitchen. The flowers of lavender

Jamaica flower (*Hibiscus sabdariffa*).

can be used fresh or dried to impart their scent to sugar or ice cream. Crystallised flowers can also be used as wonderful embellishments on cakes.

Rose

Rose petals can be boiled in water or sugar syrup and used to flavour food, or crystallised and used for decoration. All rose petals are edible as long as they haven't been sprayed with any chemicals. Rose-water, made from a distillation of petals, is used in the Middle East and India to flavour dishes such as Turkish delight, baklava and lassi. It gives a sweet fragrance to curries and rice dishes. The thicker, sticky sugar syrup is used in Middle Eastern sweets and pastries.

ROSE SUGAR SYRUP ➤ Put 500 g (1 lb 2 oz) caster sugar in a heavy-based saucepan. Add 1 cup water and 2 teaspoons lemon juice. Bring the mixture to the boil, stirring frequently. When the sugar has all dissolved, reduce the heat and simmer for about 10 minutes, or until the mixture is syrupy. Do not stir while the liquid is simmering. Stir in 1 tablespoon rose-water, then remove from the heat and cool.
➤ Makes 500 ml (17 fl oz)

Saffron

Saffron is the orange-red stigma of one species of the crocus plant (*Crocus sativus*), and the most expensive spice in the world. Each flower consists of three stigmas, which are hand-picked, then dried – a labour-intensive process. Its flavour is pungent and aromatic, and its colour intense, so only a little is used. It gives flavour and colour to such dishes as bouillabaisse, paella, risotto and pilaf. Saffron is sold in both powdered and thread form (the whole stigma). But beware – there is no such thing as cheap saffron. The best comes from Spain, Iran and Kashmir.

Cooking saffron Saffron threads are usually soaked in warm water, stock or milk for a few minutes to infuse. The mixture is then either strained or added, with the threads, to the dish. The threads can also be added at the end of cooking.

lemon grass
Cymbogon citratus

thai basil
Ocimum basilicum 'Anise'

perennial coriander
Eryngium foetidum

vietnamese mint
Polygonum odoratum

curry leaf plant
Murraya koenigii

lemon basil
Ocimum basilicum 'Sweet Dani'.

ASIAN HERBS

Asian herbs have experienced a surge in popularity with gardeners, just as various Asian cuisines have in restaurants. It is now easy to buy Thai basil, coriander, Vietnamese mint and perilla to use as fresh foliage; chillies, kaffir lime, lemon grass, curry leaf plant, curry plant and cardamom for pepping up dishes; and the wonderful root herbs such as galangal, ginger and turmeric for authentic flavour. Bear in mind that many of these tropical herbs are annuals in temperate climates and need frost protection in winter.

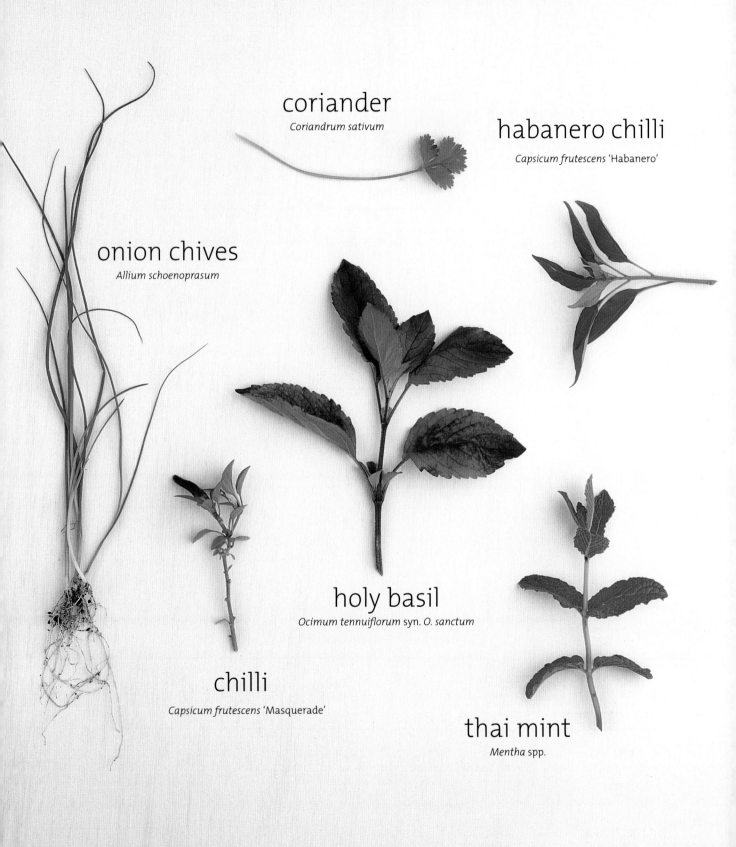

coriander
Coriandrum sativum

habanero chilli
Capsicum frutescens 'Habanero'

onion chives
Allium schoenoprasum

holy basil
Ocimum tennuiflorum syn. *O. sanctum*

chilli
Capsicum frutescens 'Masquerade'

thai mint
Mentha spp.

Salade lyonnaise.

SALADE LYONNAISE ➤ Tear 2 handfuls dandelion leaves into pieces and place them in a large bowl. Fry 4 rashers streaky bacon, cut into pieces, and add to the leaves. Cut 2 slices bread into cubes and fry in the bacon pan to make croutons, then add to the salad. Make a vinaigrette dressing and add 1 teaspoon mustard, then toss through the salad. Poach 4 eggs and serve on top. ➤ Serves 4.

Elderberry

The elderberry is the tart red, purple or black fruit of the elder tree (*Sambucus nigra*). Elderberries can be eaten raw but their slight sourness makes them better suited to being cooked in jams, pies or in wine. The creamy white, honey-scented flowers are also edible and can be used to flavour cordials or sorbets; infused in tea; used as decoration in salads; or dipped in batter and deep-fried.

ELDERFLOWER CORDIAL ➤ Make a sugar syrup by boiling 2 L (3½ pints) water with 1 kg (2 lb 4 oz) sugar until the sugar dissolves and the syrup thickens slightly (the syrup will feel greasy when you rub your finger and thumb together). Pour the syrup onto 6 elderflower heads in a glass container and leave to steep overnight. Strain and add lemon juice to taste, and keep bottled in the fridge for a few days. Dilute with water, if necessary. ➤ Makes 2 L (3½ pints)

Left to right, dried elderflower, and elderflower jelly and cordial.

Dandelion

The dandelion usually seen in supermarkets and used as a salad green is a cultivated version of the wild variety. The younger, tender leaves of wild dandelion (*Taraxacum officinale*) are edible too, but only if you're sure they haven't been treated with pesticides. Cook the leaves like spinach or use them raw in salads, dressed with a strong-flavoured oil such as hazelnut or olive oil. The word 'dandelion' is derived from the French *dents de lion*, 'lion's teeth', referring to its jagged leaves. In France, it's called *pissenlit* or 'wet-the-bed', on account of the plant's diuretic qualities.

Galangal lasts for months in the fridge.

Galangal

A spicy root, similar to ginger in appearance and preparation, galangal (*Alpinia galanga*) is used in Southeast Asian cooking, especially in Thailand, Indonesia and Malaysia. There are two types. The most widely known is greater galangal from Indonesia, a knobbly root with creamy white flesh and a delicate peppery ginger flavour. Lesser galangal, from south China, is smaller, with an orange-red flesh and a pungent and more peppery flavour.

Galangal has a tougher, woodier texture than ginger and needs to be chopped finely before use. Cut it into thin slices and add it to soup, and use it in curry pastes or in recipes that call for ginger. Buy galangal with pinker stems as these are fresher than the browner ones. Galangal is also available dried, ground or in brine – in which form it is easier to use.

Ginger

Ginger is the knobbly, beige-coloured rhizome of a tropical plant (*Zingiber officinale*). Ginger is indigenous to Southeast Asia, but is now grown all over the world in tropical climates. It was originally used in Europe in powdered, dried, crystallised or preserved form, but as Chinese, Indian, Middle Eastern and Caribbean cooking spread, ginger became increasingly available and can now be bought fresh year-round.

Store fresh ginger in the fridge tightly wrapped in plastic wrap. Unless it is extremely fresh, ginger is usually first peeled, then grated or sliced. If it's fibrous, it may be easier to grate it, preferably with a bamboo or ceramic grater.

Ginger goes well with coconut milk, coriander, garlic, lemon, lime juice, pear, rhubarb, soy sauce and spring onion.

Types of ginger

FRESH At its best when young and juicy – the root is covered in a tender skin and has a sweet, peppery flavour. As ginger gets older, the flavour strengthens but the flesh becomes more fibrous. Add to curries or Asian dishes.

GROUND (POWDERED) Mainly used in baked goods such as gingerbread, ginger cake and biscuits.

PRESERVED AND CRYSTALLISED Pieces of ginger that have been boiled in sugar syrup to preserve them. Crystallised ginger is then removed from the syrup. Use in baking, or drizzle the syrup on ice cream or fruit.

PICKLED Thin slices of young ginger, pickled and often dyed pink. This form is eaten as a palate cleanser between pieces of sushi.

MIOGA A close relative of ginger that is noted for its fragrant buds and stems, mioga is sliced thinly and used to garnish or give flavour to soups, tempura and sashimi.

GINGERBREAD MEN ➤ Mix 350 g (12 oz) plain flour with 2 teaspoons ground ginger and 1 teaspoon bicarbonate of soda. Rub in 115 g (4 oz) butter and add 150 g (5½ oz) dark brown sugar, 1 beaten egg and 4 tablespoons golden syrup. Mix to a dough. Cover and chill for 30 minutes. Roll out the dough to 5 mm (¼ in) thick, then cut out the men with a cutter. Push currants in the dough for the eyes. Bake at 220°C (425°F) for 8–10 minutes. Cool and decorate with glacé icing.
➤ This recipe makes about 20 men.

Clockwise from bottom left, ginseng root, ginseng tea, tea granules and ginseng drink.

BELOW Fresh horseradish and horesradish cream

Ginseng

Ginseng (*Panax ginseng*) is an aromatic root found in Asia and North America. In the past, it was thought that its human-like shape was a sign that it was a remedy for ailments afflicting all parts of the body. Ginseng is still widely recognised for its health-giving properties. The Chinese consider it to be 'the root of life' and add it to soups. In Korea it is infused for tea.

Horseradish

A plant cultivated for its pungent, spicy root, horseradish (*Armoracia rusticana*) is generally grated – the greatest concentration of flavour is just under the skin – and used as a condiment or in sauces. Folded into cream, horseradish makes a good accompaniment to roast beef, but also goes well with smoked fish and other meats. The young leaves can be used in salads. When not available fresh, it can be bought bottled or dried. Once peeled, it can be stored for a few days in vinegar.

HORSERADISH CREAM ➤ Lightly whisk 150 ml (5 fl oz) double cream. Fold in 2 tablespoons grated fresh or bottled horseradish, 2 teaspoons lemon juice, a pinch of salt and sugar. Don't overwhisk the cream as the acid from the lemon juice and horseradish will act as a thickener – if the cream is heavily whisked from the start, it may separate.
➤ Makes about 185 ml (6 fl oz).

Popular kitchen herbs

Basil

There are several types of basil (*Ocimum* spp.), all of which have a different flavour. Genoa or sweet basil is the best known. It has a spicy flavour and is used extensively in Italian cooking. Opal basil has purple leaves, Greek basil has smaller leaves and a pungent flavour, and Thai or holy basil complements Thai and Southeast Asian dishes. Basil should be torn, not chopped, and added to hot food at the last moment to preserve the flavour. It doesn't dry well.

PESTO ➤ Put 2 crushed garlic cloves in a mortar and pestle, add a pinch of salt and 50 g (1¾ oz) pine nuts. Pound to a paste. Gradually add 50 g (1¾ oz) basil leaves and pound the leaves against the side of the bowl. Stir in 70 g (2½ oz) grated Parmesan, then gradually add 150 ml (5 fl oz) olive oil. Use immediately or store covered in the fridge for one week. If storing, cover the pesto surface with a thin layer of olive oil. ➤ Serve with pasta or barbecued meat. Makes 250 ml (9 fl oz).

Chervil

Chervil (*Anthriscus cerefolium*) has delicate, lacy, pale green leaves that deteriorate quickly, so they should be added to hot dishes just before serving. One of the classic *fines herbes*, it has a subtle parsley flavour with a hint of aniseed. Use it with fish, in salads or with creamy dishes.

Comfrey

Comfrey (*Symphytum* spp.) belongs to the same family as borage. Its smaller leaves, dipped in batter and fried, can be eaten as a vegetable.

Coriander

The roots of coriander (*Coriandrum sativum*) are used in curry pastes, the stems are used when a strong coriander flavour is needed, and the leaves are added at the end of cooking, both as a flavouring and as a garnish. Coriander is used extensively in Asian, South American, Mexican, Middle Eastern and Mediterranean cuisines. It goes very well with chilli, lime juice and meat dishes. Coriander freezes well.

Marjoram and oregano

Traditionally used to flavour tomato sauces in Italian and Greek cooking, marjoram and oregano (*Origanum* spp.) are usually used dried. They can be added to sausages and stuffings. Both herbs should be used sparingly.

Mint

Traditionally used in British cooking to go with lamb, mint (*Mentha* spp.) also goes well in salads and with steamed fish. There are several types of mint, including apple mint, peppermint and spearmint.

Parsley

Available as flat-leaf (Italian) or curly-leaf, parsley (*Petroselinum* spp.) can be used as an ingredient as well as a garnish. Flat-leaf parsley tends to be stronger in flavour but the two can be used interchangeably.

Rosemary

Rosemary (*Rosmarinus officinalis*) is a strong-flavoured herb: either chop it very finely or use small sprigs and remove them before serving. Rosemary goes well with roast lamb and pork, and in breads.

Sage

Sage leaves are traditionally used with onion to stuff goose and in Italian cuisine to flavour butter served with pasta, as well as in pork, veal and liver dishes. Use sage (*Salvia officinalis*) sparingly as the flavour can be strong.

Tarragon

Tarragon (*Artemisia dracunculus*) has a hint of aniseed to its flavour and is used in many classic French dishes. It is important to use French tarragon and not Russian, which has a coarser flavour.

Thyme

There are many varieties of thyme (*Thymus* spp.) and all have the same small leaves that can be used as a flavouring in casseroles and soups. Thyme gives a rich, aromatic flavour to slow-cooked food and roasts.

Kuzu.

Kuzu

Both the stem and leaves of the kuzu plant (*Pueraria lobota*) are edible, but the vine is mainly grown for its tubers, which are ground to make a grey starch powder called kuzu. Similar in texture and function to cornflour, kuzu is used mainly in Chinese and Japanese cuisine as a thickener in soups, sauces and glazes, and for dusting food before it is fried.

Lemon grass

With a subtle lemon flavour and fragrance, lemon grass (*Cymbopogon citratus*) adds a refreshing taste to many Thai and other Southeast Asian dishes. Strip off tough outer layers and use whole in soups by lightly bruising the stems (remove before serving); finely chop and use in curry pastes; thinly slice the paler lower part of the stem and add it to salads; or use whole as skewers for cooking meat, prawns and chicken.

Store lemon grass by wrapping it in plastic and storing it in the fridge for up to two weeks. Lemon grass can also be bought dried in sticks or in powdered form, when it is called sereh powder. If lemon grass is unavailable, you can use grated lemon zest instead. Lemon grass goes with chicken, chilli, coconut, ginger, pork and seafood.

Mastic

Mastic is a resin collected from *Pistacia lentiscus* bushes on the Greek island of Chios. Related to the pistachio, it has an earthy, aromatic flavour and is used for flavouring Turkish delight and ice cream. It is also used in a Greek liqueur called mastika, and in Egyptian and Moroccan cuisine. It was probably the original chewing gum, and the source of the verb 'masticate'.

Millet

Millet (*Panicum miliaceum*) is a grass seed which is used as a cereal in many African and Asian countries as it can grow in areas of extreme aridity and heat. Millet can be boiled in water, milk or stock, makes a good accompaniment to spicy casseroles and is used to thicken soups. The flour is used for flat breads and griddle cakes, but as it lacks gluten it is not suited to many types of baking. Millet can also be fermented and made into a crude beer, or malted and made into a more sophisticated brew.

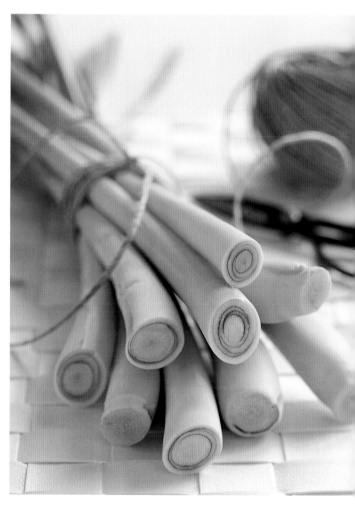

The thick, bulbous base of the lemon grass stem can be used instead of lemon zest to flavour desserts.

Clockwise from bottom left to centre, smooth mustard, mustard oil, mustard powder, yellow and brown mustard seeds, and wholegrain mustard.

Mustard

Made from the ground seeds of the mustard plant (*Brassica* spp.), mustard is a condiment. There are many species, but it is usually the black (the hottest and most pungent), brown and white (sometimes called yellow) seeds that are commonly used. Prepared mustard is made by macerating the seeds in liquid – such as water, vinegar or wine – then grinding them to a fine paste. Some mustards are flavoured with other ingredients such as herbs, honey, chilli or garlic. The pungency, colour, flavour and texture of the mustard will depend on the type of seeds used and the style of mustard.

Whole mustard seeds are used to flavour marinades and sauces, and in a host of Asian recipes. They are widely used in pickling. In Indian cooking they are fried in oil until they pop. Mustard oil (extracted from the seeds) is also popular. Mustard powder is simply ground mustard seeds and can be added to salad dressings, mayonnaise and sauces. It helps the emulsification of sauces such as mayonnaise and vinaigrette. The powder can be mixed with water and used in the same way as prepared mustard, which should be stored in the fridge as it loses its flavour at room temperature. Store mustard seeds and powder in a cool, dry place.

Types of mustard

FRENCH These most famous mustard varieties include Dijon, Bordeaux and Meaux. Dijon is a strong, smooth, pale yellow to light brown mustard. The seeds are blended with white wine or verjuice (the juice of unripe vine grapes). Meaux is a milder mustard of unmilled crushed seeds.

AMERICAN A mild mustard, sometimes flavoured with sugar, vinegar or white wine, often served with hot dogs and hamburgers.

GERMAN Typically dark, medium to hot, usually eaten with German sausages or cold meats.

ENGLISH Made from brown and white seeds, smooth and very hot. Use with roast beef and ham, with hard cheeses such as Cheddar, or as a condiment with sausages, herring or mackerel. Often prepared from mustard powder.

Serving suggestions

- Rub a little of your favourite mustard onto ham before baking it, or onto a chicken before roasting.
- Add some to a white sauce or soup for extra flavour.
- Combine some mustard with a little oil, chilli and soy sauce for a quick meat marinade.
- Mix mustard with softened butter, add some chopped fresh herbs and use on top of beef or pork steaks.
- Cook some cocktail sausages. Add 1 tablespoon wholegrain mustard and 1 tablespoon honey and toss everything together.

Nettle (*Urtica* spp.).

Nettle

Despite its reputation as a stinging weed, the nettle (*Urtica* spp.) is actually edible. The stings are caused by little hairs on the leaves, which lose their irritating properties when cooked. Nettles are rarely available commercially, so if picking them from the wild, ensure they aren't from areas that have been sprayed with pesticides. Wear gloves and choose plants with small leaves and soft stems. Prepare nettle in the same way as you would spinach and use it in soups, braise it with onions or use it to stuff ravioli.

Peppercorn

True pepper (vine pepper) is black, green or white in colour. The three varieties come from the same plant (*Piper nigrum*) but are picked at various stages of ripeness (see 'Types of pepper', right). Red pepper, Sichuan pepper, cayenne pepper and other peppers are not true peppers but were so called because pepper was an expensive commodity. Pepper contains piperine, which is an alkaloid, and it is this that gives pepper its distinctive flavour. Pepper is sold whole, cracked and coarsely or finely ground. Freezing makes the flavour of pepper more pronounced.

Storing pepper

Freshly ground black pepper is more pungent than pre-ground, which loses its flavour quickly and should not be stored longer than four months. Whole peppercorns will last about one year in a cool, dark place.

Types of pepper

GREEN PEPPER Picked when unripe and usually preserved by artificial drying or by bottling in brine, vinegar or water. Poivre rose are green peppercorns that have just begun to turn reddish.

BLACK PEPPER From berries that are red, but not completely ripe. When left to dry, they shrivel and take on a dark colour. This is the most pungent and flavourful of peppers.

WHITE PEPPER From ripe, red berries that are soaked in salt water until soft, then the white seed is removed and dried. White pepper is less aromatic than black but hotter and sharper, so use it sparingly. Useful for seasoning white sauces.

Sago

Sago is a starch extracted from Southeast Asian palms (*Cycas* spp.), processed into a flour or granulated into little balls called pearl sago. Pearl sago is commonly made into milky baked or steamed puddings in the West. In Southeast Asia, sago is used both as a flour and in pearl form to make desserts such as the Malay dessert, gula melaka, a mixture of sago, palm sugar and coconut milk.

Green peppercorns.

Black peppercorns.

White peppercorns.

Clockwise from top left, toasted sesame seeds, roasted sesame oil, gomasio (made from sea salt and toasted sesame seeds), white and black sesame seeds, and sesame seed biscuits.

SAGO PUDDING ➤ Put 125 ml (4 fl oz) golden syrup, 70 g (2½ oz) sago, 400 ml (14 fl oz) milk and 350 ml (12 fl oz) cream in a saucepan and bring to the boil, stirring. Simmer for 10 minutes, then allow to cool. Stir in 2 eggs, 1 teaspoon vanilla essence, 1 teaspoon grated lemon rind and 2 teaspoons lemon juice. Transfer mixture to an ovenproof dish and bake at 170°C (325°F) for 1 hour. ➤ Serves 6.

Sassafras

Sassafras is a North American native tree (*Sassafras albidum*) whose virtues were much lauded by the Indians and early Spanish colonists. Sassafras leaves are dried and used to make sassafras tea and filé powder, a flavouring and thickening agent in the Creole stew of gumbo. The fragrant lemon-scented oil extracted from the bark of the root is used in the cosmetic industry for its perfume; to flavour soft drinks, root beer, ice cream and confectionery; and in the health food industry.

Sesame seed

Sesame seeds come from a tropical or subtropical plant (*Sesamum orientale*) that produces seed pods which, when dried, burst open. They are then shaken to encourage the release of hundreds of tiny seeds. Sesame seeds are usually cream in colour, but may also be yellow, reddish or black, depending on the variety. The seeds can be used raw, but when toasted, take on a nutty, slightly sweet flavour. Bake in the oven at 180°C (350°F) for 15 minutes. Sesame seeds are used in cooking throughout the world – scattered over burger buns, on bread, and as garnishes for salads. In the Middle East, they are used in halvah, are crushed to make tahini or ground with chickpeas to produce hummus. In Japan, sesame seeds form the basis of seasonings such as gomasio.

Because of their high oil content, the seeds become rancid quickly. Purchase them in small amounts or store them in the fridge for up to three months. Sesame seeds may also be frozen.

milkweed
Sonchus oleraceus

plaintain weed
Plantago major

wild fennel
Foeniculum vulgare

pigweed
Portulaca oleracea

wild mustard
Sinapsis alba

marshmallow
Althaea officinalis

watercress
Nasturtium officinale

EDIBLE WEEDS The term 'weed' makes one think of a useless plant, but the definition is actually an 'unwanted plant'. Calling weeds wild plants is perhaps a better term, unless they have become an environmental menace. Many weeds are beneficial to your health and make delicious eating. Therefore, they are worth more consideration than how best to remove them.

wild mustard
Sinapsis alba

dandelion
Taraxacum officinale

Sumac

A reddish purple berry used extensively as a spice in Lebanese and Turkish cooking, sumac (*Rhus eoriaria*) has a fruity but mildly astringent lemony flavour. The seeds are dried, then crushed or powdered. Sumac is used in many dishes to add flavour and colour to meat, fish, pilafs and vegetables. (See the recipe for marinated sardines, below; sumac is an ingredient of ras el hanout.)

MARINATED SARDINES ➤ Mix 1 crushed garlic clove with ½ teaspoon salt and 2 teaspoons ras el hanout. Add enough oil to make a paste and rub into 18 sardine fillets. Fry in oil until browned; remove from pan. Cook 1 chopped onion with 3 chopped tomatoes, 2 teaspoons sumac and 1 chopped chilli for 5 minutes. Add 185 ml (6 fl oz) water and cook a further 5 minutes. Add 4 tablespoons lemon juice and season. Pour over the sardines and cool to room temperature.
➤ Serves 6.

Tamarind

The tropical tamarind tree (*Tamarindus indica*) is prized for its pods, each containing a sticky, fleshy sweet–sour pulp wrapped around small hard seeds. The pulp is used in Indian curries and chutneys, or in sauces such as Worcestershire sauce. It may be sweetened into syrups and sweetmeats. Tamarind is sold in ready-made concentrated paste in jars, or in blocks or cakes that still contain the seeds.

Cut off a little, mix it with hot water and press it through a sieve to extract the pulp. Store the paste in the fridge, where it will last up to a year.

Vanilla

True vanilla comes from the pod of a climbing orchid vine (*Vanilla planifolia*) native to Central America. The pods are picked when green, when they have no flavour, then they are left to sweat and dry in the sun. This process causes the vanilla pods to shrivel, turn deep brown and acquire a light coating of small, white vanillin crystals. True vanilla is expensive, partly because of the labour-intensive methods of obtaining it and also because the flowers are hand-pollinated on the only day of the year that they open.

Good quality vanilla pods have a warm, caramel vanilla aroma and flavour, and should be soft, not hard and dry. Bury a pod in a jar of sugar and let the flavour infuse the sugar, or soak the whole pod in hot milk and use it for custards and ice cream. For extra flavour, use the tip of a knife to slice down the pod to allow some of the tiny, potently flavoured seeds to escape.

Vanilla is sold as pods or distilled into pure vanilla extract (or essence). In these forms, vanilla is quite expensive. Synthetic or imitation vanilla flavouring – which must be labelled as such – is cheaper, but the flavour is inferior.

Cooking with vegetables

Vegetables offer a nutritious and tasty way to balance the diet and provide many of the vitamins and minerals essential to health. Nature ensures variety because a different vegetable will reach its peak cropping time every month of the year. Let the seasons be your guide to cheap flavoursome food.

The cooking times of vegetables vary according to the method used and the quality, size, quantity and freshness of the vegetables. Wherever possible, cook vegetables in their skins for extra good health.

Artichoke

Baby artichokes may be eaten whole, even raw in salads; a more mature bud may be stuffed, quartered, boiled or fried; and finally, as a large artichoke, it may be boiled and eaten one leaf at a time (suck or scrape the flesh off the fibrous base with your teeth), dipped into vinaigrette or hollandaise sauce. In all but the baby artichoke, care must be taken to discard the prickly choke, above the fleshy (and delicious) base, also known as the heart. Choose heavy artichokes with firm heads and stems, and leaves that are tightly overlapping.

When preparing artichokes, rub the cut surfaces with lemon or vinegar to stop them from turning brown. Always cut artichokes with a stainless steel knife to avoid staining the flesh. It's also important to wash your hands after handling the stem as it gives off a bitter flavour.

Asparagus

Asparagus shoots need to be cooked with care so as not to damage the fragile tips: stand them upright in a special asparagus steamer (which allows the spears to cook in water and the tips to cook in steam), or lie them flat in a large pan filled with lightly salted water. Once cooked, serve asparagus with melted butter and Parmesan, or add to risottos, quiches, stir-fries or salads. Fresh asparagus has firm, bright green spears with tight tips. Check the cut ends are not split or dried out.

Types of asparagus

GREEN This is the most common type of asparagus and is cut above ground when the shoots are 15 cm (6 in) long.

WHITE White asparagus is cut while the asparagus is below the ground (the lack of light prevents it from

Artichokes may be eaten raw in salads when young, but are cooked when older.

Asparagus with Parmesan: steam or boil asparagus spears until tender. Serve them with butter and shavings of fresh, good-quality Parmesan.

producing chlorophyll and turning green). It is more tender than the green variety and is popular in parts of Europe. Before cooking, white asparagus needs to be peeled up to the tip as the skin is tough.

PURPLE Purple when fresh, this type turns green when it is cooked.

SPRUE Young, thin asparagus.

Beans

Green beans are native to tropical America and were cultivated in Mexico and Peru more than 7000 years ago. There are hundreds of varieties and they can be steamed, boiled, stir-fried or cooked for use in salads. Cook beans in plenty of lightly salted water until they are just tender.

Types of beans

BROAD BEANS Also known as fava beans, young broad beans can be eaten in their pods like snow peas (mangetout), but as they get older, the pods become tougher. Older beans need to be removed from their pods before cooking and should also be double-podded to remove the grey skins. To do this, blanch the beans for a couple of minutes, drain and cool under running cold water, then slip off the skins. When buying broad beans, remember that most of the weight is the pods, which you will be throwing away. Frozen broad beans are also available.

RUNNER BEANS These flat beans should snap crisply when fresh, and most need to be stringed down each side unless they are very young. Though it is common to chop or slice the beans before cooking, this will cause the nutrients to leach out during cooking.

Green beans.

Braised green beans.

YARD LONG BEANS Also known as snake beans, these long beans are like French beans and are generally sold in bundles. Often used in Asian cuisine.

FRENCH BEANS Also known as green beans and string beans, these are usually fine, thin green beans, but they are also available in yellow waxy pods, purple or cream pods, and green and purple pods. Make sure the pods snap crisply to check for freshness.

BORLOTTI BEANS Popular whether dried or fresh, borlotti beans have distinguishable cream and red pods with beans the same colour. Borlotti beans are popular in Italy where they are mainly used in soups or stewed with olive oil and garlic as a side dish.

MUNG BEANS Small, olive-green beans sold dried as pulses or after the seed has sprouted as mung bean sprouts. As a pulse, mung beans may be cooked in soups and casseroles or in purées. The Chinese use the sprouts in sweet cakes or ferment them to make sauces. In Southeast Asia, mung beans are ground to make a flour used for sweets and doughs. The starch is used for making fine thread noodles.

BRAISED GREEN BEANS ➤ In a large frying pan, fry 1 chopped onion with 1 crushed garlic clove in 3 tablespoons olive oil, until soft. Add 500 g (1 lb 2 oz) green beans and fry. Add 400 g (14 oz) tinned chopped tomatoes and simmer until the beans are tender. Season well. ➤ Serves 4.

Beetroot

Native to the Mediterranean, beetroot, or beet, is a root vegetable originally cultivated for its young leaves, but now grown for its sweet-flavoured, purplish red root.

When cooking beetroot, take care to prevent them from bleeding. Don't cut or peel before they are cooked, and wash them carefully to prevent the skin breaking. In order to avoid getting the pink stain all over your hands, wear rubber gloves when handling this vegetable. Beetroot is remarkably versatile: grate it raw and add to salads; bake, steam or boil it; or purée it with oil and spices to make a dip. It is also used to make the eastern European soup, borscht. Cook and use the leaves as you would spinach: blanch them and add to soups, salads or pasta sauces. Store beetroot in the crisper drawer of the fridge for up to 2 weeks, and 1–2 days for the leaves.

BEETROOT MASH ➤ Boil beetroot until tender (this can take up to 2 hours), rub off the skins and mash with an equal quantity of cooked potatoes. Season. Add chopped chives and a knob of butter. Serve with fish, chicken or meat.

Beetroot goes well with balsamic vinegar, chives, orange, potato, sherry and sour cream.

Bitter melon.

Asian vegetables

Bitter melon

Used in Chinese, Southeast Asian and Indian cooking, bitter melon, or bitter gourd, is usually sliced and salted to remove the bitter juices, then braised or stuffed with pork and served with black bean sauce or cooked in curries.

Bok choy

A member of the cabbage family with a slightly mustardy taste, bok choy is also known as Chinese chard, Chinese white cabbage and pak choy. Separate the leaves, wash well and use both leaf and stem in soups and stir-fries, steam and serve with oyster sauce or fry in sesame oil with garlic and ginger. A smaller type is Shanghai bok choy, or baby bok choy, which is used in the same way.

Chinese broccoli

Chinese broccoli, or Chinese kale or gai larn, is distinguished by its small white flowers. It can be steamed whole and served with oyster sauce, or cut up the leaves and stems and add it to soups and stir-fries. Young stalks are crisp and mild; thicker stalks need to be peeled and halved.

Chinese cabbage.

Chinese cabbage

A versatile vegetable with a mild, sweet flavour. It can be shredded and eaten raw, steamed, used in stir-fries, soups and curries, or used to make cabbage rolls. Chinese cabbage is also used to make Korean kimchi. It is also known as celery cabbage, Chinese leaves, napa cabbage, Peking cabbage or wong bok.

Chinese keys

A member of the ginger family, Chinese keys is a reddish brown root vegetable that has thick, tapering roots which grow in a cluster, resembling a bunch of keys. Its spicy flavouring is used mainly in curries and pickles in Thai and Indonesian cooking.

Choy sum

Choy sum, or Chinese flowering cabbage, has mild, mustard-flavoured leaves and small yellow flowers. Steam or stir-fry whole and serve with oil and garlic and oyster sauce, or chop and add to soups.

Chinese keys.

Chrysanthemum greens

The young leaves of chrysanthemum greens, or garland chrysanthemum, are used in salads and stir-fries and the edible flowers are used in Chinese cooking.

Gai choy

A strong, bitter cabbage that is generally pickled as Sichuan pickled cabbage or used in pork-based soups. Another variety, jook gai choy, can be used in soups and stir-fries. It is also known as mustard greens, Oriental mustard or swatow mustard cabbage.

Hairy melon

A relative of the winter melon that looks like a cucumber covered in tiny hairs and is sometimes called fuzzy melon. It is used in Cantonese cookery. Remove the hairs by scrubbing or peeling it, then bake or boil the flesh; cut it into strips and stir-fry; cut into large pieces, core and fill with a meat stuffing; or use in braised dishes.

Sin qua.

Shiso

Widely used in Japanese cooking, shiso leaves can be red, green or purple in colour. The green leaves are used in sushi, battered and fried in tempura, wrapped around meat or fish and also added to salads; the red leaves are used to give colour and flavour to pickled plums. It is also known as beefsteak plant or perilla.

Sin qua

Similar to a cucumber in shape, but with ridges, this vegetable tastes similar to okra and zucchini (courgette). To use, peel off the ridges and some of the skin. It can then be baked, boiled or used in curries and braised dishes. It is also known as angled luffa, Chinese okra or vegetable gourd.

Tatsoi.

Tatsoi

Tatsoi, or rosette pak choy, has small, dark-green, shiny leaves with a white stem. The leaves need to be thoroughly washed and can be steamed or stir-fried and are often used in soups.

Water spinach

An aquatic plant popular in Southeast Asia, which is cooked like spinach and used in soups, curries and stir-fries. It is sometimes steamed and served as a side dish. It is also known as ong choy, kang kong, swamp cabbage or water convolvulus.

Water spinach.

Winter melon

This is a very large vegetable used like a squash and stir-fried or used in braised dishes or soups. It is also known as Chinese bitter melon, wax gourd or white gourd.

Broccoli

Broccoli can be eaten raw, steamed or boiled, and the stalks, which are quite sweet, can be peeled and diced and used in the same way as the florets. Drain well before serving as the florets hold lots of water.

ROAST BROCCOLI ➤ Toss 800 g (1 lb 12 oz) broccoli florets in 1 tablespoon ground cumin, 1 tablespoon ground coriander, 5 crushed garlic cloves, 2 teaspoons chilli powder and 4 tablespoons oil. Spread out the broccoli on a baking tray and roast at 200°C (400°F) for 20 minutes, or until cooked through. ➤ Serves 4.

Brussels sprouts

Brussels sprouts can be steamed or boiled, or shredded and used in a stir-fry. To boil them, remove the outer leaves and soak in salted water for a few minutes to remove any bugs. Cooking in lots of boiling water with the lid off helps them to stay green.

BRUSSELS SPROUTS WITH BACON ➤ Fry 400 g (14 oz) shredded Brussels sprouts in a little oil until tender. Add 4 finely chopped bacon rashers and fry together until crisp. To serve, season with pepper and sprinkle a few chopped almonds over the Brussels sprouts. ➤ Serves 4.

Red and white cabbage.

Cabbage

This stalwart vegetable is a member of a family that includes cauliflower, broccoli, Brussels sprouts and many Asian greens. There are loose-leaved and hearted varieties of cabbages. Loose-leaved cabbages tend to be green or tinged with red, and firm cabbages are red, white or green. White-hearted cabbages are good raw and shred easily; green wrinkly savoy cabbages can be eaten steamed or boiled as a vegetable.

Cabbage can be grated finely and eaten raw in coleslaw or salads; it can be cooked in stir-fries, braised, steamed or added to soups. Cabbage leaves can be used to wrap fillings, or the whole cabbage can be stuffed and baked. Red cabbage, when shredded and cooked with onions, stock, red wine and vinegar, is a classic accompaniment to game and pork dishes. Cabbage is also shredded and salted to make sauerkraut. Sauerkraut should be rinsed and drained before use to remove any excess salt.

The hard white core in the centre of the cabbage can be tough and should be removed before cooking. Cut into quarters, then cut off the base of each quarter to remove the core. Don't cook cabbage for too long or in lots of boiling water as this causes it to lose its colour and nutrients, as well as giving off a sulphurous smell. Adding a bay leaf to the cooking water may help with the smell. To prevent red cabbage from turning grey, cut it with a stainless steel knife. You can also add a little lemon juice or vinegar to the cooking water, or sprinkle it over the leaves if using raw.

Cabbages are regarded as one of the health super foods, since they contain a number of therapeutic compounds. Cabbages also contain active antiviral and antibacterial compounds that are useful for fighting infection.

COLESLAW ➤ Toss together 225 g (8 oz) finely shredded white cabbage and 2 grated carrots. Mix in 5 tablespoons mayonnaise with 2 teaspoons French mustard and 2 teaspoons sugar. Season well.
➤ Serves 4.

Cardoon

A popular vegetable in southern Europe, the cardoon (*Cynara cardunculus*) is an edible thistle related to the artichoke. Cardoons are cultivated for their fleshy, ribbed stalks, similar in flavour to a combination of celery and artichoke. Like celery, cardoon is blanched (that is, covered while growing to exclude light) as this makes the stalks more tender.

When cooking cardoons, peel off any tough outer ribs before using them. They brown very quickly, so cut them into pieces with a stainless steel knife and put immediately into water with a squeeze of lemon juice. Cardoons can be braised or baked, but are usually boiled slowly, then baked with butter. They can be topped with Parmesan, béchamel sauce or anchovy butter. In Italy, tender young cardoons are traditionally eaten raw with bagna cauda – a dip made with olive oil, butter, chopped anchovies and garlic – or deep-fried in batter and served as antipasto. They can also be used to top bruschetta or be mixed with cheese as a filling for ravioli or tortellini.

Carrot

New crop or baby carrots are best for eating raw in salads and only need to be cleaned with a stiff brush before use. Remove their fine green tops for longer storage. Larger, older carrots are best peeled and cooked. They can be steamed and served with butter, used in soups, puréed, or added to sweet dishes such as cakes and muffins.

Revive limp carrots by soaking them in iced water for 30 minutes.

VICHY CARROTS ➤ Peel 800 g (1 lb 12 oz) young carrots and cut into thin rounds. Put in a shallow pan, just cover with water and add 1½ teaspoons each salt and sugar and a knob of butter. Cover and cook over low heat until carrots are nearly tender, then remove the lid and boil until any remaining liquid evaporates. Serve sprinkled with finely chopped parsley and small knobs of butter. ➤ Serves 4.

Cauliflower

A member of the cabbage family, the cauliflower has a large head of tight flower buds (known as 'curds'). Cauliflowers are usually creamy white, but there are also green and purple varieties, as well as miniature ones. Cauliflower can be eaten raw as crudités or steamed, boiled, stir-fried, pickled or used in soups. Remove the leaves and store in the vegetable crisper in the fridge.

Prepare the florets or the whole cauliflower by soaking it in salted water to get rid of any bugs. Cook in a non-aluminium saucepan (aluminium reacts with cauliflower and can turn it yellow). Cauliflower can be steamed or boiled, but steaming is better as it keeps the florets intact. If cooking a whole cauliflower, cut a cross in the base of the stalk or cut out the core to help it cook evenly.

Cauliflower contains a natural chemical that breaks down into a sulphur compound when cooked. To prevent this, cook until just tender with a bay leaf – the longer it cooks, the stronger the smell will become.

CAULIFLOWER CHEESE ➤ Steam a whole head of cauliflower until tender, then cut into quarters and put in a baking dish. Melt 30 g (1 oz) butter in a saucepan, add 30 g (1 oz) flour. Mix and cook until bubbling then add 300 ml (11 fl oz) milk off the heat and whisk well. Return to the heat and simmer for 2 minutes. Add 150 g (5½ oz) grated cheese to the milk and mix in. Season, then pour the sauce over the cauliflower, sprinkle with a little extra cheese and place under a hot grill until golden and bubbling. ➤ Serves 6.

Celeriac root and celeriac remoulade.

Celeriac

A winter vegetable, also known as celery root or knob celery, celeriac is a type of celery but, unlike celery, only the knobby root is eaten. To prepare celeriac, peel and cut it into cubes or strips. The flesh discolours on contact with air, so soak or cook celeriac in water with a squeeze of lemon juice to prevent this.

Celeriac can be eaten raw in salads, or used in soups and stews. Cooked and mashed with garlic and potatoes, it is perfect served with game or meat. For better storage, remove the leaves and store celeriac in the crisper drawer of the fridge for up to 1 week.

CELERIAC REMOULADE ➤ In a bowl mix 450 g (1 lb) coarsely grated celeriac, 5 tablespoons mayonnaise, 2 tablespoons mustard and 2 tablespoons baby capers. Season; add lemon juice to taste. Serve the remoulade with bread or as a vegetable with meat dishes. ➤ Serves 4.

Cauliflower cheese.

Celery

Celery is grown for its stalks, roots and seeds. The ancient Greeks, Egyptians and Romans used wild celery for its medicinal properties and used celery leaves, like bay leaves, to crown their victorious athletes. In the 16th century, the first cultivated form of celery was developed, and was usually eaten cooked.

Celery grows as a cluster of long ridged stalks, which vary in colour from white to green. It is often grown under cover to prevent the stalks from becoming too dark and too strong in flavour. The stalks are eaten raw in salads, as crudités, cooked and served as a vegetable, braised in tomato or cream, or used as a base flavour in stocks and sauces. Celery leaves are used in soups, such as cream of celery, and the tender inner leaves can be used in salads or eaten with the stalk.

Celery has a high water content so it should be stored in the crisper drawer of the fridge wrapped in plastic. To revive wilted celery, sprinkle it with water and put it in the fridge until it becomes crisp again.

Chicory

Not one but a group of leafy vegetables cultivated from European wild chicory, all of which share differing degrees of bitterness. Chicory (endive) vary from long-leaved varieties, through the various radicchios to the witlof (Belgian endive) type, which is blanched (grown in the dark) to control the bitterness. Leafy chicory is good in salads and witlof can be grilled, braised in stock and caramelised.

Cook witlof in stock until tender, drain well, then barbecue or grill it until browned and caramelised, or fill a cooked pastry case with chicory cooked in stock and drained, sprinkle with blue cheese, drizzle with cream and cook until heated through. All types of chicory can be used as salad leaves but bear in mind their bitterness and use in moderation.

Radicchio is the Italian name for red chicory. There are several varieties, but two of the most common sold in Italy are rosso di Verona, a pink, flower-like chicory that looks similar to a round cabbage and is usually called radicchio in other countries, and rossa di Treviso, deep red and creamy streaked and usually called red chicory elsewhere. Red chicory is not as bitter as white, and it adds wonderful colour to salads. Sauté lightly in olive oil and balsamic vinegar.

Corn

Corn is usually yellow but can also be blue, red, white, orange and purple. Blue corn may be ground into flour and used to make corn chips and tortillas.

When cooking sweet corn, do not salt the water as it prevents the kernels softening as quickly. Cook in slightly sweetened water or add a little milk to retain flavour and softness.

To remove the kernels from sweet corn, stand the cob on one end and slice downwards, as close to the cob as possible. To barbecue, strip back the husk and remove the silk, then replace the husk and soak it briefly in water. The husk will burn off as it cooks. This will stop the corn from burning.

CORN FRITTERS ➤ Mix 150 g (5½ oz) polenta with 40 g (1½ oz) plain flour, 1 teaspoon bicarbonate of soda and 500 ml (17 fl oz) milk. Stir in 300 g (10½ oz) corn kernels, 1 tablespoon melted butter and 1 tablespoon finely chopped spring onions. Whisk 2 egg whites until soft peaks form and stir in. Season well. Heat some oil in a frying pan and fry spoonfuls of the mixture. Fry until brown on both sides and cooked through. Serve with roasted tomatoes.
➤ Makes about 30 fritters.

Many varieties are grown for pickling as dill pickles, gherkins and French cornichons. Store cucumbers in the refrigerator wrapped in plastic to prevent their odour from spreading to other foods.

Cucumbers have a refreshing flavour and are a key ingredient in raita, which is a cooling side dish served with curry.

RAITA MIX ➤ Combine 1 large grated cucumber, 1 finely chopped tomato, 1¼ cups plain yoghurt with 1 tablespoon black mustard seeds toasted in oil. Sprinkle with fresh chopped coriander leaves.

Edible weeds

An amazing number of common garden weeds are gourmet foods in their own right, healthful and free for the taking. Weeding is anything but a thankless task when you know the gourmet secrets of weeds.

Types of edible weed

Among weeds well worth sampling are nettles used as a spinach substitute, fat hen or Good King Henry (*Chenopodium album*), which is also excellent as a spinach substitute, corn salad or lamb's lettuce which is a superb salad green for cooler months, dandelion leaves which are excellent sautéed as wilted greens or as a slightly bitter green in salads, wild sorrel which makes an excellent creamed soup or salad addition, and the ubiquitous chickweed (*Stellaria media*) which is a delicious addition to salads and reputed to have a regulating effect on the thyroid gland. Succulent purslane (*Portulaca oleracea*) flourishes in sunny dry garden soils. The tender young leaves are excellent raw in salads, and can also be used like spinach as the flavour is somewhere between watercress and spinach.

A tradition of gathering wild greens exists in Mediterranean countries such as France, Italy and Spain, as well as the Middle East, and each country has its own repertoire of dishes created from wild greens. Among Italy's favourite wild greens are borage (*Borago officinalis*), sea kale (*Crambe maritima*), wall rocket (*Diplotaxis tenuifoliia*) and wild rocket (*Diplotaxis*

Cucumber

One of the oldest cultivated vegetables and, many would say, one of the most refreshing, cucumbers, like other members of the cucurbit family, have a high water content of 96 per cent. The cucumber today exists in over 100 varieties – including at least one described as 'burpless' – as well as many shapes.

Cucumber can be eaten raw; in salads; cooked in a soup; mixed with yoghurt as raita, used as an accompaniment to curries; or added to yoghurt and garlic to make Greek tsatsiki.

Cucumber is the traditional accompaniment to cold salmon, and the main ingredient for a doria garnish for classic fish recipes. Sliced paper thin in white bread sandwiches, the cucumber represents the height of old-fashioned English gentility at afternoon tea.

erucoides), wild sorrel (*Rumex acetosa*), corn salad or lamb's lettuce (*Valerianella locusta*), the fresh shoots of wild hops (*Humulus lupulus*) and wild garlic or ramsons (*Allium ursinum*).

Other countries around the world have their own wild pantry too. New Zealand is rich in wild foods and Maori techniques for their preparation, with foods like pikopiko and the near-asparagus-flavoured fiddlehead fern. Australia also has an ancient tradition of wild foods, many of which have gained an international reputation in recent times. Both these countries are adding their indigenous wild foods to an emerging Pacific Rim cuisine.

Thinnings

Thinnings from the vegetable garden, which you remove when reducing overcrowding can also be eaten, rather than thrown away or put on the compost heap. The seedlings of chicory (endive), turnips, radish, kale, Swiss chard (silverbeet), sorrel, beetroot and mustard can be used in salads or wilted like spinach.

Eggplant (aubergine)

Eggplants, or aubergines, can be served hot or cold, puréed, fried, stuffed or battered, and they are the main ingredient of many famous dishes such as moussaka, imam bayildi, baba ghanoush and ratatouille.

Eggplants vary in size and shape from small, round pea shapes to large, fat, pumpkin-shaped fruit. Their colour ranges from green, cream or yellow to pale or dark purple. Look for firm, heavy eggplants with shiny, smooth skins with no brown patches and a distinct cleft in the wider end.

Most eggplants don't need peeling or degorging (salting followed by draining) to reduce their bitterness, but this can reduce the amount of oil they absorb as they cook. Blanching in boiling water also helps prevent this. To degorge, cut into slices and put in a colander. Sprinkle heavily with salt and weight down with a plate (to speed up the removal of liquid). Leave for 30 minutes, then rinse in cold water. Dry well with paper towels. Always cut with a stainless steel knife to stop them discolouring.

BABA GHANOUSH ➤ Roast a large eggplant at 200°C (400°F) for 30 minutes or until soft. Allow to cool, then peel and cut into cubes and process with 1 tablespoon tahini, 1 crushed garlic clove and plenty of lemon juice. Season well. Serve with crackers. ➤ Serves 6.

Fennel

Native to the Mediterranean but now widely grown, fennel is cultivated for its aromatic leaves and seeds, similar in flavour to aniseed. The fine feathery leaves can be snipped like dill and used to flavour fish dishes, dressings or sauces. Florence fennel, known as finocchio in Italy, is cultivated for its thick stems and bulbous base, both of which may be eaten raw like celery, or the base may be braised, sautéed or added to soups.

BRAISED FENNEL ➤ Cut 4 baby fennel bulbs into quarters and blanch them in boiling water for 5 minutes. Drain well. Fry the fennel in butter until browned, then add 1 teaspoon brown sugar and caramelise. Add 1 tablespoon white wine vinegar and 150 ml (5 fl oz) chicken stock. Cover and simmer until the bulbs are tender. Boil until the liquid is reduced and stir in 2 tablespoons double cream. ➤ Serves 4.

Fiddlehead fern.

AÏOLI ➤ Place 6 peeled garlic cloves, 2 egg yolks and a pinch of salt into a blender and blend the ingredients until a thick paste forms. With the motor running, add about 1 cup olive oil, drop by drop, until the aïoli is thick and creamy. However, it if gets too thick, add a little lemon juice. Season to taste. This recipe can also be made using a mortar and pestle. ➤ Serves 6.

Fiddlehead fern

The young fronds or croziers of the oyster or ostrich fern (*Osmunda cinnamomea*), which grows wild in Europe and America, have a flavour that is similar to asparagus. The young shoots are usually boiled and served with a sauce, added to stir-fries or eaten raw in salads. Fiddlehead ferns are sold fresh or tinned.

Garlic

Each head of garlic is made up of a cluster of 10–16 cloves, and both head and individual bulbs are covered with a paper-like skin. There are many varieties of garlic, each differing in size, pungency and colour. In dishes such as aïoli, tapenade and pesto, garlic is indispensable, and it adds a pungent flavour to a variety of sauces, stews and meats. Don't be tempted to use more than the specified amount, as garlic will overpower the other flavours.

Garlic is freshest in summer when the bulbs are firm and the cloves harder to peel. Discoloured garlic or bulbs that are sprouting will have a rancid flavour. The green shoots of garlic can be used rather like chives and snipped onto salads and stir-fries. Garlic can also be eaten as a vegetable, barbecued or roasted whole or broken up into cloves.

Raw garlic is more potent than cooked. When garlic is cooked, some of the starch converts to sugar, making the garlic less pungent. Be careful not to overbrown or burn it as it can become very bitter. Chopping or crushing garlic releases the flavours. Crush a whole garlic clove by putting it under the flat blade of a knife and banging the knife with your fist. If the clove has sprouted, cut out the green sprout from the centre. Flavour oil with garlic by frying slices in oil, then discard the slices.

Garlic and aïoli.

Jerusalem artichoke

Neither from Jerusalem nor an artichoke, this winter root is actually a native of Peru and a relative of the sunflower (in Spanish, 'girasol' – mispronounced in English as 'Jerusalem'). It has a mildly sweet, smoky flavour. Finely slice and add raw to salads, boil or roast like potatoes or use to make wonderful, velvety soups and mashes. When cut, drop into water with a squeeze of lemon juice to stop them going brown. Jerusalem artichokes have a reputation for causing flatulence. This can be countered with a pinch of asafoetida.

ROASTED JERUSALEM ARTICHOKES ➤ Scrub 750 g (1 lb 10 oz) Jerusalem artichokes, then toss them in 2 tablespoons olive oil with plenty of seasoning. Put them on a baking tray and roast at 200°C (400°C) for about 40 minutes, or until tender in the centre, then drizzle with a little hazelnut or walnut oil. Serve as a vegetable or for a salad, toss with rocket leaves and fried cubes of bacon. ➤ Serves 4.

Jicama (yam bean)

Jicama, or yam bean, is a bulb-like root vegetable, similar in appearance to a very large turnip, with thin, beige, leathery skin and sweetish, crisp white flesh. A native to Mexico, jicama is also eaten extensively in Southeast Asian cuisine. To use it, peel the skin including the fibrous flesh directly under it, then slice and use raw in salads, add to stews, or cut into cubes and use in stir-fries as a substitute for water chestnuts – which it resembles in flavour. Jicamas are a good source of starch and, like potatoes, if stored in the fridge for too long will convert their starch to sugar. Jicama is also known as Mexican potato or Mexican turnip.

Kale

A relative of the cabbage, with a similar but stronger flavour and, depending on the variety, dark green or purple, smooth or curly leaves. As it grows happily in colder climates, kale has long been a popular winter vegetable in northern European countries, and is eaten widely in the southern United States as 'collard greens'. Use as you would cabbage or stir into soups and stews.

Kohlrabi

The bulbous stalk and the leaves of this cabbage family member are edible. The stalk is like turnip, and can be eaten in the same way, grated or sliced raw, added to stir-fries or stews, mashed or cooked in chunks and tossed in butter. The flesh is crisp and mild in flavour. Kohlrabi is more popular in Asia and continental Europe, particularly Germany, than Britain and the United States.

Leek

The leek is a mild-flavoured member of the onion family. The thick white stems of cultivated leeks are blanched by piling up dirt around them as they grow. Smaller leeks are best as the green tops are still tender. Some recipes call for just the white part, but most of the leek can be used if it is young and the green leaves are not too tough.

Jicama (yam bean).

Leeks are particularly good in creamy sauces and soups, most famously vichyssoise (a potato, cream and leek soup that is traditionally served cold). Like onions, they need to be cooked for a reasonable amount of time or they will be crunchy rather than tender and sweet; if overcooked, they will go slimy. Leeks can be boiled, steamed or braised in butter and cooked. Whole cooked leeks can be wrapped in pieces of ham or covered in a béchamel sauce and grilled. The leek is also the national emblem of Wales.

Leeks often contain soil and grit between their layers and therefore need to be washed thoroughly. Trim the roots, remove any coarse outer leaves, then wash well in a colander under running water. If using whole leeks, carefully separate out the leaves to rinse – making a cut halfway through the stalk to open the leaves. Wash the leek, leaf end down, so all the dirt runs out.

LEEKS À LA GRECQUE ➤ In a large frying pan, simmer together 1 cup water, 50 ml (2 fl oz) olive oil, 30 ml (1 fl oz) white wine, 1 tablespoon tomato paste, ¼ teaspoon sugar, 1 crushed garlic clove, a sprig of thyme, 1 bay leaf, 4 peppercorns and 4 crushed coriander seeds for 5 minutes. Add 12 thin leeks and cook until tender in the middle. Remove leeks, add a squeeze of lemon juice and 100 ml (3½ fl oz) water and boil until the liquid thickens and forms a sauce. Stir in 1 tablespoon chopped parsley, then return to the pan. Cool before serving. ➤ Serves 6.

Lettuce

Lettuces vary greatly in colour and texture: from light green to deep red, from those with loose, floppy leaves to those with crisp leaves and firm stems. Lettuce is

OPPOSITE Leeks and leeks à la grecque.

ABOVE Loose and crisp-leaved lettuce varieties.

mainly used fresh in salads or sandwiches but can also be cooked. In France, lettuce is cooked with baby onions and peas in stock and in China lettuce is a common cooked vegetable. In a green salad, lettuces are generally interchangeable, but when adding other ingredients, pick a leaf type that will suit them – floppy leaves won't go well with heavy ingredients like potatoes, and crisp firm leaves need a fairly robust dressing. Always dress lettuce just before you serve it.

Lettuce leaves need to be washed and dried before use. Either dry them in tea towels or paper towels or use a salad spinner, as any moisture left on the leaves will dilute the dressing. Don't leave lettuce to soak for any length of time as the leaves will absorb water and lose their flavour.

CAESAR SALAD ➤ Tear a large cos (romaine) lettuce into pieces and place it in a large bowl. In a blender, blend 1 egg yolk with 1 garlic clove and 4 anchovy fillets. Gradually add 170 ml (5½ fl oz) olive oil, then add 1 tablespoon lemon juice and a dash of Worcestershire sauce. Toss the dressing through the lettuce, then add some chunky croutons and Parmesan shavings ➤ Serves 4.

Lotus

The lotus is from the waterlily family (*Nymphaea* spp.), with beautiful white and pink flowers. In cooking, it is the root that is most commonly used. When sliced horizontally, it displays a floral-like pattern of holes. This decorativeness, along with its crisp, delicately flavoured flesh, is much appreciated in Chinese and Japanese cuisine.

First peel the root, then slice it before eating it raw or cooked. You can add it to salads or stir-fries, or cut it into chunks, stuff it, or serve it as a vegetable. Store in water with a squeeze of lemon juice to prevent it from turning brown. The seeds are also edible, eaten out of the hand or used in Chinese desserts and soups, and the leaves are used to wrap food such as whole fish for cooking. Lotus root can be bought fresh, dried, frozen and canned.

LOTUS ROOT AND VEGETABLE STIR-FRY ➤ Thinly slice 1 peeled lotus root and 2 zucchini (courgettes). Heat a small amount of oil in a frying pan, then briefly fry 2 crushed garlic cloves and 1 tablespoon grated ginger. Add the lotus root and zucchini (courgettes), and stir-fry for 2 minutes, then add 1 chopped carrot, 1 chopped red pepper (capsicum) and 12 snow peas (mangetout), cut in half, and fry for a further 2 minutes. Add 2 tablespoons oyster sauce, 1 tablespoon soy sauce, 1 teaspoon sesame oil and toss together. Add some snowpea sprouts and toss everything together until the sprouts are wilted. Serve the vegetables with noodles or rice. ➤ Serves 4.

Marrow

From the same family as the squash, pumpkin and cucumber, marrows, or vegetable marrows, are best eaten young as their flavour tends to deteriorate and becomes more watery as they get bigger. Marrows are best stuffed, either halved lengthways or cut into rings with stuffing in the middle. Use stuffings that will absorb water without going soggy, such as rice or couscous. A whole marrow is baked for about 2–3 hours, depending on its size.

STUFFED MARROW ➤ Cut a marrow into thick rings, scoop out any seeds and blanch for 5 minutes. Fry 1 chopped onion with 250 g (9 oz) minced lamb, add 70 g (2½ oz) cooked rice, 1 chopped tomato, 2 tablespoons chopped parsley and ½ teaspoon cinnamon; season. Fill the rings and put on a baking tray, drizzle with olive oil, cover and bake at 180°C (350°F) for 30 minutes. Serve with yoghurt. ➤ Serves 6.

Mesclun

Originally a mixture of the leaves and shoots of young plants, served as a salad, today mesclun is a Provençal mixture of assorted, small, young salad leaves and various herbs. A typical one may include lettuce, sorrel, rocket and dandelion leaves, curly endive, mustard greens, spinach and chervil. It is seasoned with a vinaigrette of olive oil, *fines herbes* and garlic. A mesclun salad provides a contrast of both flavour and textures by combining mild and bitter tastes and soft and crunchy textures. Only young leaves should be used. In Provence, France, mesclun is served with baked goat's milk cheeses, pieces of bacon, croutons, or chicken livers fried in butter.

The word 'mesclun' is derived from the French Nice dialect word *mesclumo*, meaning 'mixture'. A similar mixture in Rome is called mescladisse.

Mushrooms

Some of the most exciting food known to humanity is found in dark, damp habitats, on forest floors, living off live, decaying and dead organic matter. Mushrooms are the fruit of the fungus that grows above ground. There are countless varieties of edible mushroom, some cultivated, others gathered from the wild.

The most common types of cultivated mushrooms are small button mushrooms, larger open-cup mushrooms and flat (open or field) mushrooms.

Types of wild mushroom

CEP (PORCINI) Also known as penny bun, these have a brown cap and thick white stem. They have a rich, sweet and nutty flavour and are sold fresh and dried (usually called porcini). Cep are good in risottos and stews or raw in salads.

CHANTERELLE Also known as girolles, these are golden yellow with a concave cap. The underside has blunt, gill-like waves and folds. Chanterelle is a good all-round mushroom.

ENOKI Also known as enokitake, these grow and are bought in clumps. They have tiny cream caps on slender stalks, and a delicate flavour and crisp texture. The base of the clump can be sliced off or the whole clump can be cooked together.

HORN OF PLENTY Also known as black trumpet and trompette des morts, these saggy, leather-like mushrooms have a strong, earthy taste. Slit down the side to clean them. Fry them in butter and garlic or try them in cream sauces with chicken.

MOREL These short, stubby mushrooms, resemble a domed sponge; usually found dried. They are good with chicken or veal and make an excellent creamy mushroom sauce.

OYSTER These are wild mushrooms, now cultivated widely. Tear large oyster mushrooms into long pieces along the lines of the gills. Add to stir-fries or fry quickly and add to leafy salads.

SHIITAKE With dark-brown caps, shiitake mushrooms are available in fresh and dried form. Dried shiitake are best with a crazed top. Fresh are best when very smelly. Cut a cross in the top of the cap of large mushrooms to

Okra goes well with eggplant (aubergine), onion, pepper (capsicum) and tomato.

allow them to cook through the thickest part.

SHIMEJI Also known as beech, these are small oyster mushrooms with long stalks. When cooked they retain a slightly crunchy texture and are good in mushroom mixtures, such as stir-fries.

STRAW These are grown on beds of straw. They are small and globe-shaped with an internal stem. They are usually found canned.

Mushrooms do not keep for long. Wild mushrooms are best eaten on the day they are picked and will last no longer than a day in the fridge; cultivated mushrooms will last up to 5 days.

Okra

Okra (*Abelmoschus esculentus*) is a slender, five-sided pod that contains numerous white seeds. When young, okra is eaten as a vegetable; the older pods are usually dried, then powdered and used as a flavouring. When cooked, okra releases a sticky, gelatinous substance, which serves to thicken stews and soups such as the Cajun and Creole dish, gumbo. Okra is also used extensively in India, the Caribbean, Southeast Asia and the Middle East. It can be eaten raw in salads or blanched, then dressed in a vinaigrette.

Buy pods that are tender and healthy green in colour. They should snap rather than bend and should be no more than 10 cm (4 in) long. If too ripe, the pod will feel very sticky. To prepare, gently scrub okra with paper towel or a vegetable brush. Rinse and drain, then slice off the top and tail. If using as a thickener, blanch okra whole first, then slice and add it to the dish about 10 minutes before the end of cooking. In some recipes, the pod is used whole, thus preventing the release of the sticky substances within. Okra goes with eggplant (aubergine), onion, pepper (capsicum) and tomato.

Onion

One of the most important ingredients in the kitchen, onions are used in just about every nation's cuisine, adding a depth of flavour to dishes, although they are a delicious vegetable in their own right. Onions grow as single bulbs (globe) or in clumps (aggregate). Dry onions are left in the ground to mature where they develop a papery brown skin; green (spring or salad) onions are pulled out while young and the bulb is still small. Store in a cool dark place.

Red onions are good for eating raw, due to their naturally sweet flavour. They can also be barbecued or grilled.

Types of onions

YELLOW The most common kind of onion, sometimes called brown onion. Varieties include a sweet onion called vidalia, Spanish onions, pickling onions and cipolline – small flat onions.

WHITE Generally mild and slightly sweet. Can be used for cooking or salads. Pearl onions are small white onions ideal for pickling, but can also be added whole to stews and casseroles.

RED Delicious in salads, adding both flavour and colour. Good for barbecues and grilling. When cooked, red onions have less flavour than other varieties, although they can be slightly sweeter.

SPRING ONION This is an immature onion that if left in the ground would grow to full size. Depending on when it is picked, it has a small, white bulb of varying size and long green tops. There is also a variety called a Welsh onion with a papery brown skin. Spring onions have a mild, delicate flavour and both the green tops and the white bulb can be sliced and added to salads or omelettes, tossed into stir-fries or shredded finely and used as a garnish on fish or in noodle dishes. Store wrapped in plastic in the fridge. Also known as salad onion, green onion, scallion and, erroneously in some countries, shallot.

Pandanus

Long, flat pandanus leaves (*Pandanus* spp.) are used for their colour and fragrance and as a food container – which also imparts flavour – in Southeast Asian cooking, particularly in Indonesia and Malaysia. The leaves are crushed and added to dishes such as rice or curries during cooking or tied in a knot so they fit easily into the pot, then removed before the dish is served. For colouring (in Malaysian and Indonesian sweets, for example), the leaves are boiled and the colour extracted.

Pandanus leaves are sold in bundles and are available both dried and frozen. Dried ones lack the intensity of flavour and the frozen leaf is much less fragrant.

Pandanus leaf essence, called bai toey in Indonesia, is a brilliantly coloured, fragrant flavouring used in cakes and sweet dishes. In sweet dishes, vanilla extract is an acceptable substitute.

Pandanus leaves impart their flavour and aroma to fish or meat during grilling, baking or barbecuing.

Parsnip

The parsnip is a root vegetable with a nutty, sweet flavour. It has creamy yellow flesh and can be served roasted, mashed or added to casseroles and soups. Parsnips are an autumn/winter vegetable and they become sweeter after the first frosts. Leave the skin on for cooking, then peel once cooked. If peeled before cooking, store in water with a squeeze of lemon or vinegar (acidulated water) as their flesh darkens on contact with the air. Particularly large or old parsnips may need their core removed before cooking as they can be hard, flavourless and very fibrous. Parsnips will keep in the fridge for about 4 weeks.

CURRIED PARSNIP SOUP ➤ Heat 2 tablespoons olive oil in a large saucepan. Add 2 large, peeled and chopped parsnips and 1 chopped onion. Cook over medium heat for 5 minutes. Add 2 teaspoons good quality curry paste, such as Madras, and cook, stirring, for 1 minute. Add vegetable stock or water to cover. Cover with a lid, bring to the boil, then simmer for about 20 minutes until the parsnips are tender. Cool slightly, then blend in a food processor until smooth. Return to the pan, stir in 500 ml (17 fl oz) water and 3 tablespoons double cream or fromage frais. Check seasoning and serve with crusty bread. ➤ Serves 4.

If harvested too late, peas become dry and lose their sweetness.

Pea

The three main varieties of pea are the garden pea, the field or grey pea (these are dried and not eaten fresh) and the wild Mediterranean pea. Peas should be cooked quickly in boiling water or a little butter. They are usually served hot as a vegetable or added to soups and risottos. Both pease pudding, made from split peas boiled in a pudding cloth, and mushy (mashed) peas are eaten in the United Kingdom.

Types of garden peas

PEA SHOOTS (PEA LEAF) These are the tender leaves of the garden pea that have been prevented from flowering or shooting to encourage the growth of the small leaves. Good in stir-fries. They only last 2 days.

PETITS POIS Not a different variety, these are just peas that have been harvested young. The peas are shelled before cooking.

SNOW PEA A variety of pea, also called mangetout, eaten pod and all (top and tail before eating). They have a flat, thin pod and are eaten raw in salads or used in stir-fries.

SUGAR SNAP PEA Similar to snow pea, but with a more rounded pod as they are more developed. Use whole, in stir-fries or noodle dishes.

Peppers (capsicums)

The fruit of a tropical plant (*Capsicum annuum*) was deliberately misnamed pepper (pimiento in Spanish) by Columbus in order to sell its close relation, the chilli, as an alternative to the spice pepper that was, at the time, much sought after. Although peppers are a fruit, they are treated more as a vegetable or salad ingredient. They are also known as bell peppers, capsicums or sweet peppers.

Peppers vary in appearance but they are all basically smooth, shiny and hollow, containing thin white membranes and seeds. Most peppers are green at first, they then later turn red, yellow or orange or even purple–black, depending on the variety. Other types include wax peppers, which are yellow or white; cherry peppers, which are small, round peppers; and anaheim and poblano peppers (ancho when dried), which are usually classed as chillies although they are actually sweet peppers.

Preparing peppers

Peppers can be prepared in many ways. Simply cut them into slices, chunks or quarters, and eat them raw in salads; stuff or fry; skinned peppers can be sliced and added to salads, or drizzle with olive oil for the antipasto table. Eat raw peppers as crudités or use in soups, stews and stir-fries. Peppers feature in ratatouille, peperonata and gazpacho.

When stuffing whole peppers, cut a slice off the top and remove the seeds and white veins. Blanch each pepper for 2 minutes. Fill the pepper with the stuffing, replace the top slice and bake.

Roasting or grilling peppers makes them sweeter and also gives them a smoky flavour if you use a chargrill or barbecue. To remove the skin of peppers, put whole or halved peppers under the grill until the skin blackens and blisters. Turn the pepper so that all sides are blackened. Alternatively, roast them whole at 180°C (350°F) for 15–20 minutes. Allow to cool, then peel away the skin. Peeled, seeded peppers can be kept covered in oil in the fridge for 1 week.

To make pepper sauces, grill and remove the skins (as explained above), then purée or push the flesh through a sieve.

CHOPPING CHILLIES

1 Wearing rubber gloves, carefully cut the chillies in half and scrape out any seeds.

2 Cut away the membrane, then chop or slice the chillies.

STUFFED PEPPERS ➤ Fry 2 finely chopped onions in 4 tablespoons olive oil until soft. Stir in 3 crushed garlic cloves, 1 teaspoon each of cinnamon and paprika and 2 tablespoons currants. Cook for 1 minute. Cook 125 g (4½ oz) mixed wild rice and long-grain rice. Stir this into the onion mixture and season. Slice the tops off 4 medium red peppers, discard the seeds and fill with the stuffing. Replace the tops, stand in a baking dish and drizzle with olive oil. Cover with foil and bake at 200°C (400°F) for 1 hour. ➤ Serves 4.

Chilli peppers

Each chilli has its own flavour and varies in its degree of 'hotness'. Mexican recipes usually call for the skin to be removed after roasting as it can be bitter. Roasting also gives a smoky flavour to the flesh. Drying chillies intensifies the flavour. Dried chillies are often roasted before soaking to reconstitute them (be careful not to burn them when you roast them).

Types of chillies (with heat rating from 1–10)
ANAHEIM (2) Come in green and red and have a mild, sweet flavour. Used to make rellenos and also used in soups and stews.

ANCHO (3) A dried poblano chilli, dark red and mildly sweet. Used widely in Mexican cuisine, often with mulato and pasilla to form the 'Holy Trinity' of chillies used in mole sauces.

BANANA (2) These are mild and sweet, large, long chillies, creamy yellow or orange red in colour. Use them split in half and grilled. Also called Hungarian wax peppers.

CASCABEL (4) Small, plum-shaped chillies sold dried. Reconstitute and use chopped in salsas, or in soups and stews.

HABANERO (10) Looks like a mini pepper (capsicum) and can be green, red or orange. They are very, very hot. Use in salsas and marinades.

JALAPEÑO (5) Oval-shaped chilli with thick, juicy flesh and a wheel shape when sliced. Very hot if seeds and membrane are used. Ripens to red and when dried is called chipotle.

PASILLA (3–4) A dried black chilli often used in mole.

PEPPERONCINI (4–5) From south Italy, sweet and mildly hot, and usually available dried. Crumble into pasta sauces and stews.

POBLANO (3) A dark green, almost black, long chilli with thick flesh that ripens to red. Dried versions are mulato and ancho.

SERRANO (7) A common Mexican chilli, cylindrical in shape, red or green, and often used in salsas or pickled.

THAI (8) Also called bird's eye chillies, these are tiny, either red or green, and very hot. Use in Thai curries or sliced raw onto Asian salads.

> **CHILLI CON QUESO** ➤ Seed 1 ancho or pasilla chilli and flatten into one piece. Gently fry on both sides in 1 tablespoon oil, then allow to cool and crispen. Break the chilli into small pieces. Add 1 cup sour cream to the pan and cook for 2 minutes. Add 100 g (3½ oz) cubed Cheddar, stir until melted, then add the chilli. Serve with corn chips. ➤ Serves 4.

Potato

Native to South America, the potato is now a staple in the global diet. Potatoes are cheap, hardy and easy to grow, and are high in starch, protein and vitamins. Almost all nationalities have a traditional dish based on potatoes, such as the French gratin dauphinois, the Swiss rösti and Irish stew. There are thousands of varieties of potatoes, but only a hundred or so are grown for commercial use.

Potatoes can be divided into new crop (early) potatoes and old (main crop) potatoes and their texture can be floury or waxy. Some potatoes are good all-round types, others are more suitable for specific recipes. Potatoes are never eaten raw but must be cooked first as they contain 20 per cent indigestible starch, which, when cooked, converts into sugar.

Preparing and storing potatoes

It's important to scrub potatoes well before preparing, to remove dirt, and cut off any green parts and any 'eyes'. It is the thin layer immediately underneath the skin that is the most nutritious, so leave the skin on potatoes, where possible. Store potatoes in paper bags to allow moisture to escape and to keep light out. Keep in a cool and dry, dark, well ventilated place to prevent them from sprouting. If exposed to light, potatoes turn green – these will be bitter and indigestible and can

Potatoes Anna.

be poisonous. If stored in the fridge, potatoes become sweeter than if stored at room temperature.

Types of potatoes

FLOURY These have a low moisture and sugar content and are high in starch. They are good for baking, roasting, mashing and chips, gnocchi and in bread, but disintegrate when boiled. They include Russet (Idaho), Pentland Squire and King Edward.

WAXY These have a high moisture content and are low in starch. They hold their shape when boiled or roasted but don't mash well. Use in salads or stews. They include Roseval, Charlotte, Pink Fir Apple, Kipfler and Cara.

SALAD These are waxy, have a distinct flavour and are not usually peeled. Boil or roast. These include Kipfler, Pink Fir Apple, Jersey Royal and La Ratte.

ALL-PURPOSE Use these in recipes that don't specify the type of potato needed. These include Desiree, Nicola, Maris Piper, Romano, Wilja, Bintje, Spunta, Pontiac and Pink Eye.

> **POTATOES ANNA** ➤ Arrange thinly sliced, patted-dry potatoes in circles in a dish. As each layer is added, add butter and season. Cover the dish with foil and weight the top down to force the layers together. Bake until golden brown in a 230°C (450°F) oven then turn out onto a plate. ➤ Serves 4

Pumpkin

A member of the gourd family classified as a winter squash, often with orange skin and flesh as used in Halloween lanterns. Their flesh has a pronounced sweet flavour and is used in both sweet and savoury dishes. Pumpkins can be boiled, steamed, roasted or mashed. In some countries, all squashes are referred to as pumpkins; in others, only the large round segmented ones are.

If boiling pumpkin, remove the skin and seeds. If roasting larger pieces, the skin can be left intact for cooking. The seeds of pumpkins are dried and used in both sweet and savoury food. They are delicious toasted and sprinkled on salads and soups, or they can be eaten as nibbles, just like nuts. The roasted seeds are also used

Thai pumpkin and coconut soup.

to make a thick, dark brown oil with a strong flavour and aroma, used as a salad dressing and seasoning. Store whole at room temperature for around 1 month. Wrap cut pumpkin in plastic wrap and store in the fridge.

When making pumpkin purée or mash, steam or roast it to give a better flavour as boiling it tends to make the flesh a little watery.

> **THAI PUMPKIN AND COCONUT SOUP** ➤ Heat 2 tablespoons olive oil in a large saucepan and gently fry 1 finely chopped onion for 5 minutes. Add 1 tablespoon red curry paste and 1 tablespoon tomato purée and fry for 30 seconds. Add 450 g (1 lb) cubed pumpkin flesh and fry for 5 minutes. Add 400 ml (14 fl oz) coconut milk and 500 ml (17 fl oz) vegetable stock. Cover and simmer for 15 minutes. Remove lid and simmer for a further 5 minutes. Cool slightly, then purée in a food processor until smooth. Return to a clean saucepan and reheat. Stir in 3 tablespoons chopped coriander and garnish with sliced red Thai (bird's eye) chilli. ➤ Serves 4.

green cayenne
Capsicum annuum

peppercorns
Piper nigrum

brown mustard
Brassica spp.

thai chilli
(bird's eye)
Capsicum frutescens

orange habanero chilli
Capsicum chinense

horseradish
Armoracia rusticana

radish
Raphanus sativus

dried chilli
Capsicum annuum

yellow mustard
Brassica spp.

ornamental chilli
Capsicum annuum

cascabel chilli
Capsicum annuum

red cayenne
Capsicum annuum

dried thai chilli
(bird's eye)
Capsicum frutescens

red habanero chilli
Capsicum chinense

serrano chilli
Capsicum annuum

HOT FOODS
If hot and spicy is the way you like it, grow some vegetables that bite back! Radish, both red and white, has a kick. Horseradish, too, is another root crop that will add spice. Best known for heat, however, are chillies. They come in various strengths from fiery hotness to a milder intensity. The seeds and membrane are the hottest parts of the fruit.

red cayenne
Capsicum annuum

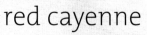

white radish (daikon)
Raphanus sativus var. *longipinnatus*

ABOVE Radish.   BELOW French shallot.

Radish

A peppery root vegetable related to the mustard plant, whose many varieties are grouped under red, black or white radishes. Red are the mildest and are crisp and juicy, usually eaten raw in salads. Black radishes have a stronger flavour, and are often peeled before use to reduce their pungency. Add to stir-fries and soups.

White radish (daikon)

White radish, or daikon, has a firm, crisp flesh and a mild flavour, similar to a white turnip. Some varieties have a slight peppery taste, while others are slightly sweeter. Raw white radish can be diced and added to salads, or used like a potato or turnip and added to soups, stews or stir-fries. In Japan, grated raw white daikon is formed into a small pile and is the traditional accompaniment to sashimi or tempura or it may be eaten as pickles.

Rocket

Rocket, or arugula, is a slightly bitter salad leaf with a nutty, peppery flavour. Younger leaves are milder than the mature, which can get quite hot. Rocket is used predominantly as a salad ingredient, and is one of the traditional ingredients of Provençal mesclun salad; it can be used as a pizza topping, added to soups and purées or served wilted as a vegetable. Rocket wilts quickly but will keep in the fridge wrapped in plastic for up to 2 days.

> **ROCKET AND PARMESAN SALAD** ➤ Put 2 bunches of washed and dried rocket in a serving dish. Mix 4 tablespoons olive oil with 1 tablespoon balsamic vinegar. Pour dressing over the rocket and mix well. Use a vegetable peeler to shave off pieces from a block of Parmesan. Scatter over the rocket, sprinkle with a little coarse salt and pepper. ➤ Serves 4.

Shallot

A relative of the onion, but with a milder flavour, shallots grow in clusters and are joined with a common root end. There are several types including the grey or common shallot, with grey skin and a purple head; the Jersey shallot, a round bulb with pink skin; the French shallot, also called banana shallot, which has golden copper-coloured skin and an elongated bulb; and Asian shallots, which are a lighter pink.

Shallots can be used as a garnish, thinly sliced and eaten raw in salads, or peeled and cooked whole as a vegetable. In France, shallots are used in sauces as the flesh dissolves well when cooked; in Asia, they are made into pickles. Store in a cool, well ventilated place for up to 1 month. In some countries, such as Australia, spring onions are erroneously called shallots.

To skin shallots, blanch them in boiling water for 1 minute, then peel. If leaving whole, then only trim the root or they will fall apart. When browning shallots, make sure they are well browned all over as the colour will wash off if they are added to a liquid.

With its tart, lemony flavour, sorrel makes a delicious addition to mayonnaise. Serve it with shellfish.

Sorrel

Sorrel (*Rumex acetosa*) is a leafy green plant that grows wild in northern Asia and Europe. There are many species, including common sorrel and round-leafed (French) sorrel, the mildest in flavour. Sorrel has large, spinach-like leaves that have a lemony, acidic, slightly bitter taste, due to the presence of oxalic acid. It can be used in a mixed green salad; cooked like spinach; made into soups, purées and sauces; or used as a flavouring herb in omelettes.

Soy beans and byproducts

The most nutritious and versatile of all beans, soy beans have been cultivated in their native China for thousands of years. Soy beans (or soya beans) contain a higher proportion of protein than any other legume, even higher than that of red meat, making them an important part of vegetarian diets and in Japanese, Chinese and Southeast Asian cooking where little meat is used. Soy beans may be red, green, yellow, black or brown. The beans are eaten fresh or dried but are also used as a

ABOVE Clockwise from top, shelled soy beans, fermented soy bean paste, dried soy beans, soy bean pods, soy bean sprouts.

BELOW Tofu, or bean curd, is a white, cheese-like curd made from soy beans, first prepared by the Chinese about 2000 years ago.

source of oil, milk, curd, pastes, sauces and flavourings. They may also be cracked, sprouted and even roasted and ground as a coffee substitute.

Dried soy beans contain a trypsin inhibitor, which must be destroyed by first soaking and cooking them for a long time before they are digestible. Soak dried beans for at least 6–8 hours before use. Yellow beans need longer soaking than black. Discard the soaking water before cooking.

Preparing soy beans

Soy beans have little flavour and a slightly oily texture and benefit from being cooked with strong flavours such as chilli, garlic and soy sauce.

As with other pulses, soy beans can also be puréed, added to casseroles or used in soups and salads. Fresh soy bean pods can be rubbed with salt, then boiled. These are eaten as a snack with beer in China and Japan.

SOY BEAN DIP ➤ Cook 200 g (7 oz) frozen soy beans in 2 cups vegetable stock for about 10–12 minutes. Drain, reserving ¼ cup of stock. Mix the beans in a food processor with 1 clove of garlic, ½ cup chopped fresh basil, I tablespoon extra virgin olive oil and the reserved stock, occasionally scraping down the sides, until smooth. Serve warm with crostini or crusty bread. ➤ Makes 1½ cups.

Spinach

Originally native to Persia, spinach is a green leafy plant with slender stems. The young leaves are used in salads; the older ones are cooked. The vegetable contains iron and vitamins A and C, but also oxalic acid, which is responsible for the slightly bitter taste and which acts as an inhibitor to the body's ability to absorb calcium and iron. This knowledge has somewhat diminished its famous 'Popeye' reputation. Cook spinach in the minimum of water – the water that is left on the leaves after washing is often enough. Steam or cook in a covered pan. Spinach that is to be added to dishes needs to be squeezed dry. This is best done by pressing it between two plates.

SAUTÉED GARLICKY SPINACH ➤ Wash 1 kg (2 lb 4 oz) spinach thoroughly and shake dry, leaving just a little water clinging to the leaves. Heat 2 tablespoons olive oil in a frying pan and add 1 finely chopped garlic clove. Cook for a few seconds and then add to the spinach. Cover the pan for a minute to create some steam. Remove the lid and turn up the heat, stirring the spinach until all the liquid has evaporated. Season before serving. ➤ Serves 4.

Squash

Squash belong to the marrow family, which includes melons, marrows, gourds, gherkins and cucumbers. They come in a wide variety of colours, sizes and shapes. Squash are divided into winter and summer types. Generally, winter squash have hard skin and flesh and summer squash have a softer skin and more watery flesh. Squash are often stuffed and baked or roasted, puréed, braised, boiled, steamed or fried in batter or breadcrumbs. Add them to soups, casseroles or gratins.

Types of squash
PATTYPAN A saucer-shaped squash, yellow or green in colour with white flesh. It is usually picked when young and very small; it does not need to be peeled and cooks quickly.

Sautéed garlicky spinach.

Clockwise from bottom right, sweet dumpling squash, pattypan squash, golden nugget squash, spaghetti squash, acorn squash.

SWEET DUMPLING Dark green with deep ridges and yellow markings. The flesh is yellow-orange in colour.

SPAGHETTI Has a hard yellow skin and a flesh that is made up of fibres. Steam or bake, then gently pull out the fibres – these resemble spaghetti.

GOLDEN NUGGET These are small squash that look like baby Halloween pumpkins. They have a hard skin and can be baked whole or in halves. Best cooked with their skins on.

TURBAN A large squash with a crown at the top and a hard, dark skin that can be dark green or orange. It has a dry, sweet, orange flesh with a nutty flavour.

HUBBARD Has a hard, coarse skin that may be ridged and varies in colour from green to bluish-green to red. The flesh is pale orange.

Sweet potato

This is the tuberous root of a tropical vine which, although also native to Central and South America like the potato, is not a true potato. Today, sweet potatoes are an important crop in the southern United States, South America, Asia, Japan, the Mediterranean, Hawaii, Australia and New Zealand, where one variety, orange in colour, is known as kumara, close to the original Peruvian name of 'kumar'. There are several varieties of sweet potato and their flesh, which may be white, orange or yellow, ranges from meaty to moist and watery, and their skins may be white, yellow, red, purple or brown. Orange-fleshed sweet potatoes are softer when cooked.

Sweet potatoes can be cooked as you would a potato (roasted, boiled, mashed or fried), but their soft, slightly sweet flesh makes them an ideal ingredient in cakes and sweet dishes, breads, soups and casseroles. A simple cooking method is to sprinkle them with brown sugar and butter and roast.

Sweet potatoes will not store for as long as potatoes but will last 1 week if kept in a cool, dry place.

Swiss chard (silverbeet)

Swiss chard, or silverbeet, is a relation of the sugar beet and is mostly grown and eaten around the southern Mediterranean. Swiss chard has fleshy stalks and large leaves, both of which can be prepared as for spinach. The leaves may be eaten raw in salads or cooked and the stalks may be served in a sauce, added to soups or sautéed.

There is a great range of chards available, many of which have colourful stalks. Ruby chard has a red stalk and can be cooked in the same way as regular Swiss chard.

Store covered and unwashed in the fridge for up to 4 days. Swiss chard is sometimes sold under the name of 'spinach' in Australia. It is also known as chard, leaf beet, seakale beet, spinach beet and white beet.

Tomatillo

A relative of the tomato that is used as a vegetable, either raw or cooked, this fruit may be green, yellow or purple. Tomatillos are used in Mexican cuisine in salsa verde and are essential in a proper guacamole. Like physalis, the tomatillo has a papery calyx.

Tomato

Although botanically a fruit, the tomato, another gift of inestimable value to the cuisines of the world – especially Italian – from South America, is used mainly as a vegetable. So thoroughly has the tomato been assimilated that it's difficult to imagine life in the western world (no tomato sauce or pizza!) before it arrived in Naples in the 16th century. At first the tomato was thought of as a medicinal plant, and it took a generation before it began to appear on the table. Today, tomatoes are grown worldwide, America and Italy being the largest producers for canning, sauces, pastes and purées. There are more than 1000 varieties, in numerous sizes, shapes and colours. Most varieties are red, although others are yellow or pink. Unripe green tomatoes are used in pickles and chutneys.

PEELING TOMATOES

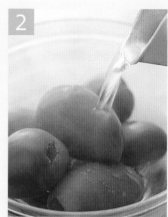

1 Remove the stems of the tomatoes and score a cross in the bottom of each one with a knife, cutting just through the skin. Blanch in boiling water for 30 seconds or so.

2 Test a tomato to see if the skin will come off easily, otherwise leave them to soak for a few seconds more. Don't leave them for too long or they might start to cook.

3 Transfer to a bowl of cold water then peel the skin away from the crosses – it should slip off easily.

Tomato salad.

ROUND This is the most common type of tomato, commercially bred to be round and red. It can be bought vine-ripened and in different varieties such as the striped tigerella or even yellow or orange coloured. The round tomato is an all-purpose tomato.

> **TOMATO SALAD** ➤ Slice 6 large ripe tomatoes. Arrange the tomatoes on a plate and scatter over 1 finely chopped shallot and 2 tablespoons chopped chives. Drizzle with extra virgin olive oil and top with torn basil leaves. If your tomatoes are not highly flavoured, add a few drops of balsamic vinegar to the olive oil. ➤ Serves 4.

The best flavoured tomatoes are those that are ripened on the actual vine. For immediate use, tomatoes should be firm and bright coloured, with no wrinkles and a strong tomato smell. Buy only in small quantities (unless making sauce), or buy some greener than others and allow to ripen on the kitchen windowsill. For salads and pasta sauces, buy only the reddest and ripest of tomatoes. Remember, uniformity of shape or colour has no relation to flavour.

Types of tomatoes

CHERRY Cherry tomatoes come in various sizes but essentially are a tiny variety of tomato. Some are red, others are yellow and some are pear-shaped and yellow. Good for salads or use whole or halved in stews and pasta sauces.

PLUM Also known as egg or Roma, these are commercially used for canning and drying. They have few seeds and a dry flesh, which makes them ideal in sauces and purées. A good variety is San Marzano.

BEEF STEAK These are larger tomatoes, either smooth and rounded or more irregular and ridged in shape. Beef steak tomatoes can be used for stuffing or sliced in salads. Marmande is an especially good variety.

Turnip

A relative of the cabbage, grown both for its root and the green tops, which are used as a spring vegetable. The turnip is one of the earliest cultivated European vegetables. Turnips spread across the globe early on, and appear in the cuisine of many countries: in Chinese and Japanese recipes, and as pickles in Korean and Middle Eastern cooking. In France they are eaten mostly when young. There are many varieties, long or rounded, white tinged with green or purple, but all have white flesh.

Although turnips are usually relegated to ingredient status in soups and stews, they make excellent eating on their own. When young, grate them raw into salads, braise them, or make Chinese-style turnip cake. Older turnips can be roasted, which gives them a sweeter flavour. Turnip tops (greens) are boiled as for cabbage and served with butter. Turnips are also available salted and sun-dried in Asian stores. Store unwashed and refrigerated in a perforated plastic bag for up to 2 weeks.

> **GLAZED TURNIPS** ➤ Peel 4 turnips and cut them into quarters, or trim 16 baby turnips. Boil for 8–10 minutes until tender but still firm, then drain well. Heat 2 tablespoons butter in a frying pan; add turnips, sprinkle on 1 tablespoon sugar and fry until turnips are golden and caramelised (be careful the sugar does not burn). Serve with roast meats or baked ham. ➤ Serves 4.

Zucchini (courgette)

Zucchinis, or courgettes, are baby marrows, and are usually dark green in colour, but there are also light green and yellow varieties. Young zucchini can be sliced thinly, dressed in olive oil and lemon juice and eaten raw in salads. Use larger zucchini in stir-fries. You can also steam or boil them, coat slices in batter and deep-fry them, or hollow out, stuff and bake them. If using zucchini in fritters or frying, you should salt them first to degorge them so they soak up less oil. Storage in the fridge makes the texture of zucchinis deteriorate.

MARINATED ZUCCHINI ➤ Thinly slice 500 g (1 lb 2 oz) zucchini diagonally. Heat 1 tablespoon olive oil in a frying pan and fry the slices on both sides until browned. Remove with a slotted spoon and drain. Place the zucchini in a non-metallic dish and add 1 tablespoon finely chopped parsley, 1 sliced garlic clove and 1 tablespoon balsamic vinegar. Season with salt and pepper and leave for a few hours. Serve with grilled or roast meats or as antipasto. ➤ Serves 4

ABOVE Zucchini flower and deep-fried zucchini flowers.

LEFT Left to right, glazed turnips, raw turnips.

Zucchini flowers are edible too, available in the male (the flower has a stalk) or female (the flower has a baby zucchini attached) form. These are usually stuffed before being baked or fried. They are sold at specialty fruit and vegetable shops. Wash them before use and make sure there are no insects hidden inside.

DEEP-FRIED ZUCCHINI FLOWERS ➤ For batter, whisk 2 eggs with 60 g (2¼ oz) flour. For stuffing, mix 125 g (4½ oz) ricotta with 1 tablespoon chopped basil, 2 tablespoons grated Parmesan, 2 tablespoons breadcrumbs and an egg yolk. Season. Stuff the mixture into 10 flowers. Dip flowers in batter and deep-fry. ➤ Serves 4

8

Herb
directory

YARROW Yarrow is a low, mat-forming perennial that has dense, dark green, fern-like foliage. Flat heads of small flowers appear on top of tall, mostly leafless stems during the later summer months and in autumn. They may be white, pink or yellow.

GARLIC Garlic grows from a bulb that consists of several segments. These are the strongly aromatic cloves that have led to its widespread culinary use. This perennial plant also has a long list of medicinal uses, and it is a renowned companion plant and source of pest control in the garden.

Achillea millefolium

yarrow
ASTERACEAE/COMPOSITAE

CONDITIONS

Climate Best grown in cool climates where winters are always frosty, but grows reasonably well in warmer areas. It is not suitable for the tropics.

Aspect Full sun is essential. This vigorous grower is well suited to growing in rockeries or on banks.

Soil Well drained, not-too-rich soil is ideal. Plants will rot if the soil stays wet for long periods after rain or watering.

GROWING METHOD

Planting Propagate by dividing the roots of mature plants in early spring or autumn, or by sowing seed in spring in trays or punnets of moist seed-raising mix. Barely cover the seed and place the containers in a warm, bright but shaded spot until germination is complete. Gradually expose containers to more and more sun, then transplant seedlings into their final site when they are big enough to handle.

Watering Water deeply but occasionally; yarrow has deep roots that will find water at lower levels in the soil.

Fertilising No fertilising is necessary.

Problems No particular problems.

Pruning Cut plants to the ground in middle to late autumn or after frosts have started. New growth will appear in spring.

HARVESTING

Picking Harvest leafy stems and flowers on a dry morning when plants are in the early stages of full bloom. Tie them together and hang upside down in a dry, dim, airy place. If they are intended for dried arrangements, hang each flower separately.

Storage When the stems are dry, remove the flowers and leaves from their stems, crumble the leaves and break up all the stems into small pieces. Mix stems, leaves and flowers together and store the mixture in airtight jars.

Freezing Not suitable for freezing.

USES

Culinary Young, small leaves have a slight, pleasantly bitter flavour. Add a few chopped young leaves to salads or sandwiches.

Medicinal Herbal tea made from the dried stems, leaves and flowers is a good general pick-me-up, blood cleanser, tonic for the kidneys and, reputedly, a slimming aid.

Gardening Yarrow is a good choice for informal or meadow-style plantings, or for planting on dry, infertile banks where other flowers are difficult to grow. It has the slightly unkempt look of a wildflower.

Allium sativum

garlic
LILIACEAE

CONDITIONS

Climate Grows well in a wide range of climates, but dislikes the high summer heat, humidity and rainfall of the tropics, where it can be grown in deep pots of sandy potting mix if sheltered from constant rain.

Aspect Full sun is essential.

Soil Good drainage is also essential but garlic grows in any crumbly, reasonably fertile soil. Dark, sandy loam with rotted organic matter and 1 cup of lime per square metre (square yard) is ideal.

GROWING METHOD

Planting In mid-autumn or early spring, break cloves from a fresh head of garlic. Push into soil that is well dug over and crumbly so that the pointy end is 1–2 cm (½–¾ in) below the surface. Space cloves about 20 cm (8 in) apart, cover with soil and water in well. Mulch lightly with compost, rotted manure or rotted grass clippings.

Watering Newly planted garlic needs good moisture for its developing roots but does not want to be sodden during autumn and winter. If rain does not fall, water deeply once a week. Gradually reduce watering as the weather warms up in spring as garlic bulbs need a hot, dry summer to mature.

Fertilising Apply complete plant food at planting time.

Problems Aphids may cluster on leaves and flower buds but are easily rubbed off by hand. Bad drainage or overwatering causes bulbs to rot.

HARVESTING

Picking Harvest in summer when the flower dies and the leaves begin to turn yellow. Don't cut the dead leaves off – use them to plait the bulbs together for storage. After harvest, wash the bulbs clean, then leave them in the sun for a few days to dry.

Storing Dried bulbs may be strung together and hung in a dry, airy position, ready to be used as they are needed.

Freezing Not suitable for freezing.

USES

Culinary Garlic has hundreds of uses in virtually every type of cuisine. It is an essential ingredient in many European and Asian dishes, and it is used in vinegars and herb butters. Chopped leaves can be lightly stir-fried.

Medicinal Garlic has antibiotic and antiseptic properties; it is useful in lowering blood pressure and cholesterol, and is said to have beneficial effects on the immune system. Regular intake of garlic reduces susceptibility to colds and improves the digestive system. A sliced clove rubbed over a cut will clean and sterilise the wound.

Gardening Garlic is often planted under roses to help deter aphids and other rose pests.

Allium schoenoprasum, A. tuberosum

chives

LILIACEAE

CONDITIONS

Climate Chives are very adaptable and can withstand extremes of high and low temperatures. They are frost hardy.
Aspect Grow best in full sun but tolerate partial shade. In very hot, dry climates they may require a little shade and humidity.
Soil Prepare beds well with organic matter such as compost and blood and bone fertiliser. Good drainage is essential. If growing chives indoors, use potting mix and fertiliser.

GROWING METHOD

Planting Sow seeds directly into the garden during spring. Prepare drill holes and plant about 10 seeds together as a clump, 1 cm (½ in) deep. Firm the soil over and water. Keep the soil moist during the germination period of 2–3 weeks. Thin out so that the clumps are about 20 cm (8 in) apart. Alternatively, young plants can be raised in seed beds and transplanted into the garden when one month old, again in clumps of 10, 20 cm (8 in) apart. If planting clumps in rows, space the rows 30–60 cm (1–2 ft) apart to allow inter-row cultivation. Bulbs can also be lifted and divided in autumn or spring every two years once the plant is established.
Watering Water well, especially during hot months.
Fertilising At planting time, dig in complete plant food. Apply liquid or soluble fertiliser every four weeks.
Problems Generally free of diseases but watch for aphids in hot weather. Treat with the appropriate spray.

HARVESTING

Picking Chives are ready to crop when they reach about 15 cm (6 in) high during summer and autumn (autumn to spring in tropical areas). Do not snip off just the tips or the chive will become tough and fibrous. Clip the leaves or blades close to the ground, leaving about 5 cm (2 in) still intact. Harvest chives regularly to keep the crop growing.
Storage Chives do not store very well.
Freezing Chives can be frozen for about six months. Chop them, wrap them in small packages with freezer bags and then freeze them for use when needed.

USES

Culinary Leaves of the common chive (*A. schoenoprasum*) have a delicate onion flavour. Add to soups or casseroles during the last moments of cooking. Use chopped leaves in salads, as a garnish and in the French *fines herbes*. The flowers can be eaten fresh in salads or made into delicious herb vinegars or butters. All parts of the Chinese or garlic chive (*A. tuberosum*) have a mild garlic flavour and the unopened flower bud has a special place in Asian cuisines.
Gardening Recommended companions for roses, carrots, grapes, tomatoes and fruit trees.

Aloe barbadensis, syn. *A. vera*

aloe vera

ALOEACEAE/LILIACEAE

CONDITIONS

Climate Aloe vera is best grown in tropical and warm zones.
Aspect Full sunlight and good drainage. Grow indoors in direct light. Protect from heavy frosts.
Soil Should drain rapidly and be reasonably open; roots will rot if exposed to long periods of wet soil. If soil and water are too alkaline, growth may be slow.

GROWING METHOD

Planting Can be grown from seed or by division of the parent plant. New shoots must be 'pruned' or leaves will turn bright green and grow horizontally rather than vertically. When new shoots are 10 cm (4 in) tall, break them off from the parent and repot in soil made up from equal parts of coarse river sand, garden loam and decayed garden compost or cow manure. Water well, then leave for three weeks to form a network of water-seeking roots.
Watering Allow the plant to become fairly dry in between waterings; water only very lightly during winter, and more often during the growing period when the leaves begin to thicken.
Fertilising Excessive fertilising may slow growth.
Problems Almost non-existent, but watch out for root rot in wet soils.
Pruning Aloe vera grows from the centre. Cut older, outside leaves to keep the plant in balance and in shape. These leaves do not grow back once cut.

HARVESTING

Picking Harvest leaves as required but always cut larger, lower leaves first as they have more juice. This also promotes new growth from the centre. Trim the thorny edges of the leaves and split the leaf across its width to extract the gooey gel. As the gel ceases to flow, scratch the exposed leaf and continue to do so until only the green leaf skin is left.
Storage Wrap whole or partially used leaves in foil and store in the refrigerator for several days, or bottle the extracted juice.
Freezing Can be frozen for six months.

USES

Cosmetic The juice of the leaves is applied directly to the skin as a softening agent and for minor wounds (insect bites, scratches or cuts) and sunburn. Astringent and drying, it is often combined with lanolin and vitamins A and E to intensify its soothing qualities.

CHIVES Chives are perennial herbs that make an attractive edging for a herb garden or bed of mixed annuals and perennials. They grow in clumps from very small bulbs that send up 30 cm (12 in) tall grass-like, hollow, tubular, green leaves, which taper to a point at the top. The flowers of the common chive take the form of a globular head of dense, pinkish to pale purple blossoms. Chinese or garlic chives have a flower head composed of star-like, white flowers and flat, narrow, light to dark green leaves.

ALOE VERA A bitter-juiced, succulent perennial, aloe vera grows to about 60 cm (2 ft) high and wide in the open garden but is much smaller in containers where growth is restricted. A strong, fibrous rooting system supports a single, sturdy stem. The fleshy, pale green leaves with paler blotches have spiny, toothed edges. The bell-shaped flowers are borne on long branches in summer, while the capsule-like fruit are triangular and contain many seeds.

LEMON VERBENA A large, bushy deciduous shrub that can grow at least 1 m (3¹⁄₃ ft) in height, lemon verbena has long, lemon-scented, narrow leaves. Spikes or sprays of small white to mauve flowers appear in the axils of the leaves in summer. The plant's fragrance is released when you brush against the leaves in the garden. Grow lemon verbena in containers, and indoors in cooler climates, although container plants do not reach the same height as specimens grown in the garden.

Aloysia triphylla

lemon verbena

VERBENACEAE

CONDITIONS

Climate Prefers moist, warm climates, although the high summer humidity in the tropics may cause it to be short lived. Plants are sensitive to cold weather and are best grown in containers in cooler regions.
Aspect Prefers a sheltered, sunny position with protection in winter.
Soil Likes rich soils. Needs mulching against frosts.

GROWING METHOD

Planting Grow from softwood cuttings in summer or from hardwood cuttings in autumn. Trim a 13 cm (5 in) piece from the parent bush, and remove a third of the upper leaves and a few of the lower leaves. Place in a mix of two-thirds coarse sand and one-third peat moss. Moisten the soil and cover the pot with a plastic bag to create a mini-greenhouse. Pot on into good quality potting mix when the cutting has taken root and shows renewed leaf growth. Plant out in the garden when the plant is growing strongly.
Watering The plant is reasonably tolerant of dry conditions and normal garden watering is sufficient.
Fertilising Use complete plant food every six weeks or apply controlled-release granules as directed on the packet.
Problems Spider mite and whitefly weaken the plant by sucking plant juices from the leaves and stems. Hose the leaves frequently, or use organic soap and pyrethrum or recommended chemical sprays for these pests. Watch out for powdery mildew, which causes foliage to wilt, on the upper surfaces of the leaves. Spray or remove diseased plants.
Pruning Prune each season to contain its straggly growth habit. This is an ideal plant to train into a formal shape as a standard or topiary.

HARVESTING

Picking Sprigs of leaves can be harvested all year long. If leaves are required for drying, cut the bush back during summer and early winter. Hang the branches in a cool, airy place and strip off the leaves when they are dry.
Storage Store dried leaves in airtight jars. The fragrance is retained for some years.
Freezing Wrap in plastic bags and then freeze for up to six months.

USES

Culinary Dried leaves can be used for herbal tea or in cooking where a lemon flavour is required, as with fish, poultry, marinades, salad dressings and puddings.
Craft The strong fragrance makes dried leaves a popular component of herb pot pourris and sachet fillings.
Gardening Lemon verbena is an attractive border plant.

GALANGAL A member of the ginger family, this perennial forms a clump of leafy stems up to 2 m (7 ft) tall. The leaves are glossy and light green, about 50 cm (20 in) long and lanceolate in shape. The flowers are unremarkable; they appear in summer and autumn and are followed by spherical, red fruits. The plant is native to tropical Southeast Asia. It can be grown in large containers.

Alpinia galanga

galangal

ZINGIBERACEAE

CONDITIONS

Climate Best in tropical areas but grows satisfactorily, if a little slowly, anywhere frost-free. Where winters are cold but summers long and hot, try planting after the last frost in winter or spring and lifting after the first frost of autumn.
Aspect Takes bright dappled sun or part shade in the tropics, but needs full sun and a warm, sheltered position elsewhere.
Soil Best in deep, fertile, free-draining soil with plenty of rotted organic matter. Roots rot in wet soil. Use top quality potting mix for pots.

GROWING METHOD

Planting Plant sections of fresh rhizome bought in spring from an Asian grocery store or good fruit market. Cut the rhizome into sections about 7.5 cm (3 in) long, each with an obvious green growing tip. Dry the cut ends for a few days and then plant horizontally 7.5–10 cm (3–4 in) below the surface and water in. Alternatively, lift an existing plant in late winter and replant some rhizomes as above. Growing from seed takes much longer. Sow the seeds into punnets or trays of seed-raising mix. Cover lightly, moisten and place on a heated seed-germinating pad in a bright, warm place. Keep moist. When seedlings are big enough to handle, transfer to individual containers. Plant out when 15 cm (6 in) tall.
Watering Keep plants well watered from the time growth appears in spring until autumn when the top growth begins to die back. These plants are from rainy, tropical areas and expect a lot of rain in summer. Plants in pots may need watering every day during the hotter periods of summer.
Fertilising Apply a complete plant food at planting time or when growth begins, then feed the plant each month with liquid or soluble plant food. Mulch around the plants with rotted manure. Feed potted galangal fortnightly with liquid or soluble fertiliser. Also mix 1 tablespoon of controlled-release fertiliser into the potting mix at planting time.
Problems No particular problems.

HARVESTING

Picking Galangal is usually lifted in autumn when the leaves begin to deteriorate. Detach the rhizomes for culinary use and save one or two for replanting next year's crop.
Storage Cleaned rhizomes may be stored in the crisper bin of the refrigerator for a few weeks. They can also be pickled for long-term storage and they keep reasonably well in a cool, dark, well ventilated cupboard.
Freezing Not suitable for freezing.

USES

Culinary Reminiscent of ginger but with a distinctly different flavour, galangal (or Laos powder) is a popular addition to many Indonesian, Thai and Malaysian dishes.

Anethum graveolens
dill
APIACEAE/UMBELLIFERAE

CONDITIONS

Climate Needs a warmish, dry summer but can be grown with some success in cooler regions that are frost-free.

Aspect Prefers full sun; may need support and protection from winds.

Soil Dig plenty of organic matter into the garden beds to improve water retention, as these plants mature through the drier months of spring and summer.

GROWING METHOD

Planting Plant dill by seed any time except during winter. Dill will quite often self-sow, so choose a permanent position for the initial plantings. Successive planting every fortnight is recommended to ensure that there is continuous cropping. Sow the seeds in shallow furrows, with at least 60 cm (2 ft) between the rows, and then thin the seedlings out to 30 cm (1 ft) apart when they have reached approximately 5 cm (2 in) in height.

Watering Keep the plants well watered, especially during hot weather.

Fertilising Mulch well throughout spring and summer with rotted organic matter such as compost or old manure.

Problems No particular damaging pests or diseases affect this plant.

HARVESTING

Picking Dill leaves can be picked within two months of planting. Clip close to the stem in the cooler parts of the day. Several weeks after the plant blossoms, pick the flower heads and place them in a paper bag. Store the bag in a cool, dry place until the seeds ripen and fall.

Storage Leaves and stems can be frozen and pieces cut off as required. They do not keep for more than a couple of days in the refrigerator before drooping and losing flavour. Dry leaves by spreading them thinly over a firm, non-metallic surface in a warm, dark place. After drying, place them in an airtight container. Seeds are dried in a similar manner.

Freezing Leaves can be frozen for up to six months.

USES

Culinary Dill has a pronounced tang. Use fresh leaves in salads and as a garnish. Use the seeds ground or whole in cooked dishes, as well as in the making of vinegars, pickles and herb butters. Add the dried leaves to soups or sauces. It is a great favourite in fish dishes. Tea can also be made from the seeds.

Gardening Dill is considered an ideal companion plant for lettuce, cabbage and onions.

Angelica archangelica
angelica
APIACEAE/UMBELLIFERAE

CONDITIONS

Climate Cool climates are best as the plant needs to rest over winter. In frost-free areas angelica is soon exhausted by continuous growth.

Aspect In cold climates where summers tend to be mild, grow in full sun. Where summers are hot, part shade is essential. Shelter from wind.

Soil Needs well drained but moisture-retentive, fertile soil.

GROWING METHOD

Planting Grow from seed as soon as it is ripe. Sprinkle seeds onto a tray of moist seed-raising mix and barely cover. Keep evenly moist. Expect germination in 3–4 weeks, although germination is not always reliable. For a few plants, lift two-year-old plants in early spring and divide roots into smaller sections. Replant immediately into loose, friable, fertile soil.

Watering Keep soil moist – the plant is native to cool, rainy areas.

Fertilising Apply complete plant food once in early spring when new growth begins and again in early summer. Mulch around plants with compost or rotted manure.

Problems Angelica is short lived, usually dying after two years, but if it doesn't flower it grows for up to four years: snip off flower stems as they form.

Pruning No pruning is necessary. In cold climates it dies back to the ground each winter.

HARVESTING

Picking Collect the seeds by harvesting the whole flower head just as it ripens. Place in a paper bag in a warm, dry place until the seeds fall from the head. Separate the seeds from the dross before storing. For the best flavour, cut stems after they bloom. Pick leaves at any time. Dig roots just as flowers are forming and wash clean immediately.

Storage Store seeds in an airtight jar. Crystallise stems before storage. Dry and grind leaves before storing them in airtight containers. Store clean roots in a cool, dry, dark and airy place until needed.

Freezing Not suitable for freezing.

USES

Culinary Eat crystallised stems and leaves as sweets or use them to decorate cakes. Use leaves to make a herbal tea.

Medicinal Tea made from any part of the plant can be taken to soothe nervous conditions and to ward off colds. Avoid frequent or heavy consumption of any part of the angelica plant as it is known to exacerbate certain medical conditions. Diabetics should avoid the plant altogether.

Craft Use dried stems, leaves and roots in pot pourris.

Gardening Angelica is a handsome plant that makes a fine addition to a planting of perennial flowers in cool climates.

DILL An annual herb growing to 1 m (3⅓ ft), dill looks very like fennel, with its thread-like, feathery, blue-green leaves. It has a single, thin tap root rising above the ground to form a long, hollow stalk. This stalk branches at the top to support a 15 cm (6 in) wide mass of small yellow flowers, appearing in clusters in summer. Flat oval seeds, brown in colour, are produced quickly and in great quantities.

ANGELICA Growing up to 2 m (6–7 ft) tall with a spread of around 1.5 m (5 ft), angelica is a majestic, stout-stemmed, perennial herb that has large, toothed leaves made up of several leaflets. The tiny honey-scented, green-yellow flowers are produced in clusters in spring; winged seeds follow later in the summer. All parts of angelica are subtly, sweetly aromatic.

CHERVIL Chervil is a small, hardy annual herb that has a long cropping period. Looking rather like parsley, it grows to about 30 cm (12 in), the small light green leaves turning pinkish in hot sunny weather. Only the lower leaves have stalks. The leaves are usually curly but there is a variety with plain ones. Very small, white flowers are borne in clusters (called compound umbels) in summer. The herb has a very subtle flavour, somewhere between anise and parsley.

CELERY This popular vegetable grows to 25 cm (10 in) tall with erect, succulent semicircular stems and green aromatic leaves. If it is not cropped, the plant will produce flowers and then seeds. All parts of the plant are edible and can be used in a wide range of herbal remedies.

Anthriscus cerefolium
chervil
APIACEAE/UMBELLIFERAE

CONDITIONS
Climate Grows best in a cool climate but tolerates humid tropical areas.
Aspect Prefers filtered shade during summer and survives over winter if kept in the sun. Ideal for indoors if grown in a sunny position.
Soil Rich in compost and well drained. Add lime to strongly acid soils. Mulch plants against extremes of temperature.

GROWING METHOD
Planting Successive plantings every two weeks until the weather becomes too hot ensure a long cropping period. In the garden, plant under or near larger plants that provide shade and protection. Chervil does not transplant well, so sow seeds into their final position. Cover only lightly, even exposing the seeds to the sun a little, but keep the seeds moist. Germination occurs within 10 days. Thin seedlings to 25 cm (10 in) apart when they are 5 cm (2 in) high.
Watering Water well as moisture is essential at all times.
Fertilising Side dress chervil occasionally with a soluble and nitrogen-rich fertiliser to promote leaf growth.
Problems No specific diseases, although aphids can be a pest. Treat with appropriate sprays as vigorous hosing does not seem to work.

HARVESTING
Picking Chervil leaves are ready to cut from about 6–8 weeks after planting.
Storage The leaves can be made into a herb butter. The leaves are not really suitable for drying: they can be dried rapidly in an oven but they do tend to lose their flavour.
Freezing Wrap herb butters in plastic wrap and store them in the freezer.

USES
Culinary Both stems and leaves can be used as a flavouring in foods. Use fresh whole sprigs in salads or as an attractive garnish. If you are using chervil in cooking, be sure to add it at the end of the cooking process, because long periods of heating will give it a bitter flavour. Chervil is one of the main ingredients of *fines herbes* used in French cooking. It can also be used effectively in herb butters.

Apium graveolens
celery
UMBELLIFERAE

CONDITIONS
Climate Tropical to cool climates but does best in cooler areas.
Aspect Full sun is essential.
Soil As celery should be grown fast, plant into well dug, very fertile soil. Dig in well rotted manure to improve the soil fertility and condition.

GROWING METHOD
Planting In all areas sow seeds in spring. In warm and tropical regions sow through the summer. Sow seeds 5 mm (¼ in) deep into trays or punnets of fine seed-raising mix. Water with a fine mist spray and keep evenly moist. When seedlings reach about 2.5 cm (1 in) tall, gently prick them out and pot them into small, individual containers of quality potting mix. Grow on in these containers for around two months, and then plant out into a prepared bed.
Watering Always keep plants evenly moist. If the shallow roots are allowed to dry out, the stems become bitter and stringy.
Fertilising Ensure the bed contains plenty of rotted organic matter. Feed the plants fortnightly with liquid or soluble fertiliser that contains a high proportion of nitrogen.
Problems Inspect plants frequently for signs of damage by snails, slugs, aphids and caterpillars; pick pests off by hand. If chemical control is necessary, choose a product with the lowest toxicity available (for example, pyrethrum, garlic or fatty acid-based sprays).

HARVESTING
Picking Pick outside stems individually or harvest the whole plant when mature. Pick small quantities of leaves at any time but do not continually strip the leaves. If you want seeds, let a few plants go to seed; the stems may be too stringy to eat.
Storage Store seeds and dried leaves in airtight containers. Stems are best used fresh, but can be frozen. Store cleaned roots in the crisper bin of the refrigerator for a month or more.
Freezing Stems cut into sections and blanched in boiling water can be frozen for several months.

USES
Medicinal Seeds, chewed whole or made into tea, are a diuretic and help eliminate toxins that aggravate gout and arthritis. Stems and leaf stems share this attribute and are more palatable. A tincture made from celery root has a history of use as a remedy for kidney and arthritic disorders. Juice, made from the whole plant, is said to be good for bladder infections.

Armoracia rusticana
horseradish
BRASSICACEAE/CRUCIFERAE

Artemisia dracunculus
tarragon
ASTERACEAE/COMPOSITAE

CONDITIONS
Climate Cool and warm climates are most suitable.
Aspect Full sun is essential.
Soil Grow in deep soil that has been dug over deeply – a vegetable patch is ideal. It enjoys good conditions and thrives in well drained soils that are rich in rotted manure.

GROWING METHOD
Planting Dig up the root system in late autumn and replant in spring to control the plant's ability to spread rapidly. Add new plants to the garden as root cuttings. In mild areas plant them in autumn, but plant in spring where winters are cold. Allow 30 cm (12 in) between plants. The following autumn, take 20–25 cm (8–10 in) cuttings of the straight, thin side roots. These may be replanted immediately in mild areas, but in cold places they are best kept over winter in just-damp sphagnum moss, soil or sand. Replant in spring.
Watering Keep horseradish plants moist during spring and summer. If you are growing it in the vegetable patch, give it the same watering as other vegetables.
Fertilising Mix a ration of low-nitrogen fertiliser into the planting hole and drench two or three times during the growing season with a low-nitrogen liquid or soluble plant food – one designed to promote flowering is ideal. Too much nitrogen makes excessive leaves and poor quality roots.
Problems Snails, slugs and caterpillars will strip young plants quickly if not controlled. Lay traps for snails and slugs, and either pick off and squash caterpillars or spray plants with preparations containing *Bacillus thuringiensis*, a biological control that kills only caterpillars.

HARVESTING
Picking The main harvest is in autumn, although side roots can be snipped off in summer for immediate use. Scrape soil away from the main root, replacing it when the desired roots have been cut. For the main harvest, lift the plant, ensuring that all roots are removed (or the plant will regrow). Use selected side roots for regeneration, the rest for processing.
Storage Fresh whole roots can be stored in the refrigerator for about two weeks, while the grated roots can be made into horseradish sauce or pickled in vinegar.
Freezing Whole roots can be wrapped in foil and frozen for up to six months.

USES
Culinary Use horseradish sauce as a condiment with beef, other meats and fish. Add a little to sauces and dressings.
Medicinal Horseradish clears blocked noses instantly but is not an easy medicine to take. It has antiseptic properties and is said to ward off colds if small amounts are eaten regularly. It contains high levels of vitamin C and essential minerals.

CONDITIONS
Climate Cool and warm climates provide the best conditions but tarragon grows well in hot, arid areas if it is watered regularly. If winters are not cool enough to cause the plant to go dormant, it will be short lived.
Aspect Prefers full sun or partial shade.
Soil Needs well drained, sandy soils that do not hold moisture for too long, especially over winter when the rhizomes may rot. Dig in some organic matter.

GROWING METHOD
Planting Propagate by root division. Lift the plant during spring, divide it and replant the pieces in pots or in the garden, spaced 60 cm (2 ft) apart. Tarragon needs to be replanted every few years as the plants lose their vigour over time.
Watering Keep well watered but ease off over winter. Soils should be damp but not soggy.
Fertilising Apply complete plant food once in early spring. Mulch French tarragon (*A. dracunculus*) over winter when it has died down.
Problems No specific pests but it does suffer from downy and powdery mildew. Fungal growths may appear on the leaves, which wilt and die. Remove affected plants and burn them. Root rot may also be a problem.
Pruning Pick out flower stems to promote leaf growth.

HARVESTING
Picking Pick leaves during summer but take care not to bruise them.
Storage Leaves can be dried, although much of the flavour and some of the colour will be lost in the process. Place them on racks or hang stems in bunches in a warm, dry place, and then store them in airtight containers. Leaves can also be preserved in vinegar.
Freezing Wrap leaves in plastic wrap and freeze for up to six months.

USES
Culinary Tarragon is one of the herbs in the classic French *fines herbes* used to enhance the flavours of various foods, from fish, meat and dairy foods to herbed vinegars, butters, sauces, vegetables and soups. Leaves of Russian tarragon (*A. dracunculus* var. *dracunculoides*) lack the aromatic oils of the French variety.

HORSERADISH Although it is a perennial plant, horseradish is often grown as an annual. It is a rather weedy looking plant, consisting as it does of a clump of big, soft, spinach-like leaves, and it is best grown tucked away in the vegetable patch. In spring a stem of unremarkable, off-white flowers rises from the centre of the clump.

TARRAGON The two culinary varieties grown are French tarragon and Russian or 'false' tarragon. French tarragon is a perennial herb that spreads by rhizomes, or underground stems, sending up erect stems to a height of 38–50 cm (15–20 in) or more. The leaves are olive green with an anise flavour. It dies down over winter and regenerates in spring. It must be propagated by division. The tarragon seed offered by some nurseries is Russian tarragon. This variety keeps some of its foliage and is more vigorous but has a much more bitter flavour. White or greenish flowers appear in late summer.

BORAGE A fast-growing annual or biennial that grows up to 1 m (3¹⁄₃ ft) tall, borage bears star-shaped flowers with protruding black anthers in summer. They are usually bright sky blue, although they can sometimes also be pink or white. The bush bears many sprawling, leafy branches with hollow stems, which can be quite fragile. The stems are covered with stiff white hairs and the greyish green leaves are also hairy.

Borago officinalis

borage

BORAGINACEAE

CONDITIONS

Climate Grows in all climates except extreme cold.
Aspect Prefers a sunny spot but grows in most positions, including partial shade; needs plenty of space. Has brittle stems, so plants may need staking to prevent wind damage. It grows quite well indoors if placed in a sunny corner.
Soil Grows well in most soils that are aerated, moist and mulched to keep competitive weeds down. Indoors, grow borage in a deep pot, with a moist and fertile potting mix.

GROWING METHOD

Planting Sow seed directly into the garden in clumps and thin out the seedlings later, leaving 60 cm (2 ft) between plants. Seedlings do not transplant well once established. Successive sowings of seeds every 3–4 weeks after winter frosts have disappeared will extend the harvesting period. The plant self-sows readily and its spread may need to be controlled. Take tip cuttings from a mature plant in spring and pot them up, using a coarse sandy mix. Dampen the soil and cover the pot with a plastic bag supported on sticks or a wire frame. When cuttings have taken hold, plant them out in spring or summer.
Watering Keep the soil moist at all times.
Fertilising Apply complete plant food once each spring or use controlled-release granules.
Problems Generally free of specific pest and disease problems.

HARVESTING

Picking Pick the leaves as required while they are fresh and young. Harvest the open flowers during the summer months.
Storage You must use the leaves fresh; you cannot dry and store them. You can crystallise the flowers and then store them in airtight jars.
Freezing The leaves cannot be frozen. The flowers may be frozen in ice cubes.

USES

Culinary Borage has a faintly cucumber-like taste: add young leaves to salads. Freeze flowers in ice cubes for cold drinks, or crystallise them and use to decorate cakes and desserts.
Note Borage may be a danger to health: it is now under study because of the presence of toxic alkaloids.
Gardening An excellent companion plant in the garden, especially when it is planted near strawberries.

CARAWAY Caraway is a biennial plant growing to around 60 cm (2 ft) in height on slim, faintly striped stems. Its leaves are aromatic, finely cut and ferny, and in summer the plant produces heads of small white flowers. These are followed by ridged, dark brown seeds. The edible, carrot-like roots are white.

Carum carvi

caraway

APIACEAE/UMBELLIFERAE

CONDITIONS

Climate Equally suited to cool or warm climates. In rainy tropical areas it is best grown in winter.
Aspect Full sun, but will tolerate a few hours of afternoon shade. In windy areas, shelter is desirable.
Soil Deeply dug, good quality, well drained soil allows the roots to grow straight and long. Soil that contains rotted organic matter is the most fertile.

GROWING METHOD

Planting Grow from seed sown in early spring or, where winters are not cold, in autumn, directly where the plants are to grow. Sow the seeds shallowly, 15–20 cm (6–8 in) apart, or thin to that spacing after germination. Mulch around the plants with compost, rotted manure or lucerne hay.
Watering Water deeply during dry times.
Fertilising Dig a ration of complete plant food into the soil before planting, and water plants with liquid organic or soluble fertiliser once or twice during late spring and summer.
Problems No particular pest or disease problems, but to prevent an invasion of caraway seedlings, remove the seed heads before the seeds fall.

HARVESTING

Picking Pick seed heads when thoroughly ripe but before the seeds have begun to fall. To dry them properly, place them in open containers in the sun. Pick the young spring leaves, the most palatable, as needed. Use the roots when young and small also. Pull up the whole plant in late spring.
Storage Store dry seeds in airtight jars after they have been separated from the dried seed head. Store roots in the refrigerator for a few weeks. Eat the leaves while they are fresh.
Freezing Caraway is not suitable for freezing.

USES

Culinary Use the seeds in herbal tea and in baking, and add them to many other recipes, especially vegetable and fruit dishes and curries. Add the leaves to salads; steam or boil the roots and eat them as a vegetable.
Medicinal All parts are good for the digestion and kidneys; chew the seeds after a heavy meal to relieve wind and bloating.
Gardening Sowing a succession of caraway plants in heavy, not very friable soil improves its tilth.

Chamaemelum nobile, syn. *Anthemis nobilis*
chamomile
ASTERACEAE/COMPOSITAE

Cichorium intybus
chicory
ASTERACEAE/COMPOSITAE

CONDITIONS
Climate Grows in most climates, from hot to cool.
Aspect Prefers full sun, but grows well in areas with partial shade.
Soil Prefers a lime-rich soil.

GROWING METHOD
Planting Plant the very fine seeds in spring in well fertilised beds. Or raise seedlings in trays of seed-raising mix and then prick them out into 7.5 cm (3 in) pots to harden and establish before planting them out. Dig over and rake the area before transplanting the seedlings during spring. For a chamomile lawn, prepare the area over winter, then spread or sow the seed directly into a prepared lawn bed. Finely rake the bed to cover the seed then water it in. Keep the lawn weeded. Alternatively, take rooted cuttings or offshoots of the parent plant and set them out in well manured soil, 45 cm (18 in) apart. In cold areas mulch them heavily so they will survive severe frosts.
Watering Keep the soil evenly moist; do not let it dry out.
Fertilising Give light applications of blood and bone during spring and autumn.
Problems No specific pests or diseases worry this herb.
Pruning Chamomile lawns can be mowed and will regenerate quickly.

HARVESTING
Picking Pick flowers as they appear during late spring and summer, just as the petals start to turn backwards from the central yellow disk.
Storage Dry flowers on paper on racks in a cool, airy space, then store them in airtight jars.
Freezing Flowers can be frozen for up to six months.

USES
Cosmetic Use the flowers to make face masks and hair rinses.
Culinary Chamomile is popular as a herbal tea.
Craft Use the flowers in pot pourris.
Gardening As a companion plant, chamomile keeps a range of other plants happy and healthy, especially cucumber, onions and other herbs.

CONDITIONS
Climate Suitable for most climates but not usually long lived in the monsoonal tropics.
Aspect Prefers full sun.
Soil These plants require deep, rich, friable soil for best growth. Dig in plenty of organic matter in the form of compost or decayed animal manures before planting. Keep the garden beds free of weeds.

GROWING METHOD
Planting Plant seeds in spring, into drills or trenches 2.5 cm (1 in) deep, and thin the seedlings to 30 cm (12 in) apart when they are established. Seeds may also be germinated in seed trays and seedlings transplanted into the garden during spring. Divide the mature plants in autumn, then replant in spring. Sow seeds in autumn in hot, dry tropical areas.
Watering Keep chicory well watered during spells of hot weather, especially in hot, dry areas without much natural rainfall.
Fertilising Add compost to the garden bed in midsummer, but do not provide too much nitrogen or the leaves will grow rapidly at the expense of root growth.
Problems No particular pests or diseases affect this plant.

HARVESTING
Picking Pick young green leaves of chicory when they are required. Pick flowers as they appear, early on summer mornings. Carefully dig up the roots in mid-autumn if planted in spring, and in early summer if planted in autumn.
Storage The leaves cannot be stored either fresh or dried. The root can be dried and then rendered into a powder.
Freezing Not suitable for freezing.

USES
Culinary Use young, freshly picked leaves, either in salads or in cooking. The strong, bitterish flavour is similar to dandelion. Flowers can be crystallised and used to decorate cakes and puddings. The root powder is used in beverages.

CHAMOMILE
This perennial herb is known as Roman chamomile and should not be confused with the erect and much taller growing annual form that is known as German chamomile (*Matricaria recutita*). Both forms have feathery foliage and flower from late spring to late summer. The daisy-like blossoms are white with a yellow centre, and they have many uses. Chamomile has an attractive apple-like fragrance and flavour.

CHICORY This large perennial plant sometimes reaches more than 1 m (3¹/₃ ft) in height. It bears intense sky blue, fine-petalled flowers in summer, which open in the morning but close up in the hot midday sun. The broad, oblong leaves with ragged edges, reminiscent of dandelions, form a rosette around the bottom of the tall, straggly stems. The upper leaves are much smaller, giving a bare look to the top of the plant. Chicory is an attractive background plant but it can sometimes need support to remain upright. If cultivated by forced growth and blanching, the lettuce-like heart of the chicory plant is turned into the vegetable witlof, also known as Belgian endive.

CORIANDER Also known as Chinese parsley or cilantro, this very quick-growing, bright green annual reaches a height of approximately 50 cm (20 in). Leaves on the lower part of the stem are oval with serrated edges, but as they mature on the outside branches the leaves become feathery and divided into narrow segments. The small flowers are white to pink, mauve or reddish and are borne in short-stalked clusters in summer. The spherical seeds are brownish yellow in colour, about 3 mm (1/8 in) in diameter and have a musty odour.

LEMON GRASS Also known as citronella grass, lemon grass is a perennial grass of tropical regions. The narrow, ribbon-like, leafy stalks grow in clumps up to 1 m (3 1/3 ft) or more in height. The leaves swell slightly at the base to form a fleshy stolon or underground stem. The stem is white and is also edible. The edges of mature leaves are rough and can be quite sharp – it's easy to get cut fingers when harvesting them.

Coriandrum sativum
coriander
APIACEAE/UMBELLIFERAE

CONDITIONS
Climate Likes hot, dry climates resembling those of the eastern Mediterranean region and southern Europe, but coriander will grow in cool, warm and tropical areas.
Aspect Prefers a sunny position, or partial shade in very hot climates.
Soil Well drained and mulched beds required to keep weed growth down. Coriander is a very fast growing but short lived herb which will grow in most soils that are not over-rich in fertiliser. Too much nitrogen lessens the flavour in the plant.

GROWING METHOD
Planting Successive sowings of seed several weeks apart will extend the cropping period. Autumn sowings in mild climates produce seedlings that fare much better than those germinated in spring, which may mature quickly and go to seed. Sow directly into garden beds, into holes 1 cm (1/2 in) deep and 20 cm (8 in) apart. Seedlings start to appear within 1–2 weeks, two from each seed. Thin plants to 10–15 cm (4–6 in) apart.
Watering Water evenly and do not let the soil dry out during hot, dry spells.
Fertilising No fertiliser is necessary.
Problems Coriander is prone to bacterial wilt and downy mildew. The mildew may be sprayed; otherwise, remove and burn affected plants.

HARVESTING
Picking Pick fresh leaves as required; the smaller immature leaves have the better taste. Harvest seed when leaves and flowers turn brown and the seed is ripe. Pull out the whole plant, place it upside down in a paper bag and hang it in a cool, dry, airy space. The ripened seeds will fall into the bag.
Storage Seeds are dried and stored in sealed jars or ground to a powder. The leaves cannot be dried satisfactorily.
Freezing The leaves can be frozen for up to six months.

USES
Culinary Leaves, seeds and roots are used for culinary purposes, especially in Asian cuisines. Both leaves and roots can be eaten fresh, the leaves having a pronounced sage flavour with citrus overtones and the roots having an additional nutty flavour. They also go well with meats and vegetables in cooking. Ground coriander seed is much favoured as a spice.

Cymbopogon citratus
lemon grass
GRAMINEAE/POACEAE

CONDITIONS
Climate Lemon grass prefers to grow in warm or tropical regions but will grow in cooler areas if the frosts are not too severe and if the plant is heavily mulched in autumn to protect it throughout winter.
Aspect Outside of tropical areas, lemon grass requires a protected, sunny position. In cooler climates, it can be grown in a container in a greenhouse or on a sunny, protected deck – these conditions provide enough humidity to simulate its natural environment.
Soil Rich, fertile soils. Add plenty of organic matter in the form of compost, leaves, straw or decayed animal manures to the soil before planting and mulch constantly throughout the season to retain moisture levels.

GROWING METHOD
Planting Lemon grass rarely flowers. Plant commercially purchased root stock or propagate in spring. To do this, divide the mature plant, breaking off portions from the outer edge of the clump, and then replant.
Watering Water well as this plant requires a great deal of water, especially during the earlier stages of its growth.
Fertilising In spring and summer apply liquid or soluble fertiliser monthly.
Problems Lemon grass is not attacked by any particular pests or diseases.

HARVESTING
Picking Pick leaves or remove portions of the stem in summer as required.
Storage Harvested portions will keep in the refrigerator for a few days. Lemon grass cannot be dried.
Freezing Can be wrapped in plastic wrap and frozen for up to six months.

USES
Culinary Lemon grass is widely used in the cuisines of Southeast Asia. The 'sweet–sour', lemony flavour of the leaves is used in herbal teas, or pieces can be tied together and used to flavour marinades and in cooking. The white, fleshy stem is chopped and used to flavour cooked dishes such as curries, fish or soups. If fibrous, the stem should be discarded after cooking.

Foeniculum vulgare

fennel
APIACEAE/UMBELLIFERAE

CONDITIONS
Climate Grows in most areas but does best in cool to warm climates where frosts are not very severe. Not well suited to the high levels of summer rain and humidity in the tropics.
Aspect Full sun is essential and shelter from blustery winds advisable.
Soil Most vigorous on crumbly, sandy loam with plenty of rotted organic matter. Dig in 1 cup of lime per square metre (square yard) of soil before planting as fennel prefers slightly alkaline conditions.

GROWING METHOD
Planting Most easily grown from seed sown in spring or, in frost-free areas, autumn. Sow the seeds directly where they are to grow, 5 mm (¼ in) deep and thin to about 30 cm (12 in) apart. Vigorous young plants produce the sweetest and best flavoured 'bulbs', and you should dig out and replace plants every three years.
Watering Keep well watered during spring and summer. Consistent moisture around the roots ensures succulent, sweet growth. Decrease water from about mid-autumn.
Fertilising Additional feeding is not necessary if the soil is rich and fertile. If in doubt, apply complete plant food once in early spring.
Problems No particular problems.

HARVESTING
Picking Pick leaves any time from late spring to late summer. Seeds are harvested when ripe in late summer and as this time approaches, plants should be inspected regularly so that ripe seeds can be gathered before they start to fall. The bulbous bases can be dug up as required.
Storage Store dried seeds in airtight jars. Use the leaves fresh as they lose flavour during drying.
Freezing Wrap small bunches of leaves in a freezer bag or foil and freeze for up to six months.

USES
Cosmetic Cold tea made from the seeds is a refreshing facial rinse that is said to reduce wrinkles and tone the skin.
Culinary Seeds, which are an aid to digestion, are chewed raw or used whole or ground in recipes. Add finely chopped leaves to many dishes, notably fish and carbohydrates such as pasta and potatoes, and to vinegars. Eat the fleshy, white base raw or cooked.
Medicinal All parts of fennel are said to be beneficial to the digestion, good for the eyes and a mild appetite suppressant. Tea made from the seeds is a mild laxative. Chew the seeds to freshen stale breath.

Hyssopus officinalis

hyssop
LABIATAE/LAMIACEAE

CONDITIONS
Climate Best in cool or warm areas. In the tropics, grow in pots sheltered from heavy summer rains.
Aspect Full sun produces compact growth and the strongest flavour but hyssop tolerates shade for part of the day.
Soil Likes light, fertile, well drained soils but will grow in any reasonably fertile soil as long as it drains freely.

GROWING METHOD
Planting Hyssop can be grown from seed, softwood cuttings or division of the roots. Sow seeds in spring in trays of seed-raising mix. Cover lightly, keep moist and when seedlings are big enough to handle, prick out into small, individual pots to grow on. Plant out 30 cm (12 in) apart when plants are about 20 cm (8 in) tall. Take 7.5 cm (3 in) tip cuttings in spring and insert into pots of sandy potting mix. Keep moist and in bright, sheltered shade – roots will form within a month. To divide, lift a parent plant in late autumn or early spring. Cut the root mass into smaller sections and replant immediately.
Watering Keep soil moist, especially during the warmer months, but do not overwater. Hyssop is a resilient plant that can often get by on rain.
Fertilising Complete plant food applied in spring when new growth appears is enough.
Problems No particular problems.
Pruning When new growth begins in spring, pinching out the tips of young stems will encourage the plant to become bushier and thus produce more flowers. In late autumn, the remains of the plant can be cut to ground level.

HARVESTING
Picking Pick flowers for using fresh or for drying when they are in full bloom. Harvest individual stems as needed.
Storage Store flowers and leaves dry. Cut bunches of flowering stems, tie them together and hang them upside down in a dim, airy place. When they are dry, crumble them into airtight jars.
Freezing Not suitable for freezing.

USES
Culinary Add 1–2 finely chopped fresh leaves to soups and casseroles. Fresh flowers give flavour and colour to salads.
Medicinal Tea, made from the dried stems, leaves and flowers, may relieve the symptoms of colds; hyssop leaves are often a component in mixed herbal tonics and teas.
Cosmetic Oil distilled from hyssop is used in perfumes and other commercial cosmetics. At home, add to bath water. Cooled hyssop leaf tea is a cleansing, refreshing facial rinse.
Gardening Hyssop is a decorative plant and very attractive to bees and butterflies. Use it in a border of mixed flowers or grow it as an edging to paths.

FENNEL
Fast growing and spreading, this herbaceous perennial can reach a height of nearly 2 m (7 ft). An erect, finely foliaged plant with a strong aniseed aroma, it has a bulbous, fleshy base, hollow stems and thread-like, delicate, dark olive green leaves. Flattened heads of tiny, bright yellow flowers appear on the top of the plant in summer. Fennel is an extremely invasive plant that has been declared a noxious weed in some areas. It should only be grown where an unwanted spread can be easily controlled.

HYSSOP A perennial to around 60 cm (2 ft) tall, hyssop has many erect stems clothed in narrow, lanceolate, sage green leaves. Spikes of small blue-violet, pink or white flowers appear in summer. The whole plant exudes a pungent aroma and the leaves have a bitter taste.

ORRIS ROOT
Orris root is a rhizomatous perennial iris. It consists of a fan-shaped clump of stiff, upright, sword-shaped leaves in grey-green with distinct parallel veins. The showy flowers appear in spring or summer, and are white flushed with mauve or soft lilac-blue. The plant grows to a height of approximately 45 cm (18 in). Once dried, the root exudes a strong aroma reminiscent of violets, a property not shared with other irises.

BAY TREE An aromatic, evergreen tree 10–20 m (33–66 ft) high, the bay is often grown in containers where the height can be controlled. The trunk has smooth grey bark and the short stalks bear alternate, shiny, dark green elliptical-shaped leaves with wavy edges. The leaves are the edible part of the plant; they are 2.5–5 cm (1–2 in) long and leathery in texture. The flowers, inconspicuous and yellowish green, appear in spring and produce dark purple or black one-seeded berries.

Iris x *germanica* var. *florentina*
orris root
IRIDACEAE

CONDITIONS
Climate Best suited to cool climates. Can be grown in warm areas if they are not excessively hot, wet and humid in summer.
Aspect Full sun is essential.
Soil Plants do best in well drained, slightly alkaline soil to which a proportion of rotted organic matter has been added. Take care not to over-enrich the soil with either manures or fertilisers as these plants do not grow well with high levels of nitrogen.

GROWING METHOD
Planting Grow from divisions of the rhizome taken after blooming. Lift the plant and cut its creeping rhizome into sections. Each section should have its own fan of leaves and a growing point. The old centre of the clump, which has flowered, will never do so again and should be discarded. Cut the leaves in half crosswise, and then replant the rhizomes about 35 cm (14 in) apart into soil that has been well dug over. Lay them horizontally so that about half the rhizome is above ground level – deeper planting will cause the rhizomes to rot.
Watering Keep soil evenly moist during the warmer months. Orris root is not particularly tolerant of prolonged dry conditions.
Fertilising Dig in a lean ration of complete plant food at planting time, but no other feeding will be necessary. A thin mulch of very old, rotted manure or compost may be applied.
Problems No particular problems.

HARVESTING
Picking Dig out the root in early summer. A few pieces of young rhizome can be replanted to provide future crops and the rest can then be put aside for processing.
Storage Clean the root and cut it into small segments. Dry it in the sun and then store it in an airtight jar in the fridge. The fragrance of the root does not develop fully until after about a year.
Freezing Not suitable for freezing.

USES
Craft Orris root is mainly used to give a heady violet scent to pot pourris. It also acts as a preservative in such dried material. Do take care, however, as orris root may cause sneezing, coughing and other allergic reactions in some sensitive people.

Laurus nobilis
bay tree
LAURACEAE

CONDITIONS
Climate Mediterranean-style climate with hot, dry summers and cool, wet winters.
Aspect Prefers full sun in cool to warm zones. Needs partial shade on very hot summer days if growing in tropical areas.
Soil Moderately rich and well drained soil. For a potted tree, add lime if the soil is very acid, ensure that the pot is large enough for the root ball and add decayed animal manure or compost if necessary. Mulch the top soil.

GROWING METHOD
Planting Fresh green shoots or tip cuttings taken in autumn and summer offer the best chance of success. Take a 7.5 cm (3 in) cutting from a mature plant and remove the upper and lower leaves. Dip the end in hormonal rooting powder to speed up root growth. Place the cutting in a small pot containing a mix of two-thirds coarse sand and one-third peat moss. Place the pot under a plastic bag, making a wire frame to hold the bag off the cutting. This mini-glasshouse provides a warm, humid environment. Cuttings may take nine months to take root before they can be planted in the garden.
Watering Let the soil dry out between waterings, but during hot weather keep the moisture up, especially for potted specimens.
Fertilising Apply complete plant food once in spring, and then mulch with rotted organic matter. Keep mulch away from the trunk.
Problems Scale, a small wingless insect covered with a waxy substance, may suck the sap of the plant and cause stunted growth. Secretions attract ants, promoting sooty mould. Treat with insecticidal soap sprays.
Pruning Prune only if you want to restrict the height or formalise the shape.

HARVESTING
Picking Pick leaves early in the day throughout the year and then use fresh or dried as required.
Storage Dry in a dark, airy room. Place leaves on a firm, flat surface and weigh them down to prevent curling. Leave for at least two weeks. Store dried leaves in sealed jars.
Freezing Wrap the leaves in plastic wrap; freeze for up to six months.

USES
Culinary Excellent as a flavouring in soups, stews, sauces and custards, bay is also used when cooking game, in terrines and in pickling brines. The leaves are an essential component of bouquet garni.
Gardening This very slow-growing tree casts dense shade. It can be pruned into formal shapes when grown in containers.

Lavandula spp.
lavender
LABIATAE/LAMIACEAE

CONDITIONS
Climate Best suited to cool or warm climates where most rain falls in winter. Not suited to the tropics or areas that are very humid.
Aspect Prefers full sun. Flowering spikes need protection from severe winds.
Soil Prefers well drained soil, but it need not be rich. If it is acid, add lime or dolomite.

GROWING METHOD
Planting Seed has a long germination time and may not come true to strain: taking cuttings is the best way to get the lavender you want. Take 5 cm (2 in) tip cuttings with a heel or base of old wood in autumn or late winter. Trim off the upper and lower leaves and plant in a mixture of two-thirds coarse sand to one-third peat moss. Keep soil on the dry side until the cutting has taken root and new leaf shoots appear. Then pot on into a good quality potting mix. Plant in the garden in spring about 60 cm (2 ft) apart. Or pull a lower branch of a mature plant to soil level, slightly scratch the underside and peg it into the soil. Once the branch has taken root, cut it off and transfer it to its new spot.
Watering Water only in dry weather as lavenders do not require a great deal of water.
Fertilising Applications of a complete fertiliser (NPK 5:6:7) will improve fragrance. Less cold-resistant varieties may need winter mulching.
Problems Roots are often attacked in this otherwise tough plant. Root knot nematodes can arrest the flow of nutrients and water to the plant. Companion planting with marigolds will keep nematodes down. Root rot can result from poor drainage, and diseased plants need to be removed. Leaf spot, causing yellowing leaves with whitish spots, indicates plants may be too close together and need more air circulation. Do not water over leaves.
Pruning Keep plants pruned in their first year to discourage flowering: bushier plants result.

HARVESTING
Picking Cut flowers in early spring before they open. Dry by hanging in bunches in a dry, airy, hot place.
Storage Store dried leaves and flowers in airtight jars.
Freezing Not suitable for freezing.

USES
Culinary Use fresh or dried flowers and leaves to flavour sugars, jellies, ice creams and cheeses. Flowers can also be crystallised and used as decoration on cakes.
Craft Use dried lavender spikes for their fragrance in pot pourris, perfumed sachets and dried arrangements. Lavender is also used to make essential oil and floral waters.

Levisticum officinale
lovage
APIACEAE/UMBELLIFERAE

CONDITIONS
Climate Lovage is not suitable for hot tropical areas. It grows well in cool climates, tolerating extremes of frost.
Aspect Prefers full sun or semi-shade.
Soil Moist, fertile, well drained alkaline soil. Dig plenty of compost and decayed animal manure deep into the soil and if acidity is a problem, add some lime or dolomite to the top soil. In warmer areas, mulch the soil around each plant to keep it cool, moist and free of weeds.

GROWING METHOD
Planting Sow seeds in late summer through autumn directly into the garden, or plant seedlings approximately 30 cm (12 in) apart. Propagate mature plants that have been in the garden for at least two seasons by dividing the roots in autumn or spring.
Watering Water well so that the soil is moist, especially in hot, dry weather.
Fertilising Give an application of complete plant food once in early spring.
Problems Aphids love lovage and can transmit viral diseases to the plant. Hose vigorously to break their cycle or treat with organic or recommended insecticidal sprays. Leaf miner maggots will tunnel into the leaves, causing white blotches. Remove infected leaves.
Pruning For a bushier plant, prune the flowers in summer.

HARVESTING
Picking Harvest any part of the plant as needed. Do not cut the central stem when picking leaves.
Storage Dry stems, leaves and seeds and keep them in airtight jars.
Freezing Blanch the leaves in boiling water and then quickly freeze them wrapped in small lots or frozen within ice cubes. Can be frozen for up to six months.

USES
Culinary The leaves, stems and seeds are substitutes for celery. Try leaves and stems in fresh salads and dried seeds in soups, casseroles, sauces and pickling mixtures, or savoury biscuits. Lovage is also used in teas, vinegars and butters.

LAVENDER
The many varieties of this fragrant perennial herb include *L. angustifolia* (a favourite subspecies is *L. angustifolia* 'Alba', or white lavender), *L. dentata* and *L. stoechas*. The common names English, French and Italian lavender are used, but authorities disagree as to which species is which. Heights differ but all grow into evergreen, bushy shrubs. Leaf edges are smooth or serrated, depending on the variety. Long spikes of fragrant deep purple to pinkish flowers appear in late winter to summer.

LOVAGE
A very tall perennial herb that reaches 1–2 m (3¹/₃–7 ft), this plant looks quite spectacular when growing in the garden. Dark green to yellowish leaves become smaller towards the top of the plant and break into wedge-shaped, ridged leaflets. Greenish flowers appear in summer, and are then followed by 5 mm (¼ in) long, light brown, grooved aromatic seeds. The hollow, ribbed stems of lovage look and taste like celery and there is a longish tap root that looks much like a carrot. Lovage may die back to ground level over winter but it will regenerate in the spring.

LEMON BALM A spreading perennial growing to 90 cm (3 ft) high, lemon balm has small, serrated, nettle-like leaves with a lemon scent. Spikes of inconspicuous white flowers are borne in the axils of the leaves during summer. These plants are very sensitive to frosts and may die back during winter, but established plants will regenerate in spring. Position lemon balm anywhere in the garden, and especially near trees or plants that need bees to pollinate blossoms.

MINT There are many varieties of mint, but all are perennials and all have square stems and invasive, spreading roots. They can be prostrate or upright in nature. The simple, light to dark green or mottled leaves have toothed edges and their own individual fragrance, depending on the variety. Small purple, pink or white flowers grow in whorls on terminal spikes in summer. Because of their very invasive nature, mints are best grown in containers or in garden beds that have a solid border at least 50 cm (20 in) deep.

Melissa officinalis

lemon balm
LABIATAE/LAMIACEAE

CONDITIONS

Climate Balm comes from the hot regions of North Africa and southern Europe but is now cultivated successfully in warm zones and even some cooler areas. May be grown in the cooler months in the tropics.
Aspect Prefers full sun or partial shade.
Soil Soils should be rich in organic matter and kept moist and well mulched. Before planting, dig lime or dolomite into the beds.

GROWING METHOD

Planting Balm can be propagated in three ways. Sow seeds directly into the garden in early to mid-autumn, or first germinate them in seed boxes and then transplant them during early spring. The germination period is long, and in the garden seedlings may need protection during winter. Mulching will help. Root division of the parent plant in early spring is also successful. Space the divided roots at least 60 cm (2 ft) apart. Cuttings 10–13 cm (4–5 in) long can be taken from new spring growth. Cut below a node of the parent plant and remove the top leaves of the cuttings. Plant them deeply in small pots containing a 3:1 mix of river sand and peat moss, and keep the soil moist.
Watering Keep plants well watered in hot dry spells.
Fertilising Apply complete plant food once in early spring when new growth begins.
Problems The diseases most likely to strike are fungal. Brown leaves or orange, powdery spots or pustules on the leaves' undersides indicate rust infection. In moderately dry climates, powdery mildew may form a light grey powdery coating on leaves, flowers or young shoots, causing stunting or even defoliation of the plant. Treat both diseases with recommended fungal sprays. The most common insect pest is spider mite. Spray with the appropriate insecticide.
Pruning Keep straggly clumps in shape by pruning during spring for summer growth.

HARVESTING

Picking Pick fresh leaves as required. Cut whole stems when flowers begin to emerge and then dry them. The leaves are most tender and full of flavour in spring.
Storage Dry quickly by hanging cut stems in a cool, airy space. Rub dry leaves and flowers from the stems and store in airtight jars.
Freezing Wrap in plastic wrap; freeze for up to six months.

USES

Culinary Use fresh leaves and flowers in salads; you can also use the leaves in stuffings or sauces for poultry and fish. Lemon balm herbal teas are very popular and fresh leaves can also be used to flavour cool summer drinks.

Mentha spp.

mint
LABIATAE/LAMIACEAE

CONDITIONS

Climate Grows in most climates, even in arid areas if it is watered regularly.
Aspect Prefers a semi-shaded position but will grow in full sun if the soil is kept moist. Mint can be grown indoors in a container.
Soil Moderately rich and well mulched soil that retains moisture. Too much organic matter or fresh manures added to the bed will encourage rust diseases.

GROWING METHOD

Planting Most mints can be raised from seed (although some varieties, such as spearmint, cannot be propagated in this way), but root division during spring and summer is the easiest method of propagation. Lift runners, divide them and replant in rich, moist soil.
Watering Keep the soil moist as mint must always have plenty of water.
Fertilising No fertiliser is necessary if mint is planted in well mulched soil.
Problems Mint flea beetle is a tiny, dark, oval pest that is continually on the move when disturbed. It eats holes in the leaves and its larvae will eat into the roots of the plant. To treat it, keep weeds down and spread lime around the bush. Treat spider mite with an appropriate spray. Discolouring of leaves may indicate mint rust – which can be treated with sulphur dustings – or a form of wilt that causes leaves to brown and drop. Treat the wilt by removing diseased plants and do not feed healthy plants with high-nitrogen fertilisers.
Pruning Frequent pruning of the stems forces lateral branching and healthier plants.

HARVESTING

Picking Pick young, fresh leaves at any time. The younger the leaf, the more tender and tasty it will be.
Storage Place the leaves on a rack in a cool, airy space to dry. When dry, crumble them and store in airtight jars.
Freezing Fresh leaves can be chopped and frozen in small packages or in ice cubes.

USES

Culinary Mints have a wide range of flavours, from the fruity taste of apple mint (*M. suaveolens*) to the perfume-like eau de cologne variety (*M.* x *piperita citrata*), making them very useful, especially in sauces or jellies. They can be used fresh in salads, drinks, vinegars or as a garnish to vegetables, often turning a bland taste into an exciting experience. Dried mints can be used in place of some of the salt in soups.
Gardening Some organic gardeners promote the growth of mint around apple trees to ward off moths, but there is some doubt about its effectiveness.

curry tree
Murraya koenigii

curry tree
RUTACEAE

CONDITIONS

Climate Grows best in warm and tropical regions. It tolerates light frosts but only if they are relatively infrequent.
Aspect Prefers full sun but in tropical areas will tolerate afternoon shade. In windy areas, grow it in a sheltered spot.
Soil Needs deep, fertile, moisture-retentive soil that drains freely after watering or heavy rain.

GROWING METHOD

Planting Can be raised from seed sown in spring into 15 cm (6 in) wide containers of potting or seed-raising mix. When seedlings are about 20 cm (8 in) tall, either pot them up to grow bigger or plant them out in their permanent positions. Alternatively, take firm tip cuttings in late spring or early summer. Insert them into sandy potting mix and place the containers on a heated seed-germinating pad. Keep the soil evenly moist.
Watering Trees grow fastest and best in soils that are always moist, so give regular, deep soakings during extended droughts or if rain is unreliable.
Fertilising If soil is deep and fertile, a yearly or twice yearly application of rotted organic matter beneath the foliage canopy will be sufficient. In poorer soils or the monsoonal tropics, give a ration of complete plant food once in spring and again towards the end of summer.
Problems The fruit is attractive to birds, so there's a risk of self-seeding in frost-free areas.
Pruning No pruning is necessary but the tree can be pruned at the start of spring in order to control its size.

HARVESTING

Picking Harvest the leaves at any time they are needed.
Storage You can dry the leaves but this diminishes their flavour. The longer they are stored the less flavour they have.
Freezing Not suitable for freezing.

USES

Culinary Fresh leaves are used to impart a curry-like flavour to soups, stews, pickles and marinades. They cannot be used as a substitute for curry powder, which is a different product altogether.
Medicinal In India, all parts of the tree are used medicinally. Extracts are said to be effective for the relief of headaches, diarrhoea and intestinal worms.
Gardening This attractive tree can be grown successfully in a big tub.

Nepeta x faassenii, N. cataria

catmint
LABIATAE/LAMIACEAE

CONDITIONS

Climate Grows in most climates, but is not well suited to lowland tropical regions. In arid regions water regularly.
Aspect Prefers full sun to partial shade. The fragrance is stronger in good sunlight.
Soil Best in light, organically enriched sandy loams. Dig in lime or dolomite if the soil is too acid.

GROWING METHOD

Planting Once established, catmint self-seeds readily, and can also be grown from cuttings taken in spring. Cut a 10 cm (4 in) piece from the parent plant, remove the tip and lower leaves, and place the cutting in a thoroughly moist soil medium. Cuttings take root in 1–2 weeks. They are very sturdy and can be planted out into the garden. Water in thoroughly. You can also divide mature plants into three or four clumps in early spring.
Watering Keep moist at all times. Do not stand pots in water or the plants will drown.
Fertilising For more leaf growth, feed catmint in spring with nitrogen-rich fertiliser such as poultry manure.
Problems Catmint is basically pest-free.
Pruning Prune back each year to keep bushes in shape.

HARVESTING

Picking Pick fresh leaves as required. Cut leafy stems in late summer when the plant is in bloom and hang them to dry in a cool, shady place.
Storage Strip leaves from dried stems and store them in airtight jars.
Freezing Wrap leaves in plastic wrap and freeze for up to six months.

USES

Culinary Once popular salad and herbal tea ingredients, the fresh young leaves are less of a favourite now.
Craft Use dried flowers and leaves in pot pourri mixtures, and in toys for cats.

CURRY TREE
This small evergreen tree reaches 5–6 m (17–20 ft) tall and has compound leaves about 2.5–5 cm (1–2 in) long. They are lanceolate to ovate in shape, and spicily aromatic when crushed. The small white flowers are produced during spring and summer in clusters at the ends of the branches and then are followed by dark red berries.

CATMINT There are several varieties of catmint, or catnip, and all have slightly different growing habits, but in general this is a low-growing perennial, reaching 30–90 cm (1–3 ft) tall. Fine white hairs cover both the grey-green leaves and the stem, which is square, just as in all members of the mint family. The leaves are coarse-toothed and ovate, although the base leaves are heart-shaped. The tubular summer flowers are massed in spikes or whorls. White, pale pink or purplish blue in colour, the flowers are followed by very fine seeds. Cats find some species of catmint very attractive.

BASIL Most basils are annuals, such as sweet or common basil (*O. basilicum*). But perennial varieties also grow – bush basil (*O. basilicum* 'Minimum'), lemon basil (*O. basilicum* 'Citriodorum') and sacred or holy basil (*O. sanctum*). All basils have a specific aroma and taste, depending on the variety. They can range from yellow-green to dark green and purple, and the small white flowers that appear in summer produce tiny dark brown seeds.

EVENING PRIMROSE This species includes annual, biennial and perennial plants with many upright leafy stems. From late spring to summer, each stem is topped with a cluster of golden yellow (or red, pink or white at times), sweetly fragrant flowers which open towards the end of the day. The bluish green foliage forms a rosette around the base of the plant. It is native to dry areas in the central and eastern United States. It should be planted with caution as it self-seeds most prolifically and can spread quickly in favoured locations.

Ocimum basilicum, O. sanctum

basil

LABIATAE/LAMIACEAE

CONDITIONS

Climate Warm to hot. Sensitive to cold and frost. In cold areas grow basil indoors in containers.
Aspect Full sun to partial shade. Protect from winds. In tropical areas basil needs some shade.
Soil Rich, moist, well drained soils that are not too acid. Mulch once the soil has warmed up.

GROWING METHOD

Planting Plant seed in late spring to early summer in warm zones, in cooler months in the tropics, and in summer when the soil has warmed in colder areas. Sow seeds directly into the garden, covering them with a light scattering of seed-raising mix. Firm down and moisten the soil. Thin seedlings to 20 cm (8 in) apart. Or sow seeds in trays using a moist mixture of vermiculite and perlite or a good quality seed-raising mix. Soil temperature needs to be warm: 25–30°C (77–86°F). Prick out seedlings to pots, and then transplant into open beds or larger pots from mid-spring onwards.
Watering Water regularly as basil likes moisture.
Fertilising If growing in containers, feed occasionally with a nitrogen-rich liquid fertiliser.
Problems Remove beetles and slugs by hand or put out snail traps such as shallow containers of beer in damp soil.
Pruning Keep the centres pinched to inhibit flowering and promote a bushier plant.

HARVESTING

Picking Pick fresh leaves at any time or harvest and dry them during late summer. Cut whole sprigs after the flower buds have formed but before they open.
Storage Preserve leaves and sprigs in oils or vinegars, or dry leaves and store them in airtight jars. Place bunches in water and store them for a few days in the fridge.
Freezing Wrap the sprigs in plastic wrap. They can be frozen for up to six months.

USES

Culinary Basil is a very popular culinary herb, especially in Italian, Mediterranean and Thai cuisines. Use the leaves and flowers in salads or as an aromatic garnish, or combine with other herbs in tomato, vegetable and meat dishes. Preserve leaves and sprigs in oils, vinegars or butters, to which they add their own particular flavour.
Medicinal Basil tea is a useful remedy for travel sickness.
Craft Basil is much prized for its fragrance, and is used in pot pourris and sachets. The flowering stems are sometimes used in small bouquets and other floral arrangements.
Gardening Basil is a popular companion plant with organic gardeners, who believe that planting it next to tomatoes and capsicum will improve their growth.

Oenothera spp.

evening primrose

ONAGRACEAE

CONDITIONS

Climate Evening primrose grows in cool, warm and hot, arid places.
Aspect Full sun is essential.
Soil Not very fussy about soil and grows in most places as long as the drainage is good. This plant thrives in average garden soils.

GROWING METHOD

Planting Grows from seed sown in autumn or early spring directly where it is to grow. Thin seedlings out so that there is at least 30 cm (12 in) between them.
Watering Do not overwater. Once established, plants are drought tolerant and can usually get by on rain in areas where it falls regularly.
Fertilising No fertilising is necessary. Over-rich soils can lead to excessive foliage growth and weak or deformed stems.
Problems No particular problems.
Pruning Pruning is not necessary, but snap off flower stems after the blooms have faded but before the seeds ripen. This plant self-seeds freely and can create a major weed problem. Allow one plant to seed in order to regenerate the plants, but collect the seed before it falls so that you can sow it where you want it.

HARVESTING

Picking All parts of the plant are edible. Leaves may be picked any time, while seeds are harvested when ripe in autumn. The small roots may also be dug in spring or autumn.
Storage Store the seeds in airtight containers. Use other parts of the plant fresh.
Freezing Not suitable for freezing.

USES

Culinary Use the fresh leaves in salads, or lightly steam or stir-fry them. Eat the seeds raw or use them in recipes.
Medicinal Tea made from the leaves is good for coughs and colds, and is a tonic for the liver, kidneys and intestines. An oil contained in the seeds has traditionally been credited with amazing therapeutic powers.
Gardening Evening primrose looks wonderful in a moonlit garden; it is a pretty plant and a good partner for other meadow flowers such as California poppies and paper daisies.

Origanum marjorana, syn. Marjorana hortensis

marjoram

LABIATAE/LAMIACEAE

CONDITIONS

Climate Grows in warm zones; must be well drained in areas of summer rain. Doesn't like frost but does well in containers indoors in cooler areas. In the tropics grow as a cool season annual.

Aspect Prefers full sun.

Soil Quite rich soils containing plenty of compost and decayed animal manure. Add lime or dolomite if the soil is too acid. Shallow cultivate to keep the soil free of weeds.

GROWING METHOD

Planting Seeds are slow to germinate and are usually planted in seed boxes. Pot on into small containers after the first few true leaves have formed, and then put established seedlings into the garden in spring. Plant in small clumps 15 cm (6 in) apart. Propagation by cuttings is also possible, during autumn. Take 7.5 cm (3 in) pieces of woody stem from the parent plant, trim the leaves from the cuttings and strike them in a mixture of two-thirds coarse sand to one-third peat moss. Transplant in spring when the root structure is established and new growth appears on the stems. You can also divide the roots of a mature plant in autumn.

Watering Water adequately but do not overwater.

Fertilising Little additional fertiliser is needed in soil that is well mulched. Apply liquid organic fertiliser or seaweed-based conditioner every six weeks.

Problems Damping off of seedlings can be a problem: they become water-soaked, shrivel and die. Keep seed beds warm and use good quality, sterile seed mix. Bad drainage will bring on this disease, and root rot in older plants. Pests include aphids and spider mite. Hose down, or treat with insecticide.

Pruning Flowers can be pruned at knot stage to maintain the shape of the bush.

HARVESTING

Picking Pick leaves for culinary use at any time. For drying, harvest leaves and unopened knot-like flowers in summer, and hang them to dry in a cool, shady spot.

Storage Remove leaves and buds from the stems and store them in airtight jars.

Freezing Chop leaves and buds finely, mix with a little water and freeze in ice cubes.

USES

Culinary The taste resembles that of a mild oregano, for which it can be substituted. It is often used in bouquet garni. Use the fresh leaves and flowers in salads, stuffings for meat and poultry, or in marinades. The flavour blends with most vegetable dishes and can also be used to flavour vinegars and oils. Dried, it makes a refreshing herbal tea.

Origanum vulgare

oregano

LABIATAE/LAMIACEAE

CONDITIONS

Climate Prefers warm, relatively dry climates where most rain falls in winter. In areas of summer rain, soil must be very well drained. In the tropics grow it as a cool season annual. It does not like frost but grows satisfactorily in cooler regions as a container herb.

Aspect Needs full sun or partial shade.

Soil Likes well drained garden soil that is not too rich. Mulch to keep soil moist in hot, dry weather.

GROWING METHOD

Planting Sow seeds in spring, in damp, warm seed-raising mix. For the best results, temperatures need to be above 20°C (68°F). Transplant seedlings into the garden when well established. Because this plant spreads by underground stems, it is easier to propagate by root division in late spring or to propagate by layering. Scarify the undersurface of the branch, peg it down and cover with soil. Keep damp until roots form, cut it off and replant. Replace plants every couple of years as the stems become woody.

Watering Keep plants well watered and do not let the soil dry out.

Fertilising Apply liquid organic fertiliser or seaweed-based soil conditioner every six weeks.

Problems Treat aphids, leaf miner and spider mite with appropriate insecticidal sprays. Hosing leaves may bring temporary relief but if infestations are bad, remove and burn the diseased plants. Remove plants affected by root rot, which is caused by bad drainage; rotate plants every three years.

Pruning Prune after flowering to keep plant compact.

HARVESTING

Picking Pick fresh leaves throughout the growing season as required. Cut whole stems before flowering and hang them up to dry in a cool, shady spot.

Storage Strip dry leaves from the stems and store them in airtight jars.

Freezing Wrap in plastic wrap; oregano can be frozen for up to six months.

USES

Culinary Oregano is widely used as a flavouring, especially in Mediterranean-style cooking, in sauces, soups and casseroles, as well as in vinegars and butters.

Gardening Oregano plants make excellent groundcovers.

MARJORAM This variety of marjoram, known as sweet or knotted marjoram, is most common in herb gardens. A tender, bushy perennial, it is often grown as an annual as it does not survive cold winters. It can grow to 60 cm (2 ft) or more, producing small oval leaves covered with fine hair. The leaves are light green on top and grey-green below. During summer very small white to lilac flowers appear in clusters of knot-like shapes, and produce tiny brown seeds.

OREGANO Oregano is very closely related to marjoram and is often confused with it. Three varieties of this perennial are widely grown. Common or wild oregano (*O. vulgare*) is a small shrub growing to 30 cm (12 in) high, with soft hairy leaves and tiny white flowers. Golden oregano (*O. vulgare* 'Aureum') is very decorative in the garden but tends to spread. The leaves are golden yellow and the flowers are pink. Greek or white oregano (*O. vulgare* 'Viride') is taller than the other varieties, up to 50 cm (20 in). Its leaves are dark green and covered with a white hairy bloom.

PARSLEY Parsley grows from a strong tap root with erect, 30 cm (12 in) tall stems bearing divided, feather-like, small leaves which may be flattish or curly depending on the variety. Tiny yellowish green flowers arranged in clusters are borne on tall stalks in summer, and produce small, brown, oval and ribbed seeds. Some common varieties of this biennial or short lived perennial plant include curly parsley, flat-leaved or Italian parsley, and Hamburg or turnip-rooted parsley.

Petroselinum spp.

parsley

APIACEAE/UMBELLIFERAE

CONDITIONS

Climate Parsley likes a warm to coolish climate. Grow these plants as a cool season annual in the tropics or in a container in areas where there are frosts.
Aspect Parsley prefers full sun or possibly part shade.
Soil Parsley needs only a moderately rich, well drained soil.

GROWING METHOD

Planting Grow from seed planted during the warmer months when the soil is warm – above 10°C (50°F). Because germination takes 6–8 weeks, seeds are usually brought on in seed boxes before they are planted out. Before planting, create optimum conditions by soaking the seeds in warm water for 24 hours and pouring boiling water over the soil to raise the temperature. Transplant the seedlings out, 25 cm (10 in) apart, after they have grown several true leaves. If parsley is grown in a container, the pot should be at least 20 cm (8 in) deep, and the longer tap root of Hamburg or turnip-rooted parsley (*P. crispum* var. *tuberosum*) will require an even deeper pot. Once parsley plants are established in the garden, the mature plants can be left to self-sow when they go to seed during the summer months in their second year of growth.
Watering Keep the soil moist and do not let it dry out during dry weather.
Fertilising Side feedings of a nitrogen-rich liquid fertiliser will promote more leaf growth.
Problems The main pests are parsley worm, carrot weevils and root-knot nematode, which devour the foliage, burrow into the top and root, and stunt the growth. Practise crop rotation and destroy affected plants. Watch for white fungal growth near the base of the plant and a brownish crust on the soil, indicative of crown rot. Treat as for pests.
Pruning Parsley can be kept productive by frequent pruning and by nipping out the seed stalks whenever they appear.

HARVESTING

Picking New growth comes from the centre of the stem, so always pick parsley from the outside of the plant. Pick this vitamin-rich, nutritious herb as needed.
Storage With its stronger taste, flat-leaved or Italian parsley (*P. crispum* var. *neapolitanum*) gives a better result when dried than the other varieties.
Freezing Curly parsley (*P. crispum*) freezes well. Wrap it first in plastic wrap and put it in the freezer for up to six months.

USES

Culinary Parsley is used in salads, as a garnish and in cooking. Hamburg parsley is used like a root vegetable. Fresh parsley is a breath freshener.

Pimpinella anisum

anise

APIACEAE/UMBELLIFERAE

CONDITIONS

Climate Will grow in all areas, but in the monsoonal tropics is best raised in the cooler, drier months.
Aspect Prefers full sun, sheltered from strong winds.
Soil Light, sandy, well drained soil enriched with rotted organic matter.

GROWING METHOD

Planting When spring has turned warm, sow seeds where they are to grow about 1 cm (½ in) deep and 15 cm (6 in) apart. For seeds to ripen properly, anise requires a long hot summer, so in cooler areas sow them indoors in late winter or early spring into trays of seed-raising mix. Place in a sunny spot on a heated seed-raising pad and keep lightly moist. Prick seedlings out into small pots and place these on the heated pad. Plant out only when the weather has turned warm.
Watering Never allow the soil to dry out. To avoid flattening the stems, water the soil, not the leaves.
Fertilising If soil is friable but poor, dig in complete plant food when planting. Mulch when seedlings are 20 cm (8 in).
Problems No particular problems.

HARVESTING

Picking Place the ripe seed heads in the sun to dry out. Pick the fresh leaves as they are needed.
Storage When the heads are dry, rub the seeds to separate them from the husks. Store seeds in airtight jars.
Freezing Not suitable for freezing.

USES

Culinary The seeds give a pleasant liquorice taste to many cooked foods, including cakes and pies, stewed fruits and vegetable dishes. Use fresh leaves in salads or add them late to casseroles, stews and soups.
Medicinal A good tonic for the digestive system. Regular intake of aniseed is said to help prevent colds and to banish bad breath. Taken before bed, aniseed encourages sound sleep.
Craft Aniseed is used in pot pourris and pomanders.
Gardening Anise will attract bees and butterflies to your garden.

ANISE A dainty, feathery-looking annual that may reach a height of 60 cm (2 ft), anise has rounded, mid-green leaves with distinctly toothed edges. The flat heads of white flowers appear in late spring through summer, followed by the small liquorice-flavoured seeds – aniseeds.

Polygonum odoratum

vietnamese mint
CONVALLARIACEAE/LILIACEAE

Portulaca oleracea

purslane
PORTULACACEAE

CONDITIONS

Climate Grows best in a warm or tropical climate as it is not hardy in temperatures that go much below freezing.
Aspect Plant in bright dappled shade or where it receives shade during the hotter part of the day in summer. It grows in full sun if kept well watered.
Soil Fertile, well drained soil that contains enough rotted organic matter to retain moisture. It enjoys good conditions and can get out of hand very quickly if regular care is not taken to control excess growth.

GROWING METHOD

Planting As Vietnamese mint stems root where they touch the ground, new plants are easily created by detaching the newly rooted section from the parent plant and replanting it. Cuttings also root very easily if struck in late spring and summer. The cutting can be taken from the parent plant and then inserted in the ground directly where it is to grow.
Watering Although Vietnamese mint that has withered from lack of water will recover when rewetted, it grows fastest and best where it has ample water always.
Fertilising During spring and summer, water it occasionally with soluble fertiliser that contains a high proportion of nitrogen or sprinkle it with a ration of complete plant food once in spring and again in summer.
Problems No particular problems apart from the plant's ability to spread fast.

HARVESTING

Picking Pick individual leaves or stems as required. This herb is best used fresh.
Storage This plant grows so fast, there is no need to store it.
Freezing Not suitable for freezing.

USES

Culinary A popular herb in Vietnamese and other Southeast Asian cuisines, Vietnamese mint is added during cooking and is also a salad ingredient. It has a peppery taste which is pleasant in small amounts.

CONDITIONS

Climate Purslane can be grown almost everywhere, from cool zones to tropical climates, as it is very forgiving.
Aspect Prefers full sun but will tolerate shade for some part of the day.
Soil Plants will produce succulent leaves more quickly if they are grown in fertile, sandy soil that contains some rotted organic matter.

GROWING METHOD

Planting Sow the seeds directly where they are to grow in early spring or, in cooler areas, after all danger of frost has passed. In tropical areas, sow seeds during the autumn months. Purslane can also be started from cuttings that are taken any time from mid-spring onwards. Make the cuttings about 5 cm (2 in) long, strip off the lower leaves and insert the cuttings into small containers of very sandy potting mix or seed-raising mix. Keep the containers warm and moist, and put them in a bright but not sunny spot until the roots have formed. The plants can then be planted out into their permanent positions in the garden.
Watering Having water-storing leaves and stems, purslane is well able to cope with dryness, but for the best quality leaves, keep the soil evenly moist during spring and summer.
Fertilising Fertilising will not be necessary if purslane is grown in fertile soil. Elsewhere, water the plants once a month with a high-nitrogen soluble fertiliser.
Problems No pest or disease problems, but flowers should be routinely removed to minimise unwanted spread by seed.

HARVESTING

Picking Let the plants grow until they are about 10 cm (4 in) across, then pick the stems and leaves as they are needed. Plants regrow quickly.
Storage Cut purslane stems may be stored in the refrigerator for a few days.
Freezing Not suitable for freezing.

USES

Culinary Leaves and stems contain large amounts of iron and have a fresh, acid taste. Eat them raw in salads, or lightly stir-fry or steam them as a vegetable.

VIETNAMESE MINT Vietnamese mint is a highly aromatic, creeping perennial that may grow to nearly 1 m (3⅓ ft) tall in ideal conditions. The reddish stems are jointed at leaf junctions, and wherever they touch the ground, roots will form. The lanceolate leaves are about 7.5 cm (3 in) long, olive green with a brownish red marking on the upper side. Small, pink flowers appear at the ends of the stems in spring and summer.

PURSLANE This spreading, succulent annual is extremely adaptable, growing as a weed in many parts of the world. It forms a mat-like growth, which makes it a useful groundcover in regions where it will not spread unduly. It has bright, light green, spoon-shaped leaves on trailing, fleshy stems that are reddish in colour. The small, bright yellow flowers are produced at stem junctions during the spring and summer months. They will open only when the plants are in sunlight.

ROSEMARY
A perennial, evergreen woody shrub, rosemary has thin, needle-like leaves, glossy green above and whitish to grey-green and hairy below. The fragrance is reminiscent of pine needles. In spring, small-lobed flowers appear among the leaves. They are white or pale blue to pinkish, depending on the variety. The varieties of rosemary range in habit from the upright (*R. officinalis*) to the dwarf (*R. officinalis* 'Nana') and the prostrate (*R. officinalis* 'Prostratus'). Other popular varieties include 'Blue Lagoon' rosemary and pink rosemary (*R. officinalis* 'Rosea'). Rosemary bushes can be between 50 cm (20 in) and 2 m (7 ft) high, depending on the variety.

SORREL
Broad-leaved sorrel (*R. acetosa*) is an upright clumping perennial with spear-shaped, lemony acid-tasting leaves that can grow 60–90 cm (2–3 ft) tall. French sorrel (*R. scutatus*) has heart-shaped leaves with a more delicate lemon flavour; it grows to about 50 cm (20 in). Small green flowers appear on long stalks in summer.

Rosmarinus officinalis
rosemary
LABIATAE/LAMIACEAE

CONDITIONS
Climate Grows well in warm, relatively dry climates with most rain in winter. This is a good herb to grow in containers, and it also grows well in seaside positions where not much else will grow, as it will withstand salt and wind. Tolerates cooler climates, but best grown there in containers.
Aspect Likes full sun and a reasonably dry position.
Soil Needs well drained soil to lessen the risk of root rot, and is more fragrant in alkaline soils. If acidity is a problem, dig in 200 g per square metre (7 oz per square yard) of lime or dolomite before planting.

GROWING METHOD
Planting Propagate mainly from cuttings and layering. Seeds are not often used because they have long germination times and tend not to come true to type. Take 10 cm (4 in) long cuttings in late spring (early autumn in warmer climates), trim off the upper and lower leaves, and place the cuttings in small pots containing a moist mixture of two-thirds coarse sand and one-third peat moss. Cover with a plastic dome and set aside in a semi-shaded position until roots and new leaves form.
Watering Prefers soil to be on the drier side; give average garden watering.
Fertilising Fertiliser is not needed.
Problems Look out for mealy bug, scale, spider mite and whitefly. Treat with appropriate insecticidal sprays. Botrytis blight, a fungal growth affecting all parts of the plant, and root rot can be treated by improving drainage and removing yellowing leaves and dead flowers or badly infected plants. Frequent summer rainfall can cause the shrub to rot.
Pruning Prune to keep bushes compact. The 'Blue Lagoon' variety (*R. officinalis* 'Collingwood Ingram') has a very straggly growing habit.

HARVESTING
Picking Fresh leaves or sprigs 5–10 cm (2–4 in) long can be picked as required.
Storage Dry sprigs in a cool dry place, strip leaves from stems and store in airtight jars.
Freezing Store sprigs in plastic bags and freeze for up to six months. To use, crumble before thawing.

USES
Cosmetic Rosemary hair rinses help control greasy hair.
Culinary Use fresh, dried or frozen leaves in cooking, marinades and salad dressings. The leaves are used in vinegars, oils, teas and butters. Fresh flowers are good in salads or as decorations for puddings and desserts.
Craft It is used in pot pourris and herb wreaths.

Rumex acetosa, R. scutatus
sorrel
POLYGONACEAE

CONDITIONS
Climate Prefers moist, warm climates but grows in cooler regions; tolerates some dryness. Grow as a cool season annual in the tropics.
Aspect Prefers sun or semi-shade but needs protection from winter frosts.
Soil Needs light, average soil. To promote strong leaf growth, add animal manures to the soil and mulch well. Tolerates slightly acid soils.

GROWING METHOD
Planting Sow seed directly into the garden during spring. Thin seedlings to 30 cm (12 in) apart. Mature plants can be divided in autumn or early spring. To do this, dig up older plants, trim the leaves and stems, and replant the divided portions 30–40 cm (12–16 in) apart.
Watering Water regularly. If the soil is left to dry out, the leaves wilt and burn off.
Fertilising Give an application of high-nitrogen liquid or soluble fertiliser monthly.
Problems Snails and slugs attack leaves. Pick them off by hand or set traps such as shallow containers of beer among the beds. If leaf miners attack the plant, remove and destroy the infected leaves.
Pruning If you are not growing plants for seed, pinch out the seed-bearing stalks as they appear.

HARVESTING
Picking Leaves can be picked throughout the growing season as required. Always pick from the outside of the clump.
Storage Freshly picked leaves will keep in the refrigerator for a few days if they are stored in a plastic bag.
Freezing Pack leaves in plastic wrap and freeze for up to six months.

USES
Culinary Sorrel used to be cooked and eaten like spinach. Today, because it is known to contain a lot of oxalic acid, the small lemony-flavoured leaves are only used in such dishes as salads or soups.

rue

Ruta graveolens

rue

RUTACEAE

CONDITIONS

Climate Grows in cool or warm climates, and especially well where most rain falls in winter. Dislikes summer humidity.
Aspect Needs full sun in cooler areas where summers are mild. In warmer areas, will tolerate some, but not full, shade.
Soil Deep, well drained but rather poor, sandy or gravelly soil. Over-rich soils lead to lax, rampant growth and loss of compactness.

GROWING METHOD

Planting Sow seeds in spring in trays or punnets of seed-raising mix. Keep moist and place in bright dappled shade until germination is complete. Gradually expose to greater amounts of sun before planting into the final position. Alternatively, new plants can be grown from cuttings taken towards the end of summer. Select growth that has matured but is not yet woody, and place 10 cm (4 in) cuttings into pots of very sandy potting mix. Keep the mix moist and place pots in bright shade until roots have formed. Where stems of mature plants touch the ground, they will often form roots. These rooted 'layers' can be detached from the parent plant, dug up and relocated.
Watering Water deeply every two weeks from mid-autumn to mid-spring as this simulates the plant's natural growing conditions. Water in summer only in really dry conditions.
Fertilising No fertilising is needed.
Problems Usually no pest and disease problems but high summer heat, rain and humidity can lead to fungus diseases of the leaves and root rot. The plant's sap can severely irritate sensitive skins. Wear gloves whenever handling the plant and do not let it touch your hands, face or body.
Pruning Untidy plants may be pruned hard in early spring. Using sharp secateurs, cut back to a main framework of branches. New growth will restore the plant's rounded, bushy habit. Less untidy plants may be made more compact by a light, all-over shearing in mid-spring.

HARVESTING

Picking Rue has toxic properties and must be used with extreme caution. Leaves may be picked at any time to make an insecticidal infusion.
Storage Bunch leafy stems and dry them in a dark, airy place for later use.
Freezing Not suitable for freezing.

USES

Gardening Rue is a decorative plant that infuses the garden with its herbal aroma, especially on hot days. It is a good companion for other Mediterranean plants such as lavender and echium. An insect repellent for use on ornamental or productive plants can be made from the leaves.

Salvia spp.

sage

LABIATAE/LAMIACEAE

CONDITIONS

Climate Sage plants tolerate most climates, except for the monsoonal tropics. In areas of extreme heat or cold, the plants are best grown in containers.
Aspect Most varieties prefer a sunny, sheltered, well drained position.
Soil Rich, well drained, non-clayish soil. If necessary, raise the beds to at least 20 cm (8 in) above the surrounding garden level. Prepare the beds by digging in 250 g (9 oz) of lime or dolomite, followed by plenty of organic matter, such as compost and decayed animal manure.

GROWING METHOD

Planting Plant seeds in late spring in seed-raising boxes, and when seedlings are 7.5–10 cm (3–4 in) tall, plant them out into the garden, spaced 45 cm (18 in) apart. Cuttings, 10 cm (4 in) long, can be taken in late autumn or spring. Remove the upper and lower leaves, and plant the cuttings in small pots containing a soil mix of two-thirds coarse sand and one-third peat moss. Water, then cover the pots with a plastic bag to create a mini-greenhouse. Plant out when the cuttings have developed roots and new leaves. Sage may also be layered – scarify the lower side of a branch and peg it into the soil to take root.
Watering Give a deep soaking once a week.
Fertilising At planting, apply complete plant food. Give an application each spring.
Problems Slugs can be a problem. Pick them off by hand or put out snail traps among the beds. Spider mites will need to be sprayed with an insecticide. If the plant suddenly flops over for no apparent reason, this is probably due to bacterial wilt affecting the vascular system. Remove affected plants before the disease spreads. Root rot can be avoided by providing good drainage.
Pruning Prune off flowers to stop from setting seed.

HARVESTING

Picking Leaves or flowers can be picked as required. For drying purposes, harvest leaves before flowering begins.
Storage Dry leaves on racks in a cool, airy place and then store them in airtight jars.
Freezing Chop leaves, pack in plastic wrap and freeze for up to six months.

USES

Cosmetic Regular sage hair rinses will darken grey hair.
Culinary Fresh or dried leaves are used as a flavouring in stuffings, marinades and cooking. The individual fruity flavour of pineapple sage (*S. elegans*, syn. *S. rutilans*) complements citrus fruits and the edible flowers look decorative in salads or as a garnish.

RUE Rue is a rounded, shrubby perennial with many stems rising from a woody base. It can grow to about 1 m (3$^{1}/_{3}$ ft) tall and has a similar spread. The leaves are strongly aromatic and the colour varies: it may be green, blue-green or even variegated. The foliage is finely divided and is an attractive background for the small, spicily fragrant, yellowish flowers which appear in late spring or summer.

SAGE Sage is a small, woody perennial shrub that grows to about 75 cm (2$^{1}/_{2}$ ft). The long, oval, grey-green leaves, velvety in texture, have a slightly bitter, camphor-like taste. The flowers, borne on spikes in spring, can be pink, red, purple, blue or white, depending on the variety. For there are numerous varieties of this beautiful and hardy herb. The most popular edible types are common or garden sage (*S. officinalis*), purple sage (*S. x superba*), pineapple sage and golden or variegated sage (*S. officinalis* 'Variegata'). Other sages are grown purely for their decorative qualities in the garden, chief among them being clary sage (*S. sclarea*). Sage plants become woody after about four years.

SALAD BURNET This small but bushy perennial herb grows in a clump about 50 cm (20 in) high. The roundish grey-green, toothed leaves are borne on a central stem which droops down close to the ground. Flower stems, growing to about 60 cm (2 ft) high, appear in summer and produce pinkish red, oval flowers. Salad burnet is an attractive border plant and it can also be grown successfully in pots.

ELDER A deciduous shrub or small tree, elder or elderberry is usually less than 6 m (20 ft) tall, with rough, corky bark and compound leaves composed of five or so toothed, dark green leaflets. Heads of creamy white, scented flowers appear in summer, leading to shiny blue-black berries in autumn. The flowers attract bees while the berries are eaten by birds.

Sanguisorba minor, syn. *Poterium sanguisorba*

salad burnet
ROSACEAE

CONDITIONS
Climate Warm to cold regions are best. Burnet is not suited to the tropics.
Aspect Salad burnet likes a sunny, well drained position.
Soil Most soil types are suitable. Add lime or dolomite if the soil is acid. Ensure soil is well drained at all times.

GROWING METHOD
Planting Salad burnet readily self-sows. Germinate seed in seed-raising boxes, cover the seed lightly with mix and keep the soil damp. When the seedlings are 5–10 cm (2–4 in) tall, plant them into the garden or containers, spaced 30–40 cm (12–16 in) apart. Propagation by division of the parent plant during autumn or spring is also possible.
Watering Water thoroughly in hot weather but do not overwater in winter as the plant tolerates much drier conditions then.
Fertilising Apply complete plant food once each year in early spring and water in well.
Problems Burnet suffers from root rot if the soil is not well drained. If conditions are too damp in winter, crown rot will develop and the plants will turn yellow and die.
Pruning Removal of flower stalks will stimulate new leaf growth.

HARVESTING
Picking Pick the leaves when they are still quite young and tender.
Storage Cannot be successfully stored.
Freezing Cannot be frozen.

USES
Culinary Use burnet only when fresh. The leaves have a cucumber scent and flavour, and are much prized in salads or with fresh vegetables. They can also be chopped and included in cooked soups or sauces. Freshly picked sprigs look effective as a garnish in summer drinks.
Gardening As a companion plant, burnet does very well if grown near beds of thyme and mint.

Sambucus nigra

elder
CAPRIFOLIACEAE

CONDITIONS
Climate Best in cool climates. Where autumn nights are sufficiently cold, the leaves turn brilliant colours before falling. Elder grows well enough in warm areas but does not produce much in the way of autumn colour there.
Aspect Prefers a sunny position but will tolerate bright dappled shade or a few hours of full shade each day.
Soil Friable, fertile soil that drains well yet stays moist is best, but elder accepts a wide range of soil types.

GROWING METHOD
Planting Sow from seed in spring, or dig and detach suckers, with their own roots, from the parent plant. This can be done at any time, but spring is generally best. Elders can also be propagated by cuttings. Take hardwood cuttings in winter or tip cuttings in spring. Root either type in containers of very sandy potting mix. Pot them up to grow larger and then plant them out into their permanent positions. If you are planting a group or row, leave at least 3 m (10 ft) between them to allow room for the suckers to develop.
Watering Elders like moisture at their roots at all times, especially in summer. If rainfall is reliable and reasonably regular, mature plants usually need little extra water.
Fertilising In average garden soils no special fertilising is required, especially if you mulch beneath the plants with rotted organic matter. If the soil is not very fertile, a ration of complete plant food once in early spring is sufficient.
Problems No particular problems.
Pruning No pruning is necessary.

HARVESTING
Picking Pick the flower heads in the morning but only when all the flowers on each head have bloomed. Dry them in a cool, dark, airy place. Pick the berries when they are ripe.
Storage Dried flowers can be removed from their stems and stored in airtight containers. Ripe berries can also be dried and similarly stored.
Freezing Berries that have been cooked for a few minutes may be frozen for later use.

USES
Cosmetic Cold elderflower tea splashed daily onto the face tones and soothes the skin.
Culinary Make fresh flowers into elderflower wine, jams or jellies. Use the berries for jams or jellies; the juice can be fermented into elderberry wine. Do not eat the raw berries.
Medicinal Tea from young leaves taken in small doses is a diuretic. The juice of cooked berries is taken for headaches.
Gardening Elders, with their dense growth and suckering habit, make a good privacy screen and reasonable windbreak. Use as an understorey shrub beneath tall, open trees.

Santolina chamaecyparissus

cotton lavender
ASTERACEAE/COMPOSITAE

Satureja spp.

savory
LABIATAE/LAMIACEAE

CONDITIONS
Climate Cotton lavender suits both cool and warm climates, and tolerates the heat of arid areas if watered as needed.
Aspect Full sun is essential.
Soil Good drainage is essential but it does grow well in poor, rather dry soils. If conditions are too rich it loses its dense, compact appearance and becomes straggly and lax. Cotton lavender will tolerate alkaline soils.

GROWING METHOD
Planting In late spring, take 7.5 cm (3 in) long cuttings of stems that have lost their sappy freshness but have not yet become woody. Insert the cuttings into small containers of sandy potting mix, and keep the mix moist and the container shaded until roots develop after 4–6 weeks. Harden off the cuttings by moving the container into full sun in stages so as not to burn the leaves that have become used to shade. When fully hardened, plant out the new plants about 30 cm (12 in) apart.
Watering Cotton lavender does best when the most rain falls from mid-autumn to mid-spring, with dry summers. Water to simulate these conditions. Once established, cotton lavender is tolerant of dry weather.
Fertilising No fertilising is needed.
Problems High summer rainfall and humidity can cause the plant to rot.
Pruning Shear the plant all over once or twice during the summer months and once again more heavily in autumn. This will keep it neat and very bushy.

HARVESTING
Picking Sprigs of leaves may be picked at any time, as required.
Storage Tie sprigs of the leaves together and hang them upside down in a dark, airy place to dry. Then store the dried sprigs in an airtight container.
Freezing Not suitable for freezing.

USES
Craft Dried leaves can be used in pot pourris and herbal sachets.
Gardening Cotton lavender is mostly used today as an edging plant along paths or driveways, or to border herb or vegetable gardens or other formal plantings. It can also be used as an unusual large-scale groundcover, especially if used on dry, sunny banks.

CONDITIONS
Climate Savories grow best in warm climates. Winter savory (*S. montana*) can withstand much colder temperatures than summer savory (*S. hortensis*). Neither is suited to the tropics.
Aspect Both prefer to be grown in full sun.
Soil Savories like well drained, alkaline soils. If necessary, dress beds with lime, 200 g per square metre (7 oz per square yard). Summer savory prefers slightly rich soil and is ideal in containers; winter savory likes a less rich, rather sandy soil.

GROWING METHOD
Planting Sow seeds of summer savory directly into their final garden position in spring, after the weather has warmed up. Lightly cover them with soil and keep the soil damp. When seedlings are established, thin them to 45 cm (18 in) apart and support each plant by mounding soil around the base. Winter savory is best propagated by cuttings and root division during spring or autumn. Remove the upper and lower leaves of 7.5–10 cm (3–4 in) long cuttings and plant the trimmed stem in a mixture of two-thirds coarse sand and one-third peat moss. Water the container and cover it with plastic supported on a wire frame. Plant the seedlings out when new leaves appear and a root structure has developed. Alternatively, pot up pieces of the divided root of the parent plant and transplant them later into the garden.
Watering Water regularly, although savories can bear dry conditions.
Fertilising Summer savory needs side applications of liquid fertiliser every 2–3 weeks during the spring and summer growth cycle.
Problems Root rot can sometimes affect winter savory. Good drainage is essential for these plants, and it is prudent to rotate crops every three years.
Pruning Prune winter savory in autumn after flowering (as a protection against winter cold) and again in early spring; use the cuttings to grow new plants.

HARVESTING
Picking Pick fresh leaves of both varieties at any time.
Storage Dry leaves in a cool, airy space and then store them in airtight jars.
Freezing Pack sprigs in plastic wrap and freeze for up to six months.

USES
Culinary Summer savory has a peppery flavour, and it is called the 'bean' herb because it complements beans and other vegetables. It is also used in herb vinegars and butters. Winter savory has a stronger aroma and more piney taste: use it with game meats and terrines. Either variety can be used to make savory tea.

COTTON LAVENDER
Grey, rounded and cushiony, cotton lavender is a low ground-covering shrub that usually grows about 30 cm (12 in) tall, sometimes taller. When crushed, the toothed leaves give off a strong aroma reminiscent of lavender but with a delightful difference. In summer, dull yellow flowers appear on leafless stems and make a striking contrast to the soft grey leaves.

SAVORY Summer savory is an annual plant growing to about 50 cm (20 in). Its small, narrow, greyish leaves turn slightly purple during summer and early autumn. The leaves are attached directly to a pinkish stem, and small white flowers appear on the plant in summer. The winter savories, both the upright (*S. montana*) and the prostrate (*S. montana* 'Repens') forms are perennial, with low-growing (up to 40 cm/16 in) or sprawling habits. Glossy, dark green lanceolate leaves and spikes of white to lilac flowers grow in summer.

Symphytum officinale

comfrey
BORAGINACEAE

Tanacetum parthenium, syn. *Chrysanthemum parthenium*

feverfew
ASTERACEAE/COMPOSITAE

COMFREY This large, coarse, hairy perennial grows to 1 m (3¹/₃ ft) high or more. It has dark green, lanceolate leaves that reach 25–30 cm (10–12 in) long, and clusters of yellow, white or mauve, five-lobed flowers in summer. The sticky qualities of its rhizome, which is black outside and has juicy white flesh within, gave rise to its nickname of slippery root; its other name, knit-bone, comes from its use in healing. The plant dies down during winter but makes a strong recovery in spring and can become quite invasive in the garden, overrunning other plants once it has taken hold. Confine it to distant parts of the garden, where it can form an attractive backdrop to other plants.

FEVERFEW This perennial has aromatic, finely cut leaves and clusters of small, white, daisy-like flowers appearing in spring (summer in cool areas). The plant is densely foliaged and can grow to 60 cm (2 ft). Leaves are usually a fresh, light green but a golden foliaged form is also available.

CONDITIONS
Climate Prefers moist climates in warm and cool areas. Doesn't grow well in hot, dry inland areas.
Aspect Prefers full sun but tolerates partial shade.
Soil Comfrey needs moist, rich soils. Prepare beds with plenty of compost and animal manures.

GROWING METHOD
Planting Comfrey can be propagated from spring plantings of seed, by cuttings at any stage of its life cycle or by root division in autumn.
Watering Water well as this fleshy herb requires a great deal of water.
Fertilising Requires little fertiliser or other maintenance once established.
Problems No specific pests or diseases.
Pruning Cutting the flowers will encourage more leaf growth on this plant.

HARVESTING
Picking Pick the leaves in the spring, summer and autumn.
Storage Dry the leaves and store them in airtight containers.
Freezing Can be frozen for up to six months.

USES
Culinary Culinary use is not recommended as controversy surrounds the use of young leaves in salads. Dried leaves are sometimes used to make a herbal tea.
Medicinal The plant contains unusually high concentrations of vitamin B12, but a great deal would need to be eaten daily to have any beneficial effect; some studies suggest that certain alkaloids in the plant can cause chronic liver problems.
Gardening Comfrey is best used as a liquid manure: steep fresh leaves in water for several weeks. Leaves can also be used to promote decomposition in the compost heap, so plant it close by.

CONDITIONS
Climate Best in cool to warm areas but it grows in the tropics as an annual in cooler, drier months.
Aspect Full sun is essential in cooler areas. In warmer areas it prefers light shade on summer afternoons, but plants will grow lax and flower poorly in areas that are too shady.
Soil Average, well drained garden soil is preferred. In over-rich soils, plants produce too much soft leafy growth.

GROWING METHOD
Planting Easily grown from seed sown in early spring. Press seeds just beneath the surface where the plants are to grow. Established plants can be dug up in winter and divided. Each division should have its own roots and the divisions should be replanted immediately. Soft-tip cuttings taken in mid-spring will also root easily. Make cuttings about 7.5 cm (3 in) long and insert them into small pots of very sandy potting mix. Place in a warm but shady and sheltered spot, and keep moist. Roots should form in about three weeks.
Watering Do no overwater or the plant will rot.
Fertilising A ration of complete plant food applied once each spring will meet the plant's needs. Alternatively, feed monthly with liquid or soluble plant food and water in.
Problems Slugs, snails and caterpillars can strip the foliage or eat young plants entirely. Put out snail traps during spring and autumn; pick off and squash caterpillars whenever you see them. For major infestations of caterpillars, spray plants with products containing *Bacillus thuringiensis*, a biological control that affects only caterpillars.

HARVESTING
Picking All upper parts of the plant are useful medicinally and whole plants may be harvested any time they are in full bloom. Fresh, young leaves can be harvested any time but remember that plants need their leaves to live: grow enough plants so that you do not use just one or two for picking.
Storage Dry the upper parts, including leaves, stems and flowers, in a cool, dark, airy place. When dry, coarsely chop and store in an airtight jar.
Freezing Freshly picked leaves can be wrapped in foil and frozen for up to six months.

USES
Cosmetic Feverfew makes a useful moisturiser.
Medicinal Tea made from the dried upper parts relieves indigestion and period pain. Eating one or two fresh leaves every day may help prevent the onset of migraines in sufferers but in some people this causes mouth ulcers.
Craft Flower stems placed in linen closets discourage moths.
Gardening Use for massed plantings and borders. It attracts bees and is often planted near fruit trees to assist pollination.

Tanacetum vulgare

tansy
ASTERACEAE/COMPOSITAE

CONDITIONS
Climate Tansy grows in cool and warm areas but is not well suited to the monsoonal tropics.
Aspect Full sun, part shade or bright, dappled shade are equally suitable for tansy, although full sun produces more compact growth and many more flowers.
Soil Any well drained soil will do. Tansy is a very adaptable plant, able to grow almost wherever its seed falls.

GROWING METHOD
Planting Dividing the roots of an established plant is the easiest way to start a new plant quickly. Lift the parent in early spring and cut or pull the creeping roots into sections, each with its own roots. Replant immediately into the permanent site. Tansy may also be started from seed sown in spring or early autumn or from cuttings of semi-ripe stems that are taken in late spring and rooted in a moist, sandy potting mix.
Watering Water sparingly but deeply. In coastal areas, tansy can usually get by on rain.
Fertilising No fertilising is needed.
Problems No particular problems.
Pruning Cut the plants to the ground in mid- to late autumn (early winter in warm areas). New growth will appear in spring.

HARVESTING
Picking Pick leafy stems any time during the warmer months. Cut flower stems when they are freshly opened rather than when they are old.
Storage Both the leaves and the flowers can be stored dry. To dry either, tie bunches together and hang them in a dim, well ventilated place or lay them out on drying racks. When the leaves are dry, remove them from their stems and store them in airtight jars. Take the dried flowers off the stems and store the flowers in airtight jars.
Freezing Not suitable for freezing.

USES
Cosmetic Tansy leaves can be used to make a delightful skin freshener.
Medicinal Although tansy can be taken for medicinal purposes, it must only be administered by a trained herbal practitioner. Tansy has toxic properties and can be easily taken in excess.
Gardening Tansy is a lovely, silvery green plant with very attractive flowers and an aroma that is very pleasant in the garden. Grow it in borders of mixed flowers or in big containers that will prevent its unwanted spread.

Taraxacum officinale

dandelion
COMPOSITAE

CONDITIONS
Climate Grows best in cool to warm climates, especially the higher rainfall areas. Not well suited to tropical regions.
Aspect Full sun is essential.
Soil Not particularly fussy, but you will get the biggest and best roots and less bitter leaves by growing plants in good quality, friable, well drained soil.

GROWING METHOD
Planting Sow seeds in spring directly where the plants are to grow, with a bed in an established vegetable patch being the most suitable site. Plants may also be grown in containers that are deeper than they are wide so as to accommodate the long tap root. Although they are perennials, individual dandelion plants should be dug up and discarded every 2–3 years. Replace them with fresh seedlings.
Watering Keep the soil evenly moist.
Fertilising If plants are grown in a bed that has had rotted manure dug into it, no further fertilising is required. For containers, add controlled-release fertiliser to the potting mix at planting time and feed the growing plants monthly with liquid or soluble fertiliser.
Problems No particular problems.
Pruning Remove flower stems as they rise or, if the pretty flowers are wanted, deadhead as they fade to stop unwanted seed formation, as dandelion becomes an invasive weed.

HARVESTING
Picking Pick fresh spring leaves while they are small and sweet. Bigger, older leaves are very bitter. You can reduce the bitterness by blanching – that is, excluding light. Do this by covering the plant with an upturned tin or flower pot, being sure that all holes are covered. Young leaves are ready for picking when they have lost all or most of their green colour. Harvest roots only in late autumn or winter or they will lack flavour and body.
Storage The leaves must be used fresh. Store the roots by cleaning, chopping and roasting them until dark brown, then grind and store in an airtight jar.
Freezing Roasted, ground roots will stay fresher and more flavoursome if stored in the freezer like fresh coffee.

USES
Culinary Young sweet leaves are highly nutritious and can be used in salads, stir-fries or to make teas. The roots are ground and used as a coffee substitute.
Medicinal The sticky, white sap of the dandelion is used to remove warts. Dandelion coffee is sleep inducing and a detoxicant said to be good for the kidneys and liver.

TANSY Growing more than 1 m (3¹/₃ ft) tall, tansy is a sprawling perennial with finely divided, grey-green, ferny foliage and heads of yellow button-like flowers that are produced in summer and autumn. The leaves are aromatic and bitter to the taste, and the whole plant dies back to ground level over winter. It spreads out by means of creeping roots and can become quite large over time. In smaller areas it will need to be reduced regularly.

DANDELION
A perennial plant often seen as a weed in lawns or neglected places, dandelion has a flat rosette of deeply lobed, bright green leaves that grows from a big, fleshy tap root. Bright yellow flowers are produced during spring and summer on hollow, leafless stems; these flowers develop into puffy, spherical seed heads that shatter when ripe, and the individual seeds float away on the breeze. Dandelion has a milky sap and its hollow flower stems differentiate it from other weeds.

THYME
Many varieties of this very
common garden herb are
grown. Most are low, creeping
plants, although some will
grow to 25–30 cm (10–12 in).
The shape of the bush and the
colour and aroma of the leaves
all depend on the variety. Not
all thymes are used in cooking;
the varieties used most often
include common garden thyme
(*T. vulgaris*), lemon-scented
thyme (*T. x citriodorus*), silver
posie thyme (*T. vulgaris*
'Silver Posie'), orange thyme
(*T. vulgaris* 'Fragrantissimus')
and caraway thyme (*T. herba-
barona*).

NASTURTIUM This trailing
perennial can be trained to
reach up to 2 m (7 ft) tall, but
is usually grown as an annual,
especially in colder areas and in
the tropics. The wide leaves are
roundish and dark green to
variegated in colour and have
a peppery taste. The funnel-
shaped, five-petalled and
spurred flowers appear in late
spring and summer, and range
from creamy white through
yellow to salmon, brilliant
orange and red. Some varieties
have double flowers and all
have a slight perfume.

Thymus spp.
thyme
LABIATAE/LAMIACEAE

CONDITIONS
Climate Warm, dry climates best suit thyme, although low,
creeping varieties grow better than the bushier types in
colder areas.
Aspect Prefers full sun or partial shade and a light, well
drained soil.
Soil Does not need very rich soil but adding some compost
will help to keep the soil friable. The soil should not be too
acid: if necessary, add lime to the garden bed at the rate of
120 g per square metre (4 oz per square yard).

GROWING METHOD
Planting Sow seeds in spring or autumn in clumps in flat
trays containing damp seed-raising mix. Mist spray the trays
until the seeds germinate, which is usually within a week.
When seedlings are 10 cm (4 in) tall, place the trays outside
for a week to harden the seedlings and then transplant them
into the garden. Dividing mature plants is by far the most
common method of propagation. During spring or summer,
gently lift the parent plant, cut it into two or three sections,
each with a good root formation, and then plant them in the
garden. Layering is also a satisfactory method of propagation.
Watering Do not overwater. Thymes prefer a dryish soil.
Water adequately during dry spells.
Fertiliser No fertiliser needed.
Problems Spider mite, which feeds by sucking juice, can
affect this herb. Treat with a recommended insecticidal
spray. Root rot will set in if the soil is not well drained and
becomes waterlogged.
Pruning Prune or clip to prevent woodiness.

HARVESTING
Picking Fresh leaves and flowers can be picked as required or
the whole plant can be cut back to within 5 cm (2 in) of the
ground in summer and the leaves dried.
Storage Leaves are dried on the stem by hanging branches in
a warm, airy place. Branches are then stripped and the leaves
stored in airtight containers.
Freezing Pack in small airtight containers or plastic wrap;
thyme can be frozen for up to six months.

USES
Culinary Thyme is a classic component of the French
bouquet garni. Varieties of thyme add special, individual
flavours to many dishes. Both leaves and flowers can be
eaten fresh in salads or used as garnishes or as a flavouring
in honey, vinegars, stuffings, butters or teas.
Gardening Thymes can be grown for their decorative effect
as their low, matting habit makes them excellent edging or
rockery plants.

Tropaeolum majus
nasturtium
TROPAEOLACEAE

CONDITIONS
Climate Native to South America and now cultivated in most
climates. Grow as a cool season annual in the monsoonal
tropics and as a summer annual in colder areas.
Aspect Prefers full sun, although dwarf varieties will grow
in semi-shade. Leaf growth is more pronounced in shady
situations.
Soil Nasturtiums do not like an over-rich soil but good
drainage is necessary.

GROWING METHOD
Planting Sow seeds from midsummer through to spring in
hot and tropical climates, from spring through to summer in
warm zones and during spring in colder areas. Sow several
seeds of the trailing varieties together in clumps set about
75 cm (2½ ft) apart. Plant dwarf varieties 40 cm (16 in) apart.
Sow the seeds 2.5 cm (1 in) deep directly into the garden bed
or containers where they are to grow and keep the soil just
moist.
Watering Do not water excessively, especially when plants
are well established.
Fertilising More flowers and seeds will be produced if
you hold back on the fertiliser and compost. Fertilising
encourages the growth of leaves.
Problems Sap-sucking aphids love nasturtiums. Vigorously
hose the pest off or treat the plant with an appropriate spray.
Bacterial wilt and leaf spot are two common diseases. Don't
cultivate while plants are wet and remove all diseased plants
from the garden.

HARVESTING
Picking Pick any part of the plant as required.
Storage Leaves and flowers do not store well and should be
used immediately. Buds and seeds can be pickled in vinegar,
stored in airtight jars and used at a later date.
Freezing Not suitable for freezing.

USES
Culinary All parts of this herb are edible. You can use the
fresh leaves and flowers in salads or the flowers alone as a
garnish. Use the pickled buds and seeds as a substitute for
capers.
Gardening Because nasturtiums are so attractive to aphids,
they are an excellent companion plant for vegetables such as
cabbages, broccoli and other brassicas. The aphids will flock
to the nasturtiums and leave the vegetables alone.

Viola odorata
violet
VIOLACEAE

CONDITIONS
Climate Violets grow in cool or warm climates but dislike the tropics or hot, dry summers.
Aspect Sun in winter and bright dappled shade in summer are ideal. Where summers are mild, violets will tolerate full sun. They do not tolerate hot, dry winds. The flowers are disappointing if violets are grown in too much shade.
Soil Violets need deep soil rich in rotted organic matter, preferably from composted fallen leaves. Soil must drain freely but it must also remain moist between watering.

GROWING METHOD
Planting Violets are easily established by division. Lift immediately after flowering and separate the cylindrical runners. Each division should have its own roots but these will usually form later if they are absent. Plant so that the runners are firmly in contact with the soil but not buried. Scatter seed where it is to grow or, for better germination, onto trays of seed-raising mix. Cover lightly, keep moist and place trays in a bright but shady and cool place. Transplant seedlings when they are big enough to handle.
Watering If they never go dry for long periods, violets will flourish.
Fertilising Place a mulch of rotted manure around plants, but not over the root crown, each spring (this can be hard in a densely planted area), or sprinkle a ration of complete plant food over the plants in spring. Once or twice in summer, use a liquid organic fertiliser or seaweed-based soil conditioner.
Problems Put out snail traps for slugs and snails, which eat leaves and flowers. Spider mites and aphids also damage plants. You can buy predatory mites to help control them; aphids are easily controlled with low-toxicity pyrethrum, garlic or fatty acid sprays. If plants fail to flower, the cause may be too much shade or too much high-nitrogen fertiliser.
Pruning No pruning is necessary, but if flowers fail to form, cut all leaves off in early winter to encourage spring bloom.

HARVESTING
Picking Pick the flowers as soon as they open and pick the leaves any time.
Storage Flowers may be crystallised for later use.
Freezing Not suitable for freezing.

USES
Culinary Use crystallised flowers to decorate cakes or eat them as a sweet treat.
Medicinal An infusion of the leaves and flowers may relieve the symptoms of colds.
Craft Violets are used in pot pourris.
Gardening A very desirable groundcover in partly shaded areas. Posies of cut flowers will fill a room with fragrance.

Zingiber officinale
ginger
ZINGIBERACEAE

CONDITIONS
Climate A tropical climate is best, but ginger will grow anywhere that is frost-free.
Aspect In the tropics, part or dappled shade is best. In warm areas more sun is needed, but ginger still likes shade on hot summer afternoons. Shelter from strong winds is essential.
Soil Deep, friable, well drained soil that is rich in rotted organic matter and a little alkaline: dig in 1 cup of lime per square metre (square yard) at planting time. Dig the bed over deeply, adding rotted manure or compost and complete plant food. The finished bed should be light, fine and crumbly.

GROWING METHOD
Planting Plants can be started from sections of fresh root ginger bought from a fruit market. Cut the rhizome into sections about 7.5 cm (3 in) long, ensuring that each has a pointed growth bud. Allow the cut ends to dry for a few days before planting horizontally 7.5–10 cm (3–4 in) below the surface. Water in thoroughly. In tropical areas plant in autumn; otherwise, mid-spring is better. Mulch the planted bed with compost, rotted manure or other organic matter. Don't plant rhizomes too closely together, especially in the tropics, as this spreading plant needs space.
Watering In tropical areas with dry winters, water deeply once a week. Elsewhere, keep soil lightly moist, gradually increasing the water as temperatures rise. In summer, the plant cannot be overwatered if drainage is good. After the plant has flowered, start to reduce the watering.
Fertilising As well as the fertiliser applied at planting time, ginger should be fed with liquid or soluble plant food every month from mid-spring to late summer. Replacing the mulch as it is washed into the soil also helps feed the plant.
Problems No particular problems.
Pruning In autumn, old stems can be cut out at ground level to make room for vigorous new growth.

HARVESTING
Picking Ginger is harvested in autumn. Dig up and detach the rhizomes, replanting a few to produce next year's crop.
Storage Rhizomes can be wrapped tightly in foil and stored in the crisper bin of the refrigerator for a few weeks, or they may be pickled or crystallised for long-term storage.
Freezing Not suitable for freezing.

USES
Culinary In Asian, African and Caribbean cuisines, ginger is used in everything from curries, soups and stews to salads and vegetable dishes. Crystallised, it is used as a sweet; dried, powdered ginger is added to cakes, biscuits and other foods.
Medicinal Fresh juice directly applied is said to relieve the pain of burns.

VIOLET Violets are low-growing perennials just 15 cm (6 in) tall with a wider spread. The dark green leaves are roundish or kidney-shaped with scalloped edges. Small and very sweetly fragrant flowers appear on short stalks in winter and early spring. They are usually violet in colour but there are also mauve, yellow and white forms. Violets spread very rapidly by creeping roots.

GINGER A clump-forming perennial, ginger is a native of tropical lowland rainforests. It has many erect stems that grow to about 1.5 m (5 ft) tall. Lanceolate leaves, mid-green and about 20 cm (8 in) long, are produced all along the stems. Unremarkable flowers appear in summer, after which the top growth begins to die back.

9

Vegetable
directory

OKRA Also known as gumbo or lady's finger, okra is an annual and a member of the hibiscus family. The large, hibiscus-like, yellow flowers with purplish red centres produce edible, seed-containing pods that have an unusually high gum content. Because of this, not everyone finds this vegetable to their taste. The pod is green and grows to about 7.5–10 cm (3–4 in). The bush grows to a height of 2 m (7 ft), and has hairy stems and large flattened leaves. It does not grow well in containers.

MUSHROOM Mushroom is a fungus, the edible part of which is a spore-producing head that grows up from a body of filaments that feed throughout a bed of compost below. Mushrooms have no leaves or chlorophyll and they absorb no carbon dioxide from the air. Young mushrooms have a small, white, rounded head that opens to a circular cap revealing ridges of pink gills beneath. These turn brown as spores develop between them. There are many poisonous types of fungi, and careful identification is very important when out collecting mushrooms in the field. There are also many varieties of interesting and unusual mushrooms now available in fruit markets.

Abelmoschus esculentus, syn. *Hibiscus esculentus*

okra
MALVACEAE

CONDITIONS

Climate Best grown in tropical, subtropical and hot temperate climates with long, warm growing seasons.
Aspect Prefers to be in full sun; requires well drained soil.
Soil Okra likes moderation in all things. Clay or clay loamy soils with average moisture level and neither over-fertilised nor under-fertilised are ideal.

GROWING METHOD

Planting Sow seeds in spring through to early summer in cool and warm climates. Sow all year round in tropical areas. Seeds can be germinated indoors under controlled conditions and later transplanted, but in most warm climates it is better to plant directly into garden beds. Plant seeds 2 cm (³⁄₄ in) deep and spaced 45 cm (18 in) apart. The flowers take 12–14 weeks to appear.
Watering As the plant is prone to stem rot, water sparingly around the plant and not over it.
Fertilising Lay a band of complete fertiliser in furrows 10–15 cm (4–6 in) deep. Cover with soil and leave a week before planting seed. Side feed 15 cm (6 in) around the plant when pods begin to show; this will assist growth. Water in immediately. Compost to increase the water holding capacity of the soil.
Problems Relatively few problems. Watch out for stem rot in wet conditions. Keep garden free of diseased organic plant matter. Crop rotation will prevent build-up of soil diseases.

HARVESTING

Picking Immature pods are picked when 5–7.5 cm (2–3 in) long after 3–4 months. If left on the bush too long, the pods become fibrous and tough. Pick daily to lengthen cropping period.
Storing Refrigerate for up to three days.
Freezing Blanch in boiling water for 3–4 minutes, cool, pack in freezer bags and freeze for up to 6 months.

USES

Culinary Pods may be used fresh or dried. They are widely used as a flavouring in soups and in meat cooking, or can be fried or boiled and eaten as a vegetable. It is sometimes used as a thickening agent in soups and stews.

Agaricus spp.

mushroom
AGARICACEAE

CONDITIONS

Climate The garden mushroom is mostly grown indoors or under shelter, in temperature-controlled environments. High humidity with constant, cool temperatures from 12–18°C (54–64°F) are recommended.
Aspect Prefers the dark but will tolerate some light. Direct sunlight is not necessary. The home gardener usually grows mushrooms in dark cupboards or in cellars. Good ventilation is required to remove excess carbon dioxide in the air.
Soil Use sterilised mushroom farm compost, inoculated with mushroom spores. Add a 2.5 cm (1 in) layer of sterilised topsoil or peat. This is called the casing.

GROWING METHOD

Planting The easiest way is to buy a kit with spores already in the compost medium. Simply cover tray with 2.5 cm (1 in) of commercially available (sterilised) topsoil and keep moist. Greyish coloured filaments appear in 1–2 weeks, spreading through the compost medium and growing together to form clumps called mycelium. Pinhead structures, which develop into mature mushrooms, grow from this mycelium, forcing their way upwards through the shallow casing.
Watering Keep compost moist but never too wet or soggy. Water two or three times a week.
Fertilising Do not fertilise. Initial preparation of the growing medium is satisfactory.
Problems No serious diseases if using commercially available sterilised compost. Larvae from fly infestations, mushroom mite and nematodes can infect the mycelium and fruiting bodies. Dust beds with pyrethrum every two weeks to clear.

HARVESTING

Picking About four weeks to mature, in growth waves called flushes. Button mushrooms (*A. bisporus*) are cropped before the cap opens. Mature mushrooms are ripe when the cap opens and gills are exposed. Cut stalks at soil level and pick regularly to encourage further flushes. If, after several flushes, no mushrooms appear within 14–21 days, the bed is exhausted and the cultivation cycle needs to be repeated.
Storing Store mushrooms in the fridge for 5–7 days in a paper (never plastic) bag.
Freezing Pack clean mushrooms in plastic bags and freeze for up to six months. They can be dried or pickled and stored in airtight jars.

USES

Culinary Use raw in salads or cook in white sauces. Button mushrooms are good for stir-fries. Larger mushrooms are ideal for stews and casseroles. The flat field mushrooms (*A. campestris*) are delicious grilled or stuffed, but if cooked with white meat, they may turn the dish grey.

Allium ampeloprasum Porrum Group

leek
ALLIACEAE

CONDITIONS
Climate Best grown in cool weather in temperatures below 25°C (77°F). Growth is slower in warm climates. During extreme temperature drops mulch heavily with straw.
Aspect Prefers full sun.
Soil Loose, rich, well drained soil.

GROWING METHOD
Planting Plant seeds in seed-raising boxes from spring to autumn in cool climates, and in late summer and autumn in warm and tropical regions. In areas where winters are mild, seeds can be planted directly into the garden during late summer. When seedlings reach pencil thickness and are 20–30 cm (8–12 in) tall, plant 15 cm (6 in) deep, 15 cm (6 in) apart, in rows that are a handspan apart. Roots should touch the bottom of the hole. Rather than fill the hole with soil, water regularly so as to gradually deposit soil around the roots of the young leek. Also remove the top third of the leaf structure to reduce water loss and to encourage new root growth. Alternatively, in flat garden beds, heap soil around the base of the young leek, cover stem with newspaper and pile dry soil up around it. Keep adding soil as the leek grows. A newspaper collar will prevent soil getting in among leaves.
Watering Water regularly. Moist, fertile soil encourages strong growth.
Fertilising Dig in nitrogen-rich fertiliser and large quantities of animal manure and other organic material. Regular monthly applications of urea will speed up growing time.
Problems Very few problems. Seldom affected by specific pests and diseases. If thrips appear, remove by hosing.

HARVESTING
Picking Leeks take a long time to produce large stems. The growing season takes about 4–5 months from seed stage, 3 months from seedlings. It is not necessary to wait till full maturity before picking. The younger they are, the tastier and sweeter the flesh. To crop when mature, remove top half of leaves in midsummer. Crop only as required but before any frosts set in. The best way is to pull the complete plant from the ground lengthways.
Storing Refrigerate for 7–10 days.
Freezing Pack in freezer bags; freeze for up to six months.

USES
Culinary Some recipes call for just the white part, but most of the leek can be used if it is young and the green leaves are not too tough. Leeks are very good in creamy sauces and soups, most famously vichyssoise. They need to be cooked for a reasonable amount of time or they will be crunchy rather than tender and sweet; if overcooked, they become slimy. They can be boiled, steamed or braised in butter.

Allium ascalonicum, A. cepa

shallot
ALLIACEAE

CONDITIONS
Climate Will grow in all climates.
Aspect Prefers full sun to partial shade.
Soil Well drained soil, rich in humus. Tolerates most soils but not acid soils. Dig in large quantities of animal manure and compost several weeks before planting.

GROWING METHOD
Planting As this plant does not produce viable seed, it is propagated by replanting small bulbs broken off from the parent plant each season. Do this from midsummer to mid-autumn in cold regions; from the end of summer to the end of autumn in temperate zones; and at the end of summer to the beginning of winter in warm, tropical areas. If planning to harvest in its green state, while the plant is quite young, plant the bulb quite deep to 6 cm (2½ in) and hill soil around the stem as it grows. If wanting mature bulbs, plant quite shallow so that the bulblet is level with the top of the soil. In both cases, it is best to leave about 15–20 cm (6–8 in) around each plant. The shallow, fibrous roots need light cultivation and beds need to be kept free of weeds.
Watering Water regularly so that soil does not dry out.
Fertilising Apply complete fertiliser before planting and again at mid-season.
Problems Very few pests and diseases. If thrips appear, remove them by thorough and vigorous hosing.

HARVESTING
Picking Bulbs mature in 3–4 months, but can be harvested after eight weeks if soft bulbs with white stalks and young green leaves are preferred. Shallots may be picked at any stage of growth, but care must be taken not to cut the main stem and hinder further development of the plant. Mature bulbs should be lifted when the top, leafy parts wither.
Storing Store in a cool, airy place for several months.
Freezing Separate cloves from the bulb, pack in freezer bags and freeze for up to three months.

USES
Culinary The shallot is used a great deal in French cooking, particularly for making sauces, where its subtle flavour is an asset. Young succulent leaves may be used raw in salads or as a flavouring in the same way that chives or spring onions are used. They can also be peeled and cooked whole as a vegetable. In Asia, they are made into pickles.

LEEK A relative of the onion, this vegetable has a long, white, underground stem and is slightly bulbous at the root end. Green, strap-like leaves protrude above ground. Most leeks are left to grow to a fully mature state but are much tastier if cropped earlier. The flesh is thick and mildly onion-flavoured.

SHALLOT This vegetable is not to be confused with the evergreen onion, known as the spring onion. Spring onions are very young, green onions, whereas shallots are a more mature form of onion similar to garlic in their formation. With its chestnut-brown skin, *A. ascalonicum* is aptly called the golden shallot. It has small bulbs that measure 1–3 cm (½–1¼ in) in diameter when mature. It has a similar but much more delicate flavour than an onion, although elongated varieties have a stronger flavour than the rounder varieties. The bulbs are clustered at the base of the plant, and narrow whitish stems and green leaves extend above ground. This is an easy vegetable to grow.

Allium cepa

onion

ALLIACEAE

ONION
This versatile vegetable can be grown in most soils and climates. The edible part is the fleshy bulb under the skin; it can be white, yellow or brown through to red. Spring onions are early maturing onions that are grown for their small white bulbs or their thin stems and green tops. White and brown onions are late maturing and will keep much longer than early maturing varieties.

CONDITIONS

Climate All climates are suitable, but it is important to choose varieties that suit your local conditions. Careful planting of varieties with different maturing dates is necessary to achieve cropping over a long period.

Aspect Onions do not like beds that get too hot. They are very temperature-sensitive. Warm weather and direct sunlight promote bulb development, so exposure to full sun is necessary at some stage of the growth process. Cool weather promotes top growth, so green, early maturing onions are able to tolerate partial shade.

Soil Prefer to be in non-acidic soils, about pH 6. Prepare the garden beds well ahead with large amounts of well decayed organic matter.

GROWING METHOD

Planting Onions are classified as early, mid-season or late maturing. Plant early varieties in mid- to late summer in all areas, from cold to tropical. Plant mid-season varieties in early winter in cold regions; autumn to midwinter in warm areas; and autumn in subtropical to tropical areas. Plant late maturing varieties in early winter in cold to warm zones; and in late autumn to early winter in subtropical to tropical regions. Sow seeds directly in the ground or transplant seedlings from seed beds when they are 13 cm (5 in) tall. Plant about 7.5 cm (3 in) apart, in rows 30 cm (12 in) apart. Control weeds by regular, shallow cultivation. When weeding be particularly careful not to cover the maturing bulbs with soil. The best way to do this is by hilling the soil around the bulbs rather than covering them with soil.

Watering Water regularly and evenly. Lack of water delays growth and leads to bulb splitting.

Fertilising Fertilise before planting and mid-season with dressings of urea or sodium sulphate. Nitrogenous fertilisers in the form of blood and bone or animal manures are best, but complete fertiliser is satisfactory. Avoid using nitrogen as the plant approaches maturity because it promotes foliage at the expense of the bulbs.

Problems Onion maggot thrives in fresh organic material, so fertilise with well decayed material. White stipple on leaves indicates onion thrip; use an appropriate spray. Downy mildew can be treated chemically, or remove diseased plants.

HARVESTING

Picking Onions can take more than six months to mature, depending on the variety. If you are going to store onions, wait until the most of the tops have fallen over and, using a rake, knock over the stalks that are still upright. Pull the onions out of the ground about two days later and just leave them on the ground to dry. (If the weather is wet, then you can dry them in a layer of mesh or in shallow trays in a dry place.) If any onions have thick, green stems, then use these immediately, as they will not store well. There is no need to remove the long dried stems. When the onions are fully dried, you can braid these.

Storing Store in a cool, dry place.

Freezing Peel, chop or cut into rings, pack in freezer bags and freeze for up to three months. Small onions can be frozen, still in their skins, in freezer bags. Make sure you remove all air from the bag first, then seal.

USES

Culinary Onions are used in almost every cuisine around the world, generally used to impart flavour to other ingredients. However, they can be cooked and served alone. Brown, or yellow, onions are used in sauces and stews. White onions are mild and slightly sweet: use for cooking or salads. Pearl onions are small, white onions and are ideal for pickling. They can also be added whole to stews. Red onions are good for salads, barbecues and grilling. After cooking red onions tend to have less flavour than other varieties of onion, although they are sweeter. Spring onions are simply immature onions – if they were left in the ground, they would grow to full size. They have a mild flavour and both the green tops and white bulb can be used in cooking. They are usually sliced and tossed with omelettes or with stir-fries.

Gardening Some varieties of onion produce attractive, globular pink or white flowers.

Alocasia macrorrhiza, syn. *Colocasia esculenta*
taro
ARACEAE

CONDITIONS
Climate Requires warm climate with long hot summer. Does best in tropical and subtropical areas with temperatures about 35°C (95°F). The tubers cannot be cultivated in frost-prone areas.
Aspect Prefers full sun.
Soil Fertile, friable soil containing plenty of organic material. Soil should also be moist and well drained.

GROWING METHOD
Planting Plant autumn and winter in warm zones and in midsummer to midwinter in tropical areas. If using small tubers, called 'sons of taro', hived off from the parent tuber, plant during spring. Plant in furrows or trenches 15 cm (6 in) deep and spaced 30 cm (12 in) apart in rows about 1 m (3¹/₃ ft) apart. After planting, cover tubers with 5 cm (2 in) of soil and water in. Taro is best grown near an irrigation ditch so as to benefit from water run-off. Propagation may also be by stem cuttings. Sometimes the plant is 'forced' in warm, dark conditions to produce blanched leaves, which are considered a delicacy by food lovers.
Watering Needs a great deal of regular watering during its growth cycle.
Fertilising Add a complete fertiliser to soil. Do not over-fertilise with nitrogen because this will promote excessive leaf growth at the expense of the tuber.
Problems Relatively free of specific pests and diseases.

HARVESTING
Picking Taro matures in 3–7 months, depending on the variety. At maturity, the leaves turn yellow and the plant almost dies. When this happens, carefully lift the tubers from the soil, especially if there is any danger of a cold spell because this will damage the tuber. Young leaves and stems are also edible and should be picked as soon as the leaves open. However, never strip the plant fully because some leaves are necessary for the continuing development of the tuber.
Storing Will keep for several months in a cool, dry place.
Freezing Peel and cut into pieces. Blanch for three minutes in boiling water. Cool and spread on a tray in a single layer and freeze for 30 minutes. Remove from the freezer, pack in freezer bags and freeze for up to six months.

USES
Culinary Taro root can be used in a similar way to potatoes – fried, baked, roasted, boiled or steamed. They are nuttier in flavour than potatoes when cooked.

Amaranthus tricolor
chinese spinach
AMARANTHACEAE

CONDITIONS
Climate Best grown in hot climates above 20°C (68°F). Will grow under cover where temperatures are controlled.
Aspect Prefers sunny position, sheltered from winds in cool areas. Tolerates partial shade in hot areas.
Soil Grows in light, sandy to heavy, well drained soil that is quite fertile and preferably slightly acidic. Dig in plenty of compost or decayed animal and poultry manures.

GROWING METHOD
Planting Plant seeds in spring and summer in warm and tropical areas, when the soil warms to about 20°C (68°F). The seeds are very small and before sowing should be mixed with coarse wet sand and set aside in a dark place for 1–2 days. Place the sand and seed mixture in garden trenches to a depth of 2.5 cm (1 in) and firm over. Keep trenches 25 cm (10 in) apart and thin seedlings to be 7.5–10 cm (3–4 in) apart. Successive sowings every fortnight will give a longer cropping period. Seeds can also be germinated under cover in late spring to early summer. Seedlings will appear in 2–3 weeks and can be transplanted out when about 2.5 cm (1 in) high and showing 2–3 true leaves. Chinese spinach can also be propagated from cuttings, which are usually taken from younger growth or sideshoots that have not flowered. The plant may bolt if left to dry out in hot weather; if it does, remove any flowers and seed heads that appear.
Watering Soil must be kept moist for succulent growth.
Fertilising Use a dressing of nitrogenous liquid occasionally.
Problems Young seedlings may become too damp and wither or flop. In warmer climates caterpillars and stem borer may also be a problem. Treat with appropriate sprays.

HARVESTING
Picking Takes 6–8 weeks from sowing for plant to reach cropping stage. There are several ways to harvest. Tips of larger plants can be picked while quite young. Alternatively, the whole plant may be pulled from the ground, roots and all, when about 25 cm (10 in) tall. Another method is to cut the mature plant back to 2.5 cm (1 in) above ground level, leaving some of the stem and a few basal leaves to promote regrowth.
Storing The leaves will last for three days in the refrigerator, but will go limp immediately if left out at room temperature.
Freezing Wash and trim leaves. Blanch for one minute, chill, drain, pack in freezer bags and freeze for up to six months.

USES
Culinary The leaves have a slightly pungent flavour and are used in the same way as spinach. Young shoots can be used in salads.

TARO Also known as dasheen, taro is an edible tuber with a high starch level. The flesh can be white to purplish or greenish. The tuber has a spherical shape, growing to 20 cm (8 in), with a thick, fibrous, hairy, light brown skin and divisional markings on the circumference. It is a large plant, growing up to 1–1.5 m (3¹/₃–5 ft), its large, light green, shield-shaped leaves borne on long stalks. The leaves, which are sometimes called callaloo, are edible but may be grown purely for their decorative quality. This vegetable is eaten in many tropical countries throughout the world.

CHINESE SPINACH One of a very large group of plants called amaranths, Chinese spinach, or amaranth, is a green leafy vegetable cultivated for its nutritional value. Erect and branching, this annual grows to 1 m (3¹/₃ ft) or more under ideal conditions. Soft textured leaves can grow to 15 cm (6 in). The leaves are pointed or round, light to dark green, and both the leaves and the stems have red to purple markings. The flavour is a little reminiscent of an artichoke's flavour, although older plants can develop a hot taste. It grows well in containers and looks attractive.

Apium graveolens

celery
APIACEAE

CONDITIONS

Climate Prefers mild to cool weather and cool nights. Very cold weather will inhibit growth. Seedlings are sensitive to temperatures below 13°C (55°F).
Aspect Tolerates light shade and wet weather.
Soil Soil needs neutral to alkaline pH level. Prepare beds with animal manure and compost and complete fertiliser.

GROWING METHOD

Planting Plant in spring to summer in cool areas; winter through to summer in warm zones; and summer through to autumn in tropical areas. In temperatures above 13°C (55°F), plant seed directly into open beds. Seed viability is often poor, so use fresh seeds for new plantings, sown 5 mm (¼ in) deep in seed beds. When the seedlings are about 12 cm (4 in) high, thin and plant in the garden in trenches 10 cm (4 in) deep. Leave 25 cm (10 in) between plants and 45–60 cm (18–24 in) between rows. Mound soil around young plants, with roots well covered and thoroughly watered in. Keep beds weed-free by shallow cultivation.
Watering Celery requires a great deal of water from seed to maturity; water daily during hot, dry weather. Lack of water leads to slow growth and stringy, tasteless stalks.
Fertilising Enrich beds with complete fertiliser. Fortnightly side dressings are essential throughout the growing period. This is especially important because the plant is shallow rooted and frequent watering leaches nutrients from the soil. Occasional dressings of sulphate of ammonia help growth.
Problems A fungal disease known as leaf spot or septoria may affect this plant, producing dead spots on leaves. Control with an appropriate fungicide spray. Magnesium and calcium deficiency in soil increases the risk of disease.

HARVESTING

Picking Celery matures 4–5 months after planting. Cut the whole plant at ground level before seed stalks appear, or break off outside stems as needed.
Storing Place stems in plastic wrap and store in the crisper drawer for up to 10 days. To revive wilted stems, sprinkle with water and put in the refrigerator until crisp again.
Freezing Cut stems into 2.5 cm (1 in) pieces. Blanch for two minutes in boiling water. Chill, drain, pack in freezer bags and freeze for up to six months.

USES

Culinary Celery stems are eaten raw in salads or as crudités, cooked and served as a vegetable, braised in tomato or cream, or used as a base flavour in stocks and sauces. Leaves add flavour to stocks and soups; tender inner leaves can be used in salads or eaten with the stalk. The seeds can be dried and used in soups and pickles.

CELERY Celery is a biennial that is mostly grown as an annual. It has a tight collection of green stalks or stems that are about 25 cm (10 in) tall and topped with multiple dividing leaves. Both the stalks and leaves are edible. The seeds, produced from flowers when the plant is left to grow and not cropped, are also edible. However, this is not an easy crop for the home gardener to grow.

ASPARAGUS Attractive, fern-like, feathery foliage is a feature of this hardy perennial which grows to 1 m (3⅓ ft) tall. The edible part is the tender young stem or spear. Male and female flowers appear on separate plants, with the male plants producing the larger and better spears. Female plants, which can be identified by their red berries, should be discarded after the second autumn of growth. This delicious vegetable is easy to grow, but is not suitable for container growing.

Asparagus officinalis

asparagus
ASPARAGACEAE

CONDITIONS

Climate Grows well in mild to cold climates and can withstand frosts, which fit in with the dormancy period.
Aspect Prefers full sun but will grow in partial shade.
Soil Fertile, well drained soil with a pH of over 6.

GROWING METHOD

Planting Plant seeds in spring in special beds. Transfer two-year-old seedlings during winter or spring to a permanent position. Alternatively, buy and plant two-year-old crowns in winter. Prepare permanent beds to a depth of 30 cm (12 in) with plenty of organic matter and complete fertiliser. Plant in trenches that are 25 cm (10 in) wide and deep. Set crowns 45 cm (18 in) apart in the trench and cover with 5 cm (2 in) of soil. As the fern grows, cover with soil until the trench is filled, leaving new shoots uncovered. For 'white' or blanched asparagus, mound soil over trenches to a depth of about 25 cm (10 in) in late winter. The fern dies off in winter and new shoots occur in spring.
Watering Keep soil moist, especially when spears are forming. Dry soil causes stringy stalks.
Fertilising Regularly apply high-nitrogen fertiliser during summer to encourage top growth, and in late winter for spring spear growth.
Problems Mostly problem-free. Grow rust-resistant varieties to lessen incidence of rust. Spray for asparagus beetle if this becomes a problem.

HARVESTING

Picking Harvest three-year-old plant in late winter or early spring. Cut when the spears are 15–20 cm (6–8 in) long, at just below soil level, being careful not to damage adjacent new shoots. Feathering of the spear means the harvest is too late. Harvest along the same row at two-week intervals in season, for up to eight weeks. For white asparagus, cut the spear 15 cm (6 in) below soil level when the tip has just broken the surface. Production increases annually and maturity occurs at 4–5 years.
Storing Refrigerate for up to 10 days. Break off the rough ends and stand upright in 2.5 cm (1 in) of water.
Freezing Remove woody portions. Cut into 15 cm (6 in) lengths, blanch in boiling water. Cool, place on trays in a single layer and freeze for 30 minutes. Remove from freezer, pack in freezer bags and freeze for up to six months.

USES

Culinary Cook the delicate shoots quickly and with care so as not to damage the fragile tips. Once cooked, serve asparagus with melted butter and Parmesan cheese, or add to risottos, quiches, stir-fries or salads.

Beta vulgaris

beetroot
CHENOPODIACEAE

CONDITIONS
Climate Tolerates frost and best in cooler climates, but can grow in most climates. In very hot regions, roots tend to become woody; if the weather becomes too cold, young plants may not develop roots and will run to seed. Watch planting times if these two extremes of temperature occur during the crucial stages of the growing season.
Aspect Can tolerate both full sun and partial shade.
Soil Prefers loose soils; root can grow freely. Soils need to be high in organic matter, well limed, with good drainage.

GROWING METHOD
Planting Sow in spring through to early autumn in colder areas, during spring and autumn in warm regions, and all year round in subtropical climates. Sow seeds directly into soil and stagger planting by a month for continuous supply throughout harvesting period. Prepare trenches 10 cm (4 in) deep, 7.5 cm (3 in) wide and in rows 45 cm (18 in) apart. Lay a narrow band of complete fertiliser in the trench and cover with 7.5 cm (3 in) of soil. Lay seeds on top, then fill the trench with soil. Alternatively, dig a complete fertiliser through the bed before sowing. Thin out the very young seedlings to 4 cm (1½ in) apart and later to 7.5 cm (3 in) as the root swells. Beetroot does not like weed competition, but when weeding take care not to damage developing roots.
Watering Give young beetroot plenty of water to encourage larger, tender roots. Left to dry out, the vegetable becomes tough and stringy.
Fertilising In new beds, use a complete fertiliser. Do not over-manure or over-fertilise beds that have been heavily fertilised for the previous crop because this leads to rather tasteless beetroot with a low sugar content.
Problems Seldom any problems.

HARVESTING
Picking Beetroot matures about 3–4 months after sowing, depending on area and seasonal conditions. Harvest before the plant goes to seed and when the root is sufficiently large.
Storing Refrigerate the roots for up to three weeks, the leaves for up to one week. It can also be canned or pickled.
Freezing Only freeze tender young beetroot. Cook until tender and slice, chop or leave whole. Cool, transfer to plastic containers and freeze for up to six months.

USES
Culinary Beetroot is remarkably versatile: grate it raw and add to salads; bake, steam or boil it; purée it with oil and spices to make a dip; or as in Eastern European kitchens, use it to make the soup, borscht. Cook and use the young leaves as you would spinach. Blanched, the leaves can be added to soups, salads or pasta sauces.

Beta vulgaris var. *cicla*

swiss chard
CHENOPODIACEAE

CONDITIONS
Climate All climate zones are suitable, although it is best to avoid growing in very hot or frosty cold months.
Aspect Prefers full sun or partial shade.
Soil Well drained, rich, neutral or slightly alkaline soil. Prepare beds with plenty of compost or decayed manure.

GROWING METHOD
Planting Plant late summer and during spring in colder areas, midwinter to early summer in temperate zones, and all year round in subtropical climates. Sow seeds directly into the garden in trenches 2.5 cm (1 in) deep, 10–15 cm (4–6 in) apart, along rows 40 cm (16 in) apart. Apply fertiliser along each side of the trench base, fill with soil, firm down and water in. Seedlings should appear within two weeks. When 4 cm (1½ in) high, thin so seedlings are 30 cm (12 in) apart. Swiss chard should mature within 8–12 weeks of planting and may bolt to seed in hot weather. Remove flower stems as they appear and keep beds free of weeds. Mulch in hot weather.
Watering Keep soil moist by watering regularly.
Fertilising Swiss chard likes a good complete fertiliser that is nitrogen-rich. Apply monthly side dressings of urea for vigorous growth.
Problems Swiss chard is reasonably hardy but leaf spot (grey spots with brown leaf edges) can affect spring plantings. Treat with appropriate sprays, otherwise the infected leaves should be picked and burned. Aphids and leaf miners can be controlled by vigorous hosing or by picking the insects off the plant.

HARVESTING
Picking Swiss chard will have a long cropping period if the seed is sown at the right time. Pick the mature outside leaves as the need arises and the plant will probably go on producing all season. Do not cut the stalks, but break or peel off by a downwards and sideways action. Leave younger stalks on the parent plant to encourage further growth. Alternatively, the whole plant can be cropped by cutting down to 5 cm (2 in) and then left to regenerate.
Storing Refrigerate for up to two weeks.
Freezing Wash, trim leaves and blanch in boiling water for one minute. Chill, drain, pack in freezer bags and freeze for up to six months.

USES
Culinary Eat cooked or raw in salads. Use stalks in sauces, added to soups or sautéed.
Gardening Interplant Swiss chard with flowers in a mixed ornamental and edible bed.

BEETROOT
Beetroot, or beet, is mostly cultivated as an annual. The swollen edible root can be either rounded or tapered and is red, yellow (golden beet) or white. The leaves sprout as a rosette above ground and are delicious used in salads when young. Beetroot is suitable for growing in either gardens or large containers; however, the 'Cylindrica' variety, with its long tubular roots, is not suitable for containers.

SWISS CHARD (SILVERBEET)
Also known as silverbeet, this member of the beetroot family is often mistakenly called spinach. Swiss chard has white to cream, ribbed stems supporting large, green, crinkly leaves. All these parts are edible. Different varieties, called chards, are available and their varicoloured (red, orange, gold and yellow) stems make them attractive deep container plants. This is an easy vegetable to grow in the home garden.

SWEDE

The swede belongs to a group that includes vegetables such as cabbage, Brussels sprouts and broccoli. Swede is also known by the name rutabaga and it is very similar to the turnip. It can be identified by the multiple leaf scars on its top and by the deeply lobed structure of its greyish green leaves. The large root, which is actually a swelling at the base of the plant's stem, sits on the soil surface as the vegetable grows. The skin is white, yellow or purple and the flesh is creamy to yellow.

CHINESE BROCCOLI

Chinese broccoli is known by various names, such as gai larn or kailan, and is often used in Asian cooking. This stout, leafy plant grows to about 45 cm (18 in). It has thick, crisp leaves which are blue-green to grey with a waxy look. The leaves come in different shapes and sizes, depending on the variety. The plant has medium-sized, attractive, white or yellow flowers. It is grown as a vegetable for its chunky, edible, 1–2 cm (½–¾ in) thick stem. It is only suitable for container growing if young plants are to be harvested. Older plants need to be grown in the garden. It has a small, shallow rooting system.

Brassica napus Napobrassica Group

swede

BRASSICACEAE

CONDITIONS

Climate Best grown as a cool climate crop, but all climates are suitable, depending on the variety grown.
Aspect Prefers full sun to partial shade.
Soil Fertile, well drained soil. Prepare beds with plenty of organic matter for free growth of roots. Beds that have been well fertilised and worked over for a previous crop are ideal. Do not plant in the same bed as an earlier *Brassica* crop.

GROWING METHOD

Planting For best results in cold regions have two plantings, one in midsummer and the other at the end of winter; plant late summer to early autumn in temperate zones; and plant at the end of summer to mid-autumn in hot, subtropical areas. Successive planting every three weeks ensures a longer cropping period. Sow seeds directly into the ground, no more than 1 cm (½ in) deep in rows 25 cm (10 in) apart. Cover with compost and water in. Thin plants to 13 cm (5 in) apart after seedlings appear, which should be within the first fortnight after sowing. Do not hill soil around exposed vegetable. Keep beds weed-free, being particularly careful not to damage the developing root.
Watering Give vegetables plenty of water, especially through hot weather periods to avoid plant drying out. Swedes do not do well in dry conditions.
Fertilising Prepare the bed with a light dressing of poultry manure plus a complete fertiliser that has a good amount of phosphorus. Apply side dressings of the same fertiliser about four weeks after planting.
Problems This vegetable has no serious diseases but does suffer from various pest infestations. Hose off aphids or control with appropriate sprays. Pests, such as caterpillars and grubs, which affect other brassicas, damage swedes. Spraying with a recommended insecticide every two weeks from seedling stage onwards will help to control pests.

HARVESTING

Picking This vegetable matures in about 3–4 months, or sometimes earlier in warmer areas. When harvesting the root, pull whole roots from the ground before they become coarse and woody, otherwise they develop a very strong flavour.
Storing Store in a cool, dark place. Swedes can be waxed with melted paraffin to prevent wrinkling during storage. They will keep in the refrigerator for about four weeks.
Freezing Not suitable for freezing

USES

Culinary Use in a similar way to turnips: roast, boil or bake, although they will take longer to cook..The leafy tops of very young vegetables can be used successfully in salads.

Brassica oleracea Alboglabra Group

chinese broccoli

BRASSICACEAE

CONDITIONS

Climate Can be successfully grown in all climatic zones, even tolerating frosts once past the seedling stage.
Aspect Chinese broccoli does best in a sunny position. Needs to be protected from strong winds, which may 'lift' and move the plant because of its shallow root system.
Soil Fertile, well drained soil. Prepare the soil with organic material such as compost and animal and poultry manure.

GROWING METHOD

Planting Sow from late spring through summer to early autumn in all areas. Midsummer sowings produce the heaviest yields. If harvesting young plants, scatter seed directly into the garden or a large container, thinning later to 15 cm (6 in) apart. For plants that will be left to mature and have a longer cropping period, sow seeds directly into the garden, spacing 30 cm (12 in) apart. The plant matures in about 12–14 weeks. Secondary shoots will appear after the main flowering shoot is cut.
Watering Keep soil moist and water frequently.
Fertilising Provide extra nitrogen supplements in liquid fertiliser, especially if the soil is sandy. For plants exposed to windy conditions, firm soil up around roots for strength and protection. Dig in a generous application of poultry manure and a little complete fertiliser. Side dressings of sulphate of ammonia during the growing season or weekly applications of liquid seaweed aid growth.
Problems Susceptible to downy mildew. Treat with the appropriate fungicide. Plant leaves give cover to slugs and caterpillars. Spray, dust or put out traps for protection.

HARVESTING

Picking If left to mature, the plant can be harvested over a long period. Cut the shoots or stems when about 15 cm (6 in) long and before the flowers open. Harvest frequently in hot climates to prevent the plant bolting and shoots becoming tough. Alternatively, the whole plant can be harvested while quite young, usually about six weeks after sowing.
Storing Will keep for a long time, either in or out of the refrigerator.
Freezing Cut to required size, blanch for three minutes and chill. Drain and place on a tray in a single layer and freeze for 30 minutes. Remove from freezer, pack in freezer bags and freeze for up to six months.

USES

Culinary Steam whole or cut up the leaves and stems and add to soups and stir-fries. Young stalks are crisp and mild; thicker stalks need to be peeled and halved.

Brassica oleracea Botrytis Group
cauliflower
BRASSICACEAE

CONDITIONS
Climate Grows in most climates but does not like extremes of temperature. Like most brassicas does best in cooler areas, needing lower temperatures for the flower heads to form.
Aspect Protect from full sunlight and frosts or maturing heads will discolour.
Soil Heavy feeder, requiring rich, well drained soil that is not acidic, with plenty of well rotted manure or compost.

GROWING METHOD
Planting Sow from late spring through summer in cool areas; summer and autumn in temperate areas; and autumn in subtropical areas. Sow seeds 1 cm (½ in) deep in outdoor beds in rows 5 cm (2 in) apart. Use a number of varieties with differing maturing dates. Transplant when seedlings are 10–13 cm (4–5 in) high in cool weather; space at least 60 cm (2 ft) apart. To keep the cauliflower white, tie the largest leaves together over the head. Start this when the head is quite small and replace the leaves as the head grows larger.
Watering Keep soil moist and air humid around maturing plants, but avoid watering directly over the head, which may cause damage. The head may need protection from heavy rainfalls for the same reason.
Fertilising About four weeks before planting, prepare the bed with complete fertiliser and a good amount of dolomite or lime, which assists in the uptake of the trace element molybdenum. Apply side dressings of the same fertiliser mid-season or four weeks after transplanting seedlings. Cauliflowers will take more fertilising than other brassicas. Dressings of urea will promote growth if applied when heads are starting to form.
Problems Caterpillars of the cabbage white butterfly and aphids are a problem in warmer zones. Treat with an appropriate pesticide. Yellowing and withering of leaves is due to molybdenum or magnesium deficiency. Water seedlings with a solution of 20 g (¾ oz) sodium molybdate dissolved in 5 litres (9 pints) water.

HARVESTING
Picking Harvest 4–5 months after planting. Remove heads when about 20 cm (8 in) wide; cut before they discolour and lose their crisp firmness. Harvest young leaves.
Storing Remove the leaves and refrigerate for up to a week.
Freezing Divide into florets and blanch. Chill, drain and place on a tray in a single layer. Freeze for 30 minutes. Remove, pack in freezer bags and freeze for up to six months.

USES
Culinary Steam, boil or stir-fry or eat raw as crudités. Can also be pickled or used in soups. Use leaves as a green cooking vegetable

Brassica oleracea Capitata Group
cabbage
BRASSICACEAE

CONDITIONS
Climate Adaptable to a wide range of climates but best as a cool weather crop. Tolerates frost but not extremes of heat.
Aspect Prefers a sunny position.
Soil Well drained soil with a pH of 6.5–7.5 that has been made fertile with the addition of decomposed manure and compost. Keep garden beds well mulched.

GROWING METHOD
Planting Plant in summer and spring in cool zones and all year round in other areas. Sow seeds 1 cm (½ in) deep and 7.5 cm (3 in) apart in seed beds. Transplant into garden when seedlings are 5–6 weeks old, with 4–5 true leaves. Plant seedlings deeply, up to first leaves, 60 cm (2 ft) apart, in rows 75 cm (2½ ft) apart, depending on variety. Sugar loaf cabbages need just 30–40 cm (12–16 in) between plants. Harden off seedlings by withholding water for a couple of days just before transplanting.
Watering Keep topsoil moist at all times.
Fertilising Prepare bed several weeks before planting with a complete fertiliser and a good amount of dolomite. Spread small amounts of the same fertiliser over the garden bed one month after planting and water in at once. When cabbages start to form firm hearts, apply a light dressing of urea, especially if soils are sandy.
Problems Cabbage white butterfly caterpillars, centre grubs and corn ear worms attack cabbages and destroy growing buds. Spray every two weeks from seedling stage onwards with an appropriate insecticide. Magnesium deficiency and downy mildew are common.

HARVESTING
Picking Harvest after 14–16 weeks when the head is firm. Cut from the stem, leaving the outer leaves attached to the stem. In cool areas, harvest summer to autumn; in warm areas, harvest late spring to early summer; and in subtropical zones, harvest in autumn and winter.
Storing Refrigerate for several weeks. Can also be pickled as sauerkraut.
Freezing Remove outer leaves. Cut into thin wedges or shred. Blanch for two minutes. Drain, chill, pack in freezer bags and freeze for up to six months.

USES
Culinary Raw cabbage can be shredded finely in coleslaw or salads; use in stir-fries, braised, steamed or added to soups; leaves can be used to wrap fillings. Red cabbage cooked with onions, stock, red wine and vinegar is a classic dish with pork or game. Shredded and salted cabbage is used to make sauerkraut; rinse and drain well before serving.

CAULIFLOWER Grown as an annual, this plant has a single stalk supporting a solid head made up of a collection of edible flower buds. The heads can be white, green or purple, depending upon which variety of cauliflower is grown. Both quick and late maturing types are available. 'Mini' varieties are now on the market and require only half the growing space of the larger cauliflowers. Cauliflowers have large rooting systems and are not suited to container growing.

CABBAGE This is a very hardy vegetable, always grown as an annual. The edible part is a large, terminal bud composed of tightly packed, overlapping leaves that form a round or sometimes a pointed head. The leaves are either green or purple, depending on the variety, and have a smooth or crinkled texture. The stem is short except when the plant is left to go to seed.

BRUSSELS SPROUT The Brussels sprout belongs to the cabbage family and has very similar requirements to cabbages. The Brussels sprout's small heads measure about 5 cm (2 in) in diameter, resemble cabbages and grow from a tall, main stem, nestling among large, green leaves.

KOHLRABI
Kohl is the German word for cabbage and rabi means turnip, and these two words perfectly describe kohlrabi. It is a cabbage-like root producing a swollen white, purple or green, turnip-shaped stem above ground. Circles of edible green leaves grow from the stem. It tastes somewhere between a cabbage and turnip, although not as strong as and slightly sweeter than both. This is a favourite vegetable in Asian cuisines.

Brassica oleracea Gemmifera Group

brussels sprout

BRASSICACEAE

CONDITIONS

Climate Prefers cool growing season. Tolerates frosts but not extended cold or hot periods. Temperature range between 25°C (77°F) by day and 10°C (50°F) at night are ideal.
Aspect Garden beds should have a sunny aspect.
Soil Most soils are suitable except sandy soils, which produce loose, leafy vegetables with no heart, or waterlogged soils. Young plants will do best in soils with a pH of 6.5–7.5.

GROWING METHOD

Planting Plant during summer through autumn in cooler climates; during summer and early autumn in temperate zones. Sow seeds 1 cm (½ in) deep, well spaced, in seed boxes. When 10 cm (4 in) tall, transplant seedlings 45 cm (18 in) apart, in rows 60 cm (2 ft) apart. Protect from wind damage by hilling soil around plants. Remove the terminal bud when the plant is about 40 cm (16 in) to encourages sprouts to mature at the same time.
Watering Need a great deal of water as well as cool, moist air. Ease off on watering a week or two before harvesting.
Fertilising Prepare beds some weeks before transplanting by digging in poultry manure with a complete fertiliser. Add extra nitrogen during picking times; if heavy rains leach the soil, apply 5 g (⅛ oz) of nitrate of potash to each plant.
Problems Very prone to pests and diseases. Cabbage white butterfly caterpillars cause problems early in the season, followed by aphids, slugs and snails. Use commercial and/or organic sprays. Treat downy mildew and club root (worsened by acidic, moist soil conditions) with constant applications of fungicide. Yellowish areas around leaves are indicative of magnesium deficiency. Water soil around the plant with a solution of 30 g (1 oz) magnesium sulphate (Epsom salts) in 5 litres (9 pints) water. Many of these conditions can be avoided with proper drainage and preparation.

HARVESTING

Picking The growing season is 5–6 months. Harvest late summer through spring; if the weather is too hot, this will be shorter. Pick mature sprouts frequently, especially in warmer zones, and before they burst. Start at the bottom of the stem where mature sprouts first develop.
Storing Refrigerate for 7–10 days. Early winter sprouts left on the stem and hung in a cool, dry place keep for a month.
Freezing Remove outer leaves and cut a cross at the stem end. Blanch for three minutes, cool, drain, spread on a tray in a single layer and freeze for 30 minutes. Remove from the tray, pack in freezer bags and freeze for up to six months.

USES

Culinary Steam or boil, or shred for use in a stir-fry.

Brassica oleracea Gongylodes Group

kohlrabi

BRASSICACEAE

CONDITIONS

Climate All climates, from subzero to subtropical, suit this vegetable.
Aspect Prefers sunny, well drained beds with cool, moist soil.
Soil Soil should be well drained and rich in organic matter. Dig in plenty of well rotted animal manure. This will help to retain moisture levels in the soil, but do not hill soil around the vegetable as it matures. Aim for a pH range of 6.5–7.5.

GROWING METHOD

Planting Sow from midsummer to autumn in all areas. Early spring sowing is also viable in regions with cooler temperatures. Seedlings do not transplant readily, so it is best to plant seeds directly into prepared garden beds. Sow seeds in rows 45–60 cm (18–24 in) apart and cover with no more than 1 cm (½ in) of soil. Thin seedlings to 10 cm (4 in) apart when about 5 cm (2 in) high. Like other brassicas, kohlrabi has a shallow root system, so keep beds free of weeds by shallow cultivation.
Watering Keep topsoil evenly moist at all times, otherwise the texture of the vegetable will turn towards woodiness.
Fertilising Prepare beds several weeks before sowing with complete fertiliser and a good amount of lime or dolomite. Spread small amounts of the same fertiliser over the garden bed one month after planting and water in immediately. Light side dressings of urea help growth as the vegetable matures. Fortnightly applications may be necessary in sandy soils.
Problems Common pests are the same as those that attack cabbages, such as caterpillars of the cabbage white butterfly and centre grubs. Spray with an appropriate pesticide every two weeks from seedling stage onwards. Downy mildew and magnesium deficiency are also common.

HARVESTING

Picking The growing season for kohlrabi is short at about 8–10 weeks. Always harvest during cool weather when the vegetable has reached 5–7.5 cm (2–3 in) in diameter. It tends to bolt in cooler areas where growing season temperatures fall below 19°C (66°F).
Storing Refrigerate for 7–10 days.
Freezing Wash, peel and cut into pieces. Blanch for three minutes, chill, drain and spread on a tray in a single layer and freeze for 30 minutes. Remove from the tray, pack in freezer bags and freeze for up to six months.

USES

Culinary Kohlrabi can be grated or sliced raw, added to stir-fries or stews, mashed, or cooked in chunks and tossed in butter.

Brassica oleracea Italica Group

broccoli

BRASSICACEAE

CONDITIONS

Climate Grows anywhere except in the hottest and coldest climates, but temperate and cold climates are best because it needs a cool winter to reach maturity.

Aspect Can be grown in containers on verandahs, or even indoors, as well as in garden beds with a sunny position.

Soil Likes well drained soil with a pH range of 6.5–7.5. Prepare garden beds with manures and fertilisers, providing an extra nitrogen supplement if soil is sandy.

GROWING METHOD

Planting Sow seeds 7.5 cm (3 in) apart, 2 cm (¾ in) deep, during late spring to early summer in cold climates; in late summer to autumn in warmer zones; and in autumn to winter in tropical areas. Successive sowings a month apart will produce a longer cropping period. To raise seedlings, grow in punnets or small 10 cm (4 in) pots. After about six weeks, when seedlings are 10 cm (4 in) tall and at least four true leaves have appeared, transfer to garden beds, planting 50 cm (20 in) apart, in rows 60 cm (2 ft) apart. After initial rapid leaf growth, the edible head develops in 3–4 months. Sideshoots develop after the central head has been harvested. To encourage new growth, leave base of plant and some outer leaves on the plant after cropping.

Watering Grows quickly; keep soil moist by constant watering if necessary. Cut back watering as heads mature.

Fertilising Prepare beds with plenty of poultry manure and complete fertiliser. Side dressings of sulphate of ammonia and weekly applications of liquid seaweed fertiliser during the growing season will produce healthy plants.

Problems Broccoli is quite prone to disease; reduce the risk with seasonal crop rotation. Larvae of the cabbage white butterfly are the main pests. Control with commercial and/or organic sprays. Curling of the leaf indicates a molybdenum deficiency. Water seedlings with a solution containing 5 g (⅛ oz) sodium molybdate in 5 litres (9 pints) water. In moist, cool areas, avoid downy mildew by making sure plants are well aerated and have good sunlight penetration.

HARVESTING

Picking When buds are large, firm but not yet flowering, cut the large central head, leaving 15 cm (6 in) of stalk attached.

Storing Refrigerate for up to a week.

Freezing Divide tender young heads into sprigs. Blanch for three minutes, chill, drain, spread on a tray and freeze for 30 minutes. Pack in freezer bags and freeze for six months.

USES

Culinary Broccoli can be eaten raw, steamed or boiled. The stalks, which are quite sweet, can be peeled and diced and used in the same way as the florets.

Brassica rapa Pekinensis Group

chinese cabbage

BRASSICACEAE

CONDITIONS

Climate Best in cool temperatures from 13–20°C (55–68°F). Tropical varieties have also been developed.

Aspect Prefers open, sunny position but tolerates partial shade. Shelter from cold winds and frost.

Soil Deep, well drained soils, high in organic matter are best. Avoid both light and heavy soils, and apply lime if necessary so the pH range is between 6.5 and 7.

GROWING METHOD

Planting Plant from spring through summer in cold regions, winter through spring in warm zones, and all year round in tropical and subtropical climates. Most importantly, plant to avoid the vegetable reaching maturity in periods of frost. Plant seeds directly into the garden because seedlings do not transplant well. Sow seeds 5 mm (¼ in) deep in clumps along the row, so that when the seedlings are thinned out, plants will be 30–40 cm (12–16 in) apart. Allow 35–40 cm (14–16 in) between rows. Seedlings will emerge 1–2 weeks after planting. Slow growth leads to plants going to seed; they may bolt in hot, dry weather and where days are long. Select varieties to suit local conditions to lessen these risks. Mulch heavily to retain soil moisture and ward off bacterial rot. Bind heads with string or elastic bands as heads reach maturity to protect tender, white, inner leaves.

Watering These shallow-rooted vegetables require a great deal of watering for fast growth. Irrigate between rows and keep water off the leaves to reduce risk of fungal diseases.

Fertilising Dig in a complete fertiliser one week before planting. A month after planting, spread small amounts of the same fertiliser around the plants and water in immediately. When cabbages start to form heads, apply a light dressing of urea.

Problems This cabbage is prone to soil diseases such as club root and bacterial soft rot. Protect by liming and rotating with an unrelated crop several times over a few years. Dust or spray against caterpillars and aphids.

HARVESTING

Picking Pick in dry conditions, 2–3 months after planting. Cut when the heads feel solid; if left till seed stalks appear, the heads will split. Cut the heads just above soil level.

Storing Can be refrigerated or kept in a cool, dry place, such as a cellar, for several weeks or even a few months.

Freezing Only freeze crisp, young cabbage. Wash and shred. Blanch for two minutes. Chill, drain, place in freezer bags and freeze for up to six months.

USES

Culinary Shred and eat raw; steam or use in stir-fries, soups and curries; or use to make cabbage rolls.

BROCCOLI
Grown as an annual, broccoli looks like a green cauliflower. Flower stalks are green, purplish to white in colour and the plant has tiny yellow flowers. The edible part of broccoli is the head, which is eaten when it is green and in bud, not when yellow flowers are showing.

CHINESE CABBAGE Chinese cabbage has many names, including wong bok and celery cabbage. It has wide, thick, crisp leaves with a prominent, broad-based midrib. The plant's upright head is either loose or tight, depending on the variety. Leaf colour varies between dark and light green, with inner leaves having a creamy white colour. It can grow 30–45 cm (12–18 in) tall. Flavour ranges from mustardy to sweet and is rather like a lettuce. The plant is not suitable for containers.

TURNIP Closely associated with the swede, the turnip is a large root, or more precisely, a swelling at the base of the stem, which sits on the soil surface as the plant grows. The turnip comes in a variety of shapes and sizes. The root has white flesh and skin, and it supports a rosette of green feathery leaves. Both the leaves and the root are edible.

CAPSICUMS AND CHILLIES Capsicums (also referred to as peppers) and chillies are perennial, but are often grown as annuals. The capsicum plant grows to an erect, compact bush and the fruits may be a variety of shapes and colours. Chillies, a small form of pepper, produce green or purple fruit, which changes to bright red, yellow or orange at maturity. Capsicums and chillies make excellent container plants. The chilli is known for its fiery heat, while capsicums have a rather sweet, delicate flavour.

Brassica rapa Rapifera Group

turnip
BRASSICACEAE

CONDITIONS
Climate Best grown as a cool climate crop, but all climates suit, depending on variety.
Aspect Prefers full sun to partial shade.
Soil Well drained, loose, deep soil. Garden beds should be well prepared with plenty of organic matter before planting.

GROWING METHOD
Planting In cold regions, plant in late summer or winter to early spring. Plant midsummer to mid-autumn in temperate zones and late summer to early autumn in subtropical areas. Plant every three weeks for a longer cropping period. Sow seeds directly into the ground no more than 1 cm (½ in) deep, in rows 25 cm (10 in) apart. Cover with compost and water in. Thin plants to 10 cm (4 in) apart after seedlings appear, a fortnight after sowing. Keep weed-free, but do not damage the developing root nor hill soil around the exposed part.
Watering Requires plenty of water, especially through periods of hot weather.
Fertilising Prepare bed with a light dressing of poultry manure plus a complete fertiliser that is high in phosphorus. Apply side dressings of the same fertiliser about four weeks after planting.
Problems Turnips have no serious diseases but do suffer from pest infestations. Aphids may be hosed off or controlled with appropriate sprays. Caterpillars and grubs that affect other brassicas can also do damage to turnips. To control, spray with a recommended insecticide every two weeks from seedling stage onwards.

HARVESTING
Picking Turnips reach maturity in 2–3 months, sometimes earlier in warmer areas. Pull whole roots from the ground before they become coarse and develop an over-strong flavour. If the seeds have been sown thickly there will be an abundance of extra seedlings, which can be harvested within eight weeks of planting. The root and leaves are tender and sweet to eat at this young age.
Storing Turnips have a long storage time, in or out of the refrigerator.
Freezing Peel and trim tender, young turnips. Cut to the size required. Blanch for three minutes, chill, drain and spread on a tray in a single layer and freeze for 30 minutes. Pack in freezer bags and freeze for up to six months.

USES
Culinary When young, grate raw root and chop leafy tops into salads; braise; or make Chinese-style turnip cake. Use older turnips in soups and stews, or roast, which gives them a sweeter flavour. Boil turnip tops as you would cabbage and serve with butter.

Capsicum annuum

capsicums & chillies
SOLANACEAE

CONDITIONS
Climate Chillies will tolerate hotter climates than capsicums (peppers), which are best as warm season plants; not suitable for growing in frost-prone areas. Die-back may occur in winter, but plants shoot again in spring.
Aspect Need warmth and full sun. Ideal for container growing in sunny positions, protected from strong winds.
Soil Light, well drained soil.

GROWING METHOD
Planting Sow during spring to early summer in cooler and temperate regions; all year round, but mainly in autumn, in warmer tropical and subtropical zones. Sow seeds in the open garden, especially in colder regions, 8–10 weeks before planting out. In warm climates, sow directly in garden beds. Plant every two months to give a continuous crop. Transplant into fertilised furrows when seedlings are about 15 cm (6 in) tall; space 50 cm (20 in) apart in rows 60 cm (2 ft) apart. Support mature plants in windy areas. Rotate crops over several seasons. Do not plant in beds where vegetables from the same family have been grown previously.
Fertilising Prepare beds with plenty of organic matter and apply complete fertiliser one week before planting. Lay in furrows 15 cm (6 in) deep and cover with soil to ground level. When fruit has set, apply urea monthly, 15 cm (6 in) from the plant. Water in straight away. Do not over-fertilise; too much nitrogen leads to large plants but no fruit.
Watering To prevent flower drop, keep soil evenly moist. Overwatering can lead to waterlogged and cold soils.
Problems Aphids, fruit fly and cutworm are the main pests. Hose off aphids or use insecticides that also control the other pests. Watch for powdery mildew in hot, humid climates.

HARVESTING
Picking Plants take 3–4 months to mature. Capsicums are sweeter if left to ripen on the vine. Cut to remove, leaving a small brittle stem attached to the fruit. Pick chillies at any colour stage; they will be hotter if left to ripen fully.
Storing Refrigerate capsicums for up to one week, chillies for two or more in a sealed container. Thick-fleshed chillies can be frozen or pickled; thin-fleshed chillies can be dried.
Freezing Wash, remove seeds and cut into slices or leave whole. Spread a single layer a tray and freeze for 30 minutes. Pack in freezer bags and freeze for up to six months.

USES
Culinary Remove seeds and eat capsicums raw in salads, grilled or baked, or preserved in vinegar. Use chillies raw, roasted or dried. Mexican recipes usually call for the skin to be removed after roasting because it can be bitter. Drying chillies intensifies their flavour.

Cichorium endivia
chicory
ASTERACEAE

CONDITIONS
Climate Best as a cool season crop. Curly (frisée) chicory is the most cold tolerant of the two varieties.
Aspect Prefers direct or partial sun. In hot weather, shade transplanted seedlings if necessary.
Soil Prefers well drained, neutral to slightly acidic soils with a pH of 5–6. Make sure the garden bed has good drainage and has been well worked and manured previously.

GROWING METHOD
Planting Sow seeds in late summer and early autumn for a winter crop. In warmer climates sow from autumn to spring. If growing from transplanted seedlings, plant out well before the weather gets hot. Hot summers will force the plants to bolt and go to seed. If intending to crop when young, sow seed thickly in containers to produce less bitter chicory but do not leave to mature in these overcrowded conditions because they tend to bolt and are more susceptible to disease. In soil, which has been thoroughly watered beforehand, sow seeds 5 mm (1/4 in) deep in rows 50 cm (20 in) apart. Germination takes 10–14 days. Later, thin four-week-old seedlings out to 30 cm (12 in) apart. Chicory is best treated as an annual. It will sometimes grow back after cropping but the quality is usually not good.
Watering Water chicory regularly to encourage growth. Lack of water will prevent growth and cause bitterness in leaves. Sprinklers are not recommended because surplus water trapped inside the chicory head may cause rot.
Fertilising Two weeks before planting, prepare the garden bed by digging in complete fertiliser and a plentiful amount of poultry manure. Dig manure into the top 20 cm (8 in) of soil because the rooting system is shallow and food needs to be close to the surface.
Problems No serious diseases, but insect pests such as snails, aphids and cutworm can be a problem. Put out snail traps such as containers of beer among the beds. Hose off aphids or use an appropriate insecticide. Use plant collars to discourage cutworm.

HARVESTING
Picking If not cropping very young leaves, chicory will reach maturity in 2–3 months. Cut plant off at soil level. To reduce bitterness in leaves, cover with layers of straw several weeks before cropping. The exclusion of sunlight, called blanching, slows down production of chlorophyll in the leaves.
Storing Keeps in the refrigerator for two weeks.
Freezing Do not freeze.

USES
Culinary Use fresh in salads mixed with other salad greens to add flavour.

Cucumis sativus
cucumber
CUCURBITACEAE

CONDITIONS
Climate Best in warm zones. Grows in most areas, with a shorter growing season in cold areas.
Aspect Full sun. To save space in the garden, vine varieties can be trained up a trellis, resulting in cleaner, better-formed fruit than those grown on the ground.
Soil Light soil. Beds need to be well prepared with compost and animal manures, and heavily mulched.

GROWING METHOD
Planting Plant late spring to summer in cold climates, spring to summer in warm zones, and midwinter to mid-autumn in tropical and subtropical areas. Sow seed directly into the bed to a depth of 2 cm (3/4 in), 50 cm (20 in) apart, in rows 1 m (3 1/3 ft) apart. Alternatively, sow several seeds in shallow craters spaced 50 cm (20 in) apart. When seeds germinate, cull seedlings to two or three healthy ones.
Watering Water regularly during growing cycle. Drooping leaves during the hottest part of the day may be a temporary reaction to extreme conditions, not a sign of needing water.
Fertilising A week before planting, dig in complete fertiliser. When the vines show vigorous growth, use side dressings of urea; water in immediately. Repeat monthly when fruiting starts. Add lime to acidic soils or in areas of high rainfall to prevent molybdenum deficiency, which causes mottling or yellowing and upward curling of leaves. Spray young plants with a solution of sodium molybdate to rectify the deficiency.
Problems The banded pumpkin beetle attacks foliage and flowers. Treat with an appropriate insecticide. Spray aphids and red spider mite if natural predators cannot control infestations. Powdery mildew is common. To control, spray upper and lower surfaces with an appropriate fungicide.

HARVESTING
Picking Pick fruit at the optimum time for the variety and climate. As a general rule, when the small, spiny hairs on the fruit are easily brushed off, the fruit is ripe and ready for harvest. Leave too long and the fruit becomes tough, the seeds large and the taste bitter. Frequent harvesting will lead to greater flower production and subsequent fruiting.
Storing Choose firm cucumbers with no signs of bruising, pack in freezer bags and store in the refrigerator for up to 10 days.
Freezing Peel and chop in a food processor. Pack into plastic containers with lids and freeze for up to three months.

USES
Culinary Eat raw as crudités or in salads, cooked in soups, mixed with yoghurt as Indian raita to accompany curries, or added to yoghurt and garlic to make Greek tsatsiki.

CHICORY Chicory, or endive, is similar to lettuce in appearance but is chewier and more substantial, with slightly bitter leaves. There are two frequently grown varieties: curly (frisée) chicory is green, has a loose head, finely serrated or frilly leaf edges and white midribs; escarole (Batavian endive) has broad leaves that are thick, smooth and light green.

CUCUMBER Many types of cucumber are available, including long and short green varieties and the round and whitish apple cucumber. An easily digestible, 'burpless' variety is also popular. Some cucumber plants grow as a bush and are suited to container growing, while others grow as a vine.

SUMMER SQUASH Summer squash is a warm weather crop that is picked when immature. Left to ripen, the skin hardens, and the vegetable is then called winter squash. In its immature stage, the plant grows as more of a bush than a vine. Zucchini (courgette), a member of the summer squash family, are listed separately. Summer squash can be grown in a sunny position indoors.

ZUCCHINI
Zucchini, known as courgette in Europe, are a type of summer squash or young marrow. Generally they are picked quite young, when only about 15–20 cm (6–8 in) long. Zucchini grow on bushes and are quite prolific. They are ideal specimens for container growing. The vegetable is elongated in shape (although tear-shaped varieties exist) and dark green through to yellow.

Cucurbita pepo var. *melopepo*

summer squash
CUCURBITACEAE

CONDITIONS
Climate A warm weather crop, sensitive to cold and frosts. Grows in most areas; the colder it is, the shorter the season.
Aspect Prefers full sun to partial shade
Soil Grows in a wide range of soils. Good drainage is crucial. These are heavy feeders and like heavily fertilised soil.

GROWING METHOD
Planting In cold regions, plant seeds in early summer only. Plant in spring in temperate zones and all year round in hot, subtropical climates. Plant seeds 2 cm (³/₄ in) deep in pots of seed-raising mix 4–5 weeks before planting out. Or sow directly into the garden in the final position. Place several seeds 2 cm (³/₄ in) deep in wide, saucer-shaped depressions that are 20 cm (8 in) deep. Hill up the excavated soil as a rim around the depression. Leave 1 m (3¹/₃ ft) between hills. Thin to a few plants at seedling stage and to one healthy plant when true leaves appear. Remove seedlings by cutting stems at ground level, being careful not to disturb the delicate root structure. If planting in rows, allow 1.5–2 m (5–7 ft) space around each plant. Keep areas around the bush free of weeds and other decaying matter. Shallow cultivate to avoid disturbing the root structure. If no fruit develops, pollinate male and female flowers by hand, as for zucchini (courgette).
Watering Water well but keep away from stems and foliage, especially when fruit is setting. Lack of water may cause partly formed fruit to fall. Large leaves may wilt in hot weather but will recover if soil is moist.
Fertilising Dig in complete fertiliser just before sowing. Apply side dressings of urea when fruit first sets and water in immediately. Too much fertiliser will promote vigorous green growth at the expense of fruit development.
Problems Powdery mildew and bacterial wilt are common. To prevent, do not handle fragile vines while wet and keep the garden clean. Insects spread diseases such as viral mosaic. Infected plants should be sprayed or removed altogether. Aphids and pumpkin beetle affect early growth, especially in spring, and should be sprayed.

HARVESTING
Picking Harvest when young before skin hardens. Regular picking will prolong flowering.
Storing Store in the refrigerator crisper drawer for one week.
Freezing Peel and cook until tender. Mash, cool and pack into freezer containers. Freeze for up to three months.

USES
Culinary Stuff and bake, purée, braise, boil or steam summer squash. It is also delicious sliced and fried in batter or in breadcrumbs, or added to soups, casseroles or gratins.

Cucurbita pepo var. *melopepo*

zucchini (courgette)
CUCURBITACEAE

CONDITIONS
Climate Likes warm weather; sensitive to cold and frosts. It grows in most areas, but the colder it gets, the shorter the season. It also does well when grown indoors in containers.
Aspect Can be grown in full sun to partial shade.
Soil Grows in a wide range of soils, but good drainage is essential. This heavy feeder likes heavily fertilised soil.

GROWING METHOD
Planting In cold regions, plant seeds in early summer only. Plant in spring in temperate zones and all year round in hot, subtropical climates. To sow seeds, follow the same method as for summer squash. If planting in rows, leave about 1 m (3¹/₃ ft) between plants. Keep areas around the bush free of weeds and other decaying matter that might harbour disease. Shallow cultivate to avoid disturbing the delicate root structure. If no fruit develops, it may be because of unsuitable weather or lack of bee activity around flowers, often the case indoors. Should this occur, hand-pollinate male and female flowers using a soft-bristled brush. Dust the male flower (the one with a flower but no fruit on the stem), then dust the inside of the female flower.
Watering Keep water up to the plant but avoid the stems and foliage, especially when the fruit is setting. Lack of water may cause partly formed fruit to fall. Leaves wilt during hot weather but recover if soil is kept moist.
Fertilising Dig in complete fertiliser just before sowing. Apply side dressings of urea when fruit first sets; water in immediately. Too much fertiliser will promote vigorous green growth at the expense of fruit development.
Problems Powdery mildew and bacterial wilt are common. Treat with appropriate sprays. To prevent, do not handle fragile vines while wet and keep the garden clean. Insects spread diseases such as viral mosaic. Spray infected plants on the upper and lower leaves or remove altogether. Aphids and pumpkin beetle affect early growth, especially in spring, and should be sprayed.

HARVESTING
Picking Harvest when 10–15 cm (4–6 in) long and skin is soft. Regular picking will prolong flowering.
Storing Refrigerate for up to one week. Can be pickled.
Freezing Slice into 2.5 cm (1 in) slices and sauté gently in a little melted butter until tender. Cool, then pack into plastic containers and freeze for up to three months.

USES
Culinary Young zucchini can be sliced thinly and eaten raw in salads. Use larger ones in stir-fries, steam or boil them, coat slices in batter and deep-fry, or hollow out, stuff and bake them. Zucchini flowers can be lightly battered and fried.

Cucurbita spp.

pumpkin
CUCURBITACEAE

CONDITIONS
Climate Pumpkin likes warm weather and is sensitive to cold and frosts. It can be grown in most areas, but the colder it gets, the shorter the season.
Aspect Pumpkin prefers to be grown in full sun to partial shade.
Soil Rich, well drained soil. Good drainage is essential. A long growing season is needed for pumpkin, so dig in plenty of well rotted manure and compost several weeks ahead of planting.

GROWING METHOD
Planting Sow seeds in early summer in cold regions, during spring in warm zones, and all year round in hot, subtropical climates. Sow seeds as for summer squash, either in deep pots or directly into the garden. Thin to two or three plants at seedling stage and to a single plant when true leaves appear. Remove seedlings by cutting stems at ground level. Lightly cultivate to keep the area free of weeds and other decaying matter. If no fruit develops, hand-pollinate male and female flowers, as for zucchini (courgette).
Watering Water well but keep the water off the stems and foliage. Large leaves wilt during hot weather but will recover if soil is kept moist.
Fertilising Dig in complete fertiliser just before sowing. Apply side dressings of urea when fruit first sets; water in immediately. Do not over-fertilise.
Problems Powdery mildew and bacterial wilt are common. Treat with an appropriate spray. To prevent, do not handle fragile vines while wet and keep the garden clean. Insects spread diseases such as viral mosaic. Spray infected plants on upper and lower leaves or remove altogether. Aphids and pumpkin beetle affect early growth, especially in spring, and should be sprayed.

HARVESTING
Picking Maturity is reached in 14–16 weeks. The vine dies down, leaving hard, dry stalks. Crop before frosts: cut the pumpkin free of the vine, leaving a portion of stem on the pumpkin.
Storing Keeps for several months in a cool, airy place. Wrap cut pumpkin in plastic wrap and store in the refrigerator.
Freezing Peel and cook until tender. Mash, cool, then pack in plastic containers and freeze for up to three months.

USES
Culinary Pumpkin can be boiled, steamed, roasted or mashed.

Cucurbita spp.

marrow
CUCURBITACEAE

CONDITIONS
Climate Marrow like warm weather and are sensitive to cold and frosts. They can be grown in most areas but the colder it gets, the shorter the season.
Aspect Prefers full sun to partial shade.
Soil Grows in a wide range of soils. Good drainage is essential. Dig in plenty of well rotted manure and compost several weeks before planting.

GROWING METHOD
Planting Plant seeds in early summer in cool regions; in spring in warm zones; and all year round in hot, subtropical climates. Plant seeds 2 cm (³/₄ in) deep in pots of seed-raising mix 4–5 weeks before planting out. Or sow directly into the garden in the final position. Place several seeds 2 cm (³/₄ in) deep in wide, saucer-shaped depressions that are 20 cm (8 in) deep. Hill up the excavated soil as a rim around the depression. Leave 1 m (3¹/₃ ft) between hills. Thin to a few plants at seedling stage and to one healthy plant when true leaves appear. Carefully remove seedlings by cutting stems at ground level. If planting in rows, allow 1.5–2 m (5–7 ft) space around each plant. Keep areas around the bush free of weeds by shallow cultivation. If no fruit develops, hand-pollinate male and female flowers, as for zucchini (courgette).
Watering Keep water up to the plant but away from stems and foliage, especially when the fruit is setting. Sandy soil requires more watering than heavier soil. Lack of water may cause partly formed fruit to fall. Large leaves may wilt in hot weather but will recover if soil is moist.
Fertilising Dig in complete fertiliser just before sowing. Apply side dressings of urea when fruit first sets; water in immediately. Do not over-fertilise.
Problems Powdery mildew and bacterial wilt are common. Treat with appropriate sprays. To prevent, do not handle fragile vines while wet and keep the garden clean. Insects spread diseases such as viral mosaic. Spray infected plants on upper and lower leaves or remove altogether. Pumpkin beetle and aphids affect early growth and should be sprayed.

HARVESTING
Picking Marrows reach maturity in 2–3 months. Crop before frosts set in and skin hardens. Fruit is usually 6 cm (2½ in) round, but can grow much larger.
Storing Store in the crisper drawer for up to one week.
Freezing Peel, cut into pieces and blanch in boiling water. Cool, place in freezer bags and freeze for up to three months.

USES
Culinary Eat marrows young; their flavour becomes watery as they get bigger. Marrows are best stuffed, either halved lengthways or cut into rings with stuffing in the middle.

PUMPKIN The vegetables we commonly refer to as pumpkins include small to medium-sized pumpkin varieties, which belong to the species *C. pepo*, and a mammoth variety of winter squash, *C. maxima*. They are grown on long, rambling prostrate vines of 6 m (20 ft) or more. Large, male and female yellow flowers appear on the same vine. Female flowers have short, thick stems showing immature fruit just below the petals. The fruit has a dry texture and sweet taste, and ranges from yellow to orange-gold. Skins vary from dark green, through whitish grey to creamy yellow, depending on the variety. The spaghetti squash is a member of the *C. pepo* pumpkin species.

MARROW Marrow is a type of bush pumpkin or summer squash. The skin is mostly white and turns slightly yellow when mature. There is little difference in taste between varieties, although the cooked texture of the flesh varies. Male and female flowers, yellow in colour, appear on the same vine. Female flowers have short, thick stems showing immature fruit just below the petals.

ARTICHOKE The artichoke is a grey-green perennial, 1–1.25 m (3¹⁄₃–4 ft) tall, with decorative compound leaves resembling those of the Scotch thistle. The edible parts are the young, tender, globe-shaped flower buds, which are harvested and eaten before they open. These attractive plants require plenty of space.

CARROT
This hardy plant is grown as an annual. A feathery, green rosette of leaves above soil level grows from an edible, underground taproot that is golden orange in colour. Round and short varieties may be grown in a container, but the long, tapering variety, which grows to about 20 cm (8 in), requires friable soil in the open garden. 'Baby' carrots grow to no more than 10 cm (4 in) in length and about 2 cm (¾ in) in diameter. Carrots are easy to grow in the home garden.

Cynara scolymus

artichoke
ASTERACEAE

CONDITIONS
Climate Best grown in areas with mild, relatively frost-free winters and damp, cool summers. Ideal range is 10°C (50°F) at night to 23°C (73°F) by day.
Aspect Prefers full sunlight.
Soil Rich, well drained soils. Garden beds should be prepared with fertiliser and animal compost to improve drainage. Keep mulch and water up to plants during growing season and especially in summer after harvesting.

GROWING METHOD
Planting Plant in midwinter in cooler climates, in late winter in warm regions, and in spring in subtropical areas. For best results buy shoots or suckers of disease-resistant varieties from a good nursery. Planting seed is possible, but success is variable and the plant takes about one year from sowing to harvesting. Place shoots or suckers in beds 1 m (3¹⁄₃ ft) apart, in rows about 1 m (3¹⁄₃ ft) apart. Apply ½ cup of fertiliser around each; water in. In cool areas, cut back to 25–30 cm (10–12 in) in autumn and heavily mulch to protect the root structure in winter.
Watering Keep soils evenly and constantly moist, carefully monitoring this throughout the spring and summer months.
Fertilising Prepare garden beds with low-nitrogen fertiliser. Repeat this application again mid-season.
Problems Good drainage during growth is essential or crown rot may develop, principally as a result of the heavy mulching needed during winter. Handle the plants as little as possible and remove any infected or diseased specimens immediately.

HARVESTING
Picking Artichokes take 2–3 months to reach maturity when grown from shoots or suckers. In many areas, harvesting takes place from mid- to late spring when buds are tight and about 7.5 cm (3 in) across. Cut well below the bud, keeping 2.5 cm (1 in) of stem still attached. The optimum bearing period is the second year after planting. Every third year, divide adult plants and replant.
Storing Sprinkle with water, seal in a plastic bag and store in the vegetable crisper for up to two weeks. Or store upright in water, like flowers, for several days.
Freezing Remove outer leaves, wash, trim stalks and remove 'chokes'. Blanch for seven minutes. Cool, drain, pack in freezer bags and freeze for up to six months.

USES
Culinary When very young, the artichoke can be eaten whole and even raw in salads. When buds are more mature, stuff, boil or fry. Boil large artichokes and eat one leaf at a time, sucking or scraping the flesh off the fibrous base with your teeth. Dip into vinaigrette or hollandaise sauce if desired.

Daucus carota

carrot
APIACEAE

CONDITIONS
Climate Cold tolerant and prefers cooler zones; nevertheless, can be grown in most climates.
Aspect Likes full sun but tolerates partial shade. Above all, prefers a garden bed positioned for coolness.
Soil Deep, light soil. Older garden beds which have friable soils and decayed organic matter offer best results. Roots can grow deep and smooth without blemishes in sandy to loamy soils. If soils are acidic, add lime to improve root colour. In subtropical zones, mulch to keep soil temperatures cool.

GROWING METHOD
Planting Sow seed from spring to the end of summer in cold regions; mid-spring to the end of summer in warm zones; and throughout the year in subtropical regions, except at the height of summer. Prepare furrows 25 cm (10 in) apart and sow seeds 5 mm (¹⁄₄ in) deep. Cover with seed-raising mix and water lightly. When seedlings are about 5 cm (2 in) high, thin out to 2.5 cm (1 in) apart. When these reach 15 cm (6 in), thin out to 5 cm (2 in) apart. Companion plant with radishes in alternate rows to protect seedlings from burn-off.
Watering Watering is important, but during the first eight weeks of growth, use only small amounts to encourage the downwards growth of roots. Then water heavily only when soil dries out. Too much water induces root crack.
Fertilising Beds that have been heavily manured the previous season work best. If necessary, dig in a complete fertiliser one week before sowing. Do not over-fertilise; too much nitrogen leads to excess leaf growth and poor colour.
Problems Control carrot aphids with a registered pesticide. Root nematodes cause leaves to curl and turn deep red or yellow. Pull out diseased plants and burn. Fumigate the bed.

HARVESTING
Picking Carrots can be cropped at whatever size you want them. Full maturity occurs about four months after planting, depending on the variety and area. Use a garden fork to lift carrots gently out of the ground when soil is moist to prevent the roots from snapping.
Storing Store for several weeks in the refrigerator in plastic bags. Don't store near apples, pears or potatoes as the ethylene gas they produce causes carrots to turn bitter. Carrots can be pickled or bottled.
Freezing Scrub and slice. Blanch for three minutes, chill, drain, spread on a tray and freeze for 30 minutes. Pack in freezer bags and freeze for six months.

USES
Culinary Eat raw, steam and serve with butter, use in soups, casseroles and stews, or add to cakes and muffins. Use in Indian desserts, such as halwa.

Eleocharis dulcis

water chestnut
CYPERACEAE

CONDITIONS
Climate Best grown in climates with hot summers – ideally, above 30°C (86°F) during the leafy stage of growth and above 20°C (68°F) when corms are forming.
Aspect Grows in shallow water containers or ponds and is usually not affected by weather extremes.
Soil Use only rich, clay or peaty, fertile soils. The ideal pH is 6.9–7.3, so add a couple of handfuls of lime or dolomite if necessary. However, water chestnuts will tolerate a variety of conditions, even those of slight salinity.

GROWING METHOD
Planting Plant in spring after any cool snaps have passed. Place corms in any shallow, freshwater aquatic environment – such as dams, garden ponds, aquariums or containers that will hold water – and heap soil around, holding or fixing it in place with small stones. Add at least 10 cm (4 in) of soil and cover with 4 cm (1½ in) of water. Very little care is needed except to make sure that the water in the container or pond does not dry out. Rhizomes spread horizontally under the soil surface, turning up to form suckers and new plants. Later, food-producing rhizomes or corms develop. After summer harvest, store some corms in moist sand or loose, damp soil for planting the following season.
Watering Not essential when in aquatic environment.
Fertilising No chemical fertilising is required as long as the soil has been enriched with a lot of well composted organic matter and old animal manure.
Problems No diseases are known. The plant is very hardy but because it is grown in water, mosquito larvae may be a problem. Introduce goldfish or tadpoles into the aquatic environment or sprinkle quassia chips over the water surface.

HARVESTING
Picking After about six months, the stem tops of the water chestnut turn brown and die down, which means they are ready to pick. The darkish skin should be tight and taut; if the flesh texture is mushy, the nut is too old.
Storing Refrigerate in plastic bags for up to two weeks.
Freezing Bring to the boil, drain and peel off shells. Pack in freezer bags or containers and freeze for up to six months.

USES
Culinary Water chestnut corms are peeled and then eaten raw or cooked. They are excellent in stir-fries.

Eruca vesicaria subsp. *sativa*

rocket (arugula)
BRASSICACEAE

CONDITIONS
Climate Best suited to cool and warm climates but grows reasonably well in tropical winters.
Aspect During spring, grow rocket in full sun, but in summer and in the tropics, a cooler, partly shaded spot helps slow the plant's rush to seed and thus lengthens its useful life.
Soil Grow in fertile, well drained soil enriched with rotted manure or compost. Rocket will grow in poor soils too, but its leaves will be tough and more bitter.

GROWING METHOD
Planting In cool regions, sow seeds in early spring and continue sowing until about mid-autumn; in the tropics, start sowing in late autumn and continue until the end of winter. Sow seeds 2.5 cm (1 in) deep, then thin the young plants to about 15 cm (6 in) apart. If sharp frosts are likely, sow indoors in trays or punnets of seed-raising mix placed in a sunny window. Plant out when the seedlings are big enough to handle light frosts or when frosts have passed. Rocket grows fast and young leaves are the most palatable, so pick regularly and make new sowings about every four weeks. When the latest batch of seedlings is big enough to pick from, pull out the previous batch.
Watering For the fastest growth and the sweetest-tasting leaves, keep the plants well watered. Plants enjoy consistent moisture but do not like waterlogged roots, so make sure soil drains well.
Fertilising Dig in a ration of complete plant food at sowing time and then water the plants every two weeks or so with a soluble, high-nitrogen fertiliser.
Problems Snails and slugs may damage the leaves of freshly sown plants in early spring and autumn. Either pick them off by hand or lay snail traps. As rocket can quickly become an invasive weed, it is important to prevent flowering except to provide seeds for resowing. On most plants, snap off flower stems as they rise or, better still, replace flowering plants with new, young plants.

HARVESTING
Picking Start picking young leaves about five weeks after seedlings have emerged, sooner in summer when growth is faster. Harvest seeds when the pods have plumped out and are beginning to look dry.
Storing Seeds may be stored in airtight jars but leaves must be used fresh.
Freezing Do not freeze.

USES
Culinary Young leaves give green salads an appealing piquancy. Add them to stir-fries.

WATER CHESTNUT
This is a root vegetable, which does not belong to the chestnut family at all. A perennial, reed-like plant, the slender, thinly hollow, cylindrical leaves, 1–1.5 m (3⅓–5 ft) in length, act as air pumps, taking oxygen to the roots and helping to purify the water in which the plant grows. The edible corm, about the size of a walnut, grows underwater at the end of horizontal rhizomes. The corm changes from pale to dark mahogany brown as it matures. The whitish flesh has a sweet, nutty flavour, similar to that of coconut or macadamia. Corms are peeled before eating raw or cooked. They have a firm, crisp texture.

ROCKET Rocket (arugula) is an annual with long, deeply lobed, dark green leaves that are often tinted red, and simple, cross-shaped, creamy white flowers. The leaves have a pleasant, peppery, nutty flavour. They form a dense rosette at the base of the plant, from which rise branching flower-bearing stems up to 1 m (3⅓ ft) tall. Plump seed heads shatter when dry, each dispersing hundreds of seeds. Rocket grows very fast and several crops may be raised during spring and summer.

JERUSALEM ARTICHOKE
A very hardy perennial from the sunflower family, the Jerusalem artichoke has edible tubers resembling young, gnarled potatoes. Although perennial by nature, it may be planted as an annual, with the mature tubers lifted during winter and then replanted. Above ground, the plant can grow to 2.5 m (8 ft) and produces attractive dark-centred yellow flowers with small seeds. As a crop, it has a tendency to take over the garden if it is not checked.

SWEET POTATO
This frost-tender, warm season perennial, grown as an annual, is an ornamental vine with small, white or pink to dark purple flowers. Edible parts are the thick, elongated tubers that can have white, creamy yellow or deep orange flesh. Sweet potatoes are classified as being moist or dry, depending on their cooking texture. Those with moist flesh are sometimes called yams. Sweet potato is also known as kumara, particularly in New Zealand. Sweet-tasting, it may be cooked in a variety of ways and is an excellent vegetable to have in the home garden. It is not suitable for containers.

Helianthus tuberosus

jerusalem artichoke

ASTERACEAE

CONDITIONS

Climate Most areas are suitable, but special care needs to be taken during very cold winters or if frosts abound.
Aspect Prefers dry, sunny to semi-shaded locations. The plants will require staking if conditions are windy.
Soil Dig in plenty of organic matter and complete fertiliser. Add a little lime just before planting.

GROWING METHOD

Planting Plant in late winter to mid-spring in cool regions, midwinter in warm areas, and winter through to mid-spring in tropical areas. Purchase new bulbs or tubers or plant saved ones from the previous year's crop. Plant 10–15 cm (4–6 in) deep, 60 cm (2 ft) apart, in rows 90 cm (3 ft) apart. Shoots should appear within 2–4 weeks. The plant needs little attention during the growing period, but bigger tubers will result if the garden bed is well prepared before planting. To improve quality, nip out flower heads at the bud stage. Just before harvest, the tall flower stems should be cut off close to the ground. In cold climates cover with mulch to keep an even soil temperature.
Watering Do not water too much. It may be necessary to keep the soil moist during seasonal dry spells.
Fertilising These hardy plants require little help, but better yields are obtained if some animal manure is dug into the soil and a complete fertiliser is added before planting.
Problems Snails and slugs may appear as shoots form. Use commercial preparations, remove them by hand or trap them in small containers of beer sunk to soil level.

HARVESTING

Picking Harvest the plants after 4–5 months in most areas, once the leaves wilt and the stalks begin to die back.
Storing As with other root crops, the simplest method of storing is to leave the tuber in the ground, digging it up only when needed. Store in the refrigerator for several days.
Freezing Peel and slice. Blanch for two minutes, chill, drain, spread on a tray in a single layer and freeze for 30 minutes. Remove from the tray, pack in freezer bags and freeze for up to six months.

USES

Culinary Finely slice and add raw to salads, boil or roast like potatoes, or use to make soups and mashes.
Gardening Leaves and stalks are good for mulching.

Ipomoea batatas

sweet potato

CONVOLVULACEAE

CONDITIONS

Climate Needs warm days and nights and to be free of frosts for at least 4–6 months during the growing season. Sweet potato is hard to grow in cool to cold climates.
Aspect Prefers to be grown in full sun; does not like cool soil.
Soil Grows best in sandy or sandy loam soils. It is important to control weed growth before vines start their rapid growth. Sweet potatoes have a deep root system, so garden beds may need to be raised, especially when grown in areas with heavy clay soils.

GROWING METHOD

Planting Plant from spring to midsummer in subtropical and warm, coastal regions, and throughout the year in tropical zones. Sweet potatoes are grown from rooted sprouts or shoots, called slips, which are taken from mature, healthy tubers. Place tubers in propagating beds and cover with 7.5 cm (3 in) of sand or light soil. Keep the bed moist and warm. When shoots appear and have grown to 15 cm (6 in), gently pull out and transplant. Tubers will usually produce a second lot of slips for transplanting. Plant slips, not too deeply, in open garden beds 35 cm (14 in) apart, with 1 m (3¹/₃ ft) between rows. The rows should be ridged or hilled to a height of 25 cm (10 in) for best results. Water the plants immediately.
Watering Water well at the initial planting stage, and maintain even soil moisture levels throughout the growing period. Do not overwater or tuber rot may set in. Stop watering a month before harvest.
Fertilising Before planting, dig in a complete fertiliser. A side dressing of urea two months after planting can help. Do not fertilise with nitrogenous fertilisers or poultry manure: this promotes leaf growth instead of tuber development.
Problems There are generally no problems, but it is advisable to rotate sweet potato crops every 2–3 years. Maintaining general garden health is a wise preventative measure.

HARVESTING

Picking Pick after 5–6 months, when tubers reach maturity; white-fleshed tubers take longer to mature than orange-fleshed varieties. Harvest before any cold snaps and do not damage the thin skins when lifting tubers from the ground.
Storing Sweet potatoes will keep for up to four months if stored unwashed. Do not refrigerate.
Freezing Scrub, peel and bake until just tender. Drain and cool, pack in freezer bags and freeze for up to three months.

USES

Culinary Cook as you would a potato – roasted, boiled, fried or mashed. Their soft, slightly sweet flesh makes them ideal in cakes or sweet dishes, and in breads, soups and casseroles.

Lactuca sativa

lettuce
ASTERACEAE

CONDITIONS
Climate Because there are many different varieties, lettuce can be grown in all climates at any time of the year.
Aspect Prefers sun to partial shade. Lettuces do not like excessively hot beds, and in cold climates a protective cloche may be needed to help the vegetable mature.
Soil Lettuces like non-acidic, well drained soils, enriched with decayed animal or poultry manure. Apply lime or dolomite to neutralise soil acidity.

GROWING METHOD
Planting Plant year round in all areas, depending on variety. Grow quickly for best results. If a variety is planted out of season it will run to seed, especially in hot weather. Sow successively from early spring to midsummer to ensure a continuous crop. Avoid sowing in very hot weather. You can sow in containers for later transplanting, but direct sowing into garden beds is preferred. Sow several seeds in a shallow depression 25 cm (10 in) apart and lightly cover with no more than 1 cm (½ in) of compost or seed-raising mix. Keep soil moist. Thin out to single plants when seedlings are 7.5 cm (3 in) tall in rows 30 cm (12 in) apart. Mulch will keep weeds under control and help keep the shallow roots cool.
Watering Keep evenly moist. Overwatering may cause fungal diseases. Lack of water can reduce head size, cause bolting in hot weather and increase bitterness in leaves.
Fertilising A week before planting, dig in complete fertiliser. Side dress with a small amount of urea after thinning seedlings and then again when the plant is half-grown. Do not let fertiliser touch leaves. Wash off if necessary.
Problems Aphids appear early and slow plant growth. Control with appropriate sprays. Sclerotinia rot, which develops in wet, shaded conditions, is a white, cottony fungal growth that appears around the stem at ground level. Treat with suitable sprays fortnightly. Treat downy mildew and septoria, or leaf spot, with appropriate sprays. Burn dead leaves. Keeping plants well spaced during the growing period with access to full sun, especially where ground tends to be soggy, will help keep them healthy.

HARVESTING
Picking Lettuces reach maturity in 8–10 weeks, depending on climate. Pick early when hearts start to form. Loose-leaf lettuce can be harvested a few leaves at a time. Snap off mature outer leaves as needed.
Storing Store in the crisper drawer for up to seven days.
Freezing Do not freeze.

USES
Culinary Lettuce is mainly used fresh in salads or sandwiches but can also be cooked.

Lycopersicon esculentum

tomato
SOLANACEAE

CONDITIONS
Climate Varieties of tomato have been developed that are suitable to all climatic conditions. But this is a warm season vegetable (technically a fruit), susceptible to frosts.
Aspect Prefers full sun to partial shade, but can be affected by sunscald in very hot climates. Protect from strong winds.
Soil Fertile, deep, well drained soil. Prepare the garden beds with plenty of animal manure a month before planting.

GROWING METHOD
Planting Sow seeds during spring in cold regions, late autumn to early summer in temperate zones, and all year round in warm and tropical climates. Seeds are usually germinated in seed boxes, but can be planted directly into the garden, 5 mm (½ in) deep. Seedlings will appear in about 14 days; when 10 cm (4 in) tall, transfer into small containers and harden for a fortnight. When 20–25 cm (8–10 in) tall, transplant into the open garden 60 cm (2 ft) apart, in rows 60 cm (2 ft) apart. Secure weak stems against possible wind damage and to support heavy fruit: fix 2 m (7 ft) stakes firmly in soil when planting seedlings. As the plant grows, secure the stem to the stake with soft ties at 30 cm (12 in) intervals. Prune by picking out lateral shoots that appear at junctions of leaf stalks and the main stem. Single lateral shoots can be left to elongate and form another stem.
Watering Do not let soil dry out; plenty of water is needed during the growth cycle. Uneven watering leads to blossom-end rot. Do not water over the plants with sprinklers. Instead, irrigate along furrows between the rows.
Fertilising Provide phosphorus, especially at seedling stage. Lack of it leads to low yields. Dig in complete fertiliser before planting, or fertilise under seedlings.
Problems Prone to spotted wilt, spread by thrips. Leaf or target spot is common in wet seasons but is also caused by excessive use of nitrogen. Mites, tomato caterpillar and fruit fly are other pests. All can be controlled by appropriate dust or sprays. Rotate crops if soil disease is endemic.

HARVESTING
Picking Crop matures in 3–5 months, depending on variety. Pick fruit when ripe on the bush, or when mature and green and ripen indoors.
Storing Store tomatoes at room temperature for three days, or refrigerate for up to three weeks. They can also be bottled.
Freezing Wash, remove stems, cut in half or leave whole, dry, pack into freezer bags and freeze for up to six months.

USES
Culinary Use raw in salads, or cook this versatile vegetable in sauces, especially pasta sauces, soups and stews. Tomatoes are an excellent base for pickles and chutneys.

LETTUCE A cool season crop, lettuce is in greatest demand as a salad vegetable during hot months. New varieties to suit all seasons are now available. Lettuce has either compact or loosely arranged leaves forming a light green to reddish brown head. The commonly available iceberg lettuce and brown and green mignonettes are compact forms. Butterhead and oak-leaf varieties have soft, loose leaves, whereas cos (romaine) lettuce has strong, rigid leaves and a distinctively elongated head. Loose-leaf lettuce, or any of the small varieties, grow well in containers.

TOMATO Tomato has a weak, soft-stemmed structure with alternate lobed and toothed leaves. Mature plants have a vine-like or bush-growing habit. Yellow flowers grow in clusters and produce fruit of varying size, which may be red, yellow or orange to creamy white, depending on the plant variety. Tomatoes are a heavy-yielding crop and a favourite of home gardeners. They are also well suited to containers.

WATERCRESS
Although European in origin, watercress is now widely used in Asian cuisines. It is a perennial that grows to just 20 cm (8 in) with a spreading habit. The round, dark green leaves composed of several leaflets have a peppery mustard flavour and are carried on fleshy stems. The plants usually grow in water, and clusters of small, white flowers start to appear in early summer.

PARSNIP This is a popular garden vegetable because of its high yields, economic growing space and lengthy cropping period. A fleshy, cream to white underground tap root grows to 20 cm (8 in) and has celery-like leaves that protrude above the ground. The edible root contains a lot of sugar, most of which is lost during cooking, but it retains a distinctive sweet taste and aroma that is unusual for a vegetable. This is a traditional favourite for some vegetable growers and is a tasty and nutritious addition to any vegetable plot. It is not suited to container growing.

Nasturtium officinale

watercress

BRASSICACEAE

CONDITIONS

Climate Warm, moist climates are ideal.
Aspect Prefers a wet shady place that is protected from both strong winds and winter frosts. A pot or tub that can be kept damp is also suitable.
Soil Wet, well limed soil, rich in humus. For container growing, use very damp, rich soil and top it up occasionally with well rotted garden compost.

GROWING METHOD

Planting Plant through spring and autumn in cool zones and mostly in winter in warm zones. Sow seeds by placing them on a constantly damp seed-raising mix. Transplant seedlings to a permanent position when they are about 7.5 cm (3 in) tall. Either float or submerge in shallow, moving water or root in rich, wet soil. Watercress can also be grown by root division of a mature plant or propagated from stem pieces in temperate climates. Stem pieces will root easily in wet soil; place into a container with good quality potting mix and then lower it into a waterbed. Do not let the water stagnate: drain off some of the water once a week and top it up with fresh water each time. The water should be alkaline and at a temperature of around 10°C (50°F). Pick leaves regularly and do not leave to flower.
Watering Requires a great deal of water.
Fertilising Apply soluble plant food that is high in nitrogen every two weeks while growing.
Problems Watercress sometimes gets fungal diseases, which cause rotting of the stems and death of the leaves. Remove infected plants.

HARVESTING

Picking Pick leaves as required.
Storing Freshly picked leaves will keep in fresh cold water or sealed plastic bags in the refrigerator for a couple of days.
Freezing Do not freeze.

USES

Culinary Watercress is rich in iron and vitamin C. Use it raw in salads, sandwiches or as a garnish. The peppery taste adds flavour to other salad greens. The Chinese tend to cook watercress in tasty soups.

Pastinaca sativa

parsnip

APIACEAE

CONDITIONS

Climate Prefers cool weather but grows in all climates.
Aspect Full sun to partial shade
Soil Well drained, organically enriched, deep, sandy loams. Incorporate plenty of well rotted animal manure to keep soil friable well ahead of planting. Use a garden bed that has been heavily fertilised and mulched for a previous crop.

GROWING METHOD

Planting Sow seeds in spring through to early summer in cold climates, in midwinter to mid-autumn in temperate zones, and from autumn through winter in tropical and subtropical areas. Seed is not usually viable over long periods, so obtain fresh stock each season. Plant seeds 5–10 mm (¼–½ in) deep in rows 40 cm (16 in) apart in the garden. Otherwise, sow in seed beds, keeping damp until seedlings appear. Plant out when seedlings are 13–15 cm (5–6 in) high, spacing them 5 cm (2 in) apart. Before planting, beds should be well turned to a depth of 25–30 cm (10–12 in) to ensure a healthy tap root. Avoid deep cultivation while growing because it will damage roots. Hand weed if necessary. In very hot areas, mulch to keep soil cool and to stop short root growth.
Watering Water generously during early stages of growth but ease off as root thickens. Too much water induces root crack; too little leads to slow development and even stunting of root.
Fertilising Dig in complete fertiliser a week before sowing seeds or transplanting seedlings. Do not over-fertilise because too much nitrogen leads to heavy leaf growth at the expense of developing roots.
Problems No serious diseases, but insects can be a nuisance. Control aphids, which turn leaves curly and reddish brown, with sprays.

HARVESTING

Picking Harvest after 4–5 months. Using a garden fork, lift the root gently out of the soil when there is a thickness of about 4–5 cm (1½–2 in) across the crown of the vegetable.
Storing Parsnips can be kept in the ground for 2–3 months after reaching maturity; or refrigerate for 2–3 weeks.
Freezing Peel and dice. Blanch for two minutes, chill, drain and spread on a tray in a single layer and freeze for 30 minutes. Remove from tray, pack in freezer bags and freeze for up to six months.

USES

Culinary Parsnip can be served roasted, mashed or added to casseroles and soups.

Phaseolus vulgaris

bean
FABACEAE

CONDITIONS
Climate A warm season vegetable that does not like frosts. In subtropical climates it can be grown all year round. If hotter than 27°C (80°F), bean pods may not set.
Aspect Prefers sunny spots where the soil is warm.
Soil Soils should be rich in humus, moderately fertilised and well drained. Dig in plenty of organic matter if soil is too sandy. If soil has a low pH, add lime a month before sowing.

GROWING METHOD
Planting Warm weather lovers, beans are best planted mid-spring through to late summer. Sow seeds directly into beds 2.5–5 cm (1–2 in) deep; climbing beans 15 cm (6 in) apart, in rows 1 m (3⅓ ft) apart; dwarf varieties 6 cm (2½ in) apart, in rows 60 cm (2 ft) apart. Hill rows with soil during early growth to safeguard against windy conditions. When planting, set in trellises that are at least 2.4 m (8 ft) tall. Tie vines as necessary to trellis. Weed carefully so as not to disturb the shallow roots. Mulch with compost to protect roots and to promote water retention. Some varieties are suitable for medium to large container growing – check with your local nursery.
Watering Seeds sown in moist soils do not require watering until the seedlings appear, but water well in sandy soils. At flowering time, beans like humid conditions.
Fertilising Apply complete fertiliser that is not high in nitrogen as a 5 cm (2 in) wide layer either side of young plants. Or apply as a band, covered by soil, under newly sown seeds. Apply liquid fertiliser when flowering commences.
Problems Aphids and red spider mite in midsummer to mid-autumn, and bean fly, are the main pests. Beans are also susceptible to blight mosaic and anthracnose. Control pests and diseases by spraying or dusting with insecticides, especially on the undersides of leaves. Remove dead plant material and seasonally rotate crops.

HARVESTING
Picking Dwarf beans will mature in about 10 weeks and climbing beans in 10–12 weeks. Pick frequently to increase flowering and yields. Be careful not to damage vines. The pods are ready when they snap easily between the fingers and the seeds are not yet fully developed. Avoid harvesting during either very hot or cold spells.
Storing Store in the crisper drawer for up to one week.
Freezing String, top and tail. Blanch for two minutes, chill, drain, spread on a tray and freeze for 30 minutes. Remove, pack in freezer bags and freeze for up to six months.

USES
Culinary Steam, boil, cook in stir-fries, or blanch for use in salads.

Pisum sativum

pea
FABACEAE

CONDITIONS
Climate Most climates are suitable. Cool months give best results, but avoid cropping in winter in frost-prone areas.
Aspect Prefers sun to partial shade. In cooler zones, where summer growing is possible, shade protection during the hottest part of the day may be necessary.
Soil Loose, well drained soil. Enrich beds with organic matter. Treat acid soils with lime to bring them to a pH level of 6.5. Rotate crops because peas fix nitrogen in the soil and this will affect subsequent pea crops negatively.

GROWING METHOD
Planting Sow seeds directly into garden from winter to early spring in cold climates; in autumn through winter in warm zones; and in autumn to early winter in warm, subtropical areas. Succession planting every 2–3 weeks extends cropping time. Plant 2.5 cm (1 in) deep and 5 cm (2 in) apart in cooler climates where rainfall is plentiful (deeper, to 5 cm/2 in, in warmer regions), in rows 60 cm (2 ft) apart. Fill trenches with soil, firm down and wet, but do not overwater. Protect seedlings from birds with wire netting. Trellis most varieties for easy cultivation and harvesting. Lightly cultivate beds to keep weeds down. After harvesting, dig whole plant into soil as green manure.
Watering Water carefully as plants need adequate, but not excessive, water at soil level. Avoid watering over the top of mature leaves and flowers.
Fertilising Apply complete fertiliser to improve soil fertility.
Problems Rotate crops to inhibit fungal diseases, which peas are susceptible to, especially in wet weather. Discolouration of the leaves and pods and the appearance of blackish streaks on the stems indicate disease. If disease is present, remove all vines after harvesting (healthy or otherwise) and burn them. Fungicide dusting of seeds before sowing will avert seed rot and damping-off, especially in areas where winter sowings are in cold soils. Hose aphids off vines or destroy all infected foliage. Control grubs that attack pods with appropriate pesticide.

HARVESTING
Picking Pick when the pods are full, firm, shiny bright green and 5–7.5 cm (2–3 in) long. Frequent harvesting from the bottom of the plant prolongs the cropping season.
Storing Fresh peas keep for 2–3 days in the refrigerator.
Freezing Shell, wash and blanch for one minute. Chill, drain, spread on a tray in a single layer and freeze for 30 minutes. Remove, pack in freezer bags and freeze for up to six months.

USES
Culinary Boil peas or add them to soups and risottos.

BEAN Annuals of both climbing and dwarf varieties of bean have edible leaves composed of three small leaflets, and edible flowers that come in a variety of colours. The immature pod is the part of the plant that we generally eat. It can be green, yellow or purple, depending on the bean variety, and comes in stringed and stringless forms. Climbing beans give a heavier crop over a longer period than dwarf varieties.

PEA Mainly climbing annuals with pretty flowers and green tendrils clinging to a trellis for support, peas are an attractive addition to the home vegetable garden. There are many types. The garden pea is grown for the seeds contained in its fibrous pod; snow peas (mangetout) (*P. sativum* var. *macrocarpon*) or sugar snap peas (*P. sativum* var. *macrocarpon* ser. cv.) are grown for the pods themselves. Flowers and habit differ, but all pea varieties have similar requirements for successful growth.

Raphanus sativus
radish
BRASSICACEAE

RADISH The radish is a round to globular and sometimes cylindrical root vegetable with winter and summer varieties. The longer root form grows to 15 cm (6 in) in length and is good for cooking. The smaller, rounder summer radish is usually eaten fresh in salads and is perfect for growing in containers. They grow quickly and have sweet flesh, which turns bitter and hot to the taste if left in the ground too long. The thin skin ranges from red through to white. This is an easy vegetable for the home gardener to cultivate.

DAIKON
This oriental white radish is known by its Japanese name, daikon, which means 'big root'. It is a member of the mustard family and various types are used in Japanese and Chinese cuisines. The leaves, stems, seed pods, seedlings and tap root are used in Asian food. The swollen tap root varies from spherical to elongated and triangular, depending on the variety; its flesh is white to greenish. The plant itself has an erect habit, generally growing 30–60 cm (1–2 ft) tall, but will reach 1 m (3⅓ ft) when left to flower. The non-branching stem supports a leafy rosette.

CONDITIONS
Climate Grows in all climates.
Aspect Likes a moist, shady place. In high summer, may need protection from direct sunlight for a few hours of the day.
Soil Rich, deep, sandy loams with high moisture holding capacity are needed for rapid growth. The ideal pH is 6.5. Add lime to soil if necessary. Soil that has been manured and fertilised for a previous crop is ideal. Heavily mulch garden bed during hot weather.

GROWING METHOD
Planting Plant in spring, summer and early autumn in colder regions; throughout the year except in early winter in warm temperate zones; and all year round in tropical to subtropical areas. Plant seed directly into the soil 5 mm (¼ in) deep, 5 cm (2 in) apart, in rows 15 cm (6 in) apart. Or dig a shallow furrow along the length of the planting row, lay fertiliser along the bottom, cover with a little soil and then plant seed. Fill in the furrow with light compost or seed-raising mix and water in. Seedlings take 1–2 weeks to appear. Thin to 5 cm (2 in) apart (7.5 cm/3 in for winter radish) at second leaf stage. Sow successively every few weeks for a continuous crop. Weed by regular, shallow cultivation. The plant has a tendency to bolt or go to seed in hot summer weather.
Watering Water thoroughly to keep soil moist during growing stage.
Fertilising Use a complete fertiliser for furrow planting, otherwise dig into garden bed. Feed with a recommended liquid fertiliser every week at the seedling stage. Once seedlings are established, do not add further manure.
Problems Caterpillars of the cabbage white butterfly are the main pests to watch out for. Early spraying with appropriate insecticide is recommended. Club root can affect winter radish because this variety is left in the ground longer than other varieties. Aphids and other insects can be controlled by using pyrethrum or other approved sprays. Discontinue use of spray a week before harvesting.

HARVESTING
Picking Pull the whole plant from the ground at around 3–5 weeks for salad radishes and 6–8 weeks for the longer root form. It is a good idea to undertake test pullings to judge size and firmness of fruit when anticipated maturity time is reached. Harvest before the radish gets old and tough.
Storing Refrigerate radishes, trimmed of greens, wrapped in plastic bags, for up to 10 days.
Freezing Do not freeze.

USES
Culinary Eat summer radishes raw in salads; braise winter radishes with a knob of butter.

Raphanus sativus var. *longipinnatus*
daikon (white radish)
BRASSICACEAE

CONDITIONS
Climate Best grown as a cool weather crop in temperatures around 20°C (68°F). The most important thing to remember is to choose the variety most suited to your local climate.
Aspect Prefers moist, shady spots.
Soil Rich, light, well drained soils. Root shape tends to be modified by the soil character so avoid heavy clay soils, which prevent roots expanding. To counter this problem, the root in some adaptable varieties props itself above the soil level.

GROWING METHOD
Planting Sow in autumn in cool regions and twice a year in spring and autumn in warm and tropical areas. Sow seeds thinly, directly into the garden bed, 1–2 cm (½–¾ in) deep, in drills 4 cm (1¾ in) deep. Seedlings will appear in 10–14 days. Thin so that young plants are at least 10 cm (4 in) apart, depending on the variety. Really large rooting types will need up to 40 cm (16 in) of space around each plant. As seedlings grow, cover stems with soil from around the drill holes. Keep beds free of weeds and avoid damaging roots. These plants have a tendency to bolt in warm conditions after cold snaps.
Watering Water steadily and constantly and do not let soil dry out. As plants reach maturity, cut down on watering because excess water leads to cracking of roots.
Fertilising Preferably use previously fertilised beds. Use complete fertiliser beneath drill holes before planting, if necessary.
Problems Aphids, cabbage white butterfly caterpillars, nematodes and black beetle cause root damage. Control with pyrethrum sprays. Hot, wet weather can give rise to soil diseases, such as bacterial soft rot, which affects the root at ground level, gradually sending the whole root soft and mushy. To prevent, keep bed free of decaying vegetable matter. Destroy any diseased plants. Rotate crops at least every three years as a preventative measure.

HARVESTING
Picking Daikon matures within 8–10 weeks in most areas, but can be harvested at any stage of the growing cycle. Roots are ready when about 20 cm (8 in) long (for elongated varieties) or when diameter is 5–10 cm (2–4 in). Skin should be smooth and white and the flesh firm. Crop during cool weather, pulling the root whole from the ground.
Storing Refrigerate, wrapped in plastic, for several weeks. It can also be dried, pickled, fermented or preserved in brine.
Freezing Do not freeze.

USES
Culinary Raw daikon can be diced and added to salads. Cooked, use like a potato or turnip, adding it to soups, stews or stir-fries.

Sechium edule

choko (chayote)
CUCURBITACEAE

CONDITIONS
Climate Best suited to subtropical areas and warmer areas of temperate zones. Severe frosts will kill the vine, but in cooler areas the vine will die down over winter with new growth in spring.
Aspect Prefers warm, sunny spots against a wall. During cool to cold snaps, it is possible for choko to be grown in a pot. It can then be brought inside and replanted out when the weather warms up.
Soil Deep, fertile, moist, well drained soil. Dig in a lot of organic matter and fertiliser before planting.

GROWING METHOD
Planting Select a mature choko with signs of a germinating seed. During early spring in warm climates and in autumn through to spring in tropical zones, plant the whole choko 10 cm (4 in) deep, at an angle, in damp soil, with the broad or shooting end downwards and the other end showing just above soil level. Plant near a fence or other strong supporting structure. To ensure success, plant two or three plants 1 m (3$^1/_3$ ft) apart. Keep weeds down during the growing period. After harvesting and before winter sets in, cut the vine back to three or four shoots and mulch heavily to protect the tuberous root system.
Watering Give plenty of water to keep vine growing, especially during the late summer cropping period.
Fertilising Several weeks before planting, prepare bed with complete fertiliser. Side dress with the same fertiliser in midsummer. During the second year of growth, fertilise around the new shoots during early spring.
Problems Relatively free from pests and diseases. Aphids and pumpkin beetle may be a problem. Spray or dust with appropriate insecticide.

HARVESTING
Picking A warm six-month growing season is needed for fruit to reach maturity. Two crops can be harvested in tropical zones, in spring to early summer; one in summer in warm areas. The fruit is at its best when light green in colour and about 5 cm (2 in) long. Large fruit, sometimes with prickly spines on the skin, is both coarse in texture and lacking in flavour when cooked.
Storing Refrigerate for up to two weeks.
Freezing Boil sliced chokos until tender. Drain well, then mash and cool. Pack into plastic containers and freeze for up to six months.

USES
Culinary Steam, boil, bake or braise; grate young flesh raw in salads.

Solanum melongena var. *esculentum*

eggplant (aubergine)
SOLANACEAE

CONDITIONS
Climate A warm climate vegetable, needing temperatures of 25°C (77°F) and above in the growing season. Seeds need warm soil and the air temperature above 20°C (68°F) to germinate. Eggplant is extremely sensitive to frost. Extended cool periods will retard growth.
Aspect Requires full sun and protection from winds.
Soil Light, rich, well drained soil.

GROWING METHOD
Planting Plant during late spring in cool climates, spring through to early summer in temperate zones, and spring through to autumn in tropical areas. To ensure a good striking rate, especially in cold areas, sow seeds in small pots or seed boxes at least eight weeks before transplanting into the open garden during warm weather. Cold soil will shock the plant and set it back considerably. For this reason and because of the possibility of soil-borne diseases, many people grow eggplants in containers where conditions are more controllable. Thin out and choose the hardiest seedlings for transplanting. Plant in furrows 50–60 cm (20–24 in) apart, in rows 60–90 cm (2–3 ft) apart. Keep the area around the plant free of weeds by shallow cultivation.
Watering Do not overwater because the plant is susceptible to root rot. Maintain even moisture and temperature levels in soil by mulching. Increase watering as the plant matures.
Fertilising A few days before planting, dig complete fertiliser into topsoil. Fertilise furrows to a depth of 15 cm (6 in) and width of 10 cm (4 in). Fill in furrow with soil to cover fertiliser before planting. Side dress with urea when first fruit has set.
Problems Aphids, egg fruit caterpillar and spider mites are the main pests. Treat with appropriate sprays. Crop rotation may be necessary to lessen incidence of soil-borne wilt diseases. Do not grow capsicum (peppers) or tomatoes in succession with eggplants. Control leaf spot and fruit rot with fungicide sprays.

HARVESTING
Picking Pick the fruit in full colour after 3–4 months, before the seeds harden and turn brown. Skin should be tight, firm and unwrinkled. Over-ripe fruit is coarse and bitter. Cut hard, woody stems with a sharp tool to prevent damage to fruit.
Storing Refrigerate for 7–10 days. It is ideal for pickling.
Freezing Cut into slices, sprinkle with salt and allow to stand for 20 minutes. Drain off excess liquid and fry eggplant gently in butter until just tender. Cool, then pack into plastic containers and freeze for up to three months.

USES
Culinary Eggplant can be served hot or cold, puréed, fried, stuffed or battered.

CHOKO Choko is known by numerous names, the most common being chayote. The greenish white fruit looks a little like a flattened pear and is borne on a large, vigorous, rambling vine that requires considerable support. The vine produces both male and female flowers. Leaves are large and hairy to the touch. This plant requires plenty of space but is easy to grow and relatively trouble-free.

EGGPLANT Known commonly as eggplant (aubergine), this vegetable grows on small bushes to 1.5 m (5 ft) tall with large, coarse, hairy, grey-green leaves. The star-shaped flowers are an attractive mauve and the plants produce about eight fruit per bush. The fruit varies in shape and size, from long and slender to egg-shaped varieties. They are generally dark purple to black or creamy white to mauve in colour. Some of the recently released varieties include small and rounded, reddish forms and pea-sized, green varieties from Asia. Eggplants can be grown successfully in containers.

POTATO Although originally from the high mountains of South America, potatoes do not do well in areas of either extreme frost or extreme heat. The potato is an underground tuber that produces a stem with hairy, tomato-like leaves above ground. Depending on the variety, the skin ranges in colour from cream through reddish brown to dark purple. The flesh is creamy white to white and either floury or waxy in texture. An easy vegetable to cultivate, it also grows quite successfully in containers.

SPINACH
Mature plants of spinach produce a rosette of dark green leaves 10–15 cm (4–6 in) long with a prominent midrib. The edible part of the vegetable is the leaves, which can be either crinkled or smooth, depending on the variety, and they grow in clusters at ground level.

Solanum tuberosum
potato
SOLANACEAE

CONDITIONS
Climate Potatoes can be grown in all climates. They need a frost-free season of 4–5 months to develop successfully.
Aspect Grows best in full sun.
Soil Well drained, fertile and friable soils with a pH of 5–5.5 are ideal. Beds should be raised if underlying ground is heavy clay. Add lime sparingly to reduce soil acidity. Too much lime increases incidence of scab disease, which infects skin.

GROWING METHOD
Planting Planting time does depend on variety used but, in general, plant when soils are warm: spring to early summer in cold regions; spring to end of summer in temperate zones; and summer through winter in warm tropical climates. Seed pieces are eyes cut from potato tubers with about 50 g (1³/₄ oz) of flesh attached. Lay seed pieces 35 cm (14 in) apart, on fertilised furrows 75 cm (2½ ft) apart. Fill furrows with soil and rake topsoil evenly. For a cleaner crop, cover sprouting tubers with 20–30 cm (8–12 in) of decomposing straw or mulch, and top with 10 cm (4 in) of rich, friable soil. Keep moist. Hill grow plants for support, exclude sunlight and protect from insects. Shallow cultivate to control weeds.
Watering Water regularly to promote smooth, bigger vegetables. Irrigate along channels between hilled rows. Reduce watering just before harvest, when plant tops die off.
Fertilising Before planting, dig furrows to 15 cm (6 in), then lay 80–100 g (3–3½ oz) of fertiliser along the base. Cover with 5 cm (2 in) soil. Use a fertiliser high in phosphorus.
Problems Potato moth attacks exposed tubers, so be sure to cover vegetable with soil. Treat aphids and Colorado potato beetle with appropriate sprays. Blight is common in humid weather: leaves and stems rot, the flesh becomes spotted, softens and rots. Spray with a registered fungicide to prevent the disease. Remove and burn diseased plants.

HARVESTING
Picking Harvest 'new' potatoes one month after flowering, when the leaves have turned yellow. 'Old' potatoes mature in the ground for about 4–5 months. Lift after plant dies down.
Storing Keep in a cool, dry, dark, well ventilated place to prevent from sprouting. Exposure to light causes potatoes to turn green, become bitter, indigestible and even poisonous.
Freezing Scrub, boil until almost cooked, drain, cool, pack in freezer bags and freeze for six months. Or deep-fry chips, drain and cool, then place on a tray in a single layer and freeze for 30 minutes. Pack in freezer bags and freeze for up to three months. Mash and freeze for up to three months.

USES
Culinary Roast, fry or boil. Different varieties lend themselves to different cooking techniques.

Spinacia oleracea
spinach
CHENOPODIACEAE

CONDITIONS
Climate Best in cool climate, but grows in most areas. Ideal temperatures are 10–15°C (50–59°F).
Aspect Prefers sun to partial shade and needs shelter from winds.
Soil Prefers non-acidic, well drained soils with a pH range of 6–7, enriched with decayed animal or poultry manure. Lime or dolomite will help neutralise acidic soil and should be dug in two weeks before planting.

GROWING METHOD
Planting Plant from autumn through winter in cold areas, late summer through autumn in temperate zones, and summer through autumn in subtropical climates. Sow seeds directly into the garden bed, 1 cm (½ in) deep, 30 cm (12 in) apart, in rows 35 cm (14 in) apart. Lightly cover seeds with compost and water in so that soil is just moist. Seedlings emerge within 2–3 weeks. Successive sowings every three weeks will ensure a continuous crop. Keep weeds down by heavy mulching. Mulching will also keep the roots cool.
Watering Soil should be moist, but avoid continual wetting of leaves.
Fertilising A week before planting, dig in a complete fertiliser. Regular side feedings of a nitrogen-rich fertiliser after the first appearance of seedlings will promote good leaf growth.
Problems Spinach blight will cause leaves to yellow and then curl up and die. Downy mildew causes pale patches on leaves. Leaf miners and mites are the main pests. All these should be controlled by an appropriate fungicide or insect sprays.

HARVESTING
Picking Crops take 8–10 weeks to mature. Pick individual leaves as required or pull the whole plant from the ground.
Storing Refrigerate for up to one week.
Freezing Wash well and trim leaves. Blanch for one minute in a small quantity of water. Chill, drain, pack in freezer bags or containers and freeze for up to six months.

USES
Culinary Use younger leaves in salads; steam or boil older leaves or cook in stir-fries.

Vicia faba
broad bean
FABACEAE

CONDITIONS
Climate Grows very well in mild temperate and cool regions, where temperatures are below 20°C (68°F). Cool weather helps to set the pods. Pods will not develop in areas that have very hot summers.
Aspect Likes full sunlight
Soil Grow in beds of alkaline soil that are well drained and rich in organic matter.

GROWING METHOD
Planting Plant autumn to winter in cooler zones and mild temperate zones and early autumn in warm temperate climates. Sow seeds directly into beds 5 cm (2 in) deep, 5 cm (2 in) apart, in rows at least 1 m (3⅓ ft) apart. When seedlings are well established, thin to 20 cm (8 in) apart. If a good crop is evident, tips of growing shoots can be nipped out to hasten maturity. The crop requires only limited attention during the 4–5 month growing season.
Watering Do not overwater. With high temperatures, wet soil conditions lead to root diseases. Seeds planted in damp soil require no further watering until seedlings appear. As plant matures, water only when soil starts to dry out.
Fertilising When preparing beds, dig in complete fertiliser that has a good amount of phosphorus. Too much fertiliser, especially in the form of animal manures, leads to pod-setting failure. As with other legumes and pulses, broad beans add nitrogen to the soil through the action of nitrogen-fixing bacteria on their roots and so, in a way, produce their own fertiliser.
Problems Control aphids and mites with recommended insecticides or organically prepared garlic sprays. Diseases include rust and broad bean wilt, which causes darkening of the growing tip, wilting, then death. Remove and burn diseased plants immediately. Protect remaining plants from aphids. Crop rotation over several seasons is recommended.

HARVESTING
Picking Young pods, which can be eaten whole, can be harvested during early spring in most areas. Mature plants are ready for harvest 4–5 months after planting.
Storing Refrigerate for up to two weeks.
Freezing Shell, wash and blanch for 1½ minutes. Cool, place on a tray in a single layer and freeze for 30 minutes. Remove, pack in freezer bags and freeze for up to six months.

USES
Culinary When harvested young, the whole pod containing half-ripe seeds can be prepared and eaten as you would climbing beans. Remove older beans from pods and steam, boil, stir-fry or cook for use in salads.

Zea mays var. *saccharata*
sweet corn
POACEAE

CONDITIONS
Climate Prefers hot, warm frost-free climates.
Aspect Needs full sun and wind breaks, if necessary.
Soil Grows in a wide range of soils, but prefers deep, well manured soil.

GROWING METHOD
Planting Plant late spring to early summer in colder regions; in spring to midsummer in temperate zones; and all year round in subtropical and tropical climates, although autumn is optimal. Prepare short rather than long rows, 50–60 cm (20–24 in) apart, to give an overall clumping effect to the garden bed. Dig seed trenches to a depth of 25 cm (10 in), layer with complete fertiliser, then cover with 10 cm (4 in) soil. Space seeds about 25 cm (10 in) apart. Soil should be damp and warm, at least 15°C (59°F). Seedlings should emerge within 14 days of seeds being sown. Remove weeds by light cultivation.
Watering Keep soil evenly moist, especially in hot weather and after pollination, when care should be taken not to wet tassels.
Fertilising Dig in plenty of poultry manure at least two weeks before planting. Give applications of fertiliser high in nitrogen and phosphate when planting and apply side dressings throughout the growing period.
Problems Many pests attack corn, including corn earworm, corn borer and cutworm, which penetrate the ears and damage the seed. Sap-sucking aphids are also a problem. At the first sign of trouble, spray with appropriate insecticide every 2–3 days when the plant is at the 'green silk' stage. Birds may also attack the ears of corn. Cover at the ripening stage.

HARVESTING
Picking Sweet corn will reach maturity within 12–14 weeks of planting. The kernels will be plump and full of milk, which oozes out when the ripe cob is cut. If the fluid is clear, it means the cob is immature.
Storing Store corn in the refrigerator, with the husks on, for up to two days.
Freezing Remove leaves and silk and cut off top of cob. Wash, blanch for 5–7 minutes, chill and drain. Wrap in plastic, place in freezer bags and freeze for up to six months.

USES
Culinary Corn can be boiled, steamed, barbecued, roasted and even microwaved.

BROAD BEAN
A hardy, winter annual growing to 1.5 m (5 ft) tall, broad beans have square stems producing small leaflets, which give the plant a bushy look. The many white flowers produce 15–20 cm (6–8 in) pods that contain edible seeds. The seeds are large and may be eaten fresh, although they are often dried. Broad beans are easy to grow in the home garden, although they are not suited to container growing.

SWEET CORN A member of the grass family, sweet corn grows to a majestic 5 m (17 ft) tall, and produces one or two ears per stalk. The ears, or cobs, are completely covered with regularly arranged seeds, called kernels, which are white to yellow in colour, although some heirloom varieties have red and black seeds or a combination of all these colours.

Index

Page numbers in **bold** print refer to main entries. Page numbers in *italics* refer to photographs and illustrations

Picture credits

John Coco 32 (top right),

Ben Dearnley/Jared Fowler 25 (right), 28, 32 (left), 33, 55 (top), 61 (right), 62, 63, 70 (right), 116–17, 120, 135, 140 (left), 148 (bottom), 149 (top), 154, 165 (right), 172, 173 (right), 263–65, 268–70, 272–75, 278–301, 304 (top), 305, 306 (top), 308, 310–11

Joe Filshie cover (front flap, far right; back flap, right), 6, 7 (bottom), 29, 35, 36, 38, 39, 40–41, 45 (bottom), 48, 70 (left), 73 (left), 78 (top left, centre and right), 80, 84 (top), 85, 87 (left), 105 (top), 125 (bottom), 129 (bottom), 130 (bottom), 131, 163 (right), 176–77, 180 (bottom right), 185, 217, 218, 229, 230, 236–37 (centre), 238, 239, 241, 242, 244, 256 (top), 316 (top), 318 (bottom), 320 (bottom), 321 (bottom), 323, 327 (bottom), 328 (bottom), 331 (bottom), 332 (bottom), 333 (top)

Getty Images: front cover

Denise Greig 55 (bottom)

Ian Hofstetter 75 (top left), 307 (bottom), 309

Andrea Jones 235

Chris L. Jones cover (front flap, second from right), 49, 130 (top), 149 (bottom), 158–59, 162, 164–65 (centre), 199, 211, 260–61, 304 (bottom)

Meredith Kirton 37

Luis Martin 94 (top), 96

Murdoch Books 10 (top), 24 (left), 108, 140 (top right), 144 (top), 160, 163 (top and bottom left), 171, 182 (bottom), 183 (left), 191 (bottom), 240, 249, 251, 257 (top), 262 (right), 314–15, 317, 318 (top), 319, 320 (top), 321 (top), 322, 324–26, 327 (top), 330 (bottom), 331 (top), 334–37, 338 (bottom), 339–57, 358 (bottom), 359–61, 362 (bottom), 363–65

Robin Powell cover (back flap, centre), 10 (bottom), 12, 13, 14, 16, 17, 51

Robert Reichenfeld 306 (bottom), 307 (top)

Lorna Rose cover (front flap, second from left; back flap, right), 7 (top), 8 (top), 9 (top), 11, 24–25 (centre), 31, 32 (bottom right), 42, 43, 50, 52, 58, 75 (top and bottom right), 76, 86, 89, 95, 97, 101, 105 (bottom), 107 (bottom), 109, 121 (right), 129 (top), 145, 146, 151, 173 (left), 213 (left), 214–15 (left), 216 (right), 222, 223, 226, 227 (bottom), 231, 245 (right), 250, 254, 257 (bottom), 358 (top)

Sue Stubbs cover (front flap, far left), 4, 9 (bottom), 15, 22, 23, 26–27, 44, 45 (top left and right), 47, 54, 56–57, 64–65, 74, 77, 78 (bottom), 81, 82–83, 84 (bottom), 87 (right), 88, 90, 91 (top), 92 (right), 94 (bottom), 98–99, 104, 106, 107 (top), 118, 119, 121 (left), 122–23, 124, 125 (top), 126, 127, 128, 132, 136–37, 138, 140 (bottom right), 144 (bottom), 147, 148 (top), 153, 155, 168–69, 178, 179, 181, 183 (right), 186, 191 (top), 192–93, 208–209, 210, 212. 2123 (right), 215 (right), 216 (left), 219, 220, 221, 224–25, 227 (top), 232–33, 234, 236 (left), 237 (right), 243, 245 (left), 246–47, 248, 252–53, 255, 256 (bottom), 262 (left), 266–67, 276–77, 302–303, 316 (bottom), 328 (top), 329, 330 (top), 332 (top), 333 (bottom), 338 (top), 362 (top)

Mark Winwood 20–21, 30, 34, 46, 53, 59, 60, 61 (left), 68–69, 71, 72, 73 (right), 91 (bottom), 92 (left), 93, 100, 103, 133, 134, 141, 150, 161, 164 (left), 166, 167, 170, 180 (top left and right), 182 (top), 184, 187, 188, 189, 190, 228

Although every care has been taken to trace and acknowledge copyright, the publisher apologises for any accidental infringement where copyright has proved untraceable. The publisher would be pleased to come to a suitable arrangement with the rightful owner in each case.